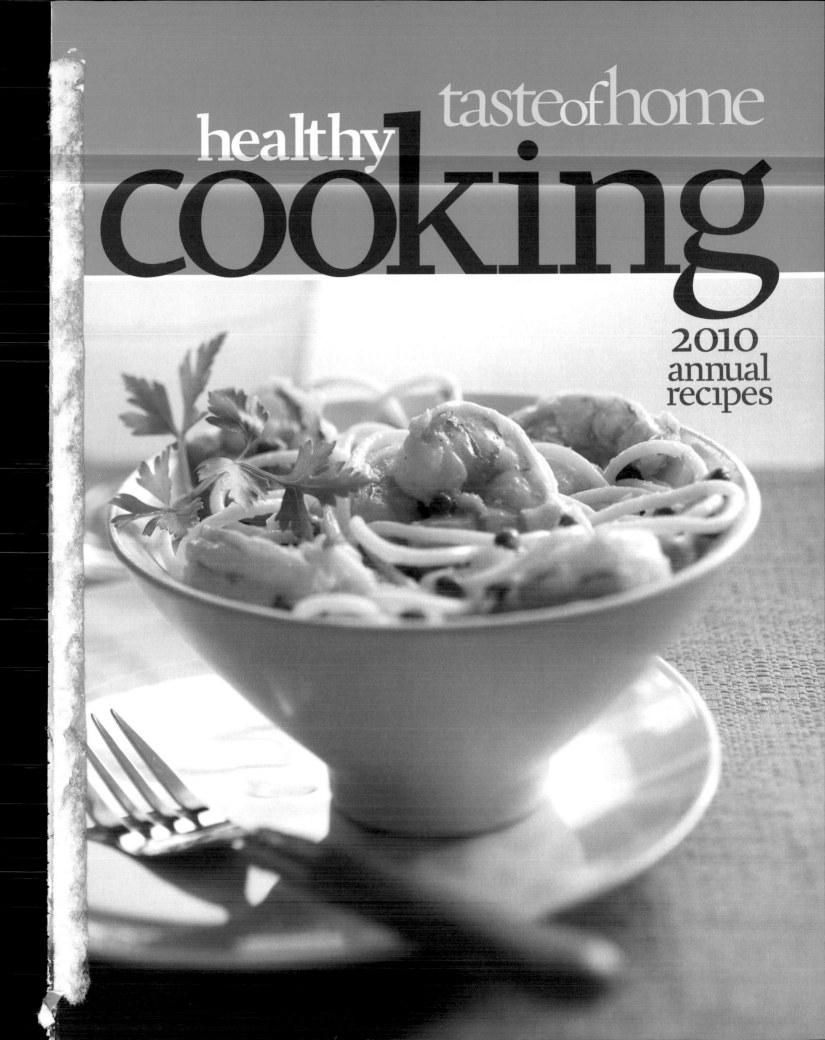

taste of home

2010 Healthy Cooking Annual Recipes

©2010 Reiman Media Group, Inc.
5400 S. 60th St., Greendale WI 53129

Taste of Home is a registered trademark of The Reader's Digest Association, Inc.

International Standard Book Number (10):
0-89821-763-6

International Standard Book Number (13):
978-0-89821-763-6

International Series Number: 1944-7736

Printed in U.S.A.
13 5 7 9 10 8 6 4 2

Cover Photography
Photographers: Jim Wieland, Grace Natoli Sheldon
Food Stylists: Sarah Thompson, Jennifer Janz
Set Stylist: Dee Dee Jacq

Pictured on Front Cover:
Enchilada Casser-Ole! (p. 122); Chicken Alfredo Veggie Pizza (p. 16); Italian Vegetable Soup (p. 41); and Makeover Chocolate Mint Layer Cake (p. 234).

Pictured on Back Cover:
Cajun Orange Pork Chops (p. 161); Crab Salad Tarts (p. 15); Spicy Chicken Breasts with Pepper Peach Relish (p. 127); and Artichoke Tomato Salad (p. 34).

To order additional copies of this book, or to purchase other *Taste of Home* books and products, visit

ShopTasteofHome.com

Editor in Chief
Catherine Cassidy

Vice President & Executive Editor/Books
Heidi Reuter Lloyd

Creative Director
Ardyth Cope

Food Director
Diane Werner RD

Senior Editor/Books
Mark Hagen

Art Director
Gretchen Trautman

Editor/Healthy Cooking
Mary Spencer

Food Editor/Healthy Cooking
Peggy Woodward RD

Production Supervisor
Julie Wagner

Design Layout Artists
Kathy Crawford, Nancy Novak

Proofreaders
Susan Uphill, Linne Bruskewitz

Recipe Asset Management Systems
Coleen Martin

Premedia Supervisor
Scott Berger

Recipe Testing & Editing
Taste of Home Test Kitchen

Food Photography
Taste of Home Photo Studio

Administrative Assistant
Barb Czysz

U.S. Chief Marketing Officer
Lisa Karpinski

Vice President/Book Marketing
Dan Fink

Creative Director/Creative Marketing
Jim Palmen

The Reader's Digest Association, Inc.
President and Chief Executive Officer
Mary G. Berner

President, U.S. Affinities
Suzanne M. Grimes

SVP Global Chief Marketing Officer
Amy J. Radin

Contents

The 2010 editon of *Healthy Cooking Annual Recipes* is loaded with all of the specialties you've come to expect. We divided all of these family-pleasing dishes into 16 chapters to make it a snap to find what you need, when you need it!

New Attitude

Eating healthy has never been easier, thanks to the 481 recipes and tips inside *Healthy Cooking Annual Recipes 2010*. The second edition in this series promises all of the full-flavored dishes you'd expect as well as a few new benefits, too.

Congratulations! You've made the decision to eat right and set deliciously heart-smart meals on your dinner table.

With this new edition of *Healthy Cooking Annual Recipes 2010*, the perfect dish is always at your fingertips—no matter what the occasion.

Take a look inside and you'll find everything you need to keep your healthy-eating goals on track. After all, we've collected 481 recipes from an entire year's worth of *Healthy Cooking* magazine. From "Starters & Snacks" to "Treat Yourself," the 16 chapters that follow make it a cinch to find the ideal recipe.

• In a hurry? Skip the drive-thru, and see "Dinner in 30" for more than 2 dozen recipes that are table-ready in half an hour. Or, see the indexes at the back of the book. Every dish that's ready in 30 minute or less is marked with a blue dot!

• Need a low-calorie eye-opener? Flip to page 80 for a lovely assortment of breakfast favorites. And just because you're counting carbs doesn't mean you have to give up bread altogether. Turn to "The Bread Basket" to see what I mean.

• You'll also find meal ideas sized right for two, complete dinner menus and a fantastic assortment of salads, sandwiches and soups, all trimmed down with tasty results.

• As you might expect, *Healthy Cooking Annual Recipes* has you covered when your sweet tooth comes calling. Page through "Cakes, Pies & More" and "Treat Yourself" for over 60 unbeatable goodies. These specialties make terrific desserts, but you should also consider them the next time you need a bake-sale or potluck contribution.

• This edition of *Healthy Cooking Annual Recipes* also includes an assortment of lactose- and gluten-free dishes. Not only did these delightful specialties pass our tests, but they're sure to score points with everyone in your family— whether they follow a special diet or not!

• Our at-a-glance nutrition icons easily spotlight those items that are significantly low in fat, sodium or carbohydrates, as well as dishes that are meatless.

• We also offer Nutrition Facts with every recipe, and you'll even discover Diabetic Exchanges for items that are suitable for people with diabetes.

• You'll also notice more than 300 color photographs, including this year's addition of full-page photos. Finding a recipe that's right for you is easier than ever!

We're so excited to bring you this much-anticipated cookbook. I truly hope it brings a little bit of healthy cooking into your kitchen and plenty of flavor to your life.

Peggy Woodward, RD

Food Editor, *Healthy Cooking*

Nutrition Facts Nuggets

Nutritional Guidelines

Every recipe in *Healthy Cooking Annual Recipes* fits the lifestyle of health-conscious cooks. The recipes represent a variety of foods that will fit into any meal plan that is within the standards of the USDA's "My Pyramid Plan" for moderately active adults (see box below). The target nutritional content of entrees, on a per serving basis, is:

- 400 calories (or less)
- 12 grams of fat (or less)
- 800 mg sodium (or less)
- 100 mg cholesterol (or less)

How We Calculated the Nutrition Facts

- Whenever a choice of ingredients is given in a recipe (such as 1/3 cup of sour cream or plain yogurt), the first ingredient listed is always the one calculated in the Nutrition Facts.
- When a range is given for an ingredient (such as 2 to 3 teaspoons), we calculate the first amount given.
- Only the amount of marinade absorbed during preparation is calculated.
- Garnishes listed in recipes are generally included in our calculations.

Diabetic Exchanges

All recipes in this book have been reviewed by a Registered Dietitian. Diabetic Exchanges are assigned to recipes in accordance with guidelines from the American Diabetic and American Dietetic Associations. The majority of recipes in *Healthy Cooking Annual Recipes* are suitable for diabetics.

Special Diet Indicators

To help those on restricted diets easily find dishes to suit their needs, we clearly indicate recipes that are low in carbohydrates, fat or sodium or those that contain no meat. You'll find these colored special diet indicators after the recipe title where appropriate:

F One serving contains 3 grams or less of fat

S One serving contains 140 milligrams or less of sodium

C One serving contains 15 grams or less of carbohydrates

M Appetizers, salads, savory breads, side dishes and entrees that contain no meat

---

Makeover Madness!

Recipe makeovers are one of the most popular features of *Healthy Cooking* magazine, and you'll find 37 of them in this cookbook.

From coast to coast, readers send their favorite recipes to the *Healthy Cooking* Test Kitchen, with the hopes that our home economists can lighten up their dishes without losing any of the flavor.

When a recipe arrives for a makeover, the home economists quickly review it, making sure it's a challenge they're ready to face. Once they determine how the dish can be trimmed down, they roll up their sleeves and get to work.

They start by preparing the full-fat recipe just as it was sent. Next, they create a lighter version, noting all of the changes they've made. Sometimes, a dish needs to be prepared a few times to create the perfect replica of the original submission.

Once the team feels the new version captures the flavor, appearance and texture of the full-fat dish, the makeover is set before the *Healthy Cooking* Tasting Panel.

This group of editors samples both the full-fat and lighter dishes to be sure the one accurately reflects the other. Once it's passed the taste test, a lighter version of a reader's family favorite is born!

Daily Nutrition Guide

	Women 25–50	Women over 50	Men 50–65
Calories	2,000	1,800	2,400
Fat	67 g or less	60 g or less	80 g or less
Saturated Fat	22 g or less	20 g or less	27 g or less
Cholesterol	300 mg or less	300 mg or less	360 mg or less
Sodium	2,400 mg or less	2,400 mg or less	2,400 mg or less
Carbohydrates	300 g	270 g	360 g
Fiber	20-30 g	20-30 g	20-30 g
Protein	50 g	45 g or less	60 g

This chart is only a guide. Calorie requirements vary, depending on age, weight, height and amount of activity. Children's dietary needs vary as they grow.

FRESH PEACH SALSA

GOAT CHEESE CROSTINI

CHEESE-STUFFED MUSHROOMS
MANDARIN TURKEY PINWHEELS

Starters & Snacks

With these 27 appetizers and snacks, you can party hearty and not feel an ounce of guilt the next day. Whether you need a tasty nibble for a casual get-together or an hors d'oeuvre for a formal event, the recipes in this chapter have you covered.

Mandarin Turkey Pinwheels

F **C**

PREP: 15 min. + chilling **YIELD:** 2-1/2 dozen

LORIE MINER • KAMAS, UTAH

This light appetizer has sophisticated flavor. My cousin shared the recipe, and we made dozens for an open house. People came back for seconds and thirds!

- 1 pkg. (8 oz.) reduced-fat cream cheese
- 1/2 cup mandarin oranges, drained and chopped
- 1/2 tsp. curry powder
- 3 flour tortillas (12 in.), room temperature
- 1/2 lb. sliced deli smoked turkey
- 3 cups fresh baby spinach
- 2 green onions, chopped

1. In a small bowl, beat cream cheese until smooth. Stir in oranges and curry. Spread 1/2 cup mixture over each tortilla. Layer with turkey, spinach and green onions; roll up tightly. Wrap in plastic wrap and refrigerate for 2 hours or until firm.

2. Unwrap and cut each into 10 slices. Refrigerate leftovers.

Nutrition Facts: 1 appetizer equals 50 calories, 2 g fat (1 g saturated fat), 8 mg cholesterol, 149 mg sodium, 4 g carbohydrate, 1 g fiber, 3 g protein.

Cheese-Stuffed Mushrooms

F **S** **C** **M**

PREP: 25 min. **BAKE:** 15 min. **YIELD:** 2 dozen

CATHY BARGER • CLARKSVILLE, MICHIGAN

There are never leftovers when I serve these! This recipe is from a friend, but I modified it for a slimmer version that tastes as good as the original.

- 24 medium fresh mushrooms
- Butter-flavored cooking spray
- 3 Tbsp. chopped shallot
- 2 tsp. olive oil
- 1/2 cup white wine *or* reduced-sodium chicken broth
- 1/4 cup plus 6 Tbsp. shredded reduced-fat Swiss cheese, *divided*
- 1/4 cup grated Parmesan cheese
- 3 Tbsp. dry bread crumbs
- 2 to 3 Tbsp. fat-free milk
- 2 Tbsp. dried parsley flakes
- 1/2 tsp. dried tarragon
- 1/4 tsp. salt
- 1/4 tsp. pepper

1. Remove stems from mushrooms and finely chop. Place caps on a foil-lined baking sheet; spritz with cooking spray. Set aside.

2. In a small skillet, saute the shallots and chopped mushrooms in oil until tender. Stir in wine; bring to a boil. Reduce heat; simmer, uncovered, for 10-12 minutes or until liquid is absorbed. Remove from the heat.

3. Stir in 1/4 cup Swiss cheese, Parmesan cheese, bread crumbs, milk, parsley, tarragon, salt and pepper. Spoon into reserved mushroom caps. Sprinkle with remaining cheese and spritz with cooking spray.

4. Bake at 375° for 15-20 minutes or until mushrooms are tender and cheese is melted.

Nutrition Facts: 1 stuffed mushroom equals 26 calories, 1 g fat (trace saturated fat), 2 mg cholesterol, 54 mg sodium, 2 g carbohydrate, trace fiber, 2 g protein.

Goat Cheese Crostini **S** **C** **M**

PREP/TOTAL TIME: 10 min. **YIELD:** 32 appetizers

REBECCA EBELING • NEVADA CITY, CALIFORNIA

My husband got this crostini recipe from a friend at work. At first, I thought the flavors wouldn't work well together, but they blend deliciously!

- 1 cup crumbled goat cheese
- 1 tsp. minced fresh rosemary
- 1 French bread baguette (10-1/2 oz.), cut into 1/2-in. slices and toasted
- 3 Tbsp. honey
- 1/4 cup slivered almonds, toasted

1. In a small bowl, combine cheese and rosemary; spoon over toast slices. Drizzle with honey; sprinkle with almonds.

Nutrition Facts: 1 appetizer equals 76 calories, 4 g fat (2 g saturated fat), 6 mg cholesterol, 92 mg sodium, 9 g carbohydrate, 1 g fiber, 3 g protein. **Diabetic Exchanges:** 1/2 starch, 1/2 fat.

Curried Cran-Orange Snack Mix

PREP: 15 min. **BAKE:** 40 min. + cooling
YIELD: 5-1/2 cups

MARY BETH HARRIS-MURPHREE • TYLER, TEXAS

A new sweet/salty twist on an old party favorite, this mix includes pistachios, dried cranberries and a mild curry flavor that make it irresistible!

> 2 cups Wheat Chex
> 1-1/2 cups Corn Chex
> 1 cup chow mein noodles
> 1/3 cup shelled pistachios
> 2 Tbsp. butter, melted
> 2 Tbsp. orange juice
> 2 tsp. curry powder
> 1 tsp. salt
> 1 tsp. garlic powder
> 1 tsp. dried basil
> 1 tsp. grated orange peel
> 1/4 tsp. pepper
> 3/4 cup dried cranberries

1. In a large bowl, combine the cereals, noodles and pistachios; set aside. In a small bowl, combine the butter, orange juice, curry, salt, garlic powder, basil, orange peel and pepper. Drizzle over cereal mixture; toss to coat.

2. Transfer to a 15-in. x 10-in. x 1-in. baking pan coated with cooking spray. Bake at 275° for 40 minutes or until golden brown, stirring every 10 minutes. Stir in cranberries. Cool on wire racks. Store in an airtight container.

Nutrition Facts: 1/2 cup equals 125 calories, 5 g fat (2 g saturated fat), 5 mg cholesterol, 347 mg sodium, 19 g carbohydrate, 2 g fiber, 2 g protein. **Diabetic Exchanges:** 1 starch, 1 fat.

Chicken Fajita Pizza

PREP: 25 min. **BAKE:** 10 min. **YIELD:** 6 servings

REBECCA CLARK • WARRIOR, ALABAMA

This pizza is packed with flavorful seasonings, but it's the cilantro that gives it the fresh burst of flavor. If you like Southwestern foods and pizza, too, this one is for you!

> 1 tube (13.8 oz.) refrigerated pizza crust
> 1 lb. boneless skinless chicken breasts, cubed
> 3 tsp. canola oil, *divided*
> 1 tsp. fajita seasoning mix
> 1 medium sweet red pepper, julienned
> 1 medium green pepper, julienned
> 1 medium onion, halved and sliced
> 1 garlic clove, minced
> 1/2 cup salsa
> 1/4 tsp. pepper
> 1-1/2 cups (6 oz.) shredded reduced-fat Mexican cheese blend
> 2 Tbsp. minced fresh cilantro

1. Unroll crust into a 15-in. x 10-in. x 1-in. baking pan coated with cooking spray; flatten dough and build up edges slightly. Bake at 425° for 7-10 minutes or until golden brown.

CURRIED CRAN-ORANGE SNACK MIX

CHICKEN FAJITA PIZZA

2. Meanwhile, in a large nonstick skillet, saute chicken in 2 tsp. oil until no longer pink. Sprinkle with seasoning mix; cook 30 seconds longer. Remove and keep warm.

3. In the same skillet, saute the peppers and onion in remaining oil for 3 minutes. Add garlic; cook 2 minutes longer or until vegetables are crisp-tender. Remove from the heat; stir in the salsa, pepper and reserved chicken.

4. Spoon chicken mixture over crust; sprinkle with cheese. Bake for 6-10 minutes or until cheese is melted. Sprinkle with cilantro.

Nutrition Facts: 1 slice equals 382 calories, 12 g fat (4 g saturated fat), 62 mg cholesterol, 807 mg sodium, 38 g carbohydrate, 2 g fiber, 30 g protein.

Hoisin Cocktail Meatballs
F S C

PREP: 20 min. **BAKE:** 20 min. **YIELD:** 32 appetizers

DEIRDRE DEE COX • MILWAUKEE, WISCONSIN

These upscale, Asian-inspired meatballs are ideal for appetizer parties or get-togethers with friends.

2 Tbsp. hoisin sauce
1 Tbsp. reduced-sodium soy sauce
1 tsp. sesame oil
1/4 cup dry bread crumbs
3 Tbsp. chopped green onions
3 Tbsp. minced fresh parsley
2 garlic cloves, minced
1 tsp. minced fresh gingerroot
1-1/2 lbs. lean ground beef

SAUCE:
1/4 cup rice vinegar
1/4 cup hoisin sauce
2 Tbsp. water
2 Tbsp. sesame oil
2 Tbsp. reduced-sodium soy sauce
1 Tbsp. honey
2 garlic cloves, minced
1 tsp. minced fresh gingerroot

1. In a large bowl, combine the first eight ingredients. Crumble beef over mixture and mix well.

2. Shape into 32 meatballs. Place in a 13-in. x 9-in. baking dish coated with cooking spray. Bake, uncovered, at 350° for 20-25 minutes or until meat is no longer pink.

3. Meanwhile, in a small saucepan, combine the sauce ingredients; heat through. Serve with meatballs.

Nutrition Facts: 1 meatball equals 56 calories, 3 g fat (1 g saturated fat), 13 mg cholesterol, 121 mg sodium, 3 g carbohydrate, trace fiber, 4 g protein.

MEXICAN CHICKEN MEATBALLS

Mexican Chicken Meatballs
F S C

PREP: 20 min. **BAKE:** 15 min. **YIELD:** 5 dozen

KATRINA LOPES • LYMAN, SOUTH CAROLINA

These low-fat meatballs taste fabulous on their own, but if you want to kick things up a notch, serve with a dip of melted Velveeta cheese and salsa. You could also sub in ground white turkey for chicken.

1/2	cup egg substitute
1	can (4 oz.) chopped green chilies
1	cup crushed cornflakes
1	cup (4 oz.) shredded reduced-fat Mexican cheese blend
1/2	tsp. seasoned salt
1/4	tsp. cayenne pepper
1	pkg. (1 lb.) ground chicken

Salsa, optional

1. In a large bowl, combine the first six ingredients. Crumble chicken over mixture and mix well. Shape into 1-in. balls. Place on baking sheets coated with cooking spray.

2. Bake at 375° for 12-15 minutes or until golden brown, turning occasionally. Serve with salsa if desired.

Nutrition Facts: 1 meatball (calculated without salsa) equals 21 calories, 1 g fat (trace saturated fat), 6 mg cholesterol, 49 mg sodium, 1 g carbohydrate, trace fiber, 2 g protein.

Trail Mix **S**

PREP/TOTAL TIME: 10 min. **YIELD:** 4 cups

MICHAEL VYSKOCIL • GLEN ROCK, PENNSYLVANIA

This recipe is so fast and fun that the kids can help you put it together! It makes a great little present for teachers, coaches and even scout leaders.

1/2	cup unblanched whole almonds
1/2	cup coarsely chopped walnuts
1/2	cup golden raisins
1/2	cup chopped dates
1/2	cup dried apple slices, chopped
1/2	cup dried apricots, chopped
1/2	cup semisweet chocolate chips
1/2	cup Honey Nut Cheerios

1. In a large bowl, combine all ingredients. Store in an airtight container.

Nutrition Facts: 1/3 cup equals 169 calories, 8 g fat (2 g saturated fat), 0 cholesterol, 15 mg sodium, 24 g carbohydrate, 3 g fiber, 4 g protein.

Yummy S'more Snack Cake

PREP: 20 min. **BAKE:** 20 min. + cooling
YIELD: 20 servings

DEBORAH WILLIAMS • PEORIA, ARIZONA

My delicious snack cake is a close second to yummy s'mores enjoyed by the campfire.

- 2-1/2 cups reduced-fat graham cracker crumbs (about 15 whole crackers)
- 1/2 cup sugar
- 1/3 cup cake flour
- 1/3 cup whole wheat flour
- 2 tsp. baking powder
- 1/4 tsp. salt
- 3 egg whites
- 1 cup light soy milk
- 1/4 cup unsweetened applesauce
- 1/4 cup canola oil
- 2 cups miniature marshmallows
- 1 cup (6 oz.) semisweet chocolate chips

1. In a large bowl, combine the first six ingredients. In a small bowl, whisk the egg whites, soy milk, applesauce and oil. Stir into dry ingredients just until moistened. Transfer to a 13-in. x 9-in. baking pan coated with cooking spray.

2. Bake at 350° for 12-15 minutes or until a toothpick inserted near the center comes out clean. Sprinkle with marshmallows. Bake 4-6 minutes longer or until marshmallows are softened. Cool cake on a wire rack for 10 minutes.

3. In a microwave, melt chocolate chips; stir until smooth. Drizzle over cake. Cool cake completely on a wire rack.

Nutrition Facts: 1 piece equals 168 calories, 6 g fat (2 g saturated fat), 0 cholesterol, 159 mg sodium, 28 g carbohydrate, 2 g fiber, 3 g protein. **Diabetic Exchanges:** 2 starch, 1 fat.

Creamy Dill Dip F C M

PREP/TOTAL TIME: 10 min + chilling **YIELD:** 1-1/3 cup

CORKY HUFFSMITH • INDIO, CALIFORNIA

Beau Monde seasoning is the secret ingredient that adds a little special zing to this low-fat, classic dill dip. I usually double the recipe since it only gets better after a couple of days in the fridge.

- 2/3 cup fat-free mayonnaise
- 2/3 cup reduced-fat sour cream
- 1 Tbsp. chopped green onions
- 1 Tbsp. dried parsley flakes
- 2 tsp. Beau Monde seasoning
- 2 tsp. dill weed

Assorted fresh vegetables

1. In a small bowl, combine the first six ingredients. Cover and refrigerate overnight. Serve with assorted fresh vegetables.

Nutrition Facts: 3 Tbsp. (calculated without vegetables) equals 49 calories, 3 g fat (1 g saturated fat), 10 mg cholesterol, 371 mg sodium, 5 g carbohydrate, 1 g fiber, 2 g protein.

"Beau Monde" is French for "beautiful world," and just as its name implies, the seasoning blend is a delightful balance of onion, celery and salt. Feel free to use it with any savory dish you may be preparing.

YUMMY S'MORE SNACK CAKE

CREAMY DILL DIP

Spiced Apple Tea ⓕ ⓢ ⓒ

PREP/TOTAL TIME: 25 min. **YIELD:** 5 servings

SHARON DELANEY-CHRONIS • SOUTH MILWAUKEE, WISCONSIN

I love to try new recipes for my husband and our friends. This spiced tea is one of our favorites. I enjoy it warm, and I refrigerate and serve it cold, too.

- 2 cups unsweetened apple juice
- 6 whole cloves
- 1 cinnamon stick (3 in.)
- 3 cups water
- 5 individual tea bags

Additional cinnamon sticks (3 in.), optional

1. In a small saucepan, combine the apple juice, cloves and cinnamon stick. Bring to a boil. Reduce heat; simmer, uncovered, for 10-15 minutes.

2. Meanwhile, in a large saucepan, bring water to a boil. Remove from the heat; add tea bags. Cover and steep for 5 minutes. Discard tea bags. Strain juice mixture, discarding cloves and cinnamon. Stir into tea. Serve warm with additional cinnamon sticks for garnish if desired.

Nutrition Facts: 1 cup equals 47 calories, trace fat (trace saturated fat), 0 cholesterol, 3 mg sodium, 12 g carbohydrate, trace fiber, trace protein. **Diabetic Exchange:** 1 fruit.

Crunchy Spiced Nuts

PREP: 20 min. **BAKE:** 45 min. + cooling **YIELD:** 3 cups

SUZANNE WOOD • HOUSTON, TEXAS

These flavor-packed nuts provide vitamin E and omega-3 fatty acids. You'll love 'em!

- 2 egg whites
- 2 Tbsp. water
- 2 cups confectioners' sugar
- 3 Tbsp. ground cinnamon
- 2 Tbsp. ground ginger
- 1 Tbsp. ground cloves
- 2 tsp. salt
- 1 tsp. ground nutmeg
- 1 cup unblanched almonds
- 1/2 cup pecan halves
- 1/2 cup walnut halves

1. In a shallow bowl, whisk egg whites and water. Sift together the confectioners' sugar, cinnamon, ginger, cloves, salt and nutmeg; place sugar mixture in another shallow bowl. Coat nuts in egg mixture, then dip in sugar mixture.

2. Transfer to a baking sheet coated with cooking spray. Bake at 250° for 45 minutes, stirring nuts occasionally. Cool completely. Store nuts in an airtight container.

Nutrition Facts: 1/4 cup equals 182 calories, 12 g fat (1 g saturated fat), 0 cholesterol, 243 mg sodium, 17 g carbohydrate, 3 g fiber, 4 g protein.

SPICED APPLE TEA

SHRIMP WITH ORANGE PINEAPPLE SAUCE

Shrimp with Orange Pineapple Sauce F S C

PREP/TOTAL TIME: 15 min
YIELD: about 2-1/2 dozen (2/3 cup sauce)

RADELLE KNAPPENBERGER • OVIEDO, FLORIDA

This is a very light appetizer that's easy to make. I've been asked for the recipe many times. In fact, my husband even likes it as a main dish!

1/4	cup pineapple preserves
1/4	cup orange marmalade
1/4	cup lemon juice
1	Tbsp. water
1	tsp. cornstarch
1	lb. cooked medium shrimp, peeled and deveined

1. In a small saucepan, combine the first five ingredients. Bring to a boil; cook and stir for 2 minutes or until thickened. Chill until serving. Serve with shrimp.

Nutrition Facts: 1 shrimp with 1 tsp. sauce equals 29 calories, trace fat (trace saturated fat), 22 mg cholesterol, 23 mg sodium, 4 g carbohydrate, trace fiber, 3 g protein.

Easy Buffalo Chicken Dip S C

PREP/TOTAL TIME: 30 min   **YIELD:** 4 cups

JANICE FOLTZ • HERSHEY, PENNSYLVANIA

Guys of all ages will simply devour this savory and delicious dip. The spicy kick makes it perfect football-watching food. It always brings raves. Serve it with crackers or even celery sticks.

1	pkg. (8 oz.) reduced-fat cream cheese
1	cup (8 oz.) reduced-fat sour cream
1/2	cup Louisiana-style hot sauce
3	cups shredded cooked chicken breast

Assorted crackers

1. In a large bowl, beat the cream cheese, sour cream and hot sauce until smooth; stir in chicken.

2. Transfer to an 8-in. square baking dish coated with cooking spray. Cover and bake at 350° for 18-22 minutes or until heated through. Serve dip warm with crackers.

Nutrition Facts: 3 Tbsp. (calculated without crackers) equals 77 calories, 4 g fat (2 g saturated fat), 28 mg cholesterol, 71 mg sodium, 1 g carbohydrate, trace fiber,

Spinach & Black Bean Egg Rolls F M

PREP/TOTAL TIME: 30 min. **YIELD:** 20 egg rolls

MELANIE SCOTT • AMARILLO, TEXAS

Black beans and spinach both provide folate, iron and potassium in these delicious baked egg rolls. Rolling them up is a cinch, too! Try one—you'll see! They're great with salsa or ranch salad dressing on the side.

      2 cups frozen corn, thawed
      1 can (15 oz.) black beans, rinsed and drained
      1 pkg. (10 oz.) frozen chopped spinach, thawed and squeezed dry
      1 cup (4 oz.) shredded reduced-fat Mexican cheese blend
      1 can (4 oz.) chopped green chilies, drained
      4 green onions, chopped
      1 tsp. ground cumin
    1/2 tsp. chili powder
    1/2 tsp. pepper
     20 egg roll wrappers
Cooking spray
Salsa and reduced-fat ranch salad dressing, optional

1. In a large bowl, combine the first nine ingredients. Place 1/4 cup mixture in the center of one egg roll wrapper. (Keep remaining wrappers covered with a damp paper towel until ready to use.) Fold bottom corner over filling. Fold sides toward center over filling. Moisten remaining corner with water; roll up tightly to seal. Repeat.

2. Place seam side down on baking sheets coated with cooking spray. Spray tops of egg rolls with cooking spray. Bake at 425° for 10-15 minutes or until lightly browned. Serve warm with salsa and dressing if desired. Refrigerate leftovers.

Nutrition Facts: 1 egg roll (calculated without salsa and dressing) equals 147 calories, 2 g fat (1 g saturated fat), 7 mg cholesterol, 298 mg sodium, 26 g carbohydrate, 2 g fiber, 7 g protein. **Diabetic Exchanges:** 1-1/2 starch, 1 very lean meat.

Crab Salad Tarts F S C

PREP/TOTAL TIME: 25 min. **YIELD:** 15 appetizers

DONNA ROBERTS • SHUMWAY, ILLINOIS

These little bites are as easy as they are elegant. Guests will never know you made and froze them weeks ago!

- 1 can (6 oz.) lump crabmeat, drained
- 1/3 cup shredded reduced-fat Swiss cheese
- 1/4 cup Miracle Whip Light
- 2 Tbsp. finely chopped celery
- 2 Tbsp. finely chopped red onion
- 1 tsp. dried parsley flakes
- 1/4 tsp. pepper
- 1 pkg. (1.9 oz.) frozen miniature phyllo tart shell

1. In a small bowl, combine crab-meat, cheese, Miracle Whip Light, celery, onion, parsley and pepper.

2. Spoon filling into tart shells. Cover and freeze for up to 3 months. Or, place tart shells on an ungreased baking sheet. Bake at 350° for 10-12 minutes or until shells are lightly browned. Serve warm.

3. To use frozen tarts: Place on an ungreased baking sheet. Bake at 350° for 13-15 minutes or until tart shells are lightly browned.

Nutrition Facts: 1 appetizer equals 47 calories, 2 g fat (trace saturated fat), 3 mg cholesterol, 115 mg sodium, 5 g carbohydrate, trace fiber, 2 g protein.

Spinach & Crab Dip C

PREP/TOTAL TIME: 25 min. **YIELD:** 4 cups

SANDIE HEINDEL • LIBERTY, MISSOURI

We love this recipe! I've lightened it considerably without losing flavor, and no one can tell the difference. Give the dip a try on baked potatoes as well.

- 1 pkg. (10 oz.) frozen chopped spinach, thawed and squeezed dry
- 1 pkg. (8 oz.) reduced-fat cream cheese, cubed
- 1 cup (8 oz.) plain yogurt
- 1/2 cup grated Parmesan cheese
- 1/2 cup reduced-fat salad dressing
- 2 garlic cloves, minced
- 1 tsp. crushed red pepper flakes
- 1/4 tsp. salt
- 1/4 tsp. pepper
- 1 can (6 oz.) lump crabmeat, drained

Assorted crackers or baked tortilla chip scoops

1. In a large saucepan over low heat, combine the first nine ingredients. Cook and stir until cream cheese is melted. Stir in crab; heat through.

2. Transfer to a serving bowl; serve with crackers. Refrigerate leftovers.

Nutrition Facts: 1/4 cup (calculated without crackers) equals 89 calories, 6 g fat (3 g saturated fat), 26 mg cholesterol, 256 mg sodium, 3 g carbohydrate, 1 g fiber, 6 g protein.

If Spinach & Crab Dip is making an appearance on your appetizer buffet, consider a tip from Sandie Heindel. "The zesty dip is great with crackers, but I like it with slices of **sourdough and French bread**. It's also good with wedges of pumpernickel."

SPINACH & CRAB DIP

CRAB SALAD TARTS

Fresh Peach Salsa F S C M

PREP: 15 min. + chilling **YIELD:** 4 cups

SHAWNA LAUFER • FT. MYERS, FLORIDA

With just a few minutes in the food processor, this fresh salsa takes almost no time to make. It pairs well with grilled chicken or fish.

- 4 medium peaches, peeled and pitted
- 2 large tomatoes, cut into wedges and seeded
- 1/2 sweet onion, cut into wedges
- 1/2 cup fresh cilantro leaves
- 2 garlic cloves, peeled and crushed
- 2 cans (4 oz. *each*) chopped green chilies
- 4 tsp. cider vinegar
- 1 tsp. lime juice
- 1/4 tsp. pepper

Baked tortilla chip scoops

1. In a food processor, combine the first five ingredients; cover and pulse until coarsely chopped. Add the chilies, vinegar, lime juice and pepper; cover and pulse just until blended. Transfer to a serving bowl; chill until serving. Serve with chips.

Nutrition Facts: 1/4 cup (calculated without chips) equals 20 calories, trace fat (trace saturated fat), 0 cholesterol, 58 mg sodium, 5 g carbohydrate, 1 g fiber, 1 g protein. **Diabetic Exchange:** Free food.

FRESH PEACH SALSA

Chicken Alfredo Veggie Pizza

PREP: 45 min. + rising **BAKE:** 25 min. **YIELD:** 8 servings

NANCY LINDSAY • NEW MARKET, IOWA

The name of this incredible pizza says it all. I created this recipe myself, and it's become one of our all-time favorites! The vegetables' bright colors make it very appealing, particularly when sliced into thin wedges and set on an appetizer tray. It also makes a comforting dinner for casual get-togethers.

- 1 pkg. (1/4 oz.) active dry yeast
- 1 cup warm water (110° to 115°)
- 1 Tbsp. canola oil
- 2 tsp. sugar
- 3/4 tsp. salt, *divided*
- 1/2 tsp. garlic-herb seasoning blend
- 1/2 cup whole wheat flour
- 2-1/4 to 2-1/2 cups bread flour
- 1 Tbsp. cornmeal
- 1 cup fresh baby spinach
- 4 tsp. all-purpose flour
- 1-1/4 cups 2% milk
- 1-1/2 cups cubed cooked chicken breast
- 1/3 cup shredded Parmesan cheese

Dash white pepper

- 1 cup sliced fresh mushrooms
- 1 plum tomato, seeded and chopped
- 1 small onion, diced
- 1/2 cup chopped green pepper
- 1/4 cup sliced ripe olives
- 1 cup (4 oz.) shredded part-skim mozzarella cheese
- 1/2 cup shredded Colby-Monterey Jack cheese

1. In a bowl, dissolve yeast in warm water. Add oil, sugar, 1/2 teaspoon salt, seasoning blend, whole wheat flour and 2-1/4 cups bread flour. Beat until smooth. Stir in enough remaining flour to form a stiff dough.

2. Turn onto a floured surface; knead until smooth, about 6 minutes.

3. Place in a bowl coated with cooking spray, turning once to coat the top. Cover and let rise for 20 minutes.

4. Punch dough down; roll into a 15-in. circle. Sprinkle cornmeal over a 14-in. pizza pan coated with cooking spray. Transfer dough to pan; build up edges slightly. Bake at 425° for 12 minutes or until edges are lightly browned.

5. Meanwhile, in a saucepan, bring 1/2 in. of water to a boil. Add spinach; cover and boil for 3 minutes or until wilted. Drain and squeeze dry.

6. In a saucepan, combine flour and milk until smooth. Bring to a boil; cook and stir for 2 minutes or until thickened. Add chicken, Parmesan cheese, remaining salt, pepper and reserved spinach. Cook and stir over medium heat until cheese is melted.

7. Spread over crust; top with remaining ingredients. Bake for 10 minutes or until cheeses are melted.

Nutrition Facts: 1 slice equals 317 calories, 9 g fat (4 g saturated fat), 40 mg cholesterol, 476 mg sodium, 38 g carbohydrate, 3 g fiber, 22 g protein. **Diabetic Exchanges:** 2-1/2 starch, 2 lean meat, 1/2 fat.

CHICKEN ALFREDO VEGGIE PIZZA

Light and Delicious Guacamole C M

PREP/TOTAL TIME: 10 min. **YIELD:** 2-1/2 cups

LISA SIEVERS • PHILIPSBURG, PENNSYLVANIA

Dips and spreads can be high in calories and fat, so I was happy to find this lightened-up version of guacamole. Now we can enjoy this classic dip without feeling any guilt. I love the avocado flavor, and my husband told me this is the best guacamole he's tasted! If you don't have lemon juice on hand, lime will work, too.

2	medium ripe avocados, peeled and pitted
1	pkg. (8 oz.) fat-free cream cheese
1	can (4 oz.) chopped green chilies, drained
1/4	cup chopped onion
1	Tbsp. lemon juice
1	garlic clove, peeled and halved
1/4	tsp. salt
2	plum tomatoes, seeded and finely chopped

Baked tortilla chip scoops

1. In a food processor, combine the first seven ingredients. Cover and process until blended. Stir in tomatoes. Serve with chips.

Nutrition Facts: 1/4 cup (calculated without chips) equals 87 calories, 6 g fat (1 g saturated fat), 2 mg cholesterol, 231 mg sodium, 6 g carbohydrate, 3 g fiber, 4 g protein.

Zesty Hot Chocolate F

PREP/TOTAL TIME: 20 min. **YIELD:** 2 qt.

JOY WEINSTEIN • BOULDER, COLORADO

Chili powder gives a subtle spiciness to this chocolate sipper that's sure to warm any chilly guest from head to toe.

1/2	cup sugar
1/4	cup baking cocoa
1	tsp. ground cinnamon
1	tsp. chili powder
3/4	tsp. ground cloves
1/4	tsp. salt
6	cups fat-free milk
2	cups water
1	tsp. vanilla extract
1/2	cup reduced-fat whipped topping
1/4	tsp. ground nutmeg

1. In a large saucepan, combine the first six ingredients. Gradually add milk and water; cook and stir until heated through. Remove from the heat; stir in vanilla. Ladle into mugs; top each serving with whipped topping and sprinkle with nutmeg.

Nutrition Facts: 1 cup hot chocolate with 1 Tbsp. whipped topping equals 132 calories, 1 g fat (1 g saturated fat), 4 mg cholesterol, 155 mg sodium, 25 g carbohydrate, 1 g fiber, 7 g protein. **Diabetic Exchanges:** 1 starch, 1/2 fat-free milk.

Party Pretzels F

PREP/TOTAL TIME: 25 min. **YIELD:** 12 cups

CARRIE SHAUB • MOUNT JOY, PENNSYLVANIA

Not only are these a perfect mid-morning or afternoon snack at work, they're ideal for hungry kids just home from school. Plus, they make for fantastic party food!

   1 pkg. (16 oz.) fat-free miniature pretzels
1/4 cup canola oil
   3 tsp. garlic powder
   1 tsp. dill weed
1/2 tsp. lemon-pepper seasoning

1. Place pretzels in an ungreased 15-in. x 10-in. x 1-in. baking pan. Combine the oil, garlic powder, dill and lemon-pepper; drizzle over pretzels and toss to coat. Bake at 350° for 12 minutes, stirring twice. Cool on a wire rack. Store in an airtight container.

Nutrition Facts: 1/2 cup equals 89 calories, 2 g fat (trace saturated fat), 0 cholesterol, 290 mg sodium, 16 g carbohydrate, 1 g fiber, 2 g protein. **Diabetic Exchanges:** 1 starch, 1/2 fat.

Cranberry Popcorn Deluxe
S C

PREP: 15 min. **BAKE:** 15 min. + cooling **YIELD:** 8 cups

CAROLYN SYKORA • BLOOMER, WISCONSIN

I created this recipe when I needed a festive treat for the holidays. Everyone finds the combination irresistible!

   8 cups air-popped popcorn
3/4 cup dried cranberries
1/4 cup slivered almonds
1/4 cup pecan halves
1/4 cup honey
   3 Tbsp. butter
   2 Tbsp. maple syrup
1/4 tsp. almond extract

1. In a shallow roasting pan, combine the popcorn, cranberries, almonds and pecans.

2. In a small saucepan, combine the honey, butter and syrup. Cook and stir over medium heat until butter is melted. Remove from the heat; stir in the almond extract. Drizzle over popcorn mixture and toss to coat.

3. Bake at 325° for 15 minutes, stirring every 5 minutes. Cool on a wire rack, stirring occasionally. Store in an airtight container.

Nutrition Facts: 1/2 cup equals 96 calories, 4 g fat (2 g saturated fat), 6 mg cholesterol, 16 mg sodium, 14 g carbohydrate, 1 g fiber, 1 g protein. **Diabetic Exchanges:** 1 starch, 1 fat.

It's easy to trim down your own dip and spread recipes. Start by using naturally light and flavorful ingredients such as **veggies and herbs**. A small amount of fat lends a richness to dips and spreads, so use a combination of reduced-fat and fat-free dairy products.

PARTY PRETZELS

CRANBERRY POPCORN DELUXE

White Chocolate Popcorn Deluxe

PREP: 15 min. + cooling **YIELD:** 2 qt.

KAY SCOTT • HICO, TEXAS

This recipe is so fast and simple. I take it to potlucks and for the teacher's table at work. I love to try different types of chocolate and other mix-ins, too!

- 8 cups air-popped popcorn
- 2 squares (1 oz. *each*) white baking chocolate
- 1 tsp. butter
- 1/3 cup dried cranberries
- 1/4 cup chopped walnuts
- 3/4 tsp. salt

1. Place popcorn in a large bowl. In a microwave, melt white chocolate and butter; stir until smooth. Pour over popcorn mixture and toss to coat. Add the cranberries, nuts and salt.

2. Spread onto waxed paper. Cool until set. Store in an airtight container.

Nutrition Facts: 1 cup equals 114 calories, 6 g fat (2 g saturated fat), 3 mg cholesterol, 233 mg sodium, 15 g carbohydrate, 2 g fiber, 2 g protein.

Golden Pineapple Salsa
F S C M

PREP: 10 min. + chilling **YIELD:** 2-1/2 cups

BRYNNE GARMAN • BELLEVUE, WASHINGTON

In addition to being a great appetizer, this delicious salsa is an excellent accompaniment to fish and chicken.

- 2 cups chopped fresh pineapple
- 1/3 cup finely chopped sweet onion
- 1/4 cup finely chopped green pepper
- 2 Tbsp. lime juice
- 2 garlic cloves, minced
- 2 Tbsp. minced fresh mint
- 1/4 tsp. salt
- 1/4 tsp. ground cumin
- 1/8 tsp. cayenne pepper

1. In a small bowl, combine the pineapple, onion, green pepper, lime juice and garlic. Stir in the mint, salt, cumin and cayenne. Cover and refrigerate for at least 1 hour. Serve with your favorite pork chops, fish or poultry.

Nutrition Facts: 1/4 cup equals 20 calories, trace fat (trace saturated fat), 0 cholesterol, 60 mg sodium, 5 g carbohydrate, 1 g fiber, trace protein. **Diabetic Exchange:** Free food.

Cool and Creamy Spinach Dip
F C M

PREP: 10 min. + chilling **YIELD:** 2-1/2 cups

MELISSA HANSEN • ROCHESTER, MINNESOTA

I always keep this easy dip on hand—it encourages me to eat more fresh veggies. The light cottage cheese adds protein and calcium without the fat.

COOL AND CREAMY SPINACH DIP

WHITE CHOCOLATE POPCORN DELUXE

- 1 cup (8 oz.) 2% cottage cheese
- 1 pkg. (10 oz.) frozen chopped spinach, thawed and squeezed dry
- 1 cup (8 oz.) fat-free sour cream
- 2 Tbsp. fat-free milk
- 1 Tbsp. grated Parmesan-Romano or Parmesan cheese
- 1 Tbsp. prepared reduced-fat ranch salad dressing
- 1/4 tsp. dill weed
- 1/8 tsp. garlic powder

Assorted fresh vegetables

1. In a food processor, cover and process cottage cheese until smooth. Transfer to a small bowl; stir in the spinach, sour cream, milk, Parmesan-Romano cheese, ranch dressing, dill and garlic powder. Cover and refrigerate for 3-4 hours. Serve with vegetables.

Nutrition Facts: 1/4 cup (calculated without vegetables) equals 56 calories, 1 g fat (trace saturated fat), 8 mg cholesterol, 145 mg sodium, 7 g carbohydrate, 1 g fiber, 5 g protein. **Diabetic Exchange:** 1/2 starch.

Roasted Pepper Dip F S C M

PREP: 10 min. + chilling **YIELD:** 2 cups

AMY BRASLEY • MERIDIAN, IDAHO

I've brought this creamy dip to many events in our community, to family get-togethers and to the elementary school where I work as a school psychologist. I'm always asked for the recipe.

- 4 oz. fat-free cream cheese
- 1/2 cup reduced-fat sour cream
- 1/2 cup chopped roasted sweet red peppers
- 1/2 cup grated Parmesan cheese
- 1/3 cup shredded pepper Jack cheese
- 1/4 cup finely chopped onion
- 1/8 tsp. garlic powder
- 1/8 tsp. pepper

Assorted crackers

1. In a small bowl, beat cream cheese and sour cream until smooth. Stir in the peppers, cheeses, onion, garlic powder and pepper. Refrigerate for at least one hour. Serve with crackers.

Nutrition Facts: 2 Tbsp. (calculated without crackers) equals 42 calories, 2 g fat (1 g saturated fat), 8 mg cholesterol, 126 mg sodium, 2 g carbohydrate, trace fiber, 3 g protein.

When serving dip on a hot day, **keep it cool.** Fill a serving bowl with ice cubes. Fill a smaller bowl with dip and set it over the ice. If travelling, put the dip in a bowl, cover with plastic wrap and set it in a cooler. Assemble the ice-filled serving bowl when you arrive.

GREEK INSPIRED QUINOA SALAD

BLACKBERRY SPINACH SALAD

CANTALOUPE CHICKEN SALAD

Salads

Whether crisp and refreshing or cool and creamy, salads are a popular staple with today's family cooks. Surprise your gang tonight with one of the following green leaf delights, pasta specialties or any of the other enticing salads found here.

Cantaloupe Chicken Salad

PREP/TOTAL TIME: 20 min. **YIELD:** 2 servings

GINGER SULLIVAN • CUTLER BAY, FLORIDA

I found this recipe several years ago, and my son and I enjoy it often. It's just right for a cool-me-down lunch.

1/4	cup fat-free mayonnaise
2	Tbsp. fat-free sour cream
1-1/2	tsp. sugar
1/2	tsp. grated lemon peel
1/2	tsp. lemon juice
1/4	tsp. ground ginger

Dash salt and pepper

1	cup cubed cooked chicken breast
1/2	cup sliced celery
1/2	cup seedless red grapes, halved
2	green onions, chopped
1	small cantaloupe, halved and seeded
1/4	cup slivered almonds, toasted

1. In a large bowl, combine the mayonnaise, sour cream, sugar, peel, lemon juice, ginger, salt and pepper. Add the chicken, celery, grapes and onions; toss to coat. Spoon 1 cup salad mixture into each cantaloupe half; sprinkle with almonds.

Nutrition Facts: 1 serving equals 350 calories, 11 g fat (2 g saturated fat), 60 mg cholesterol, 417 mg sodium, 40 g carbohydrate, 5 g fiber, 27 g protein. **Diabetic Exchanges:** 3 very lean meat, 2 fruit, 1-1/2 fat, 1/2 starch.

Carrot Raisin Salad F S M

PREP: 15 min. + chilling **YIELD:** 4 servings

ELIZABETH BORGEMENKE • MASON, OHIO

Vanilla yogurt gives this simple and traditional salad a special twist. It's wonderful with grilled chicken, and it makes a great lunch side with your favorite sandwich.

2-1/2	cups shredded carrots
1	celery rib, chopped
1/2	cup raisins
1	carton (6 oz.) vanilla yogurt

1. In a small bowl, combine all ingredients. Cover and refrigerate for at least 4 hours. Stir before serving.

Nutrition Facts: 3/4 cup equals 127 calories, 2 g fat (1 g saturated fat), 4 mg cholesterol, 85 mg sodium, 27 g carbohydrate, 3 g fiber, 3 g protein. **Diabetic Exchanges:** 1 vegetable, 1 fruit, 1/2 starch.

Blackberry Spinach Salad C M

PREP/TOTAL TIME: 20 min. **YIELD:** 6 servings

MARY LOU TIMPSON • COLORADO CITY, ARIZONA

This delightful salad is a delicious combination of nutritious ingredients, including fresh spinach, blackberries, tomatoes and walnuts. A sprinkle of feta cheese and a flavorful homemade dressing make it seem like you fussed.

6	cups fresh baby spinach
1	cup fresh blackberries
1	cup cherry tomatoes, halved
1	green onion, sliced
2	Tbsp. chopped walnuts, toasted
2	Tbsp. olive oil
1	Tbsp. balsamic vinegar
2-1/2	tsp. honey
1	garlic clove, minced
1	tsp. Dijon mustard
1/4	tsp. salt
1/4	tsp. pepper
2/3	cup crumbled feta cheese

1. In a large salad bowl, combine the spinach, blackberries, tomatoes, onion and walnuts.

2. In a small bowl, whisk the oil, vinegar, honey, garlic, mustard, salt and pepper. Drizzle over salad and toss to coat. Sprinkle with cheese. Serve immediately.

Nutrition Facts: 1 cup equals 116 calories, 8 g fat (2 g saturated fat), 7 mg cholesterol, 266 mg sodium, 9 g carbohydrate, 3 g fiber, 4 g protein. **Diabetic Exchanges:** 1 vegetable, 1 fat, 1/2 lean meat.

Sausage Potato Salad

PREP: 20 min. **COOK:** 15 min. **YIELD:** 5 servings

GINETTE STARSHAK • DECATUR, ILLINOIS

I like making this cool potato recipe on warm days. I reduced the oil quite a bit and added a little more honey mustard, giving it a richer taste. Sausage, too, adds good flavor to this delicious salad, giving it a richer taste! It's a wonderful dish alongside soup or a sandwich.

- 1 lb. small red potatoes
- 2 Tbsp. olive oil
- 2 Tbsp. honey mustard
- 1 Tbsp. white vinegar
- 1 Tbsp. minced fresh parsley
- 1 tsp. minced fresh tarragon or 1/4 tsp. dried tarragon
- 1/4 tsp. salt
- 1/4 tsp. pepper
- 1/4 lb. smoked turkey sausage, halved and sliced
- 1 small onion, chopped

1. Scrub potatoes; place in a small saucepan and cover with water. Bring to a boil. Reduce heat; cover and cook for 15-20 minutes or until tender.

2. For dressing, in a small bowl, combine the oil, honey mustard, vinegar and seasonings. Set aside. In a small nonstick skillet coated with cooking spray, cook and stir sausage until heated through.

3. Drain potatoes; cool slightly. Cut into 1/4-in. slices and place in a bowl. Add the onion, sausage and dressing; toss to coat. Serve warm or chilled.

Nutrition Facts: 2/3 cup equals 162 calories, 7 g fat (1 g saturated fat), 14 mg cholesterol, 398 mg sodium, 19 g carbohydrate, 2 g fiber, 6 g protein. **Diabetic Exchanges:** 1-1/2 fat, 1 starch.

Fruited Mixed Greens Salad S M

PREP/TOTAL TIME: 15 min. **YIELD:** 6 servings

ANN YARBER • GOLDSBY, OKLAHOMA

Thanks to all the fruits and veggies in this attention-getting side salad, you'll enjoy a good dose of antioxidants.

- 1 pkg. (5 oz.) spring mix salad greens
- 2 cups fresh baby spinach
- 1 cup fresh arugula *or* additional fresh baby spinach
- 1 can (11 oz.) mandarin oranges, drained
- 2/3 cup chopped walnuts
- 1/2 cup fresh raspberries
- 1/2 cup canned diced beets
- 1/2 cup fresh blueberries
- 1/4 cup sliced radishes

DRESSING:
- 2/3 cup fat-free poppy seed salad dressing
- 3 Tbsp. red raspberry preserves
- 1 tsp. white wine vinegar

1. In a large bowl, combine the first nine ingredients. In a small bowl, whisk the dressing ingredients. Drizzle over salad; toss to coat. Serve immediately.

Nutrition Facts: 1-2/3 cups equals 197 calories, 8 g fat (1 g saturated fat), 4 mg cholesterol, 116 mg sodium, 28 g carbohydrate, 3 g fiber, 6 g protein. **Diabetic Exchanges:** 1 starch, 1 vegetable, 1 fat, 1/2 fruit.

Summer-Fresh Quinoa Salad M

PREP: 25 min. + chilling **YIELD:** 14 servings

LIZ GADBOIS • WOODVILLE, WISCONSIN

This light and refreshing salad is easy to prepare and perfect for hot summer days. I often add zucchini or summer squash and use fresh tomatoes instead of sun-dried.

- 2 cups quinoa, rinsed
- 1 cup boiling water
- 1/2 cup sun-dried tomatoes (not packed in oil)

- 1 medium cucumber, peeled, seeded and chopped
- 1 *each* medium green, sweet red and yellow peppers, chopped
- 6 green onions, thinly sliced
- 1 pkg. (4 oz.) crumbled garlic and herb feta cheese
- 1/2 cup reduced-fat sun-dried tomato salad dressing, *divided*

1. Cook quinoa according to package directions. Transfer to a large bowl; cool completely. In a small bowl, combine water and tomatoes; let stand for 5 minutes. Drain and chop tomatoes; add to quinoa. Stir in the cucumber, peppers, onions, cheese and 1/4 cup salad dressing.

2. Cover and refrigerate for 2 hours. Just before serving, stir in remaining salad dressing.

Editor's Note: Look for quinoa in the cereal, rice or organic food aisle.

Nutrition Facts: 3/4 cup equals 148 calories, 5 g fat (117 g saturated fat), 6 mg cholesterol, 254 mg sodium, 22 g carbohydrate, 2 g fiber, 5 g protein. **Diabetic Exchanges:** 1-1/2 starch, 1 fat.

Feed your brain with **antioxidants** such as foods that offer lots of vitamin A, C and E. Give Fruited Mixed Greens Salad a try. It's loaded with the fruits and veggies that can help fight age-related memory loss.

FRUITED MIXED GREENS SALAD

SUMMER-FRESH QUINOA SALAD

Thai-Style Black Bean Salad Ⓜ

PREP: 15 min. + chilling **YIELD:** 4 servings

JENNIFER WICKES • PINE BEACH, NEW JERSEY

A little lime juice brightens and binds all the flavors in this salad, chock-full of good-for-you ingredients and fresh herbs.

- 1 cup frozen corn
- 1 can (15 oz.) black beans, rinsed and drained
- 1 small onion, chopped
- 1 celery rib, thinly sliced
- 1 small sweet red pepper, chopped
- 1/4 cup minced fresh cilantro
- 1 jalapeno pepper, seeded and finely chopped
- 2 Tbsp. sesame oil
- 1 Tbsp. rice vinegar
- 1 Tbsp. lime juice
- 2 garlic cloves, minced
- 1 tsp. minced fresh gingerroot
- 1/2 tsp. salt

> Need a quick dish for a **summer potluck** or casual get-together? Double or triple the ingredients for the bean salad. It travels well and is popular with all ages.

1. Cook corn according to package directions. Transfer to a small bowl; add the beans, onion, celery, red pepper, cilantro and jalapeno.

2. In a small bowl, whisk the oil, vinegar, lime juice, garlic, ginger and salt. Pour over bean mixture and toss to coat. Cover and refrigerate for at least 1 hour.

Editor's Note: When cutting hot peppers, disposable gloves are recommended. Avoid touching your face.

Nutrition Facts: 3/4 cup equals 198 calories, 7 g fat (1 g saturated fat), 0 cholesterol, 517 mg sodium, 27 g carbohydrate, 6 g fiber, 7 g protein. **Diabetic Exchanges:** 1-1/2 starch, 1 vegetable, 1 fat.

Buffalo Chicken Salad

PREP/TOTAL TIME: 25 min. **YIELD:** 4 servings

CORI COOPER • FLAGSTAFF, ARIZONA

Delicious and, even better, quick! This is truly a summer staple at our house.

- 1 lb. boneless skinless chicken breasts, cut into 1/2-in. cubes
- 1 Tbsp. olive oil
- 2 Tbsp. Louisiana-style hot sauce
- 1/4 tsp. salt
- 1/4 tsp. pepper
- 1 bunch romaine, chopped
- 2 celery ribs, chopped
- 1 cup shredded carrots
- 1/2 cup fat-free ranch salad dressing

1. In a large nonstick skillet, saute the chicken in oil until no longer pink; drain. Stir in the hot sauce, salt and pepper.

2. In large bowl, combine the romaine, celery and carrots. Divide among four plates. Top with chicken. Serve with ranch dressing.

Nutrition Facts: 1 serving equals 229 calories, 7 g fat (1 g saturated fat), 63 mg cholesterol, 644 mg sodium, 16 g carbohydrate, 3 g fiber, 25 g protein. **Diabetic Exchanges:** 3 very lean meat, 1 starch, 1 vegetable, 1/2 fat.

THAI-STYLE BLACK BEAN SALAD

BUFFALO CHICKEN SALAD

Fresh & Chunky Chicken Salad

PREP: 20 min. + marinating **GRILL:** 10 min.
YIELD: 4 servings

CAROL DOGGETTE • LOS ANGELES, CALIFORNIA

I've served this a few times to special guests at dinner parties, and everyone loved it!

- 1 Tbsp. lime juice
- 2 tsp. olive oil
- 1/2 tsp. salt
- 1/2 tsp. garlic powder
- 1/2 tsp. onion powder
- 1/4 tsp. pepper
- 3 boneless skinless chicken breast halves (4 oz. *each*)

SALAD:
- 1/2 cup diced apple
- 2 Tbsp. orange juice
- 1/4 cup fat-free plain yogurt
- 1/4 cup fat-free mayonnaise
- 1/8 tsp. pepper
- 1 cup diced cantaloupe
- 1 medium peach, peeled and diced
- 1 celery rib, diced
- 1/4 cup raisins
- 1/4 cup chopped walnuts, toasted
- 1 green onion, chopped
- 4 lettuce leaves

1. In a large resealable plastic bag, combine the first six ingredients; add chicken. Seal bag and turn to coat. Refrigerate for 20 minutes.

2. Meanwhile, in a small bowl, toss apple with orange juice; set aside. In a large bowl, whisk the yogurt, mayonnaise and pepper until blended. Stir in the cantaloupe, peach, celery, raisins, walnuts, onion and apple mixture. Cover and refrigerate.

3. Coat grill rack with cooking spray before starting the grill. Drain chicken if necessary, discarding any excess marinade. Grill chicken, covered, over direct medium heat for 4-7 minutes on each side or until juices run clear.

4. Dice chicken and stir into yogurt mixture. Serve immediately over lettuce leaves.

Nutrition Facts: 1 cup equals 247 calories, 9 g fat (1 g saturated fat), 49 mg cholesterol, 480 mg sodium, 22 g carbohydrate, 3 g fiber, 21 g protein. **Diabetic Exchanges:** 2 very lean meat, 1-1/2 fat, 1 fruit, 1/2 starch.

Greek-Inspired Quinoa Salad M

PREP: 30 min. + chilling   **YIELD:** 10 servings

JULIE STOCKEL • FARMINGTON HILLS, MICHIGAN

Packed with flavorful power foods, this salad is as delicious as it is pretty and good for you. Served cold, it's perfect for picnics and outdoor gatherings.

- 1 cup quinoa, rinsed
- 2 cups water
- 1 pkg. (10 oz.) frozen chopped spinach, thawed and squeezed dry
- 1-1/2 cups (6 oz.) crumbled feta cheese
- 1 cup grape tomatoes
- 3/4 cup canned black beans, rinsed and drained
- 1/2 cup chopped seeded peeled cucumber
- 1/2 cup sliced pepperoncinis
- 1/2 cup Greek olives, pitted and halved
- 3/4 cup reduced-fat Greek *or* Italian salad dressing, *divided*

1. In a small saucepan, bring quinoa and water to a boil. Reduce heat; cover and simmer for 12-15 minutes or until water is absorbed. Remove from the heat; fluff with a fork. Let stand for 10 minutes.

2. In a large bowl, combine quinoa, spinach, cheese, tomatoes, beans, cucumber, pepperoncinis and olives. Pour 1/2 cup dressing over quinoa mixture and toss to coat. Cover and refrigerate for at least 1 hour.

3. Just before serving, drizzle remaining dressing over salad; toss to coat.

Editor's Note: Look for quinoa in the cereal, rice or organic food aisle.

Nutrition Facts: 3/4 cup equals 184 calories, 8 g fat (2 g saturated fat), 9 mg cholesterol, 472 mg sodium, 19 g carbohydrate, 4 g fiber, 7 g protein. **Diabetic Exchanges:** 1-1/2 fat, 1 starch, 1 lean meat.

Macaroni Coleslaw M

PREP: 25 min. + chilling **YIELD:** 16 servings

SANDRA MATTESON • WESTHOPE, NORTH DAKOTA

This recipe comes from my friend Peggy. She brought it to a picnic, and everyone liked it to so much, we all just had to have the recipe.

- 1 pkg. (7 oz.) ring macaroni or ditalini
- 1 pkg. (16 oz.) coleslaw mix
- 2 medium onions, finely chopped
- 2 celery ribs, finely chopped
- 1 medium cucumber, finely chopped
- 1 medium green pepper, finely chopped
- 1 can (8 oz.) whole water chestnuts, drained and chopped

DRESSING:
- 1-1/2 cups reduced-fat salad dressing
- 1/3 cup sugar
- 1/4 cup cider vinegar
- 1/2 tsp. salt
- 1/4 tsp. pepper

1. Cook macaroni according to package directions; drain and rinse in cold water. Transfer to a large bowl; add the coleslaw mix, onions, celery, cucumber, green pepper and water chestnuts.

2. In a small bowl, whisk the dressing ingredients. Pour over salad; toss to coat. Cover and refrigerate for at least 1 hour.

Nutrition Facts: 3/4 cup equals 150 calories, 5 g fat (1 g saturated fat), 6 mg cholesterol, 286 mg sodium, 24 g carbohydrate, 2 g fiber, 3 g protein. **Diabetic Exchanges:** 1 starch, 1 vegetable, 1 fat.

Butter Bean Salad M

PREP/TOTAL TIME: 15 min. **YIELD:** 8 servings

SANDRA JACKSON • MOBILE, ALABAMA

This is a nice summery side that uses olive oil and tastes fresh, even though it relies on convenient canned beans. It's sure to perk up any picnic spread.

- 1 can (15-1/4 oz.) lima beans, rinsed and drained
- 1 can (15 oz.) butter beans, rinsed and drained
- 1 large sweet red pepper, chopped
- 1 medium green pepper, chopped
- 1 large onion, chopped
- 4 garlic cloves, minced
- 1/4 cup lemon juice
- 1/4 cup olive oil
- 2 Tbsp. cider vinegar
- 2 tsp. ground cumin
- 1/4 tsp. pepper

1. In a large bowl, combine the beans, peppers, onion and garlic. In a small bowl, combine the remaining ingredients. Pour over bean mixture and toss to coat. Chill until serving.

Nutrition Facts: 3/4 cup equals 147 calories, 7 g fat (1 g saturated fat), 0 cholesterol, 360 mg sodium, 19 g carbohydrate, 5 g fiber, 5 g protein. **Diabetic Exchanges:** 1 starch, 1 vegetable, 1 fat.

BUTTER BEAN SALAD

MACARONI COLESLAW

Balsamic Green Bean Salad S C M

PREP: 30 min. + chilling **YIELD:** 16 servings

MEGAN SPENCER • FARMINGTON HILLS, MICHIGAN

Serve up those green beans in a whole new way! The tangy flavors and crunch of this eye-appealing side complement any special meal or holiday potluck.

2	lbs. fresh green beans, trimmed and cut into 1-1/2-in. pieces
1/4	cup olive oil
3	Tbsp. lemon juice
3	Tbsp. balsamic vinegar
1/4	tsp. salt
1/4	tsp. garlic powder
1/4	tsp. ground mustard
1/8	tsp. pepper
1	large red onion, chopped
4	cups cherry tomatoes, halved
1	cup (4 oz.) crumbled feta cheese

1. Place beans in a Dutch oven and cover with water. Bring to a boil. Cover and cook for 8-10 minutes or until crisp-tender. Drain and immediately place beans in ice water. Drain and pat dry.

2. In a small bowl, whisk the oil, lemon juice, vinegar, salt, garlic powder, mustard and pepper. Drizzle over beans. Add the onion; toss to coat. Cover and refrigerate for at least 1 hour. Just before serving, stir in tomatoes and cheese.

Nutrition Facts: 3/4 cup equals 77 calories, 5 g fat (1 g saturated fat), 4 mg cholesterol, 112 mg sodium, 7 g carbohydrate, 3 g fiber, 3 g protein. **Diabetic Exchanges:** 1 vegetable, 1 fat.

Blue Cheese Waldorf Salad M

PREP: 20 min. + chilling **YIELD:** 12 servings

DEBORAH WILLIAMS • PEORIA, ARIZONA

Blue cheese perks up this version of a traditional Waldorf salad. Serve over lettuce leaves for a great lunch.

4	large apples, chopped
2	cups green grapes, halved
1-1/3	cups chopped celery
1/2	cup raisins
1	Tbsp. lemon juice
2/3	cup fat-free mayonnaise
2/3	cup buttermilk
1/3	cup crumbled blue cheese
1	Tbsp. sugar
1/4	cup chopped walnuts, toasted

1. In a large bowl, combine the apples, grapes, celery, raisins and lemon juice.

2. In a small bowl, combine the mayonnaise, buttermilk, blue cheese and sugar. Pour over apple mixture and toss to coat. Cover and refrigerate for at least 1 hour.

3. Just before serving, sprinkle with walnuts.

Nutrition Facts: 3/4 cup equals 126 calories, 4 g fat (1 g saturated fat), 5 mg cholesterol, 192 mg sodium, 24 g carbohydrate, 3 g fiber, 3 g protein. **Diabetic Exchanges:** 1 fruit, 1/2 starch, 1/2 fat.

Grecian Garden Salad C M

PREP: 20 min. + chilling **YIELD:** 6 servings

MELISSA SIPHERD • SALT LAKE CITY, UTAH

My mom often makes this for guests. Colorful and healthy, it doesn't taste light because of the generous amount of cheese.

1-1/2	cups cut fresh asparagus (1-in. pieces)
3	medium tomatoes, seeded and chopped
2	Tbsp. balsamic vinegar
4-1/2	tsp. minced fresh basil *or* 1-1/2 tsp. dried basil
1	Tbsp. olive oil
1	tsp. salt
1/2	tsp. pepper
1	cup (4 oz.) crumbled feta cheese

BLUE CHEESE WALDORF SALAD

BALSAMIC GREEN BEAN SALAD

1. In a large saucepan, bring 3 cups water to a boil. Add asparagus; cover and boil for 3 minutes. Drain and immediately place asparagus in ice water. Drain and pat dry. Transfer to a serving bowl. Stir in the tomatoes.

2. In a small bowl, whisk the vinegar, basil, oil, salt and pepper. Drizzle over vegetables; toss to coat. Cover and refrigerate for at least 1 hour. Just before serving, stir in cheese.

Nutrition Facts: 2/3 cup equals 92 calories, 5 g fat (2 g saturated fat), 10 mg cholesterol, 579 mg sodium, 6 g carbohydrate, 2 g fiber, 5 g protein. **Diabetic Exchanges:** 1 vegetable, 1 fat.

Southwest Crunch Chicken Salad C

PREP/TOTAL TIME: 30 min. **YIELD:** 13 servings

SALLY SIBTHORPE • SHELBY TOWNSHIP, MICHIGAN

It's hard to believe that this party-perfect chicken salad with cashews and turkey bacon is low in carbs, high in protein and only contains 3 g of saturated fat per serving! Enjoy it as is, on a bed of lettuce or wrapped in a tortilla.

1-1/3	cups fat-free mayonnaise
1/2	cup minced fresh cilantro
1/4	cup lime juice
1/4	cup orange juice
2	garlic cloves, minced
1-3/4	tsp. ground cumin
3/4	tsp. grated orange peel
1/2	tsp. salt
9	cups cubed cooked chicken breast
1-3/4	cups julienned peeled jicama
1-3/4	cups chopped celery
1-3/4	cups chopped sweet red peppers
1	cup chopped cashews
1/2	lb. turkey bacon strips, diced and cooked

1. In a small bowl, combine the first eight ingredients. In a large bowl, combine the remaining ingredients. Add mayonnaise mixture; toss to coat. Chill until serving.

Nutrition Facts: 1 cup equals 286 calories, 12 g fat (3 g saturated fat), 95 mg cholesterol, 653 mg sodium, 11 g carbohydrate, 3 g fiber, 33 g protein. **Diabetic Exchanges:** 4 very lean meat, 1-1/2 fat, 1 starch.

Thai Pasta Side Salad M

PREP/TOTAL TIME: 25 min. **YIELD:** 10 servings

LAURIE DAVISON • CLEARWATER, FLORIDA

A tasty peanut dressing lightly coats pasta and cabbage in this easy-to-make side dish that's perfect for potlucks or outdoor events.

2	cups uncooked bow tie pasta
4	cups chopped red cabbage
1	medium green pepper, chopped
1	medium sweet red pepper, chopped
4	green onions, thinly sliced
1/4	cup rice vinegar
1/4	cup reduced-fat creamy peanut butter
4-1/2	tsp. reduced-sodium soy sauce
1	Tbsp. honey
1-1/2	tsp. olive oil
1/2	cup dry roasted peanuts

1. Cook pasta according to package directions. Meanwhile, in a large bowl, combine the cabbage, peppers and onions. In a small bowl, whisk the vinegar, peanut butter, soy sauce, honey and oil.

2. Drain pasta and rinse in cold water; add to cabbage mixture. Pour dressing over salad; toss to coat. Just before serving, sprinkle with peanuts.

Nutrition Facts: 3/4 cup equals 161 calories, 7 g fat (1 g saturated fat), 0 cholesterol, 194 mg sodium, 21 g carbohydrate, 3 g fiber, 6 g protein. **Diabetic Exchanges:** 1-1/2 starch, 1 fat.

Layered Salad with Curry Dressing F C M

PREP/TOTAL TIME: 20 min. **YIELD:** 16 servings

KERRI PELZ • HENDERSONVILLE, NORTH CAROLINA

Light mayonnaise and yogurt cut calories and fat in this lighter version of seven-layer salad. Curry powder adds a unique twist and complements the other ingredients.

1	pkg. (10 oz.) ready-to-serve salad greens
2	celery ribs, chopped
1/2	cup chopped green pepper
1/2	cup chopped cauliflower
2	green onions, thinly sliced
1	pkg. (10 oz.) frozen peas, thawed
3/4	cup fat-free mayonnaise
3/4	cup (6 oz.) reduced-fat plain yogurt
1	Tbsp. lemon juice
1	tsp. curry powder
3/4	cup shredded reduced-fat cheddar cheese
1/2	cup sliced almonds

1. In a 3-qt. glass bowl, layer the salad greens, celery, pepper, cauliflower, green onions and peas. In a small bowl, whisk the mayonnaise, yogurt, lemon juice and curry; carefully spread over salad. Sprinkle with cheese. Chill until serving. Just before serving, sprinkle with almonds.

Nutrition Facts: 3/4 cup equals 67 calories, 3 g fat (1 g saturated fat), 6 mg cholesterol, 161 mg sodium, 7 g carbohydrate, 2 g fiber, 4 g protein.

Crunchy Apple Salad F S M

PREP: 15 min. + chilling **YIELD:** 5 servings

KATHLEEN LAW • BELLINGHAM, WASHINGTON

With fiber-rich fruit, light dressing and crunchy walnuts, this is a great snack. Try it with low-fat granola.

6	Tbsp. fat-free sugar-free vanilla yogurt
6	Tbsp. reduced-fat whipped topping
1/4	tsp. plus 1/8 tsp. ground cinnamon, *divided*
2	medium red apples, chopped
1	large Granny Smith apple, chopped
1/4	cup dried cranberries
2	Tbsp. chopped walnuts

1. In a large bowl, combine the yogurt, whipped topping and 1/4 tsp. cinnamon. Add apples and cranberries; toss to coat. Refrigerate until serving. Sprinkle with walnuts and remaining cinnamon before serving.

Nutrition Facts: 3/4 cup equals 109 calories, 3 g fat (1 g saturated fat), trace cholesterol, 12 mg sodium, 22 g carbohydrate, 3 g fiber, 2 g protein. **Diabetic Exchanges:** 1 fruit, 1/2 starch, 1/2 fat.

Fruit & Cream Layered Salad S M

PREP/TOTAL TIME: 25 min. **YIELD:** 13 servings

APRIL LANE • GREENEVILLE, TENNESSEE

I love salads, especially fruit salads, and try to cook light meals. I found a similar recipe to this one a few years ago and have revised it to make it a lot healthier.

3	oz. reduced-fat cream cheese
1	Tbsp. sugar
2	tsp. lemon juice
1/4	tsp. almond extract
1	carton (6 oz.) strawberry yogurt
2	cups reduced-fat whipped topping
3	medium peaches, peeled and sliced
2	cups halved fresh strawberries
2	cups fresh blueberries
2	cups green grapes
1	can (11 oz.) mandarin oranges, drained
1/4	cup sliced almonds, toasted

Fresh strawberries, optional

1. In a small bowl, beat the cream cheese, sugar, lemon juice and extract until smooth. Add yogurt; beat until blended. Fold in whipped topping.

2. In a 3-qt. trifle bowl, layer the peaches, strawberries and blueberries. Top with half of the whipped topping mixture. Layer with grapes, oranges and remaining whipped topping mixture. Refrigerate until serving. Sprinkle with almonds just before serving. Garnish with strawberries if desired.

Nutrition Facts: 3/4 cup (calculated without optional strawberries) equals 124 calories, 4 g fat (2 g saturated fat), 5 mg cholesterol, 37 mg sodium, 22 g carbohydrate, 2 g fiber, 2 g protein. **Diabetic Exchanges:** 1 fruit, 1/2 starch, 1/2 fat.

Over the past years, blueberries have received notice in the press for being a **power food**. And for good reason; the berries are loaded with vitamins, minerals and fiber.

CRUNCHY APPLE SALAD

FRUIT & CREAM LAYERED SALAD

Herbed Potato Salad F M

PREP: 40 min. + chilling   **YIELD:** 10 servings

JUDY GREBETZ • RACINE, WISCONSIN

Calcium-rich cheese, and potatoes and peppers packed with vitamin C make this picnic-and-potluck favorite something to smile about!

3	lbs. small red potatoes, cubed
1/2	cup cubed reduced-fat cheddar cheese
1/4	cup chopped dill pickle
1/4	cup chopped red onion
1/4	cup chopped green pepper
1/4	cup chopped sweet red pepper
1	jalapeno pepper, seeded and minced
3/4	cup fat-free mayonnaise
1	Tbsp. minced fresh basil
1	Tbsp. snipped fresh dill
1	Tbsp. minced fresh tarragon
1/2	tsp. salt
1/2	tsp. pepper
1	hard-cooked egg, chopped

1. Place potatoes in a large saucepan and cover with water. Bring to a boil. Reduce heat; cover and simmer for 10-15 minutes or until tender. Drain and cool to room temperature.

2. In a large bowl, combine the potatoes, cheese, pickle, onion and peppers. In a small bowl, combine the mayonnaise, basil, dill, tarragon, salt and pepper. Pour over salad and toss to coat. Cover and refrigerate until chilled. Garnish with chopped egg.

Editor's Note: When cutting hot peppers, disposable gloves are recommended. Avoid touching your face.

Nutrition Facts: 3/4 cup equals 142 calories, 3 g fat (1 g saturated fat), 27 mg cholesterol, 371 mg sodium, 25 g carbohydrate, 3 g fiber, 5 g protein. **Diabetic Exchange:** 1-1/2 starch.

Artichoke Tomato Salad C M

PREP/TOTAL TIME: 20 min.   **YIELD:** 8 servings

DEBORAH WILLIAMS • PEORIA, ARIZONA

For a little zip, crumble feta over the top of this combination. Add shredded rotisserie chicken for a beautiful main dish.

5	large tomatoes (about 2 lbs.), cut into wedges
1/4	tsp. salt
1/4	tsp. pepper
1	jar (7-1/2 oz.) marinated quartered artichoke hearts, drained
1	can (2-1/4 oz.) sliced ripe olives, drained
2	Tbsp. minced fresh parsley
2	Tbsp. white wine vinegar
2	garlic cloves, minced

1. Arrange tomato wedges on a large serving platter; sprinkle with salt and pepper. In a small bowl, combine the remaining ingredients. Spoon over tomatoes. Refrigerate leftovers.

Nutrition Facts: 3/4 cup equals 74 calories, 5 g fat (1 g saturated fat), 0 cholesterol, 241 mg sodium, 7 g carbohydrate, 2 g fiber, 1 g protein. **Diabetic Exchanges:** 1 vegetable, 1 fat.

ARTICHOKE TOMATO SALAD

HERBED POTATO SALAD

Spinach Bean Salad With Maple Dressing F C

PREP/TOTAL TIME: 15 min. **YIELD:** 11 servings

SALLY MALONEY • DALLAS, GEORGIA

Warm maple dressing slightly wilts the spinach in this salad, giving it a delightful texture and flavor. It's quick and easy to make, plus it's healthy and oh-so tasty!

1/4	cup maple syrup
3	Tbsp. cider vinegar
1	Tbsp. olive oil
1	Tbsp. Dijon mustard
1/4	tsp. salt
1/4	tsp. coarsely ground pepper
1	can (15-1/2 oz.) great northern beans, rinsed and drained
2	pkg. (6 oz. *each*) fresh baby spinach
4	green onions, thinly sliced
1	small sweet red pepper, chopped
5	bacon strips, cooked and crumbled

1. For dressing, in a small microwave-safe bowl, combine the first six ingredients; set aside. Place beans in another microwave-safe bowl. Microwave, uncovered, for 1-2 minutes or until heated through.

2. In a large salad bowl, combine the spinach, onions, red pepper, bacon and beans. Microwave the dressing, uncovered, for 30-60 seconds or until heated through. Whisk until smooth; drizzle over salad and toss to coat.

Nutrition Facts: 1 cup equals 90 calories, 3 g fat (1 g saturated fat), 3 mg cholesterol, 272 mg sodium, 13 g carbohydrate, 3 g fiber, 4 g protein. **Diabetic Exchanges:** 1 starch, 1 vegetable.

If you have leftover poultry or cooked beef in the refrigerator, add a few slices to the spinach salad for a fast change-of-pace entree.

CHICKEN CAESAR WRAPS

CRANBERRY CHICKEN FOCACCIA

VEGETABLE PORK SOUP

Soups & Sandwiches

Hearty lunches and casual dinners alike, few culinary combinations have stood the test of time like the delightful pairing of soup and sandwich. You can still enjoy this comforting duo even if you're watching your weight. Just turn the page!

Smoked Turkey & Slaw Wraps

PREP/TOTAL TIME: 15 min. **YIELD:** 4 servings

DEBORAH WILLIAMS • PEORIA, ARIZONA

Crunchy, colorful coleslaw adds a tangy twist to these quick-and-easy wraps. They're equally great for lunch or dinner!

1	cup shredded green cabbage
1/2	cup shredded red cabbage
1	small carrot, grated
1	green onion, thinly sliced
3	Tbsp. reduced-fat mayonnaise
1	Tbsp. lemon juice
2	tsp. Dijon mustard
1/4	tsp. sugar
4	whole wheat tortillas (8 in.), room temperature
1/2	lb. sliced deli smoked turkey
1	small tomato, sliced

1. In a small bowl, combine the first four ingredients. Combine the mayonnaise, lemon juice, mustard and sugar; pour over cabbage mixture and toss to coat.

2. Spoon cabbage mixture down the center of each tortilla. Top with turkey and tomato; roll up.

Nutrition Facts: 1 wrap equals 260 calories, 8 g fat (1 g saturated fat), 24 mg cholesterol, 761 mg sodium, 28 g carbohydrate, 3 g fiber, 17 g protein. **Diabetic Exchanges:** 2 very lean meat, 1-1/2 starch, 1 vegetable, 1 fat.

Chicken Caesar Wraps

PREP/TOTAL TIME: 15 min. **YIELD:** 6 servings

NANCY PRATT • LONGVIEW, TEXAS

This classic wrap with tender chicken, Parmesan cheese and chopped Caesar croutons features the perfect amount of dressing for a tasty meal any night.

3/4	cup fat-free creamy Caesar salad dressing
1/4	cup grated Parmesan cheese
1/2	tsp. garlic powder
1/4	tsp. pepper
3	cups cubed cooked chicken breast
2	cups torn romaine
3/4	cup Caesar salad croutons, coarsely chopped
6	whole wheat tortillas (8 in.)

1. In a large bowl, combine the dressing, cheese, garlic powder and pepper. Add the chicken, romaine and croutons. Spoon 2/3 cup chicken mixture down the center of each tortilla; roll up.

Nutrition Facts: 1 wrap equals 332 calories, 7 g fat (1 g saturated fat), 57 mg cholesterol, 689 mg sodium, 37 g carbohydrate, 4 g fiber, 27 g protein. **Diabetic Exchanges:** 3 very lean meat, 2-1/2 starch, 1/2 fat.

Cranberry Chicken Focaccia

PREP: 25 min. **BAKE:** 40 min. + cooling **YIELD:** 6 servings

CHARLENE CHAMBERS • ORMOND BEACH, FLORIDA

Take chicken to new heights with this idea. Combining some of our favorite ingredients, it's a real hit with everyone I serve it to.

1-3/4	lbs. bone-in chicken breast halves
6	fresh thyme sprigs
1/2	tsp. salt
1/4	tsp. pepper
1	cup fresh or frozen cranberries, thawed
1/2	cup orange segments
2	Tbsp. sugar
1	loaf (12 oz.) focaccia bread
1/3	cup crumbled goat cheese
3	large lettuce leaves
1/4	cup chopped pecans, toasted

1. With fingers, carefully loosen skin from the chicken breast to form a pocket. Place thyme sprigs under the skin and sprinkle with salt and pepper. Place in an 11-in. x 7-in. baking dish coated with cooking spray. Bake, uncovered, at 350° for 40-45 minutes or until a meat thermometer reads 170°.

2. Set chicken aside until cool enough to handle. Remove meat from bones; discard bones and slice chicken. Place the cranberries, orange segments and sugar in a small food processor; cover and process until blended.

3. Cut focaccia in half horizontally. Layer with cheese, lettuce, cranberry mixture, chicken and pecans; replace top. Cut into six wedges.

Nutrition Facts: 1 wedge equals 363 calories, 11 g fat (4 g saturated fat), 63 mg cholesterol, 628 mg sodium, 40 g carbohydrate, 3 g fiber, 27 g protein. **Diabetic Exchanges:** 3 very lean meat, 2-1/2 starch, 1 fat.

My Favorite Burger

PREP: 25 min. **GRILL:** 15 min. **YIELD:** 4 servings

KRISTEN SWIHART • PERRYSBURG, OHIO

After having a burger similar to this at a diner years ago, I tried to lighten it up without losing the great taste. Now I can enjoy one more often without feeling guilty!

1/4	cup grated onion
1/2	tsp. garlic powder
1/4	tsp. salt
1/4	tsp. pepper
1	lb. lean ground beef
1	cup sliced fresh mushrooms
1/2	cup sliced sweet onion
4	kaiser rolls, split
4	oz. fat-free cream cheese
2	bacon strips, cooked and crumbled

1. In a large bowl, combine the onion, garlic powder, salt and pepper. Crumble beef over mixture and mix well. Shape into four patties.

2. If grilling the burgers, coat grill rack with cooking spray before starting the grill. Grill, covered, over medium heat or broil 4-6 in. from the heat for 4-6 minutes on each side or until a meat thermometer reads 160° and juices run clear.

3. Meanwhile, in a small skillet coated with cooking spray, cook and stir mushrooms and onion over medium heat until onion is golden brown. Grill rolls for 1-2 minutes or until lightly toasted.

4. Spread rolls with cream cheese; top with burgers and mushroom mixture. Sprinkle with bacon.

Nutrition Facts: 1 burger equals 410 calories, 13 g fat (5 g saturated fat), 75 mg cholesterol, 737 mg sodium, 37 g carbohydrate, 2 g fiber, 33 g protein.

Portobello Crab Open-Faced Sandwiches

PREP: 45 min. + standing **BAKE:** 15 min.
YIELD: 4 servings

ROSALIND POPE • GREENSBORO, NORTH CAROLINA

A roasted red pepper sauce tops this hearty sandwich with a yummy crab filling.

1	large sweet red pepper
1/2	cup fat-free plain yogurt
1	tsp. sherry or reduced-sodium chicken broth
1	garlic clove, crushed
1/2	tsp. hot pepper sauce
1/4	tsp. salt

STUFFED MUSHROOMS:

1	small onion, finely chopped
1	small sweet red pepper, finely chopped
1	tsp. canola oil
1	egg, lightly beaten
3	Tbsp. fat-free plain yogurt
1/2	tsp. Worcestershire sauce
1	cup crushed saltines (about 30 crackers)
1	Tbsp. minced fresh parsley
2	tsp. Dijon mustard
1/2	tsp. seafood seasoning
1/2	tsp. paprika

Dash pepper

1	can (6 oz.) lump crabmeat, drained
4	large portobello mushrooms (4 to 4-1/2 in.), stems removed

FOR SERVING:

2	hamburger buns, split and toasted
1	cup watercress

1. Broil the large red pepper 4 in. from the heat until skin blisters, about 5 minutes. With tongs, rotate pepper a quarter turn. Broil and rotate until all sides are blistered and blackened. Immediately place pepper in a small bowl; cover and let stand for 15-20 minutes.

MY FAVORITE BURGER

PORTOBELLO CRAB OPEN-FACED SANDWICHES

2. Peel off and discard charred skin. Remove stems and seeds. Place in a food processor; add the yogurt, sherry, garlic, pepper sauce and salt. Cover and process until blended. Set aside.

3. For stuffing, in a small nonstick skillet, saute the onion and the chopped red pepper in oil until tender. In a small bowl, combine the egg, yogurt, Worcestershire sauce, saltines, parsley, mustard and seasonings. Stir in onion mixture; fold in crab. Spoon filling into mushroom caps. Place in a 15-in. x 10-in. x 1-in. baking pan coated with cooking spray.

4. Bake at 400° for 15-20 minutes or until stuffing is golden brown and mushrooms are tender. Serve on bun halves with watercress and the reserved red pepper sauce.

Nutrition Facts: 1 sandwich with 3 Tbsp. sauce equals 268 calories, 6 g fat (1 g saturated fat), 92 mg cholesterol, 794 mg sodium, 36 g carbohydrate, 4 g fiber, 19 g protein. **Diabetic Exchanges:** 2 very lean meat, 2 vegetable, 1-1/2 starch, 1/2 fat.

Beef and Tortellini Soup

PREP: 20 min. **COOK:** 40 min.
YIELD: 6 servings (2-1/4 qt.)

BARBARA KEMMER • ROHNERT PARK, CALIFORNIA

This is my mom's recipe. My family loves it and so does everyone else who tries it.

- 5 Tbsp. all-purpose flour, *divided*
- 1/2 lb. boneless beef top sirloin steak, cut into 1/2-in. cubes
- 3 tsp. butter, *divided*
- 1 medium onion, chopped
- 1 celery rib, chopped
- 1 medium carrot, chopped
- 2 garlic cloves, minced
- 1 can (28 oz.) diced tomatoes, undrained
- 2 cans (14-1/2 oz. *each*) reduced-sodium beef broth
- 1-1/2 cups water, *divided*
- 1 tsp. dried thyme
- 1/2 tsp. white pepper
- 1/4 tsp. salt
- 2 cups frozen beef tortellini

1. Place 2 Tbsp. flour in a large resealable plastic bag. Add beef, a few pieces at a time, and shake to coat. In a nonstick Dutch oven, brown beef in 2 tsp. butter; remove and keep warm.

2. In the same pan, saute the onion, celery, carrot and garlic in remaining butter until tender. Add the tomatoes, broth, 1 cup water, thyme, pepper, salt and reserved beef. Bring to a boil. Reduce heat; cover and simmer for 20 minutes. Add the tortellini; cook 5-10 minutes longer or until tender.

3. Combine remaining flour and water until smooth. Stir into the pan. Bring to a boil; cook and stir for 2 minutes or until thickened.

Nutrition Facts: 1-1/2 cups equals 265 calories, 9 g fat (4 g saturated fat), 109 mg cholesterol, 706 mg sodium, 27 g carbohydrate, 4 g fiber, 19 g protein. **Diabetic Exchanges:** 2 lean meat, 2 vegetable, 1 starch, 1/2 fat.

Fruited Turkey Salad Pitas

PREP: 30 min. + chilling **YIELD:** 8 servings

DONNA NOEL • GRAY, MAINE

I often fill a loaf of Italian bread with this turkey salad. It disappears fast at parties!

1/2	cup reduced-fat plain yogurt
1/2	cup reduced-fat mayonnaise
2	Tbsp. lemon juice
1/2	tsp. pepper
4	cups cubed cooked turkey breast
2	celery ribs, thinly sliced
1	medium apple, peeled and chopped
1/2	cup finely chopped fresh spinach
1/3	cup dried cranberries
1/3	cup chopped pecans
8	pita breads (6 in.), halved
16	romaine leaves
8	slices red onion, separated into rings

1. In a small bowl, combine the yogurt, mayonnaise, lemon juice and pepper. In a large bowl, combine the turkey, celery, apple, spinach, cranberries and pecans. Add yogurt mixture and stir to coat. Cover and refrigerate until chilled.

2. Line pita halves with lettuce and onion; fill each with 1/2 cup turkey mixture.

Nutrition Facts: 2 filled pita halves equals 393 calories, 11 g fat (2 g saturated fat), 66 mg cholesterol, 501 mg sodium, 45 g carbohydrate, 3 g fiber, 29 g protein. **Diabetic Exchanges:** 3 starch, 3 very lean meat, 1-1/2 fat.

Sausage Bean Soup F

PREP: 20 min. **COOK:** 20 min. **YIELD:** 6 servings

HEALTHY COOKING TEST KITCHEN

Cozy up to my rich and rustic soup to take the chill off any evening. Multigrain pasta increases fiber, but whole wheat pasta works well, too.

1/2	lb. Italian turkey sausage links, casings removed
1	medium green pepper, chopped
1	medium onion, chopped
2	garlic cloves, minced
2	cans (14-1/2 oz. *each*) reduced-sodium chicken broth
1	can (15 oz.) pinto beans, rinsed and drained
1	can (14-1/2 oz.) no-salt-added diced tomatoes
4	oz. uncooked multigrain spaghetti, broken into 2-in. pieces
1	tsp. Italian seasoning
1/4	tsp. pepper

1. In a Dutch oven, saute the sausage, green pepper and onion until meat is no longer pink; drain. Add garlic; cook 1 minute longer. Stir in the remaining ingredients. Bring to a boil. Reduce heat; cover and simmer for 10-15 minutes or until spaghetti is tender.

Nutrition Facts: 1 cup equals 225 calories, 4 g fat (1 g saturated fat), 23 mg cholesterol, 752 mg sodium, 32 g carbohydrate, 6 g fiber, 16 g protein. **Diabetic Exchanges:** 2 starch, 2 lean meat, 1 vegetable.

Italian Vegetable Soup **F**

PREP: 15 min. **COOK:** 25 min. **YIELD:** 7 servings

LEA REITER • THOUSAND OAKS, CALIFORNIA

Laced with a splash of white wine, this hearty soup is packed with garden-fresh nutrition and veggies! Leafy escarole adds color and plenty of vitamin A. You could substitute spinach or kale for the escarole if you wish.

- 2 celery ribs, sliced
- 1 medium onion, chopped
- 1 medium carrot, halved and sliced
- 1 Tbsp. olive oil
- 2 cups water
- 1 can (15 oz.) white kidney *or* cannellini beans, rinsed and drained
- 1 can (14-1/2 oz.) diced tomatoes, undrained
- 1 can (14-1/2 oz.) reduced-sodium chicken broth
- 1/2 cup marsala wine *or* additional reduced-sodium chicken broth
- 1 tsp. *each* dried basil, marjoram, oregano and thyme
- 1/4 tsp. salt
- 1/4 tsp. pepper
- 1 cup uncooked bow tie pasta
- 6 cups torn escarole (1 small head)

1. In a Dutch oven, saute the celery, onion and carrot in oil until tender. Stir in the water, beans, tomatoes, broth, wine and seasonings. Bring mixture to a boil. Stir in pasta.

2. Reduce heat; simmer, uncovered, for 13-15 minutes or until the pasta is tender, adding escarole during last 3 minutes of cooking.

Nutrition Facts: 1 cup equals 164 calories, 3 g fat (trace saturated fat), 0 cholesterol, 426 mg sodium, 26 g carbohydrate, 5 g fiber, 6 g protein. **Diabetic Exchanges:** 1-1/2 starch, 1 vegetable, 1/2 fat.

Grilled Veggie Sandwiches **M**

PREP/TOTAL TIME: 25 min. **YIELD:** 4 servings

MELISSA WILBANKS • MEMPHIS, TENNESSEE

Get a grip on lunch! Here's a fun recipe for using up those summer garden veggies. Beef-eaters won't even miss the meat in these hearty, fresh-tasting, grilled sandwiches.

- 1 small zucchini
- 1 small yellow summer squash
- 1 small eggplant

Cooking spray

- 1 medium onion, sliced
- 1 large sweet red pepper, cut into rings
- 4 whole wheat hamburger buns, split
- 3 oz. fat-free cream cheese
- 1/4 cup crumbled goat cheese
- 1 garlic clove, minced
- 1/8 tsp. salt
- 1/8 tsp. pepper

1. Coat grill rack with cooking spray before starting the grill. Cut the zucchini, squash and eggplant into 1/4-in.-thick strips; spritz with cooking spray. Spritz onion and red pepper with cooking spray.

2. Grill vegetables, covered, over medium heat for 4-5 minutes on each side or until crisp-tender. Remove and keep warm. Grill buns, cut side down, over medium heat for 30-60 seconds or until toasted.

3. In a small bowl, combine the cheeses, garlic, salt and pepper; spread over bun bottoms. Top with the vegetables. Replace bun tops.

Nutrition Facts: 1 sandwich equals 262 calories, 8 g fat (4 g saturated fat), 13 mg cholesterol, 477 mg sodium, 39 g carbohydrate, 10 g fiber, 13 g protein. **Diabetic Exchanges:** 3 vegetable, 1-1/2 starch, 1 lean meat, 1 fat.

GRILLED VEGGIE SANDWICHES

ITALIAN VEGETABLE SOUP

Roast Pork Sandwiches With Peach Chutney

PREP: 15 min. **BAKE:** 35 min. **YIELD:** 4 servings

LILLIAN JULOW • GAINESVILLE, FLORIDA

This combination of roast pork with peach chutney used to be a favorite Sunday dinner. Since my big family's on their own now, I cut the recipe down for sandwiches.

- 1 pork tenderloin (1 lb.)
- 2 Tbsp. spicy brown mustard

PEACH CHUTNEY:
- 1/4 cup peach preserves
- 3 Tbsp. finely chopped onion
- 2 Tbsp. red wine vinegar
- 1 small garlic clove, minced
- 1/4 tsp. mustard seed
- 1/8 tsp. salt
- 1/8 tsp. ground ginger
- 1/8 tsp. ground cinnamon
- Dash cayenne pepper
- Dash ground cloves
- 1/4 cup fat-free mayonnaise
- 4 onion rolls, split and toasted
- 4 lettuce leaves

1. Brush pork with mustard; place on a rack in a shallow roasting pan. Bake at 425° for 35-40 minutes or until a meat thermometer reads 160°. Let stand for 5 minutes before slicing.

2. Meanwhile, for chutney, in a small saucepan, combine the preserves, onion, vinegar, garlic and seasonings. Bring to a boil. Reduce heat; simmer, uncovered, for 7-8 minutes or until thickened. Set aside to cool. Spread mayonnaise over roll bottoms. Layer with lettuce, pork slices and chutney. Replace tops.

Nutrition Facts: 1 sandwich equals 357 calories, 7 g fat (2 g saturated fat), 65 mg cholesterol, 589 mg sodium, 42 g carbohydrate, 2 g fiber, 29 g protein. **Diabetic Exchanges:** 3 lean meat, 2-1/2 starch.

ROAST PORK SANDWICHES WITH PEACH CHUTNEY

Italian BLTs

PREP/TOTAL TIME: 20 min. **YIELD:** 2 servings

JOYCE MOUL • YORK HAVEN, PENNSYLVANIA

The brilliant method of toasting BLTs in a coating of crispy bread crumbs takes these sandwiches from satisfying to spectacular.

- 2 turkey bacon strips, diced
- 4 slices Italian bread (1/2 in. thick)
- 2 slices reduced-fat provolone cheese
- 2 lettuce leaves
- 1 small tomato, sliced
- 4 tsp. prepared fat-free Italian salad dressing
- 1/3 cup panko (Japanese) bread crumbs
- Butter-flavored cooking spray
- 1/2 tsp. olive oil

1. In a small skillet, cook bacon over medium heat until crisp. Layer two bread slices with cheese, bacon, lettuce and tomato; top with remaining bread. Brush outsides of sandwiches with salad dressing. Place bread crumbs in a shallow bowl. Coat sandwiches with bread crumbs; spray with butter-flavored cooking spray.

2. In a large skillet over medium heat, toast sandwiches in oil for 2-3 minutes on each side or until bread is lightly browned.

Nutrition Facts: 1 sandwich equals 272 calories, 11 g fat (4 g saturated fat), 25 mg cholesterol, 761 mg sodium, 30 g carbohydrate, 2 g fiber, 13 g protein. **Diabetic Exchanges:** 2 starch, 2 lean meat.

Southwest Chicken Corn Chowder

PREP/TOTAL TIME: 25 min.
YIELD: 9 servings (2-1/4 qt.)

EILEEN ROBITAILLE • RIVERSIDE, CALIFORNIA

My family really enjoys this recipe. It's super fast, easy and filling! It's a great starter for a Southwestern meal or a hearty lunch with a piece of cornbread.

- 1 large onion, chopped
- 1 garlic clove, minced
- 1/2 tsp. olive oil
- 1 can (14-1/2 oz.) reduced-sodium chicken broth
- 1 can (10-3/4 oz.) reduced-fat reduced-sodium condensed cream of chicken soup, undiluted
- 2 cups cubed cooked chicken breast
- 1 can (4 oz.) chopped green chilies, drained
- 2 cans (14-3/4 oz. *each*) cream-style corn
- 1 can (12 oz.) fat-free evaporated milk
- 1/2 tsp. chili powder
- 1/2 tsp. ground cumin
- 6 Tbsp. shredded reduced-fat cheddar cheese
- 4-1/2 tsp. chopped cilantro

1. In a large nonstick saucepan, saute onion and garlic in oil until tender.

2. Stir in the broth, soup, chicken and chilies until blended. Bring to a boil. Reduce heat; stir in the corn, milk, chili powder and cumin. Heat through (do not boil). Sprinkle each serving with cheese and cilantro.

Nutrition Facts: 1 cup soup with 2 tsp. cheese equals 206 calories, 5 g fat (2 g saturated fat), 35 mg cholesterol, 669 mg sodium, 27 g carbohydrate, 2 g fiber, 16 g protein. **Diabetic Exchanges:** 2 starch, 1 very lean meat.

Open-Faced Tuna Melts

PREP/TOTAL TIME: 25 min. **YIELD:** 2 servings

ALICE STRAPP-MEISTER • NEW ROSS, NOVA SCOTIA

Casting about for a way to get your family to eat more fish? These simple open-faced sandwiches are rich in healthy omega-3 oils and flavor. I've enjoyed this recipe for 20 years and usually serve it for Sunday lunch.

1/4	cup fat-free mayonnaise
2	Tbsp. chopped green pepper
1-1/2	tsp. chopped onion
1-1/2	tsp. chopped celery
1-1/2	tsp. prepared mustard
1/4	tsp. Worcestershire sauce
1	can (6 oz.) tuna, drained and flaked
2	hamburger buns, split and toasted
4	slices tomato
2	Tbsp. shredded reduced-fat cheddar cheese

1. In a small bowl, combine the first six ingredients; stir in tuna. Spread over each bun half; top with a tomato slice. Sprinkle with cheese. Place on a baking sheet. Broil 3-4 in. from the heat for 3-5 minutes or until lightly browned and cheese is melted.

Nutrition Facts: 2 sandwich halves equal 276 calories, 5 g fat (2 g saturated fat), 34 mg cholesterol, 833 mg sodium, 28 g carbohydrate, 2 g fiber, 28 g protein.

Southwest Black Bean Soup

PREP: 15 min. **COOK:** 35 min. **YIELD:** 6 servings

JILL HEATWOLE • PITTSVILLE, MARYLAND

A friend brought this recipe to a gathering, and it's been a hit with my family ever since! I use brown rice for more fiber and whole-grain goodness.

1	medium sweet red pepper, chopped
2	celery ribs, chopped
1	small onion, chopped
1	Tbsp. canola oil
2	cans (15 oz. *each*) black beans, rinsed and drained
1	can (14-1/2 oz.) reduced-sodium chicken broth
1	can (14-1/2 oz.) diced tomatoes, undrained
1	can (4 oz.) chopped green chilies
3/4	tsp. ground cumin
1-1/2	cups cooked instant brown rice
6	Tbsp. reduced-fat sour cream

1. In a large nonstick saucepan, saute the pepper, celery and onion in oil until tender. Add the beans, broth, tomatoes, chilies and cumin. Bring to a boil. Reduce heat; simmer, uncovered, for 30 minutes or until thickened.

2. Divide rice among six soup bowls; top with soup and sour cream.

Nutrition Facts: 1 cup soup with 1/4 cup rice and 1 Tbsp. sour cream equals 275 calories, 5 g fat (1 g saturated fat), 5 mg cholesterol, 660 mg sodium, 46 g carbohydrate, 9 g fiber, 12 g protein.

Breaded Eggplant Sandwiches

PREP: 30 min. **BAKE:** 25 min. **YIELD:** 6 servings

HOLLY GOMEZ • SEABROOK, NEW HAMPSHIRE

Eggplant Parmesan is one of my family's favorite comfort foods. We love this version served open-faced with a salad.

1/4	cup minced fresh basil
2	tsp. olive oil
1/4	tsp. dried oregano
1/4	tsp. pepper
1/8	tsp. salt
2	egg whites, lightly beaten
1	cup seasoned bread crumbs
1	medium eggplant
2	large tomatoes
1-1/2	cups (6 oz.) shredded part-skim mozzarella cheese
2	Tbsp. grated Parmesan cheese
1	garlic clove, peeled
12	slices Italian bread (1/2 in. thick), toasted

1. Combine the basil, oil, oregano, pepper and salt; set aside. Place egg whites and bread crumbs in separate shallow bowls. Cut eggplant lengthwise into six slices. Dip slices in egg whites, then coat in crumbs. Place on a baking sheet coated with cooking spray. Bake at 375° for 20-25 minutes or until tender and golden brown, turning once.

2. Cut each tomato into six slices; place two slices on each eggplant slice. Spoon reserved basil mixture over tomatoes and sprinkle with cheeses. Bake for 3-5 minutes or until cheese is melted.

3. Meanwhile, rub garlic over one side of each slice of bread; discard garlic. Place each eggplant stack on a slice of bread, garlic side up. Top with remaining bread, garlic side down.

Nutrition Facts: 1 sandwich equals 288 calories, 9 g fat (4 g saturated fat), 18 mg cholesterol, 628 mg sodium, 38 g carbohydrate, 5 g fiber, 15 g protein. **Diabetic Exchanges:** 2 starch, 1 lean meat, 1 vegetable, 1 fat.

Cranberry BBQ Turkey Sandwiches F

PREP: 10 min. **COOK:** 30 min. **YIELD:** 12 servings

SUSAN WILLIAMS • ROCKFORD, ILLINOIS

Keep the meat warm in a slow cooker at your next potluck, and you'll impress guests with these toasty sandwiches. No one ever suspects that cranberry sauce is my secret ingredient. It adds just a hint of tangy flavor.

1	can (14 oz.) jellied cranberry sauce
1	cup reduced-sodium beef broth
1/4	cup sugar
1/4	cup ketchup
2	Tbsp. cider vinegar
1	Tbsp. Worcestershire sauce
1	tsp. yellow mustard
1/4	tsp. garlic powder
1/8	tsp. seasoned salt
1/8	tsp. paprika
6	cups shredded cooked turkey breast
12	sandwich buns, split

1. In a large saucepan, combine the first 10 ingredients. Bring to a boil. Reduce heat; simmer, uncovered, for 20 minutes or until sauce is thickened.

2. Stir in turkey; simmer 4-5 minutes longer or until heated through. Spoon 1/2 cup onto each bun.

Nutrition Facts: 1 sandwich equals 296 calories, 3 g fat (1 g saturated fat), 61 mg cholesterol, 388 mg sodium, 41 g carbohydrate, 1 g fiber, 25 g protein. **Diabetic Exchanges:** 3 very lean meat, 2-1/2 starch.

Hearty Turkey Chili

PREP: 15 min. **COOK:** 25 min.
YIELD: 8 servings (2-1/2 qt.)

JUDY NIEMEYER • BRENHAM, TEXAS

My mother-in-law introduced our family to this chili a few years ago, and we can't seem to get enough of it! It makes a lot, so why not freeze extra portions for lunches or dinners on hectic days and nights ahead?

2	lbs. lean ground turkey
1	large onion, chopped
2	celery ribs, chopped
4	garlic cloves, minced
2	cans (16 oz. *each*) kidney beans, rinsed and drained
6	cans (5-1/2 oz. *each*) reduced-sodium V8 juice
1	cup reduced-sodium beef broth
1	can (6 oz.) tomato paste
3	tsp. ground cumin
1	tsp. salt
1/2	tsp. crushed red pepper flakes
2	bay leaves

1. In a Dutch oven, cook the turkey, onion, celery and garlic over medium heat until meat is no longer pink and the vegetables are tender; drain. Stir in the remaining ingredients. Bring to a boil.

2. Reduce heat; simmer, uncovered, for 15 minutes to allow flavors to blend. Discard bay leaves.

Nutrition Facts: 1-1/4 cups equals 329 calories, 10 g fat (3 g saturated fat), 90 mg cholesterol, 738 mg sodium, 31 g carbohydrate, 8 g fiber, 29 g protein. **Diabetic Exchanges:** 4 lean meat, 2 vegetable, 1 starch.

French Cheeseburger Loaf

PREP: 25 min. **BAKE:** 25 min. **YIELD:** 6 servings

NANCY DAUGHERTY • CORTLAND, OHIO

Once you prepare this impressive-looking, yet simple-to-make sandwich, you'll probably never look at refrigerated bread dough the same. It's just so easy!

3/4	lb. lean ground beef
1/2	cup chopped sweet onion
1	small green pepper, chopped
2	garlic cloves, minced
2	Tbsp. all-purpose flour
2	Tbsp. Dijon mustard
1	Tbsp. ketchup
1	tube (11 oz.) refrigerated crusty French loaf
4	slices reduced-fat process American cheese product
1	egg white, lightly beaten
3	Tbsp. shredded Parmesan cheese

1. In a large skillet, cook the beef, onion, pepper and garlic over medium heat until meat is no longer pink. Stir in the flour, mustard and ketchup; set aside.

2. Unroll dough starting at the seam. Pat into a 14-in. x 12-in. rectangle. Spoon meat mixture lengthwise down the center of the dough; top with cheese slices. Bring long sides of dough to the center over filling; pinch seams to seal.

3. Place seam side down on a baking sheet coated with cooking spray. Brush with egg white. Sprinkle with Parmesan cheese. With a sharp knife, cut diagonal slits in top of loaf. Bake at 350° for 25-30 minutes or until golden brown. Serve warm.

Nutrition Facts: 1 slice equals 277 calories, 7 g fat (3 g saturated fat), 33 mg cholesterol, 697 mg sodium, 30 g carbohydrate, 1 g fiber, 21 g protein. **Diabetic Exchanges:** 2 starch, 2 lean meat.

FRENCH CHEESEBURGER LOAF

Pretty Autumn Soup F M

PREP: 15 min. **COOK:** 20 min. **YIELD:** 6 servings

MARGARET ALLEN • ABINGDON, VIRGINIA

Carrots, squash and sweet potato combine to make a healthy and colorful fall soup. This one's loaded with vitamin A!

2-1/2	cups cubed peeled butternut squash
1	large sweet potato, peeled and cubed
3	medium carrots, sliced
1/4	cup orange juice concentrate
3	cups fat-free milk
1/4	tsp. salt
1/4	tsp. pepper
3	Tbsp. reduced-fat sour cream
2	Tbsp. minced chives
1	Tbsp. sesame seeds, toasted

1. Place the squash, sweet potato and carrots in a steamer basket; place in a large saucepan over 1 in. of water. Bring to a boil; cover and steam for 12-16 minutes or until tender. Cool slightly. Transfer to a food processor; add juice concentrate. Cover and process until smooth.

2. Transfer to a large saucepan; stir in the milk, salt and pepper. Cook and stir over low heat until heated through (do not boil). Top each serving with 1-1/2 tsp. sour cream, 1 tsp. chives and 1/2 tsp. sesame seeds.

Nutrition Facts: 1 cup equals 166 calories, 1 g fat (1 g saturated fat), 5 mg cholesterol, 190 mg sodium, 33 g carbohydrate, 6 g fiber, 7 g protein. **Diabetic Exchanges:** 1-1/2 starch, 1 vegetable, 1/2 fat-free milk.

Italian Beef Sandwiches

PREP: 20 min. **COOK:** 8 hours **YIELD:** 12 servings

CHER SCHWARTZ • ELLISVILLE, MISSOURI

These sandwiches are fork-tender, mouthwatering good, and so easy to fix. They always get rave reviews!

1	beef rump roast *or* bottom round roast (3 lbs.)
3	cups reduced-sodium beef broth
1	envelope Italian salad dressing mix
1	tsp. garlic powder
1	tsp. onion powder
1	tsp. dried parsley flakes
1	tsp. dried basil
1	tsp. dried oregano
1	tsp. pepper
1	large onion, julienned
1	large green pepper, julienned
4-1/2	tsp. olive oil
12	hamburger buns, split
12	slices reduced-fat provolone cheese

1. Cut roast in half; place in a 4-qt. slow cooker. Combine the broth, dressing mix and seasonings; pour over meat. Cover and cook on low for 8 hours or until tender.

2. Remove roast; cool slightly. Skim fat from cooking juices; reserve 1 cup juices. Shred beef and return to slow cooker. Stir in reserved cooking juices; heat through.

3. Meanwhile, in a large skillet, saute onion and green pepper in oil until tender.

4. Using a slotted spoon, place beef on bun bottoms; layer with cheese and vegetables. Replace bun tops.

Nutrition Facts: 1 sandwich equals 346 calories, 12 g fat (5 g saturated fat), 79 mg cholesterol, 707 mg sodium, 25 g carbohydrate, 2 g fiber, 32 g protein. **Diabetic Exchanges:** 4 lean meat, 1-1/2 starch, 1 fat.

Herbed Turkey Stock F S C

PREP: 1 hour 15 min. **COOK:** 1 hour + 30 min.
YIELD: 14 servings (3-1/2 qt.)

HEALTHY COOKING TEST KITCHEN

Spending a little extra time in the kitchen can yield big flavor, plus you'll be saving about 850 mg of sodium per cup versus store-bought chicken broth.

1	leftover turkey carcass (from a 12- to 14-lb. turkey)
2	medium onions, cut into wedges
2	celery ribs, cut into 1-in. pieces
2	medium carrots, cut into 1-in. pieces
6	garlic cloves, peeled
4	qt. plus 1 cup water, *divided*
1/2	cup packed fresh parsley sprigs
1/3	cup fresh sage leaves
1/4	cup fresh thyme sprigs
4	bay leaves
1	Tbsp. whole peppercorns

1. Place the turkey carcass, onions, celery, carrots and garlic in a shallow roasting pan coated with cooking spray. Bake, uncovered, at 400° for 1 hour, turning once.

2. Transfer the turkey carcass and vegetables to a stockpot; add 4 qt. water. Pour remaining water into the roasting pan, stirring to loosen browned bits; add to stockpot. Place the parsley, sage, thyme, bay leaves and peppercorns on a double thickness of cheesecloth; bring up corners of cloth and tie with string to form a bag; add to stockpot. Slowly bring to a boil over low heat; cover and simmer for 1-1/2 hours.

3. Discard the carcass and herb bag. Strain broth through a cheesecloth-lined colander. If using

PRETTY AUTUMN SOUP

BUTTERNUT SOUP WITH PARMESAN CROUTONS

immediately, skim fat. Or cool, then refrigerate for 8 hours or overnight; remove fat from surface before using. Broth may be refrigerated for up to 3 days or frozen for 4-6 months.

Nutrition Facts: 1 cup equals 33 calories, 1 g fat (trace saturated fat), 1 mg cholesterol, 89 mg sodium, 6 g carbohydrate, 1 g fiber, 2 g protein.

Butternut Soup With Parmesan Croutons

PREP: 50 min. **COOK:** 25 min. **YIELD:** 8 servings

JEN LEHNER • SEATTLE, WASHINGTON

Roasting creates a rich, caramelized flavor, but you can cook the squash cubes directly in the broth if you're short on time. They should pierce easily with a fork when they're done.

1   medium butternut squash (about 3 lbs.), peeled, seeded and cut into 1-in. cubes
2   Tbsp. olive oil, *divided*
1/4 tsp. pepper
1   large onion, chopped
3   celery ribs, chopped
2   Tbsp. minced fresh sage *or* 2 tsp. rubbed sage
3   cans (14-1/2 oz. *each*) reduced-sodium chicken broth

CROUTONS:
2   Tbsp. grated Parmesan cheese

2   Tbsp. olive oil
1   Tbsp. minced fresh sage *or* 1 tsp. rubbed sage
2   garlic cloves, minced
2   cups cubed French bread (1/2-in. cubes)
Cooking spray
Additional grated Parmesan cheese, optional

1. Place squash in a 15-in. x 10-in. x 1-in. baking pan lightly coated with cooking spray. Drizzle with 1 Tbsp. oil; sprinkle with pepper. Toss to coat. Bake, uncovered, at 425° for 30-35 minutes or until tender, stirring every 15 minutes. Set aside.

2. In a Dutch oven, saute the onion, celery and sage in remaining oil until tender. Stir in broth and reserved squash. Bring to a boil. Reduce heat; cover and simmer for 15-20 minutes or until heated through. Cool slightly.

3. In a blender, puree soup in batches until smooth. Return to the pan; heat through.

4. For croutons, in a small bowl, combine the cheese, oil, sage and garlic. Add bread cubes and spritz with cooking spray; toss to coat. Place on a baking sheet coated with cooking spray. Bake at 425° for 5-8 minutes or until golden brown, stirring occasionally. Serve with soup and sprinkle with additional Parmesan cheese if desired.

Nutrition Facts: 1 cup soup with 1/4 cup croutons equals 179 calories, 8 g fat (1 g saturated fat), 1 mg cholesterol, 541 mg sodium, 25 g carbohydrate, 6 g fiber, 5 g protein. **Diabetic Exchanges:** 1-1/2 starch, 1 fat.

Artichoke Chicken Pockets

PREP: 20 min. **BAKE:** 15 min. **YIELD:** 6 servings

BEVERLY O'FERRALL • LINKWOOD, MARYLAND

You'll have a hard time believing these hefty, pizza-crust pockets are light! Packed full of cheese, artichokes, chicken, spinach and fabulous flavor, they're great even without the sauce and sure to become a family favorite.

2	cups shredded cooked chicken breast
2	cups thinly sliced fresh spinach
1-1/4	cups shredded provolone cheese
3/4	cup water-packed artichoke hearts, rinsed, drained and chopped
1	garlic clove, minced
1/4	tsp. pepper
1	tube (13.8 oz.) refrigerated pizza crust
2	tsp. cornmeal

Marinara sauce, optional

1. In a large bowl, combine the first six ingredients. Unroll pizza dough; cut into six 4-1/2-in. squares. Spoon 1 cup chicken mixture onto the center of each square; brush edges of dough with water. Fold one corner of each square over filling to the opposite corner, forming a triangle. Using a fork, crimp edges to seal.

2. Sprinkle cornmeal over a 15-in. x 10-in. x 1-in. baking pan coated with cooking spray. Place pockets in pan; prick tops with a fork. Bake at 425° for 12-15 minutes or until golden brown. Serve with marinara sauce if desired.

Nutrition Facts: 1 pocket (calculated without marinara sauce) equals 355 calories, 11 g fat (5 g saturated fat), 55 mg cholesterol, 776 mg sodium, 34 g carbohydrate, 1 g fiber, 27 g protein. **Diabetic Exchanges:** 3 lean meat, 2 starch, 1 fat.

Spicy Chicken Chili

PREP: 30 min. **COOK:** 30 min. **YIELD:** 12 servings (4 qt.)

NATALIE HUGHES • YUKON, OKLAHOMA

My recipe was inspired by the fact that I've been on a low-calorie, low-fat, high-fiber diet. I entered this in a chili cookoff and had several people say that it was the best chili they'd ever had!

1	small onion, chopped
1	small green pepper, chopped
1	small sweet red pepper, chopped
2	jalapeno peppers, seeded and chopped
1	serrano pepper, seeded and chopped
3	garlic cloves, minced
1	Tbsp. olive oil

1 can (28 oz.) crushed tomatoes
1 can (14-1/2 oz.) stewed tomatoes, cut up
1 can (14-1/2 oz.) diced tomatoes with mild green chilies
1 can (16 oz.) kidney beans, rinsed and drained
1 can (15 oz.) black beans, rinsed and drained
1 carton (32 oz.) reduced-sodium chicken broth
3 Tbsp. chili powder
1 Tbsp. ground cumin
1 to 2 tsp. crushed red pepper flakes
2 to 4 Tbsp. Louisiana-style hot sauce
2-1/2 cups cubed cooked chicken breast
2 cups frozen corn
3/4 cup reduced-fat sour cream
3/4 cup shredded reduced-fat cheddar cheese

1. In a Dutch oven, saute the first six ingredients in oil until tender; add the tomatoes, beans, broth, seasonings and hot sauce. Bring to a boil. Reduce heat; simmer, uncovered, for 15 minutes. Stir in chicken and corn; heat through. Garnish each serving with 1 Tbsp. each of sour cream and cheese.

Editor's Note: When cutting hot peppers, disposable gloves are recommended. Avoid touching your face.

Nutrition Facts: 1-1/3 cups equals 242 calories, 6 g fat (2 g saturated fat), 32 mg cholesterol, 694 mg sodium, 31 g carbohydrate, 7 g fiber, 19 g protein. **Diabetic Exchanges:** 2 very lean meat, 2 vegetable, 1 starch, 1 fat.

Turkey Meatball Soup

PREP: 30 min. **COOK:** 40 min. **YIELD:** 6 servings

CHRISTIE LADD • MECHANICSBURG, PENNSYLVANIA

Every Italian-American family I know seems to have their own take on meatball soup. This recipe is based on my family's classic version.

2 egg whites, beaten
1/2 cup seasoned bread crumbs
1 Tbsp. grated Parmesan cheese
4 tsp. Italian seasoning, *divided*
1 lb. lean ground turkey
3 medium carrots, sliced
3 celery ribs, finely chopped
4 garlic cloves, minced
1 Tbsp. olive oil
3 cans (14-1/2 oz. *each*) reduced-sodium chicken broth
1/4 tsp. pepper
1/2 cup ditalini or other small pasta

1. In a small bowl, combine the egg whites, bread crumbs, cheese and 2 tsp. Italian seasoning. Crumble turkey over mixture and mix well. Shape into 3/4-in. balls. Place in a 15-in. x 10-in. x 1-in. baking pan coated with cooking spray. Bake, uncovered, at 350° for 10-15 minutes or until no longer pink.

2. Meanwhile, in a Dutch oven, saute the carrots, celery and garlic in oil until tender. Add the broth, pepper and remaining Italian seasoning. Bring to a boil. Reduce heat; cover and simmer for 20 minutes. Stir in pasta; cook 10-12 minutes longer or until vegetables and pasta are tender. Stir in meatballs; heat through.

Nutrition Facts: 1 cup equals 258 calories, 10 g fat (2 g saturated fat), 60 mg cholesterol, 783 mg sodium, 21 g carbohydrate, 2 g fiber, 21 g protein. **Diabetic Exchanges:** 2 lean meat, 1-1/2 starch, 1/2 fat.

Super-Duper Tuna Sandwiches

PREP/TOTAL TIME: 15 min **YIELD:** 4 servings

NAE BARTOLOMEO • INDIANOLA, IOWA

You can also try serving this fantastic tuna salad on tortillas for wraps or with crackers as an appetizer.

2 cans (6 oz. *each*) light water-packed tuna, drained and flaked
1/3 cup shredded apple
1/3 cup finely shredded cabbage
1/3 cup finely shredded carrot
3 Tbsp. finely chopped celery
3 Tbsp. finely chopped onion
3 Tbsp. sweet pickle relish
2 Tbsp. reduced-fat mayonnaise
8 slices whole wheat bread

1. In a large bowl, combine the first eight ingredients. Spread 1/2 cup tuna mixture over four slices of bread; top with remaining bread slices.

Nutrition Facts: 1 sandwich equals 291 calories, 5 g fat (1 g saturated fat), 28 mg cholesterol, 717 mg sodium, 31 g carbohydrate, 5 g fiber, 29 g protein. **Diabetic Exchanges:** 3 very lean meat, 2 starch, 1/2 fat.

SUPER-DUPER TUNA SANDWICHES

Vegetable Pork Soup

PREP: 20 min. **COOK:** 7 hours **YIELD:** 6 servings (2 qt.)

DEB HALL • HUNTINGTON, INDIANA

Chock-full of tender pork, veggies and savory flavor, this nutritious soup fills the house with a wonderful aroma!

- 1 pork tenderloin (1 lb.), cut into 1-in. pieces
- 1 tsp. garlic powder
- 2 tsp. canola oil
- 1 can (28 oz.) diced tomatoes
- 4 medium carrots, cut into 1/2-in. pieces
- 2 medium potatoes, cubed
- 1 can (12 oz.) light or nonalcoholic beer
- 1/4 cup quick-cooking tapioca
- 2 bay leaves
- 1 Tbsp. Worcestershire sauce
- 1 Tbsp. honey
- 1 tsp. dried thyme
- 1/4 tsp. salt
- 1/4 tsp. pepper
- 1/8 tsp. ground nutmeg

1. Sprinkle pork with garlic powder. In a large skillet, brown pork in oil; drain.

2. Transfer to a 4-qt. slow cooker. Add remaining ingredients. Cover and cook on low for 7-8 hours or until meat is tender. Discard bay leaves.

Nutrition Facts: 1-1/3 cups equals 258 calories, 4 g fat (1 g saturated fat), 42 mg cholesterol, 357 mg sodium, 34 g carbohydrate, 5 g fiber, 18 g protein. **Diabetic Exchanges:** 2 lean meat, 2 vegetable, 1-1/2 starch.

VEGETABLE PORK SOUP

Makeover Curried Chicken Rice Soup

PREP: 15 min. **COOK:** 20 min.
YIELD: 11 servings (2-3/4 qt.)

REBECCA COOK • HELOTES, TEXAS

This lighter version of our family-favorite soup boasts all the hearty texture, warm comfort and delicious flavor of the original—but less than half the fat and a fifth of the calories! That's a difference to savor!

- 1/4 cup butter, cubed
- 2 large carrots, finely chopped
- 2 celery ribs, finely chopped
- 1 small onion, finely chopped
- 3/4 cup plus 2 Tbsp. all-purpose flour
- 1 tsp. seasoned salt
- 1 tsp. curry powder
- 2 cans (12 oz. *each*) fat-free evaporated milk
- 1 cup half-and-half cream
- 4-1/2 cups reduced-sodium chicken broth
- 3 cups cubed cooked chicken breast
- 2 cups cooked brown rice

1. In a Dutch oven, melt butter. Add the carrots, celery and onion; saute for 2 minutes. Sprinkle with flour; stir until blended. Stir in seasoned salt and curry. Gradually add milk and cream. Bring to a boil; cook and stir for 2 minutes or until thickened.

2. Gradually add broth. Stir in chicken and rice; return to a boil. Reduce heat; simmer, uncovered, for 10 minutes or until vegetables are tender.

Nutrition Facts: 1 cup equals 263 calories, 8 g fat (5 g saturated fat), 54 mg cholesterol, 524 mg sodium, 26 g carbohydrate, 2 g fiber, 20 g protein. **Diabetic Exchanges:** 2 very lean meat, 1 starch, 1 fat, 1/2 fat-free milk.

Family-Pleasing Turkey Chili

PREP: 25 min. **COOK:** 4 hours
YIELD: 6 servings (2-1/4 qt.)

SHEILA CHRISTENSEN • SAN MARCOS, CALIFORNIA

My children really love this recipe, and it's become one of their best comfort foods. It's relatively inexpensive, and leftovers are wonderful!

- 1 lb. lean ground turkey
- 1 medium green pepper, finely chopped
- 1 small red onion, finely chopped
- 2 garlic cloves, minced
- 1 can (28 oz.) diced tomatoes, undrained
- 1 can (16 oz.) kidney beans, rinsed and drained
- 1 can (15 oz.) black beans, rinsed and drained
- 1 can (14-1/2 oz.) reduced-sodium chicken broth
- 1-3/4 cups frozen corn, thawed
- 1 can (6 oz.) tomato paste
- 1 Tbsp. chili powder
- 1/2 tsp. pepper
- 1/4 tsp. ground cumin
- 1/4 tsp. garlic powder

Optional toppings: reduced-fat sour cream and minced fresh cilantro

1. In a large nonstick skillet, cook the turkey, green pepper, onion and garlic over medium heat until meat is no longer pink; drain. Transfer to a 4-qt. slow cooker.

2. Stir in the tomatoes, kidney beans, black beans, broth, corn, tomato paste, chili powder, pepper, cumin and garlic powder. Cover and cook on low for 4-5 hours or until heated through. Serve with optional toppings if desired.

Nutrition Facts: 1-1/2 cups (calculated without optional toppings) equals 349 calories, 7 g fat (2 g saturated fat), 60 mg cholesterol, 729 mg sodium, 48 g carbohydrate, 12 g fiber, 26 g protein.

Pork Tenderloin Panini With Fig Port Jam

PREP: 1 hour **COOK:** 5 min. **YIELD:** 4 servings

CASEY GALLOWAY • COLUMBIA, MISSOURI

I serve these rather sophisticated, yet simple sandwiches for dinner or cut them into smaller servings for appetizers. They're great hot or cold, but if serving cold, I like to add some watercress for a bit more color.

1/3	cup port wine or grape juice
2	Tbsp. water
2	dried figs, chopped
1	fresh rosemary sprig
1	Tbsp. honey
1/8	tsp. salt

Dash pepper

SANDWICHES:

1	pork tenderloin (3/4 lb.)
1/4	tsp. salt
1/4	tsp. pepper
8	slices sourdough bread
1/4	cup crumbled goat cheese
1	cup watercress, optional

Cooking spray

1. For jam, in small saucepan, combine the first seven ingredients. Bring to a boil. Reduce heat; simmer, uncovered, until liquid is reduced to about 1/4 cup, about 15 minutes.

2. Remove from the heat. Cool slightly; discard rosemary. Transfer mixture to blender; cover and process until blended. Cover and chill until serving.

3. Meanwhile, sprinkle tenderloin with salt and pepper; place on a rack in a shallow roasting pan. Bake, uncovered, at 350° for 40-50 minutes or until a meat thermometer reads 160°. Let stand for 10 minutes before slicing. Cut pork into 1/8-in. slices.

4. On four bread slices, layer the pork, jam, cheese and watercress if desired; top with remaining bread. Coat outsides of sandwiches with cooking spray. Cook on a panini maker or indoor grill for 3-4 minutes or until bread is lightly browned.

Nutrition Facts: 1 sandwich equals 381 calories, 8 g fat (4 g saturated fat), 59 mg cholesterol, 746 mg sodium, 48 g carbohydrate, 3 g fiber, 28 g protein.

STACY'S BLACK BEAN SOUP

Stacy's Black Bean Soup F

PREP: 35 min. + soaking **COOK:** 1-1/4 hours
YIELD: 8 servings (2 qt.)

STACY MARTI • JENKS, OKLAHOMA

We love this low-fat black bean soup! It's packed with good-for-you vegetables and beans. To make it completely vegetarian, substitute vegetable broth for the chicken broth.

1-1/2	cups dried black beans
3	celery ribs, chopped
3	medium carrots, chopped
1	large onion, chopped
2	garlic cloves, minced
2	tsp. olive oil
6-1/2	cups reduced-sodium chicken broth
1	tsp. dried oregano
1/2	tsp. dried thyme
1/2	tsp. salt
1/4	tsp. cayenne pepper
1	bay leaf
3	Tbsp. lime juice
8	Tbsp. reduced-fat sour cream
1/4	cup minced fresh cilantro

1. Place beans in a large saucepan; add water to cover by 2 in. Bring to a boil; boil for 2 minutes. Remove from the heat; cover and let stand for 1 to 4 hours or until beans are softened. Drain and rinse beans, discarding liquid.

2. In a Dutch oven coated with cooking spray, saute the celery, carrots, onion and garlic in oil until vegetables are tender. Add the beans, broth, oregano, thyme, salt, cayenne and bay leaf. Bring to a boil. Reduce heat; cover and simmer for 1 to 1-1/4 hours or until beans are tender. Discard bay leaf. Cool slightly.

3. In a blender, cover and process soup in batches until smooth. Return to pan; heat though. Stir in lime juice. Garnish each serving with sour cream and cilantro.

Nutrition Facts: 1 cup equals 210 calories, 3 g fat (1 g saturated fat), 5 mg cholesterol, 686 mg sodium, 34 g carbohydrate, 8 g fiber, 13 g protein. **Diabetic Exchanges:** 2 starch, 1 very lean meat, 1 vegetable.

Chipotle BBQ Pork Sandwiches

PREP: 20 min. **GRILL:** 20 min. **YIELD:** 4 servings

PRISCILLA YEE • CONCORD, CALIFORNIA

I first made these for a summer cookout with guests who love traditional BBQ pork sandwiches but wanted something lighter. They loved these and didn't miss the extra calories one bit. Crunchy coleslaw tames the heat!

1/2	cup barbecue sauce
1	Tbsp. honey
2	chipotle peppers in adobo sauce, chopped
1	pork tenderloin (1 lb.)
1-1/2	cups coleslaw mix
2	Tbsp. reduced-fat sour cream
2	Tbsp. reduced-fat salad dressing
1	Tbsp. Dijon mustard
4	hamburger buns, split

1. In a small bowl, combine the barbecue sauce, honey and peppers. Set aside 1/4 cup until serving.

2. Coat grill rack with cooking spray before starting the grill. Prepare grill for indirect heat. Grill pork, covered, over indirect medium-hot heat for 20-25 minutes or until a meat thermometer reads 160°, basting occasionally with remaining barbecue sauce. Let stand for 5 minutes before slicing.

3. Meanwhile, combine the coleslaw mix, sour cream, dressing and mustard. Brush cut sides of buns with reserved barbecue sauce. Cut pork into 1/4-in. slices; place on bun bottoms. Top with coleslaw and bun tops.

Nutrition Facts: 1 sandwich equals 337 calories, 9 g fat (2 g saturated fat), 68 mg cholesterol, 753 mg sodium, 35 g carbohydrate, 2 g fiber, 28 g protein. **Diabetic Exchanges:** 3 lean meat, 2 starch, 1 fat.

One-Pot Chili

PREP: 25 min. **COOK:** 15 min. **YIELD:** 6 servings (2 qt.)

DAWN FORSBERG • SAINT JOSEPH, MISSOURI

This hearty entree is low in fat and full of flavor. I love that you can cook the dried pasta right in the chili. One less pot to wash! This also reheats in the microwave perfectly.

- 1 lb. lean ground turkey
- 1 small onion, chopped
- 1/4 cup chopped green pepper
- 1 tsp. olive oil
- 2 cups water
- 1 can (15 oz.) pinto beans, rinsed and drained
- 1 can (14-1/2 oz.) reduced-sodium beef broth
- 1 can (14-1/2 oz.) diced tomatoes with mild green chilies, undrained
- 1 can (8 oz.) no-salt-added tomato sauce
- 2 tsp. chili powder
- 1 tsp. ground cumin
- 1/2 tsp. dried oregano
- 2 cups uncooked multigrain penne pasta
- 1/4 cup reduced-fat sour cream
- 1/4 cup minced fresh cilantro

1. In a large saucepan coated with cooking spray, cook the turkey, onion and pepper in oil over medium heat until meat is no longer pink; drain.

2. Stir in the water, beans, broth, tomatoes, tomato sauce, chili powder, cumin and oregano. Bring to a boil. Add pasta; cook for 15-20 minutes or until tender, stirring occasionally. Serve with sour cream; sprinkle with cilantro.

Nutrition Facts: 1-1/3 cups with 2 tsp. sour cream equals 384 calories, 10 g fat (2 g saturated fat), 64 mg cholesterol, 598 mg sodium, 47 g carbohydrate, 8 g fiber, 25 g protein.

Veggie Cheese Soup C

PREP: 15 min. **COOK:** 25 min. **YIELD:** 9 servings

JEAN HALL • RAPID CITY, SOUTH DAKOTA

My niece makes this in a slow cooker. She adds the cheese when the veggies are tender and 5 minutes later, it's ready!

- 1 medium onion, chopped
- 1 celery rib, chopped
- 2 small red potatoes, cut into 1/2-in. cubes
- 2-3/4 cups water
- 2 tsp. reduced-sodium chicken bouillon granules
- 1 Tbsp. cornstarch
- 1/4 cup cold water
- 1 can (10-3/4 oz.) reduced-fat reduced-sodium condensed cream of chicken soup, undiluted
- 3 cups frozen California-blend vegetables, thawed
- 1/2 cup chopped fully cooked lean ham
- 8 oz. reduced-fat process cheese (Velveeta), cubed

1. In a large nonstick saucepan coated with a cooking spray, cook the onion and celery over medium heat until onion is tender. Stir in the potatoes, water and bouillon. Bring to a boil. Reduce heat; cover and simmer for 10 minutes.

2. Combine cornstarch and cold water until smooth; gradually stir into soup. Return to a boil; cook and stir for 1-2 minutes or until slightly thickened. Stir in condensed soup until blended.

3. Reduce heat; add vegetables and ham. Cook and stir until vegetables are tender. Stir in cheese until melted.

Nutrition Facts: 3/4 cup equals 115 calories, 4 g fat (2 g saturated fat), 15 mg cholesterol, 682 mg sodium, 13 g carbohydrate, 1 g fiber, 8 g protein.

Don't have the ham for the **Veggie Cheese Soup** recipe? Don't worry! Save a little fat and cut back on sodium and calories by leaving it out altogether. Or, replace the ham with extra vegetables instead.

VEGGIE CHEESE SOUP

Hearty Chipotle Chicken Soup

PREP: 15 min. **COOK:** 30 min. **YIELD:** 8 servings

SONALI RUDER • NEW YORK, NEW YORK

Sweet corn and cool sour cream help tame the smoky hot flavors of chipotle pepper in this well-balanced soup that's perfect for chilly nights.

1	large onion, chopped
1	Tbsp. canola oil
4	garlic cloves, minced
4	cups reduced-sodium chicken broth
2	cans (15 oz. *each*) pinto beans, rinsed and drained
2	cans (14-1/2 oz. *each*) fire-roasted diced tomatoes, undrained
3	cups frozen corn
2	chipotle peppers in adobo sauce, seeded and minced
2	tsp. adobo sauce
1	tsp. ground cumin
1/4	tsp. pepper
2	cups cubed cooked chicken breast
1/2	cup fat-free sour cream
1/4	cup minced fresh cilantro

1. In a Dutch oven, saute onion in oil until tender. Add garlic; cook 1 minute longer. Add the broth, beans, tomatoes, corn, chipotle peppers, adobo sauce, cumin and pepper. Bring to a boil. Reduce heat; simmer, uncovered, for 20 minutes.

2. Stir in chicken; heat through. Garnish with sour cream; sprinkle with cilantro.

Nutrition Facts: 1-2/3 cups with 1 Tbsp. sour cream equals 287 calories, 4 g fat (1 g saturated fat), 29 mg cholesterol, 790 mg sodium, 42 g carbohydrate, 7 g fiber, 21 g protein. **Diabetic Exchanges:** 2 starch, 2 very lean meat, 2 vegetable.

Spiced-Up Healthy Soup F

PREP: 15 min. **COOK:** 40 min.
YIELD: 14 servings (3-1/2 qt.)

DIANE TAYMAN • DIXON, ILLINOIS

This has been a hit with family and friends. It's spicy, low-fat and filled with good-for-you ingredients.

1	medium onion, chopped
1/3	cup medium pearl barley
4	garlic cloves, minced
2	Tbsp. canola oil
5	cans (14-1/2 oz. *each*) reduced-sodium chicken broth
2	boneless skinless chicken breast halves (4 oz. *each*)
1	cup dried lentils, rinsed
1	jar (16 oz.) picante sauce
1	can (15 oz.) garbanzo beans or chickpeas, rinsed and drained
1/2	cup minced fresh cilantro
8	cups chopped fresh spinach

1. In a Dutch oven, saute the onion, barley and garlic in oil until onion is tender. Add the broth, chicken and lentils; bring to a boil. Reduce heat; cover and simmer for 15 minutes or until chicken is no longer pink. Remove chicken and set aside.

2. Add the picante sauce, garbanzo beans and cilantro to soup; cover and simmer 10 minutes longer or until barley and lentils are tender. Shred chicken with two forks. Add spinach and chicken to soup. Simmer, uncovered, for 5 minutes or until spinach is wilted.

Nutrition Facts: 1 cup equals 156 calories, 3 g fat (trace saturated fat), 9 mg cholesterol, 601 mg sodium, 21 g carbohydrate, 7 g fiber, 11 g protein. **Diabetic Exchanges:** 1 starch, 1 very lean meat, 1 vegetable, 1/2 fat.

HEARTY CHIPOTLE CHICKEN SOUP

SPICED-UP HEALTHY SOUP

SUMMER VEGGIE SUBS

Summer Veggie Subs

PREP: 30 min. + standing **YIELD:** 12 servings

JENNIE TODD • LANCASTER, PENNSYLVANIA

The best versions of this recipe have been made with fresh spinach and tomatoes from the plants I grow. When I have herbs in my container gardens, I use them, but the subs are also good with a simple oil and vinegar dressing.

4	medium sweet red peppers
1/2	cup fat-free mayonnaise
2	Tbsp. minced fresh basil
1	Tbsp. minced fresh parsley
1	Tbsp. minced fresh tarragon
2	loaves French bread (1 lb. *each*), halved lengthwise
2	cups fresh baby spinach
2	cups thinly sliced cucumbers
2	cups alfalfa sprouts
4	medium tomatoes, sliced
2	medium ripe avocados, peeled and sliced
3/4	lb. thinly sliced deli turkey
6	slices reduced-fat Swiss cheese, halved

1. Broil peppers 4 in. from the heat until skins blister, about 5 minutes. With tongs, rotate peppers a quarter turn. Broil and rotate until all sides are blistered and blackened. Immediately place peppers in a large bowl; cover and let stand for 15-20 minutes.

2. Peel off and discard charred skin. Remove stems and seeds. Julienne peppers.

3. Combine the mayonnaise, basil, parsley and tarragon; spread over bread bottoms. Top with spinach, cucumbers, sprouts, roasted peppers, tomatoes, avocados, turkey and cheese. Replace tops. Cut each loaf into six slices.

Nutrition Facts: 1 slice equals 357 calories, 9 g fat (2 g saturated fat), 19 mg cholesterol, 894 mg sodium, 53 g carbohydrate, 6 g fiber, 20 g protein.

Taking full advantage of summer's bounty, as well as refreshingly crisp items such as cucumbers and alfalfa sprouts, **Summer Veggie Subs** make great picnic entrees. Wrap the loaves in plastic wrap and cut into slices at the picnic right before serving.

SPICED RICE

MAKEOVER CORN PUDDING

ONION TRIO PASTA

Side Dishes

Nothing rounds out a meal like buttery pasta, versatile rice or vibrant vegetables. This chapter features more than 40 sensational ways to complete heart-healthy menus and ensure your table abounds with smiles each and every night.

Onion Trio Pasta M

PREP: 25 min. **COOK:** 25 min. **YIELD:** 8 servings

PRISCILLA GILBERT • INDIAN HARBOUR BEACH, FLORIDA

This is a different recipe, but I love onions and my curiosity got the best of me...so I tried it. It's wonderfully good! I fix it quite often.

2	cups chopped leeks
1-1/2	cups chopped onions
1/3	cup chopped green onions
1	Tbsp. olive oil
8	oz. uncooked linguine
1	can (14-1/2 oz.) vegetable broth
1/4	cup dried currants
1	Tbsp. balsamic vinegar
1/4	cup half-and-half cream
1/2	tsp. salt
2	cups fresh arugula *or* baby spinach
1/2	cup shredded part-skim mozzarella cheese
1	tsp. minced fresh thyme

1. In a large skillet over medium heat, cook the leeks, onions and green onions in oil over medium heat for 8 minutes, stirring frequently. Reduce heat to low; cook, stirring occasionally, 5-10 minutes longer or until onions are golden brown. Meanwhile, prepare linguine according to package directions.

2. Add the broth, currants and vinegar to the onion mixture; bring to a boil. Add cream and salt; cook, stirring occasionally, for 3-5 minutes or until slightly thickened. Stir in the arugula, cheese and thyme. Drain linguine; toss with sauce.

Nutrition Facts: 3/4 cup equals 190 calories, 5 g fat (2 g saturated fat), 8 mg cholesterol, 412 mg sodium, 32 g carbohydrate, 2 g fiber, 7 g protein. **Diabetic Exchanges:** 1-1/2 starch, 1 vegetable, 1/2 fat.

Makeover Corn Pudding M

PREP: 15 min. **BAKE:** 50 min. **YIELD:** 12 servings

ARLENE SPENCER • OCONOMOWOC, WISCONSIN

Passed down for generations, this recipe was a cherished family tradition at holidays and special gatherings. Now, with less than half the fat, sodium and cholesterol of the original, it can be served up for generations to come!

1/3	cup all-purpose flour
2	Tbsp. sugar
1	cup fat-free milk
3/4	cup egg substitute
1	Tbsp. butter, melted
1	tsp. salt
8	cups frozen corn, thawed
1	can (14-3/4 oz.) cream-style corn
1	cup (4 oz.) shredded sharp cheddar cheese

1. In a large bowl, combine flour and sugar. Whisk in the milk, egg substitute, butter and salt. Stir in the corn, cream-style corn and cheese.

2. Pour into a 13-in. x 9-in. baking dish coated with cooking spray. Bake, uncovered, at 375° for 50-55 minutes or until a knife inserted near the center comes out clean.

Nutrition Facts: 1 piece equals 197 calories, 5 g fat (3 g saturated fat), 13 mg cholesterol, 403 mg sodium, 35 g carbohydrate, 3 g fiber, 8 g protein. **Diabetic Exchanges:** 2 starch, 1 fat.

Peppered Tarragon Carrots
F C M

PREP/TOTAL TIME: 25 min. **YIELD:** 4 servings

CLARA COULSTON • WASHINGTON COURT HOUSE, OHIO

Orange juice and tarragon jazz up this basic carrot side dish and boast a healthy dose of vitamins C and A.

1	lb. fresh baby carrots, halved lengthwise
1/2	cup orange juice
1/2	tsp. salt
1/2	tsp. dried tarragon
1/4	tsp. pepper

1. Place 1 in. of water in a large saucepan; add carrots. Bring to a boil. Reduce heat; cover and simmer for 5-8 minutes or until crisp-tender. Drain carrots and discard liquid.

2. Add the remaining ingredients. Cook and stir over low heat until heated through.

Nutrition Facts: 3/4 cup equals 55 calories, trace fat (trace saturated fat), 0 cholesterol, 384 mg sodium, 13 g carbohydrate, 2 g fiber, 1 g protein. **Diabetic Exchange:** 2 vegetable.

Never-Fail Scalloped Potatoes M

PREP: 30 min. **BAKE:** 1 hour **YIELD:** 6 servings

AGNES WARD • STRATFORD, ONTARIO

Take the chill off any blustery day and make something special to serve with meaty entrees. This creamy, stick-to-the-ribs potatoes-and-onion side dish is one you'll turn to often.

2	Tbsp. butter
3	Tbsp. all-purpose flour
1	tsp. salt
1/4	tsp. pepper
1-1/2	cups fat-free milk
1/2	cup shredded reduced-fat cheddar cheese
1-3/4	lbs. potatoes, peeled and thinly sliced (about 5 medium)
1	medium onion, halved and thinly sliced

1. In a small nonstick skillet, melt butter. Stir in the flour, salt and pepper until smooth; gradually add the milk. Bring to a boil. Cook and stir for 2 minutes or until thickened. Remove from the heat; stir in cheese until blended.

2. Place half of the potatoes in a 1-1/2-qt. baking dish coated with cooking spray; layer with half of the onion and cheese sauce. Repeat layers. Cover and bake at 350° for 50 minutes. Uncover; bake 10-15 minutes longer or until bubbly and potatoes are tender.

Nutrition Facts: about 3/4 cup equals 196 calories, 6 g fat (4 g saturated fat), 18 mg cholesterol, 530 mg sodium, 29 g carbohydrate, 3 g fiber, 7 g protein. **Diabetic Exchanges:** 2 starch, 1 fat.

NEVER-FAIL SCALLOPED POTATOES

Bravo Broccoli F C M

PREP/TOTAL TIME: 20 min. **YIELD:** 4 servings

HEALTHY COOKING TEST KITCHEN

Here's a fast, delicious way to dress up crisp-tender broccoli! Just toss with a simple sweet-sour mixture that gets a slight kick from crushed red pepper flakes.

1	bunch broccoli, cut into florets
1	Tbsp. butter, melted
1	Tbsp. rice vinegar
1-1/2	tsp. brown sugar
1/4	tsp. salt
1/4	tsp. crushed red pepper flakes
1/8	tsp. garlic powder

1. Place broccoli in a steamer basket; place in a large saucepan over 1 in. of water. Bring to a boil; cover and steam for 3-4 minutes or until tender. Transfer to a large bowl.

2. Combine the remaining ingredients; drizzle over broccoli and gently toss to coat.

Nutrition Facts: 3/4 cup equals 78 calories, 3 g fat (2 g saturated fat), 8 mg cholesterol, 210 mg sodium, 10 g carbohydrate, 5 g fiber, 5 g protein. **Diabetic Exchanges:** 2 vegetable, 1/2 fat.

Hominy with Peppers M

PREP/TOTAL TIME: 25 min. **YIELD:** 6 servings

ANNA BREEDING • MARION, OHIO

This is one of my family's favorite sides. My mother-in-law hated to eat light, but she would devour this when I served it. Three types of peppers and a hint of garlic make the colorful dish a hit.

1	*each* large green pepper, sweet red and yellow peppers
2	cans (15-1/2 oz. *each*) hominy, rinsed and drained
2	Tbsp. canola oil
1-1/2	tsp. garlic pepper blend

BRAVO BROCCOLI

SPICED GLAZED CARROTS

1. In a large bowl, combine the peppers, hominy, oil and garlic pepper; toss to coat. Spread into an ungreased 15-in. x 10-in. x 1-in. baking pan. Bake at 450° for 14-16 minutes or until peppers are tender, stirring once.

Nutrition Facts: 2/3 cup equals 130 calories, 5 g fat (trace saturated fat), 0 cholesterol, 692 mg sodium, 20 g carbohydrate, 5 g fiber, 2 g protein. **Diabetic Exchanges:** 1 starch, 1 vegetable, 1 fat.

Spiced Glazed Carrots F S M

PREP/TOTAL TIME: 30 min. **YIELD:** 4 servings

NANCY ZIMMERMAN • CAPE MAY COURT HOUSE, NEW JERSEY

Packed with beta-carotene, these carrots cooked with honey, apple juice and cinnamon are hard to turn down. They boast a little kick that brings big flavor to the table!

1	lb. fresh carrots, cut into 1/2-in. slices
3/4	cup unsweetened apple juice
1	cinnamon stick (3 in.)
3/4	tsp. ground cumin
1/2	tsp. ground ginger
1/4	tsp. ground coriander

Dash cayenne pepper

2	tsp. lemon juice
2	tsp. honey

1. In a large nonstick skillet coated with cooking spray, combine the first seven ingredients. Bring to a boil. Reduce heat; cover and simmer for 5-8 minutes or until carrots are crisp-tender.

2. Discard cinnamon stick. Add lemon juice and honey to carrots. Bring to a boil; cook, uncovered, for 2 minutes or until sauce is thickened.

Nutrition Facts: 2/3 cup equals 83 calories, trace fat (trace saturated fat), 0 cholesterol, 81 mg sodium, 20 g carbohydrate, 3 g fiber, 1 g protein. **Diabetic Exchange:** 1 starch.

Preparing your own glaze for carrots, as opposed to using a jarred variety, helps keep things light. When preparing **Spiced Glazed Carrots**, pick up a bag of mini carrots to save time...you'll simply need to cut them. Save money by purchasing apple juice in drink boxes. You can use a box for the recipe instead of opening a whole bottle.

BASIL TOMATO RICE

Basil Tomato Rice F

PREP/TOTAL TIME: 25 min. **YIELD:** 6 servings

SARAH RUPE • ELDON, IOWA

Whenever my family wants something different to go with grilled beef or other entrees, I throw together this easy side. It's so fresh-tasting, and I always have the ingredients on hand. What a great way to use up leftover rice.

2	cups reduced-sodium chicken broth
2	cups uncooked instant rice
1	medium green pepper, diced
1	small onion, finely chopped
1-1/2	tsp. olive oil
2	medium tomatoes, seeded and chopped
2	tsp. dried basil
1/4	tsp. salt

1. In a large saucepan, bring broth to a boil. Stir in rice; cover and remove from the heat. Let stand for 5 minutes.

2. Meanwhile, in a small skillet, saute pepper and onion in oil until tender. Add the tomatoes, basil and salt; heat through. Stir into rice.

Nutrition Facts: 3/4 cup equals 154 calories, 2 g fat (trace saturated fat), 0 cholesterol, 295 mg sodium, 30 g carbohydrate, 2 g fiber, 4 g protein. **Diabetic Exchange:** 2 starch.

Roasted Garlic and Cheese Corn on the Cob M

PREP: 1 hour **GRILL:** 20 min. **YIELD:** 8 servings

MARY BETH HARRIS-MURPHREE • TYLER, TEXAS

This recipe is so delicious that even a veggie-hater will love it. I make it every cookout, and people rave!

1	whole garlic bulb
1/8	tsp. olive oil

Dash salt

Dash plus 1/2 tsp. pepper, *divided*

8	medium ears sweet corn in husks
1/2	cup fat-free mayonnaise
1	tsp. paprika
3/4	cup grated Romano cheese

1. Remove papery outer skin from garlic (do not peel or separate cloves). Cut top off of garlic bulb. Brush with oil; sprinkle with salt and dash pepper. Wrap bulb in heavy-duty foil. Bake at 425° for 30-35 minutes or until softened. Cool for 10 minutes. Remove cloves from bulb.

2. Carefully peel back corn husks to within 1 in. of bottoms; remove silk. In a food processor, combine the garlic, mayonnaise, paprika and remaining pepper until blended; spread over corn. Sprinkle with cheese. Rewrap corn in husks and secure with kitchen string.

3. Grill corn, covered, over medium heat for 18-22 minutes or until tender, turning often.

Nutrition Facts: 1 ear of corn equals 142 calories, 5 g fat (3 g saturated fat), 13 mg cholesterol, 344 mg sodium, 21 g carbohydrate, 3 g fiber, 8 g protein. **Diabetic Exchanges:** 1-1/2 starch, 1/2 fat.

Cajun Spiced Broccoli C M

PREP/TOTAL TIME: 15 min. **YIELD:** 4 servings

KRISTA FRANK • RHODODENDRON, OREGON

I usually make this minus the Creole seasoning, but a few weeks ago I decided to try adding a different spice just to see what would happen. I loved it! It's garlicy, spicy and crunchy!

- 1 bunch broccoli, cut into florets
- 2 Tbsp. canola oil
- 2 large garlic cloves, minced
- 3/4 tsp. Creole seasoning

1. In a large nonstick skillet coated with cooking spray, saute broccoli in oil until crisp-tender, adding the garlic and Creole seasoning during the last 2 minutes of cooking.

Editor's Note: The following spices may be substituted for 1 tsp. Creole seasoning: 1/4 tsp. each salt, garlic powder and paprika; and a pinch each of dried thyme, ground cumin and cayenne pepper.

Nutrition Facts: 1 cup equals 107 calories, 8 g fat (1 g saturated fat), 0 cholesterol, 166 mg sodium, 8 g carbohydrate, 5 g fiber, 5 g protein. **Diabetic Exchanges:** 2 vegetable, 1 fat.

Orange & Mint Snap Peas F M

PREP/TOTAL TIME: 25 min. **YIELD:** 4 servings

HEALTHY COOKING TEST KITCHEN

This classic steaming method produces vibrant, crisp-tender vegetables. The sweet taste of snap peas is accented with orange, sugar and mint. Yum!

- 1/2 cup orange juice
- 2 Tbsp. brown sugar

CAJUN SPICED BROCCOLI

- 1 Tbsp. butter
- 2 tsp. grated orange peel
- 1/2 tsp. salt
- 3 cups fresh sugar snap peas, trimmed
- 2 Tbsp. minced fresh mint

1. In a small saucepan, combine the first five ingredients; bring to a boil. Reduce heat; simmer, uncovered, until mixture is reduced by half, about 15 minutes.

2. Meanwhile, place peas in a steamer basket in a large saucepan over 1 in. of water; bring to a boil. Cover and steam for 3-5 minutes or until crisp-tender; drain. Transfer to a serving bowl. Add orange juice mixture and mint; toss to coat.

Nutrition Facts: 3/4 cup equals 117 calories, 3 g fat (2 g saturated fat), 8 mg cholesterol, 323 mg sodium, 19 g carbohydrate, 4 g fiber, 4 g protein. **Diabetic Exchanges:** 1 starch, 1 vegetable, 1/2 fat.

When preparing foods in a steamer basket, be sure not to overload the basket. Unless instructed otherwise, always arrange the food in a **shallow, even layer.** Only remove the lid to add liquid if needed. Taking the lid off greatly decreases the cooking temperature.

ORANGE & MINT SNAP PEAS

Apple Bread Stuffing [M]

PREP: 15 min. **BAKE:** 35 min. **YIELD:** 4 servings

DORIS HEATH • FRANKLIN, NORTH CAROLINA

Versatile, simple and filled with savory fall flavors, this delicious side dish pairs well with chicken, beef and a variety of entrees. Juicy apple and plump raisins keep it oh-so moist and mouthwatering!

1/3	cup finely chopped onion
4-1/2	tsp. butter
2	cups soft bread crumbs
1	cup chopped peeled tart apple
1/3	cup raisins
1/4	tsp. salt
1/4	tsp. sugar
1/8	tsp. rubbed sage
4	tsp. unsweetened apple juice

1. In a small nonstick skillet coated with cooking spray, cook onion in butter until tender. In a small bowl, combine the bread crumbs, apple, raisins, salt, sugar, sage and onion mixture. Drizzle with apple juice; toss to coat.

2. Transfer to a 3-cup baking dish coated with cooking spray. Cover and bake at 350° for 30 minutes. Uncover; bake 5-10 minutes longer or until apple is tender and top is lightly browned.

Nutrition Facts: 3/4 cup equals 158 calories, 5 g fat (3 g saturated fat), 12 mg cholesterol, 314 mg sodium, 27 g carbohydrate, 2 g fiber, 2 g protein. **Diabetic Exchanges:** 1 starch, 1 fruit, 1 fat.

Coconut-Pecan Sweet Potatoes [S] [M]

PREP: 15 min. **COOK:** 4 hours **YIELD:** 12 servings

RAQUEL HAGGARD • EDMOND, OKLAHOMA

These delicious sweet potatoes cook effortlessly in the slow cooker so you can tend to other things. Coconut gives this classic dish a new, unexpected flavor.

4	lbs. sweet potatoes, peeled and cut into chunks
1/2	cup chopped pecans
1/2	cup flaked coconut
1/3	cup sugar
1/3	cup packed brown sugar
1/4	cup reduced-fat butter, melted
1/2	tsp. ground cinnamon
1/4	tsp. salt
1/2	tsp. coconut extract
1/2	tsp. vanilla extract

1. Place sweet potatoes in a 5-qt. slow cooker coated with cooking spray. Combine the pecans, coconut, sugar, brown sugar, butter, cinnamon and salt; sprinkle over potatoes.

2. Cover and cook on low for 4 hours or until potatoes are tender. Stir in extracts.

Editor's Note: This recipe was tested with Land O'Lakes light stick butter.

Nutrition Facts: 2/3 cup equals 211 calories, 7 g fat (3 g saturated fat), 5 mg cholesterol, 103 mg sodium, 37 g carbohydrate, 3 g fiber, 2 g protein.

Potluck Baked Beans [F]

PREP: 10 min. **BAKE:** 30 min. **YIELD:** 12 servings

VIRGINIA SANDER • NORTH HOLLYWOOD, CALIFORNIA

This recipe has remained a longtime favorite for picnics and family get-togethers. For those not watching their fat intake, I often add cheddar and Parmesan cheese.

4	bacon strips, chopped
1	medium onion, chopped
1	can (28 oz.) baked beans
1	can (16 oz.) kidney beans, rinsed and drained
1	can (15 oz.) pinto beans, rinsed and drained
1/2	cup packed brown sugar
1/3	cup ketchup
2	tsp. Worcestershire sauce

1. In a large skillet, saute bacon and onion over medium heat until bacon is crisp; drain. In a large bowl, combine the beans, brown sugar, ketchup, Worcestershire sauce and bacon mixture.

2. Pour into a shallow 2-qt. baking dish coated with cooking spray. Bake at 350° for 30-35 minutes or until heated through.

Nutrition Facts: 1/2 cup equals 192 calories, 2 g fat (1 g saturated fat), 7 mg cholesterol, 528 mg sodium, 37 g carbohydrate, 7 g fiber, 8 g protein.

APPLE BREAD STUFFING

COCONUT-PECAN SWEET POTATOES

SWEET POTATO DIPPERS

Sweet Potato Dippers M

PREP: 10 min. **BAKE:** 25 min. **YIELD:** 4 servings

CHERYL MACZKO • ARTHURDALE, WEST VIRGINIA

A savory and creamy dipping sauce accents the delicious flavor of tender sweet potato slices in this change-of-pace side dish. Leftover sauce can be served with crackers.

1-1/4 lbs. sweet potatoes (about 2 medium), peeled
   1 Tbsp. olive oil
1/4 tsp. salt
1/4 tsp. pepper
DIP:
   3 oz. fat-free cream cheese
   3 Tbsp. reduced-fat sour cream 2 tsp. finely chopped green onion
   2 tsp. finely chopped seeded jalapeno pepper
GARNISH:
Additional finely chopped green onion, optional

1. Cut potatoes into 1/8-in. slices. Place in a large bowl. Drizzle with oil. Sprinkle with salt and pepper; toss to coat.

2. Arrange in a single layer in two ungreased 15-in. x 10-in. x 1-in. baking pans. Bake at 375° for 25-30 minutes or until golden brown, turning once.

3. In a small bowl, beat dip ingredients. Serve with potatoes. Garnish with additional onion if desired.

Editor's Note: When cutting hot peppers, disposable gloves are recommended. Avoid touching your face.

Nutrition Facts: 1 cup dippers with 2 Tbsp. dip equals 155 calories, 5 g fat (1 g saturated fat), 5 mg cholesterol, 280 mg sodium, 23 g carbohydrate, 3 g fiber, 5 g protein. **Diabetic Exchanges:** 1-1/2 starch, 1 fat.

Raspberry Cranberry Relish F S M

PREP: 10 min. **COOK:** 15 min. **YIELD:** 5 cups

ANITA DOUGHTY • WEST DES MOINES, IOWA

The idea of cooking cranberries in honey came from a friend. I played with the recipe, and this is my family's favorite version.

   1 pkg. (12 oz.) fresh or frozen cranberries, thawed
3/4 cup cherry-flavored dried cranberries
1/2 cup honey
1/4 cup cranberry-raspberry juice
   2 Tbsp. orange marmalade
1/2 tsp. Chinese five-spice powder
   1 pkg. (12 oz.) frozen unsweetened raspberries, thawed and drained

1. In a large saucepan, combine the first six ingredients. Cook, uncovered, over medium heat until the berries pop, about 15 minutes, stirring occasionally.

2. Remove from the heat; gently stir in raspberries. Transfer to a small bowl; cover and refrigerate for at least 2 hours before serving.

Nutrition Facts: 1/2 cup equals 125 calories, trace fat (trace saturated fat), 0 cholesterol, 4 mg sodium, 32 g carbohydrate, 3 g fiber, 1 g protein. **Diabetic Exchanges:** 1-1/2 starch, 1/2 fruit.

Green Bean Medley F S C M

PREP/TOTAL TIME: 25 min. **YIELD:** 5 servings

JUDY FERRIL • SHOREWOOD, MINNESOTA

Looking for a way to dress up fresh green beans in a flash? Consider the tasty medley of flavors in this easy recipe. If you don't have sherry vinegar for the tangy sauce, try using cider or wine vinegar instead.

1	lb. fresh green beans, trimmed
1	small sweet red pepper, finely chopped
4	green onions, chopped
1/4	cup sliced fresh mushrooms
1	Tbsp. olive oil
1	garlic clove, minced
1	Tbsp. sherry vinegar
1/2	tsp. dried basil
1/4	tsp. salt
1/4	tsp. pepper

1. Place beans in a large saucepan and cover with water. Bring to a boil. Cover and cook for 4-7 minutes or until crisp-tender.

2. Meanwhile, in a large nonstick skillet, saute the red pepper, onions and mushrooms in oil until tender. Add garlic; cook 1 minute longer. Drain beans; stir into vegetable mixture. Add the vinegar, basil, salt and pepper; heat through.

Nutrition Facts: 3/4 cup equals 59 calories, 3 g fat (trace saturated fat), 0 cholesterol, 126 mg sodium, 8 g carbohydrate, 3 g fiber, 2 g protein. **Diabetic Exchanges:** 1 vegetable, 1/2 fat.

Simple Spanish Rice M

PREP: 5 min. **COOK:** 45 min. **YIELD:** 6 servings

EMILY HOCKETT • FEDERAL WAY, WASHINGTON

I prefer this side dish to traditional recipes because it's vegetarian and lower in fat. While you're preparing the rest of your meal, it simmers on the stove, allowing the flavors to blend beautifully.

1	cup uncooked brown rice
1	large onion, chopped
1	medium green pepper, chopped
2	Tbsp. butter
1	can (14-1/2 oz.) diced tomatoes with mild green chilies, undrained
1/4	tsp. salt

1. Cook brown rice according to package directions.

2. Meanwhile, in a large nonstick skillet, saute onion and pepper in butter until tender. Stir in tomatoes and salt. Bring to a boil. Reduce heat; simmer, uncovered, for 5-10 minutes or until slightly thickened. Stir in cooked rice; heat through.

Nutrition Facts: 2/3 cup equals 183 calories, 5 g fat (3 g saturated fat), 10 mg cholesterol, 390 mg sodium, 32 g carbohydrate, 3 g fiber, 3 g protein. **Diabetic Exchanges:** 1-1/2 starch, 1 vegetable, 1 fat.

> Beef up Simple Spanish Rice with strips of steak or cubed chicken leftover from **last night's dinner**. You can also toss in some extra taco meat or cubed ham for an entree.

SIMPLE SPANISH RICE

GREEN BEAN MEDLEY

Roasted Root Vegetables

F S C M

PREP: 20 min. **BAKE:** 25 min. **YIELD:** 4 servings

HEALTHY COOKING TEST KITCHEN

Roasting and an excellent herb-pepper seasoning turn this vegetable medley into a standout side dish.

> 2 cups cubed peeled rutabaga
> 3/4 cup chopped peeled turnip
> 1 small onion, cut into wedges
> 1 small carrot, chopped
> 1/2 cup chopped peeled parsnip
> 1-1/2 tsp. olive oil
> 1/2 tsp. minced fresh thyme *or* 1/4 tsp. dried thyme
> 1/2 tsp. minced fresh oregano *or* 1/4 tsp. dried oregano
> 1/2 tsp. minced fresh rosemary *or* 1/4 tsp. dried rosemary, crushed
> 1/4 tsp. pepper
> 1/8 tsp. salt

1. In a large bowl, combine all ingredients; toss to coat. Transfer to a 15-in. x 10-in. x 1-in. baking pan coated with cooking spray.

2. Bake, uncovered, at 425° for 25-30 minutes or until vegetables are tender, stirring occasionally.

Nutrition Facts: 3/4 cup equals 72 calories, 2 g fat (trace saturated fat), 0 cholesterol, 115 mg sodium, 13 g carbohydrate, 4 g fiber, 2 g protein. **Diabetic Exchange:** 2 vegetable.

Green Beans Provence F S C M

PREP/TOTAL TIME: 20 min. **YIELD:** 4 servings

HEALTHY COOKING TEST KITCHEN

Crisp-tender green beans are paired with tomatoes for a colorful and nutritious side. Dressed with fresh basil and just enough vinegar to add a bit of tang, this dish complements most any entree.

> 1 lb. fresh green beans, trimmed
> 1 cup cherry tomatoes, halved
> 2 Tbsp. minced fresh basil *or* 2 tsp. dried basil
> 1 Tbsp. tarragon vinegar
> 2 tsp. olive oil
> 1 garlic clove, minced
> 1/4 tsp. pepper

Dash salt

1. Place beans in a large saucepan and cover with water. Bring to a boil. Cover and cook for 4 to 7 minutes or until crisp-tender. Drain and immediately place beans in ice water. Drain and pat dry.

2. In a large bowl, combine beans and tomatoes. Combine the basil, vinegar, oil, garlic, pepper and salt; drizzle over beans and toss to coat.

Nutrition Facts: 1 cup equals 60 calories, 3 g fat (trace saturated fat), 0 cholesterol, 46 mg sodium, 9 g carbohydrate, 4 g fiber, 2 g protein. **Diabetic Exchanges:** 1 vegetable, 1/2 fat.

Potato Smashers

PREP/TOTAL TIME: 20 min. **YIELD:** 2 servings

JANET STEIGER • BUCYRUS, OHIO

Try this dressed-up version of stuffed potato skins for a great side dish that no one will ever guess is light!

> 6 small red potatoes (about 3/4 lb.)
> 1/2 cup water
> 2 center-cut bacon strips
> 2 Tbsp. reduced-fat Italian salad dressing
> 1/4 cup shredded sharp cheddar cheese

Reduced-fat sour cream, optional

1. Place potatoes in a small microwave-safe dish; add water. Microwave, uncovered, on high for 8-9 minutes or until tender, stirring once.

ROASTED ROOT VEGETABLES

POTATO SMASHERS

2. Meanwhile, in a large nonstick skillet, cook bacon over medium heat until crisp. Remove to paper towels to drain. Crumble bacon and set aside.

3. With the bottom of a glass, flatten potatoes to 1/2-in. thickness. In the same skillet coated with cooking spray, cook potatoes in dressing over medium heat for 2-3 minutes or until bottoms are golden brown.

4. Turn potatoes; sprinkle with cheese and reserved bacon. Cover and cook 2-3 minutes longer or until cheese is melted. Serve with sour cream if desired.

Nutrition Facts: 3 potatoes (calculated without sour cream) equals 224 calories, 8 g fat (4 g saturated fat), 23 mg cholesterol, 314 mg sodium, 29 g carbohydrate, 3 g fiber, 9 g protein. **Diabetic Exchanges:** 2 starch, 1 lean meat, 1 fat.

Grilled Portobellos With Mozzarella Salad C M

PREP/TOTAL TIME: 30 min. **YIELD:** 4 servings

SARAH VASQUES• MILFORD, NEW HAMPSHIRE

These colorful mushrooms are so filling, they're almost a meal in themselves. They can be served as a hearty side dish or with a small garden salad as an entree.

2	cups grape tomatoes, halved
3	oz. fresh mozzarella cheese, cubed
3	fresh basil leaves, thinly sliced
2	tsp. olive oil
2	garlic cloves, minced
1/4	tsp. salt
1/4	tsp. pepper
4	large portobello mushrooms (4 to 4-1/2 in.), stems removed

Cooking spray

1. In a small bowl, combine the first seven ingredients; cover and chill until serving.

2. Coat grill rack with cooking spray before starting the grill. Spritz mushrooms with cooking spray. Grill mushrooms, covered, over medium heat for 6-8 minutes on each side or until tender. Spoon 1/2 cup tomato mixture into each mushroom cap.

Nutrition Facts: 1 serving equals 133 calories, 8 g fat (3 g saturated fat), 17 mg cholesterol, 190 mg sodium, 9 g carbohydrate, 2 g fiber, 7 g protein. **Diabetic Exchanges:** 2 vegetable, 1 lean meat, 1 fat.

Roasted Parmesan Green Beans F C M

PREP/TOTAL TIME: 30 min.   **YIELD:** 4 servings

CHRISTIE LADD • MECHANICSBURG, PENNSYLVANIA

I'm not a big fan of the traditional green-bean casserole, so I came up with this no-fuss version. It's so quick and versatile, you can make it anytime, and it goes with just about any entree you can think of.

1	lb. fresh green beans, trimmed
2	tsp. olive oil
1-1/2	tsp. Greek seasoning
2	Tbsp. shredded Parmesan cheese

1. Place beans in a 15-in. x 10-in. x 1-in. baking pan coated with cooking spray. Drizzle with oil. Sprinkle with seasoning; stir to coat.

2. Bake, uncovered, at 425° for 12-15 minutes or until beans are tender, stirring once. Sprinkle with cheese.

Nutrition Facts: 2/3 cup equals 61 calories, 3 g fat (1 g saturated fat), 2 mg cholesterol, 410 mg sodium, 7 g carbohydrate, 3 g fiber, 3 g protein. **Diabetic Exchanges:** 1 vegetable, 1/2 fat.

Cheesy Canadian Bacon & Potato Casserole C

PREP: 15 min. **BAKE:** 50 min. + standing
YIELD: 12 servings

CHRISTINA PRICE • WHEELING, WEST VIRGINIA

This hearty side dish is so rich and creamy, no one will miss the extra fat at all!

1	can (10-3/4 oz.) reduced-fat condensed broccoli cheese soup, undiluted
1	cup (8 oz.) 1% cottage cheese
1	cup (8 oz.) reduced-fat sour cream
1	pkg. (28 oz.) frozen O'Brien potatoes, thawed
1	tsp. garlic powder
1/2	tsp. pepper
1/2	lb. Canadian bacon, chopped
1/4	cup shredded reduced-fat cheddar cheese

1. In a food processor, combine the soup, cottage cheese and sour cream; cover and process until smooth.

2. In a large bowl, combine the potatoes, garlic powder and pepper; stir in Canadian bacon and soup mixture. Transfer to a 13-in. x 9-in. baking dish coated with cooking spray; sprinkle with cheddar cheese. Bake, uncovered, at 350° for 50-55 minutes or until bubbly. Let stand for 15 minutes before serving.

Nutrition Facts: 2/3 cup equals 133 calories, 4 g fat (2 g saturated fat), 17 mg cholesterol, 478 mg sodium, 15 g carbohydrate, 2 g fiber, 9 g protein. **Diabetic Exchanges:** 1 starch, 1 lean meat.

Pasta with Fresh Vegetables M

PREP: 15 min. **COOK:** 20 min. **YIELD:** 6 servings

LAURIE COUTURE • SWANTON, VERMONT

Looking for the fresh taste of summer? This delicious pasta recipe is so easy to prepare and a great way to use up your garden-fresh veggies. It's also hearty and nutritious but still lower in fat and calories!

- 8 oz. uncooked penne pasta
- 1 cup sliced fresh carrots
- 1 Tbsp. olive oil
- 1/2 tsp. minced garlic
- 3 cups chopped fresh plum tomatoes
- 1 cup fresh broccoli florets
- 1 cup sliced yellow summer squash
- 1 cup chopped green pepper
- 1 Tbsp. minced fresh basil *or* 1 tsp. dried basil
- 1 tsp. minced fresh thyme *or* 1/4 tsp. dried thyme
- 1 tsp. minced fresh oregano *or* 1/4 tsp. dried oregano
- 1/2 tsp. salt
- 1/4 tsp. pepper
- 5 tsp. grated Parmesan cheese

1. Cook pasta according to package directions; drain. Meanwhile, in a large nonstick skillet, saute the carrots in oil until crisp-tender. Add the garlic; cook for 1-2 minutes or until garlic is tender. Stir in the tomatoes, broccoli, squash, green pepper and seasonings. Bring to a boil. Reduce heat; simmer, uncovered, for 10 minutes or until vegetables are tender. Stir in pasta; sprinkle with cheese.

Nutrition Facts: 1-1/4 cups equals 205 calories, 4 g fat (1 g saturated fat), 1 mg cholesterol, 244 mg sodium, 37 g carbohydrate, 4 g fiber, 7 g protein.

Corn and Broccoli In Cheese Sauce

PREP: 10 min. **COOK:** 3 hours **YIELD:** 8 servings

JOYCE JOHNSON • UNIONTOWN, OHIO

This dish is a standby. My daughter likes to add leftover ham to it. Save room in the oven by making this savory side in your slow cooker.

- 1 pkg. (16 oz.) frozen corn, thawed
- 1 pkg. (16 oz.) frozen broccoli florets, thawed
- 4 oz. reduced-fat process cheese (Velveeta), cubed
- 1/2 cup shredded cheddar cheese
- 1 can (10-1/4 oz.) reduced-fat reduced-sodium condensed cream of chicken soup, undiluted
- 1/4 cup fat-free milk

1. In a 4-qt. slow cooker, combine the corn, broccoli and cheeses. In a small bowl, combine soup and milk; pour over vegetable mixture. Cover and cook on low for 3-4 hours or until heated through. Stir before serving.

Nutrition Facts: 3/4 cup equals 148 calories, 5 g fat (3 g saturated fat), 16 mg cholesterol, 409 mg sodium, 21 g carbohydrate, 3 g fiber, 8 g protein. **Diabetic Exchanges:** 1 starch, 1 lean meat, 1/2 fat.

CORN AND BROCCOLI IN CHEESE SAUCE

PASTA WITH FRESH VEGETABLES

Baked Ratatouille Boats C M

PREP: 30 min. + standing **BAKE:** 45 min.
YIELD: 8 servings

ROSALIND POPE • GREENSBORO, NORTH CAROLINA
This dish holds true to its French origins...with much less oil.

- 2 cups cubed eggplant
- 1 medium zucchini, chopped
- 3/4 tsp. salt, *divided*
- 1 small onion, chopped
- 3 garlic cloves, minced
- 4 tsp. olive oil
- 2 large tomatoes, chopped
- 1/4 tsp. pepper
- 4 medium green peppers
- 4 oz. reduced-fat Monterey Jack cheese *or* part-skim mozzarella cheese, cut into 8 pieces
- 2 tsp. minced fresh marjoram *or* 3/4 tsp. dried marjoram
- 1 can (8 oz.) tomato sauce

TOPPING:
- 3 Tbsp. panko (Japanese) bread crumbs
- 2 Tbsp. grated Parmesan cheese
- 1 Tbsp. olive oil
- 1/8 tsp. cayenne pepper

1. Place eggplant and zucchini in a large bowl; sprinkle with 1/2 tsp. salt and toss to coat. Cover and let stand for 30 minutes. Rinse with cold water; drain and pat dry.

2. In a large skillet, saute onion and garlic in oil until tender. Add eggplant mixture, tomatoes, pepper and remaining salt; bring to boil. Reduce heat; cover and simmer for 20 minutes. Remove from the heat.

3. Meanwhile, cut green peppers in half lengthwise; discard seeds. Place in a 13-in. x 9-in. baking dish coated with cooking spray. Place about 3 Tbsp. eggplant mixture in each pepper half; top with a piece of cheese and sprinkle with marjoram. Top with tomato sauce and remaining eggplant mixture.

4. Cover and bake at 350° for 40-45 minutes or until peppers are tender. Combine the topping ingredients; sprinkle over peppers. Bake, uncovered, 3-5 minutes longer or until topping is golden brown.

Nutrition Facts: 1 stuffed pepper half equals 128 calories, 8 g fat (3 g saturated fat), 11 mg cholesterol, 430 mg sodium, 11 g carbohydrate, 3 g fiber, 6 g protein. **Diabetic Exchanges:** 2 vegetable, 1 lean meat, 1/2 fat.

Brussels Sprouts With Bacon C

PREP/TOTAL TIME: 30 min. **YIELD:** 6 servings

PAULA YOUNG • TIFFIN, OHIO
Bacon lends a wonderful salty flavor while balsamic vinegar adds a hint of spicy tang to this tasty side. Who knew brussels sprouts could taste so good?

- 3 bacon strips
- 1-1/4 lbs. fresh or frozen brussels sprouts, thawed, quartered
- 1 large onion, chopped
- 2 Tbsp. water
- 1/4 tsp. salt
- 1/8 tsp. pepper
- 2 Tbsp. balsamic vinegar

1. In a large skillet, cook bacon over medium heat until crisp. Remove to paper towels; drain, reserving 1 Tbsp. drippings. Crumble bacon and set aside.

2. In the same pan, saute brussels sprouts and onion in reserved drippings until crisp-tender. Add the water, salt and pepper. Bring to a boil. Reduce heat; cover and simmer for 4-5 minutes or until brussels sprouts are tender. Stir in bacon and vinegar.

Nutrition Facts: 2/3 cup equals 90 calories, 4 g fat (1 g saturated fat), 6 mg cholesterol, 200 mg sodium, 11 g carbohydrate, 4 g fiber, 5 g protein. **Diabetic Exchanges:** 2 vegetable, 1 fat.

BAKED RATATOUILLE BOATS

BRUSSELS SPROUTS WITH BACON

ZUCCHINI PASTA

Zucchini Pasta M

PREP/TOTAL TIME: 25 min. **YIELD:** 6 servings

MARIA REGAKIS • SOMERVILLE, MARYLAND

The taste of this rich and creamy dish will have people convinced it's not lower in fat, but it is! Garlicky and fresh-flavored, this will be a hit. Add some cooked chicken or turkey or toss in leftover ham for a quick main course.

8	oz. uncooked linguine
4	cups coarsely shredded zucchini (about 3 medium)
4	tsp. olive oil
2	garlic cloves, thinly sliced
1/4	cup fat-free plain yogurt
3/4	cup shredded reduced-fat cheddar cheese
3/4	tsp. salt
1/4	tsp. pepper

1. Cook linguine according to package directions. In a sieve or colander, drain the zucchini, squeezing to remove excess liquid. Pat dry.

2. In a large nonstick skillet, saute zucchini in oil for 2 minutes. Add garlic; saute 1-2 minutes longer or until zucchini is tender. Transfer to a large bowl. Add the yogurt, cheese, salt and pepper. Drain linguine; add to zucchini mixture and toss to coat.

Nutrition Facts: 3/4 cup equals 219 calories, 7 g fat (3 g saturated fat), 10 mg cholesterol, 395 mg sodium, 32 g carbohydrate, 2 g fiber, 10 g protein. **Diabetic Exchanges:** 1-1/2 starch, 1-1/2 fat, 1 vegetable.

Tangy Mashed Potatoes F M

PREP: 20 min. **COOK:** 20 min. **YIELD:** 13 servings

DONNA NOEL • GRAY, MAINE

Enjoy a holiday "must have," guilt free. Green onions perk up mashed potatoes, while plain yogurt adds to their comforting texture. These will be a hit!

4	lbs. potatoes, peeled and cubed (about 12 medium)
1-1/2	cups (12 oz.) reduced-fat plain yogurt
4	green onions, minced
2	Tbsp. butter
1	tsp. salt
1/2	tsp. pepper

1. Place potatoes in a Dutch oven and cover with water. Bring to a boil. Reduce heat; cover and cook for 10-15 minutes or until tender. Drain potatoes; mash with yogurt, onions, butter, salt and pepper.

Nutrition Facts: 3/4 cup equals 114 calories, 2 g fat (1 g saturated fat), 6 mg cholesterol, 216 mg sodium, 21 g carbohydrate, 1 g fiber, 3 g protein. **Diabetic Exchange:** 1-1/2 starch.

SWEET PEAS PARMA

Sweet Peas Parma

PREP/TOTAL TIME: 20 min. **YIELD:** 4 servings

JILL ANDERSON • SLEEPY EYE, MINNESOTA

Here's a simple side with delicious Italian taste!

1	pkg. (16 oz.) frozen peas
4	thin slices prosciutto or deli ham, coarsely chopped
1	garlic clove, minced
1	Tbsp. olive oil
1	Tbsp. butter
1	medium tomato, seeded and chopped
1/4	tsp. salt
1/8	tsp. pepper

1. Place peas in a steamer basket; place in a large saucepan over 1 in. of water. Bring to a boil; cover and steam for 4 minutes.

2. Meanwhile, in a large skillet, cook prosciutto and garlic in oil and butter over medium heat until prosciutto is crisp. Add the tomato, salt and pepper; heat through. Stir in peas.

Nutrition Facts: 3/4 cup equals 181 calories, 8 g fat (3 g saturated fat), 20 mg cholesterol, 569 mg sodium, 17 g carbohydrate, 6 g fiber, 10 g protein. **Diabetic Exchanges:** 1 starch, 1 lean meat, 1 fat.

Company Wild Rice M

PREP: 70 min. **BAKE:** 30 min. **YIELD:** 8 servings

MICHELLE DAVIS • ELK GROVE, CALIFORNIA

My family loves this. We always have it during the holidays. Packed with rich, savory flavor, this makes an ideal side dish for special occasions.

3	cups reduced-sodium chicken or vegetable broth
1	cup uncooked wild rice
1	medium onion, chopped
2	Tbsp. butter
2	cups sliced fresh mushrooms
1	Tbsp. all-purpose flour
1/2	tsp. garlic salt
1/4	tsp. dried parsley flakes
1/4	tsp. pepper
1-1/2	cups half-and-half cream
3	Tbsp. slivered almonds, toasted

1. In a large saucepan, combine broth and rice. Bring to a boil. Reduce heat; cover and simmer for 60-70 minutes or until rice is tender and liquid is absorbed.

2. Meanwhile, in a nonstick skillet coated with cooking spray, cook onion in butter for 2 minutes. Stir in the mushrooms; cook 2 minutes longer. Add the flour, garlic salt, parsley flakes and pepper. Gradually stir in cream. Bring to a boil. Cook and stir for 2 minutes or until thickened. Stir in rice.

3. Transfer to an 8-in. square baking dish coated with cooking spray. Cover and bake at 350° for 30-35 minutes or until heated through. Just before serving, sprinkle with almonds.

Nutrition Facts: 2/3 cup equals 210 calories, 9 g fat (5 g saturated fat), 30 mg cholesterol, 399 mg sodium, 24 g carbohydrate, 2 g fiber, 7 g protein.

Broccoli with Walnuts and Cherries S C M

PREP/TOTAL TIME: 20 min. **YIELD:** 8 servings

JOAN RANZINI • WAYNESBORO, VIRGINIA

Power foods—broccoli, walnuts and cherries—star in this delicious, easy recipe. With its green and red colors and walnut flavor, it's ideal on the Christmas dinner table.

2	bunches broccoli, cut into florets (about 6 cups)
1/2	cup chopped walnuts
6	garlic cloves, minced
2	Tbsp. olive oil
1/3	cup dried cherries
1/4	tsp. salt
1/4	tsp. crushed red pepper flakes

1. Place broccoli in a steamer basket; place in a large saucepan over 1 in. of water. Bring to a boil; cover and steam for 3-4 minutes or until tender.

2. Meanwhile, in a large nonstick skillet coated with cooking spray, saute walnuts and garlic in oil until garlic is tender. Stir in the cherries, salt, pepper flakes and broccoli; toss to coat.

Nutrition Facts: 3/4 cup equals 140 calories, 8 g fat (1 g saturated fat), 0 cholesterol, 116 mg sodium, 14 g carbohydrate, 5 g fiber, 7 g protein. **Diabetic Exchanges:** 2 vegetable, 1 fat.

Crab-Stuffed Potatoes F

PREP: 35 min. **BAKE:** 20 min. **YIELD:** 8 servings

JOHN KENNEY • MARCO ISLAND, FLORIDA

If you love crab and need a make-ahead dish, you just hit the jackpot! This elegant side pairs perfectly with seafood or even chicken.

4	large potatoes (about 3 lbs.)
1	small onion, finely chopped
1/4	cup finely chopped celery
1	Tbsp. butter
2	garlic cloves, minced
1/2	cup reduced-fat sour cream
2	cans (6 oz. *each*) lump crabmeat, drained
1/2	cup fat-free milk
1	Tbsp. minced fresh parsley
1/2	tsp. salt
1/4	tsp. pepper

1. Scrub and pierce potatoes; place on a microwave-safe plate. Microwave, uncovered, on high for 18-22 minutes or until tender, turning once. Let stand for 5 minutes or until cool enough to handle.

2. Meanwhile, in a small skillet, saute onion and celery in butter until tender. Add garlic; cook 1 minute longer. Set aside. Cut each potato in half lengthwise. Scoop out the pulp, leaving thin shells.

3. In a small bowl, mash the pulp with sour cream. Stir in the crabmeat, milk, parsley, salt, pepper and reserved vegetable mixture. Spoon mixture into potato shells. Place on a baking sheet. Bake, uncovered, at 375° for 20-25 minutes or until heated through.

Nutrition Facts: 1 stuffed potato half equals equals 231 calories, 3 g fat (2 g saturated fat), 47 mg cholesterol, 330 mg sodium, 36 g carbohydrate, 3 g fiber, 14 g protein

CRAB-STUFFED POTATOES

COMPANY WILD RICE

BROCCOLI WITH WALNUTS AND CHERRIES

Quick Broccoli Side Dish

S C M

PREP/TOTAL TIME: 20 min. **YIELD:** 6 servings

HEALTHY COOKING TEST KITCHEN

Italian seasoning and crunchy pine nuts really jazz up the flavor of this versatile veggie specialty.

4	cups fresh broccoli florets
1	Tbsp. olive oil
1	garlic clove, minced
3	Tbsp. sherry or reduced-sodium chicken broth
1	jar (2 oz.) sliced pimientos, drained
1/2	tsp. Italian seasoning
1/4	tsp. salt
1/4	tsp. pepper
2	Tbsp. pine nuts

1. In a large nonstick skillet coated with cooking spray, saute broccoli in oil for 5 minutes. Add garlic; saute 2 minutes longer or until broccoli is crisp-tender. Add the sherry, pimientos, Italian seasoning, salt and pepper; cook and stir until heated through. Sprinkle with pine nuts.

Nutrition Facts: 1/2 cup equals 58 calories, 4 g fat (1 g saturated fat), 0 cholesterol, 113 mg sodium, 4 g carbohydrate, 2 g fiber, 2 g protein. **Diabetic Exchanges:** 1 vegetable, 1 fat.

QUICK BROCCOLI SIDE DISH

Grilled Caponata Bruschetta

S C M

PREP: 35 min. **GRILL:** 10 min. **YIELD:** 2-1/2 dozen

SONYA MILLER • AUSTIN, TEXAS

An amazing combination of vegetables goes into this flavorful grilled medley. At less than 65 calories each round, you won't have to stop at just one!

1	medium eggplant
1	celery rib
1	small zucchini
1	small sweet yellow pepper
1	small sweet red pepper
1	small onion
1	medium tomato
5	garlic cloves, peeled
1/2	cup olive oil, *divided*
30	slices French bread (1/4 in. thick)
1/4	cup golden raisins
1/4	cup tomato sauce
3	Tbsp. chopped pitted green olives
1	Tbsp. minced fresh basil
1-1/2	tsp. minced fresh oregano

1. Cut the eggplant, celery and zucchini into 3/4-in. slices; place in a large bowl. Cut the peppers, onion and tomato into wedges; add to bowl. Add garlic and 1/4 cup oil; toss to coat.

2. Transfer vegetables to a grilling grid coated with cooking spray. Grill, covered, over medium heat for 8-10 minutes or until tender, turning occasionally.

3. Brush bread slices with remaining oil; grill for 1-2 minutes on each side or until toasted. Chop vegetables into 1/4-in. pieces; transfer to a large bowl. Stir in the raisins, tomato sauce, olives, basil and oregano. Spoon 1 Tbsp. mixture over each slice of toast.

Editor's Note: If you do not have a grilling grid, use a disposable foil pan. Poke holes in the bottom of the pan with a meat fork to allow liquid to drain.

Nutrition Facts: 1 appetizer equals 63 calories, 4 g fat (1 g saturated fat), 0 cholesterol, 65 mg sodium, 6 g carbohydrate, 1 g fiber, 1 g protein. **Diabetic Exchanges:** 1 fat, 1/2 starch.

GRILLED CAPONATA BRUSCHETTA

Spiced Rice F

PREP/TOTAL TIME: 25 min. **YIELD:** 4 servings

ELLEN GOVERTSEN • WHEATON, ILLINOIS

Honey, raisins and cinnamon lend a slightly sweet taste to this moist, Mediterranean-inspired side. Try it as a lovely, low-fat addition to a summery brunch or luncheon.

2/3	cup uncooked long grain rice
1-1/4	cups water
3/4	cup chopped sweet onion
1-1/2	tsp. olive oil
1-1/2	tsp. honey
3/4	cup reduced-sodium chicken broth
1/4	cup golden raisins
1	tsp. curry powder
1/4	tsp. salt
1/4	tsp. ground cumin
1/4	tsp. ground cinnamon
1/4	cup chopped sweet red pepper

1. In a large saucepan, bring rice and water to a boil. Reduce heat; cover and simmer for 14-16 minutes or until tender.

2. Meanwhile, in a small nonstick skillet, saute onion in oil for 1 minute. Stir in honey and cook 2 minutes longer. Stir in the broth, raisins, curry, salt, cumin and cinnamon. Bring to a boil. Reduce heat; simmer, uncovered, for 5 minutes. Stir in red pepper and rice until well blended. Cook 2 minutes longer or until rice is heated through.

Nutrition Facts: 3/4 cup equals 183 calories, 2 g fat (trace saturated fat), 0 cholesterol, 259 mg sodium, 38 g carbohydrate, 2 g fiber, 4 g protein.

For fluffy long grain rice, combine 1 cup rice, 1 tablespoon reduced-fat butter and 2 cups water in a 2- to 3-quart saucepan. Heat to boiling, stirring once or twice. **Don't peek.** Reduce heat; cover and simmer for 15 minutes. If the water is not absorbed after 15 minutes, cover and continue to cook for another 2-4 minutes.

CAULIFLOWER AU GRATIN

Cauliflower Au Gratin C M

PREP: 30 min. **BAKE:** 30 min. **YIELD:** 12 servings

HEALTHY COOKING TEST KITCHEN

A lighter version of a classic white sauce coats this cauliflower dish that's perfect for a potluck buffet. Even those who don't like cauliflower love this dish.

>   3   pkg. (16 oz. *each*) frozen cauliflower, thawed
>   1   large onion, chopped
>   1/3 cup butter, cubed
>   1/3 cup all-purpose flour
>   1/2 tsp. salt
>   1/4 tsp. ground mustard
>   1/4 tsp. pepper
>   2   cups fat-free milk
>   1/2 cup grated Parmesan cheese

TOPPING:
>   1/2 cup soft whole wheat bread crumbs
>   2   Tbsp. butter, melted
>   1/4 tsp. paprika

1. In a Dutch oven, bring 1 in. of water to a boil. Add the cauliflower; return to a boil. Cover and cook for 3 minutes. Drain and pat dry.

2. Meanwhile, in a large saucepan, saute onion in butter until tender. Stir in the flour, salt, mustard and pepper until blended; gradually add milk. Bring to a boil; cook and stir for 1-2 minutes or until thickened. Remove from the heat. Add cheese; stir until melted.

3. Place cauliflower in a 13-in. x 9-in. baking dish coated with cooking spray. Pour sauce over top.

4. For topping, combine the bread crumbs, butter and paprika. Sprinkle over sauce. Bake, uncovered, at 350° for 30-35 minutes or until bubbly.

Nutrition Facts: 3/4 cup equals 142 calories, 8 g fat (5 g saturated fat), 22 mg cholesterol, 257 mg sodium, 13 g carbohydrate, 3 g fiber, 6 g protein. **Diabetic Exchanges:** 1-1/2 fat, 1 vegetable, 1/2 starch.

Hash Brown Bake

PREP: 20 min. **BAKE:** 45 min. **YIELD:** 6 servings

DARLA KAHLER • BISON, SOUTH DAKOTA

My family has no idea they're eating a low-fat recipe with this hearty casserole. It's creamy, cheesy, convenient and simply delicious! Pair it with all kinds of entrees.

> 1-1/4 cups fat-free milk
>   3 oz. reduced-fat cream cheese
>   1 envelope ranch salad dressing mix
>   6 cups frozen shredded hash brown potatoes, thawed
>   1/2 cup shredded reduced-fat cheddar cheese
>   1 bacon strip, cooked and crumbled

1. In a blender, combine the milk, cream cheese and salad dressing mix. Cover and process until smooth. Place potatoes in an 8-in. square baking dish coated with cooking spray; top with milk mixture. Cover and bake at 350° for 35 minutes.

2. Sprinkle with cheddar cheese and bacon. Bake, uncovered, 8-10 minutes longer or until cheese is melted and potatoes are tender.

Nutrition Facts: 3/4 cup equals 155 calories, 5 g fat (4 g saturated fat), 19 mg cholesterol, 552 mg sodium, 19 g carbohydrate, 1 g fiber, 8 g protein. **Diabetic Exchanges:** 1 starch, 1 lean meat, 1 fat.

Asparagus Parma F C

PREP: 20 min. **BAKE:** 15 min. **YIELD:** 6 servings

JAY GOODVIN • AUSTIN, TEXAS

Here's a full-flavored dish that's great alongside lean chicken or fish. Fresh herbs give it a special touch.

1	cup reduced-sodium chicken broth
1/2	cup dry white wine *or* additional reduced-sodium chicken broth
2	Tbsp. capers, drained
1	Tbsp. minced shallot
1	Tbsp. rubbed sage
1	Tbsp. minced fresh parsley
2	garlic cloves, minced
2	tsp. minced fresh thyme
1/4	tsp. crushed red pepper flakes
1	Tbsp. butter
2	lbs. fresh asparagus, trimmed
2	thin slices prosciutto or deli ham, cut into thin strips
2	Tbsp. grated Parmesan cheese

1. In a small saucepan, bring broth and wine to a boil. Reduce heat; simmer, uncovered, for 12-15 minutes or until reduced to about 3/4 cup. Stir in the capers, shallot, sage, parsley, garlic, thyme and pepper flakes. Return to a boil. Reduce heat; simmer 4-5 minutes longer. Stir in butter until melted.

2. Place asparagus in a 3-qt. baking dish coated with cooking spray. Pour sauce over asparagus; top with prosciutto. Bake, uncovered, at 400° for 12-15 minutes or until tender. Sprinkle with cheese before serving.

Nutrition Facts: 1 serving equals 76 calories, 3 g fat (2 g saturated fat), 11 mg cholesterol, 320 mg sodium, 5 g carbohydrate, 2 g fiber, 5 g protein. **Diabetic Exchanges:** 1 vegetable, 1 fat.

Quinoa with Peas and Onion M

PREP: 30 min. **COOK:** 10 min. **YIELD:** 6 servings

LORI PANARELLA • PHOENIXVILLE, PENNSYLVANIA

I make this a lot for my son, who's a picky eater. He loves it! What a great way to prepare quinoa.

1	cup quinoa, rinsed
2	cups water
1	small onion, chopped
1	Tbsp. olive oil
1-1/2	cups frozen peas
1/2	tsp. salt
1/4	tsp. pepper
2	Tbsp. chopped walnuts

1. In a large saucepan, bring quinoa and water to a boil. Reduce heat; cover and simmer for 12-15 minutes or until water is absorbed. Remove from the heat; fluff with a fork. Let stand for 10 minutes.

2. Meanwhile, in a small skillet, saute onion in oil until tender. Stir into cooked quinoa. Add the peas, salt and pepper; heat through. Sprinkle with walnuts.

Editor's Note: Look for quinoa in the cereal, rice or organic food aisle.

Nutrition Facts: 2/3 cup equals 174 calories, 6 g fat (1 g saturated fat), 0 cholesterol, 244 mg sodium, 26 g carbohydrate, 4 g fiber, 6 g protein. **Diabetic Exchanges:** 1-1/2 starch, 1 fat.

> Quinoa (pronounced "keen-wa") is a grain that offers **more protein** than any other grain. Best of all, quinoa is delicious and a cinch to prepare!

QUINOA WITH PEAS AND ONION

ASPARAGUS PARMA

Dilled Carrots & Green Beans
F C M

PREP/TOTAL TIME: 25 min. **YIELD:** 4 servings

HARRIETT LEE • GLASGOW, MONTANA

I never enjoyed carrots before this, but I love this dish, and so does my family. It's great for entertaining, too.

3/4	cup water
1	tsp. sugar
1/2	tsp. salt
1/2	tsp. dill weed
4	medium carrots, julienned
1/2	lb. fresh green beans
1/4	cup reduced-fat Italian salad dressing

1. In small saucepan, bring the water, sugar, salt and dill to a boil. Add the carrots and beans. Cook, uncovered, for 5-8 minutes or until the vegetables are crisp-tender; drain.

2. Drizzle with dressing; toss to coat.

Nutrition Facts: 3/4 cup equals 69 calories, 2 g fat (trace saturated fat), trace cholesterol, 298 mg sodium, 11 g carbohydrate, 4 g fiber, 2 g protein. **Diabetic Exchanges:** 2 vegetable, 1/2 fat.

To trim fresh green beans quickly, simply line up the ends of the beans; then, using a chef's knife, slice several at a time. Be careful not to overcook the beans. Cook in a small amount of water until **crisp-tender** or the beans could lose their color and become soggy.

DILLED CARROTS & GREEN BEANS

Brown Rice Pilaf **F S**

PREP: 10 min. **COOK:** 45 min. **YIELD:** 6 servings

HEALTHY COOKING TEST KITCHEN

Brown rice adds almost three times as much heart-healthy fiber to this mild, versatile side dish as white would.

1	medium onion, chopped
1	medium green pepper, chopped
1	Tbsp. olive oil
1-1/4	cups uncooked brown rice
2	garlic cloves, minced
1-1/2	cups water
1	cup reduced-sodium chicken broth
1/2	tsp. dried thyme
1/4	tsp. pepper

1. In a large saucepan, saute onion and green pepper in oil until tender. Add rice and garlic; cook and stir for 3-4 minutes or until rice is lightly browned. Add the water, broth, thyme and pepper. Bring to a boil. Reduce heat; cover and simmer for 35-40 minutes or until rice is tender. Fluff with a fork.

Nutrition Facts: 3/4 cup equals 181 calories, 3 g fat (1 g saturated fat), 0 cholesterol, 99 mg sodium, 34 g carbohydrate, 2 g fiber, 4 g protein. **Diabetic Exchanges:** 2 starch, 1/2 fat.

Veggie Mushroom Rice **F M**

PREP: 15 min. **BAKE:** 45 min. **YIELD:** 7 servings

TAMMY CONDIT • LEAGUE CITY, TEXAS

There's plenty of herb and mushroom flavor for friends and family to savor in this healthful side. It goes well with a variety of meats and main dishes. Or, add a green salad and a loaf of bread for a meatless main dish.

1	small onion, chopped
1	small green pepper, chopped
1	small sweet red pepper, chopped
1/4	cup chopped celery
1	Tbsp. canola oil
1-1/2	cups sliced fresh mushrooms
1	garlic clove, minced
1-1/4	cups uncooked long grain rice
2-1/2	cups water
1-1/2	tsp. rubbed sage
1	tsp. dried parsley flakes
1	tsp. dried thyme
3/4	tsp. salt
1/8	tsp. pepper

1. In a large nonstick saucepan, saute the onion, peppers and celery in oil for 2 minutes. Add the mushrooms and garlic; saute 3 minutes longer or until vegetables are crisp-tender. Stir in the rice, water and seasonings; bring to a boil.

2. Carefully transfer to a 2-qt. baking dish coated with cooking spray. Cover and bake at 350° for 45-50 minutes or until rice is tender.

Nutrition Facts: 3/4 cup equals 154 calories, 2 g fat (trace saturated fat), 0 cholesterol, 260 mg sodium, 30 g carbohydrate, 1 g fiber, 3 g protein. **Diabetic Exchanges:** 2 starch, 1/2 fat.

VEGGIE MUSHROOM RICE

ENERGIZING GRANOLA

TOO-YUMMY-TO-SHARE SCRAMBLE

BLUEBERRY OAT PANCAKES

Good Mornings

Not only is breakfast the most important meal of the day, but it's the tastiest when you whip up any of these 26 heart-smart eye openers. Whether you need a quick bite before work or a contribution to a brunch buffet, you'll find it here!

Blueberry Oat Pancakes F M

PREP: 20 min. **COOK:** 5 min./batch **YIELD:** 10 pancakes

CANDY SUMMERHILL • ALEXANDER, ARKANSAS

I like to grind my own oats for a fiber-filled oat flour that I use in this recipe. But oats aren't the only power food in my fluffy pancakes. You get plenty of blueberries, bursting with flavor in every bite, too!

3/4	cup quick-cooking oats, *divided*
3	Tbsp. orange juice
1	egg, lightly beaten
2/3	cup fat-free evaporated milk
1/4	cup reduced-fat sour cream
2	Tbsp. unsweetened applesauce
1/2	tsp. vanilla extract
1/2	cup whole wheat flour
1/4	cup all-purpose flour
3	Tbsp. brown sugar
1	tsp. baking powder
1/2	tsp. ground cinnamon
1/4	tsp. salt
1/4	tsp. baking soda
1	cup fresh *or* frozen unsweetened blueberries

1. In a small bowl, combine 1/4 cup oats and orange juice; let stand for 5 minutes. Stir in the egg, milk, sour cream, applesauce and vanilla; set aside.

2. Place remaining oats in a small food processor; cover and process until ground. Transfer to a large bowl; add the flours, brown sugar, baking powder, cinnamon, salt and baking soda. Stir in the wet ingredients just until moistened.

3. Pour batter by 1/4 cupfuls onto a hot griddle coated with cooking spray; sprinkle with blueberries. Turn when bubbles form on top; cook until second side is golden brown.

Nutrition Facts: 2 pancakes equals 221 calories, 3 g fat (1 g saturated fat),48 mg cholesterol, 327 mg sodium, 41 g carbohydrate, 4 g fiber, 9 g protein. **Diabetic Exchanges:** 2 starch, 1/2 fruit, 1/2 fat.

Makeover Broccoli Cheddar Brunch Bake C M

PREP: 25 min. **BAKE:** 40 min. + standing
YIELD: 12 servings

CARLA WEEKS • INDEPENDENCE, IOWA

Here's a slimmed-down version of my favorite brunch recipe. It's hearty, wholesome and boasts all the gourmet flavor of the original! No one will suspect it's light.

6	Tbsp. reduced-fat butter, cubed
8	cups chopped fresh broccoli
1	cup finely chopped onion
6	eggs, beaten
1-1/2	cups egg substitute
1-1/2	cups (6 oz.) shredded sharp cheddar cheese, *divided*
1	cup fat-free milk
1	cup half-and-half cream
1	tsp. salt
1	tsp. pepper

1. In a Dutch oven, melt butter. Add broccoli and onion; saute until crisp-tender. In a large bowl, combine the eggs, egg substitute, 1 cup cheese, milk, cream, salt and pepper. Stir in broccoli mixture. Pour into a 3-qt. baking dish coated with cooking spray.

2. Bake, uncovered, at 350° for 40-45 minutes or until a knife inserted near the center comes out clean. Sprinkle with remaining cheese. Let stand for 10 minutes before serving.

Editor's Note: This recipe was tested with Land O'Lakes light stick butter.

Nutrition Facts: 1 piece equals 178 calories, 12 g fat (7 g saturated fat), 139 mg cholesterol, 459 mg sodium, 7 g carbohydrate, 2 g fiber, 12 g protein.carbohydrate, 1 g fiber, 11 g protein.

> When trimming down a recipe, replace half of the eggs called for with **egg substitute**. This switch will lower the cholesterol without altering flavor.

Cranberry Coffee Cake Wedges

PREP: 20 min. **BAKE:** 15 min. **YIELD:** 8 servings

CAROL BARBEE • JASPER, MISSOURI

A friend gave me this recipe, but it included raisins, sugar, butter and sour cream, which I changed to cranberries, Splenda, light butter and fat-free yogurt. My husband can't tell I've changed anything but the raisins!

1/3	cup dried cranberries
1	cup boiling water
2	cups all-purpose flour
3	Tbsp. plus 1 tsp. sugar blend, *divided*
2	tsp. baking powder
1/2	tsp. baking soda
1/2	tsp. salt
5	Tbsp. cold reduced-fat butter
1	cup (8 oz.) fat-free plain yogurt
1	egg, separated
1/2	tsp. ground cinnamon

1. Place cranberries in a small bowl; add boiling water. Cover and let stand for 5 minutes. Drain and set aside.

2. In a large bowl, combine the flour, 3 Tbsp. sugar blend, baking powder, baking soda and salt. Cut in butter until mixture resembles coarse crumbs; stir in reserved cranberries. Combine yogurt and egg yolk; add to crumb mixture and stir until a soft dough forms (dough will be sticky).

3. Turn onto a floured surface; gently knead 6-8 times. Transfer to a baking sheet coated with cooking spray. Pat into a 9-in. circle; cut into eight wedges, but do not separate. Beat egg white; brush over dough. Combine the cinnamon and remaining sugar blend; sprinkle over top. Bake at 425° for 15-18 minutes or until golden brown. Remove to wire rack. Serve warm.

Editor's Note: This recipe was tested with Splenda sugar blend and Land O' Lakes light stick butter.

Nutrition Facts: 1 wedge equals 202 calories, 5 g fat (2 g saturated fat), 36 mg cholesterol, 412 mg sodium, 36 g carbohydrate, 1 g fiber, 5 g protein. **Diabetic Exchanges:** 2-1/2 starch, 1 fat.

Strawberry Mango Smoothies F S

PREP/TOTAL TIME: 10 min. **YIELD:** 4 servings

HEALTHY COOKING TEST KITCHEN

Delicious and creamy with lots of strawberry and mango flavor, these smoothies are simply delightful. They're perfect for breakfast, dessert or even an afternoon snack.

1	cup fat-free milk
1/2	cup reduced-fat vanilla yogurt
1-1/2	cups halved fresh strawberries
1	medium mango, peeled and chopped
4	to 6 ice cubes

Sugar substitute equivalent to 1 Tbsp. sugar

1. In a blender, combine all the ingredients; cover and process for 30-45 seconds or until smooth. Stir if necessary. Pour into the chilled glasses; serve immediately.

Editor's Note: This recipe was tested with Splenda no-calorie sweetener.

Nutrition Facts: 1 cup equals 100 calories, 1 g fat (trace saturated fat), 3 mg cholesterol, 47 mg sodium, 21 g carbohydrate, 2 g fiber, 4 g protein. **Diabetic Exchanges:** 1 fruit, 1/2 fat-free milk.

CRANBERRY COFFEE CAKE WEDGES

STRAWBERRY MANGO SMOOTHIES

Italian Mini Frittatas c

PREP: 25 min. **BAKE:** 25 min. **YIELD:** 1 dozen

MICHELLE ANDERSON • EAGLE, IDAHO

While these individual frittatas contain prosciutto, cheese and butter, the amounts are small so each portion stays slim. They're quick to prepare, easy to serve and will certainly become a brunch favorite.

2	Tbsp. chopped sun-dried tomatoes (not packed in oil)
1/2	cup boiling water
2	thin slices prosciutto, finely chopped
1/4	cup chopped shallots
2	garlic cloves, minced
1	tsp. butter
1/4	cup all-purpose flour
1-1/2	cups fat-free milk
4	egg whites
2	eggs
1	cup (4 oz.) shredded part-skim mozzarella cheese
1/4	cup shredded Asiago cheese
1/2	cup canned water-packed artichoke hearts, chopped
2	Tbsp. minced fresh basil or 2 tsp. dried basil
3/4	tsp. salt
1/2	tsp. white pepper

1. Place tomatoes in a small bowl; add boiling water. Cover and let stand for 5 minutes. Drain and set aside.

2. In a small nonstick skillet, saute the prosciutto, shallots and garlic in butter until shallots are tender. Remove from the heat; set aside.

3. In a large bowl, whisk flour and milk until smooth; whisk in the egg whites and eggs until blended. Stir in the cheeses, artichokes, basil, salt, pepper, and reserved tomatoes and prosciutto mixture.

4. Coat 12 muffin cups with cooking spray; fill with egg mixture. Bake at 350° for 25-30 minutes or until a knife inserted near the center comes out clean. Carefully run a knife around edges to loosen; remove from pan. Serve warm.

Nutrition Facts: 2 frittatas equals 172 calories, 7 g fat (4 g saturated fat), 93 mg cholesterol, 642 mg sodium, 11 g carbohydrate, trace fiber, 15 g protein. **Diabetic Exchanges:** 2 lean meat, 1 starch.

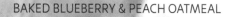
BAKED BLUEBERRY & PEACH OATMEAL

Baked Blueberry & Peach Oatmeal M

PREP: 20 min. **BAKE:** 35 min. **YIELD:** 9 servings

ROSEMARIE WELESKI • NATRONA HEIGHTS, PENNSYLVANIA

This oatmeal bake is a staple in our home. It's very easy to prepare the night before; just keep the dry and wet ingredients separate until ready to bake. I've tried a variety of fruits, but the blueberries and peaches are our favorite.

3	cups old-fashioned oats
1/2	cup packed brown sugar
2	tsp. baking powder
1/2	tsp. salt
2	egg whites
1	egg
1-1/4	cups fat-free milk
1/4	cup canola oil
1	tsp. vanilla extract
1	can (15 oz.) sliced peaches in juice, drained and chopped
1	cup fresh or frozen blueberries
1/3	cup chopped walnuts

Additional fat-free milk, optional

1. In a large bowl, combine the oats, brown sugar, baking powder and salt. Whisk the egg whites, egg, milk, oil and vanilla; add to dry ingredients and stir until blended. Let stand for 5 minutes. Stir in peaches and blueberries.

2. Transfer to an 11-in. x 7-in. baking dish coated with cooking spray. Sprinkle with walnuts. Bake, uncovered, at 350° for 35-40 minutes or until top is lightly browned and a thermometer reads 160°. Serve with additional milk if desired.

Nutrition Facts: 1 serving (calculated without additional milk) equals 277 calories, 11 g fat (1 g saturated fat), 24 mg cholesterol, 263 mg sodium, 38 g carbohydrate, 3 g fiber, 8 g protein. **Diabetic Exchanges:** 2 starch, 2 fat, 1/2 fruit.

Wake-Up Wonton Cups C M

PREP/TOTAL TIME: 20 min. **YIELD:** 10 wonton cups

GINA BERRY • CHANHASSEN, MINNESOTA

Dainty, delectable and delightfully different, these yummy breakfast bites add a fun touch to a healthy morning meal. Pepper sauce lends just a bit of heat...adjust to your liking.

10	wonton wrappers

Cooking spray

4	eggs
1/2	tsp. garlic powder
1/4	tsp. salt
1	medium tomato, seeded and chopped
10	drops hot pepper sauce

1. Press wonton wrappers into miniature muffin cups coated with cooking spray. Spritz wrappers with cooking spray. Bake at 350° for 10-12 minutes or until lightly browned.

2. Meanwhile, in a small bowl, whisk the eggs, garlic powder and salt. Heat a small nonstick skillet coated with cooking spray until hot. Add the egg mixture; cook and stir over medium heat until the eggs are completely set.

3. Spoon eggs into cups. Top each with chopped tomato and a drop of pepper sauce.

Nutrition Facts: 2 wonton cups equals 110 calories, 4 g fat (1 g saturated fat), 171 mg cholesterol, 269 mg sodium, 11 g carbohydrate, 1 g fiber, 7 g protein. **Diabetic Exchanges:** 1 starch, 1 lean meat.

Spinach Swiss Quiche

PREP: 25 min. **BAKE:** 35 min. + standing
YIELD: 6 servings

APRIL MILNER • DEARBORN HEIGHTS, MICHIGAN

My family requests this dish year-round. You can saute the bacon mixture the night before to reduce prep time on busy or eventful mornings.

1	refrigerated pie pastry
4	turkey bacon strips, diced
1/4	cup chopped onion

1/4	cup chopped sweet red pepper
1	pkg. (10 oz.) frozen chopped spinach, thawed and squeezed dry
2	cups egg substitute
1/2	cup fat-free cottage cheese
1/4	cup shredded reduced-fat Swiss cheese
1/2	tsp. dried oregano
1/4	tsp. dried parsley flakes
1/4	tsp. *each* salt, pepper and paprika
6	Tbsp. fat-free sour cream

1. On a lightly floured surface, unroll pastry. Transfer to a 9-in. pie plate. Trim pastry to 1/2 in. beyond edge of plate; flute edges. Line unpricked pastry with a double thickness of heavy-duty foil. Bake at 450° for 8 minutes. Remove foil; bake 5 minutes longer. Cool on a wire rack. Reduce heat to 350°.

2. In a small skillet, cook the bacon, onion and red pepper until vegetables are tender; drain. Stir in spinach. Spoon spinach mixture into pastry. In a small bowl, combine the egg substitute, cottage cheese, Swiss cheese and seasonings; pour over spinach mixture.

3. Bake for 35-40 minutes or until a knife inserted near the center comes out clean. Let stand for 10 minutes before cutting. Serve with sour cream.

Nutrition Facts: 1 piece with 1 Tbsp. sour cream equals 278 calories, 12 g fat (5 g saturated fat), 22 mg cholesterol, 659 mg sodium, 26 g carbohydrate, 2 g fiber, 17 g protein. **Diabetic Exchanges:** 2 lean meat, 2 fat, 1-1/2 starch.

SPINACH SWISS QUICHE

WAKE-UP WONTON CUPS

Frittata Florentine C

PREP/TOTAL TIME: 30 min. **YIELD:** 4 servings

JENNY FLAKE • GILBERT, ARIZONA

This frittata is loaded with huge flavor and is good for you. Thanks to the eggs, cheese and spinach, you get a healthy dose of calcium, too.

6	egg whites
3	eggs
1/2	tsp. dried oregano
1/4	tsp. garlic powder
1/4	tsp. salt
1/4	tsp. pepper
1	small onion, finely chopped
1/4	cup finely chopped sweet red pepper
2	turkey bacon strips, chopped
1	Tbsp. olive oil
1	cup fresh baby spinach
3	Tbsp. thinly sliced fresh basil leaves
1/2	cup shredded part-skim mozzarella cheese

1. In a small bowl, whisk the first six ingredients; set aside. In an 8-in. ovenproof skillet, saute onion, red pepper and bacon in oil until tender. Reduce heat; top with spinach.

2. Pour reserved egg mixture over spinach. As eggs set, push cooked edges toward the center, letting uncooked portion flow underneath until eggs are nearly set. Sprinkle with basil and cheese.

3. Broil 3-4 in. from the heat for 2-3 minutes or until eggs are completely set. Let stand for 5 minutes. Cut into wedges.

Nutrition Facts: 1 wedge equals 176 calories, 11 g fat (4 g saturated fat), 174 mg cholesterol, 451 mg sodium, 4 g carbohydrate, 1 g fiber, 15 g protein.

Energizing Granola S

PREP: 25 min. **BAKE:** 25 min. + cooling **YIELD:** 6 cups

NINA WISEMAN • BATAVIA, OHIO

Not only is this munchable granola packed with vitamin E, but flaxseed offers omega-3 fatty acids as well.

2-1/2	cups old-fashioned oats
3/4	cup chopped walnuts
1/2	cup unsalted sunflower kernels
1/3	cup packed brown sugar
1/4	cup flaked coconut
1/4	cup toasted wheat germ
2	Tbsp. sesame seeds
2	Tbsp. ground flaxseed
1/3	cup water
2	Tbsp. honey
2	Tbsp. molasses
1	Tbsp. canola oil
3/4	tsp. vanilla extract
1/2	tsp. salt
1/2	tsp. ground cinnamon
1/3	cup dried cranberries
1/3	cup golden raisins
1/4	cup dried banana chips

1. In a large bowl, combine the first eight ingredients. In a small saucepan, combine water, honey, molasses and oil. Heat for 3-4 minutes over medium until heated through. Remove from heat; stir in vanilla, salt and cinnamon. Pour over the oat mixture; stir to coat.

2. Transfer to a 15-in. x 10-in. x 1-in. baking pan coated with cooking spray. Bake at 350° for 25-30 minutes or until lightly browned, stirring every 10 minutes. Cool completely on a wire rack. Stir in dried fruits. Store in an airtight container.

Nutrition Facts: 1/2 cup equals 260 calories, 12 g fat (2 g saturated fat), 0 cholesterol, 110 mg sodium, 35 g carbohydrate, 4 g fiber, 7 g protein. **Diabetic Exchanges:** 2-1/2 starch, 1-1/2 fat.

FRITTATA FLORENTINE

ENERGIZING GRANOLA

Banana Pancakes M

PREP/TOTAL TIME: 25 min. **YIELD:** 10 pancakes

PEGGY GWILLIM • STRASBOURG, SASKATCHEWAN

My daughter Karen created these pancakes, and they've become a favorite at our house. We love how the cardamom and brown sugar complement the flapjacks.

      2   cups all-purpose flour
      2   Tbsp. brown sugar
      1   tsp. baking soda
    1/2   tsp. salt
    1/2   tsp. ground cardamom
      2   eggs, lightly beaten
      2   cups buttermilk
      2   Tbsp. canola oil
      1   tsp. vanilla extract
      1   small firm banana, finely chopped

1. In a small bowl, combine the flour, brown sugar, baking soda, salt and cardamom. Combine the eggs, buttermilk, oil and vanilla; stir into dry ingredients just until moistened. Fold in banana.

2. Pour batter by 1/4 cupfuls onto a hot griddle coated with cooking spray. Turn when bubbles form on top; cook until second side is golden brown.

Nutrition Facts: 2 pancakes equals 342 calories, 9 g fat (2 g saturated fat), 89 mg cholesterol, 619 mg sodium, 53 g carbohydrate, 2 g fiber, 11 g protein.

Baked Oatmeal M

PREP: 15 min. **BAKE:** 30 min. **YIELD:** 4 servings

DIANE BELL • MANCHESTER, NEW HAMPSHIRE

You can top this oatmeal bake with vanilla yogurt, milk, applesauce or syrup, but it's also comforting on its own!

      2   cups quick-cooking oats
    1/3   cup packed brown sugar
  1-1/2   tsp. baking powder
    1/2   tsp. salt
      1   cup fat-free milk
    1/2   cup egg substitute
      2   Tbsp. canola oil
    1/4   tsp. ground cinnamon
Yogurt and fruit, optional

1. In a large bowl, combine the oats, brown sugar, baking powder and salt. Combine the milk, egg substitute and oil; add to the dry ingredients and stir until blended. Let stand for 5 minutes.

2. Transfer to an 8-in. square baking dish coated with cooking spray. Bake, uncovered, at 350° for 30-35 minutes or until a knife inserted near the center comes out clean. Sprinkle with cinnamon. Serve with yogurt and fruit if desired.

Nutrition Facts: 1 serving (calculated without yogurt and fruit) equals 316 calories, 10 g fat (1 g saturated fat), 1 mg cholesterol, 542 mg sodium, 49 g carbohydrate, 4 g fiber, 11 g protein.

Too-Yummy-To-Share Scramble C M

PREP/TOTAL TIME: 15 min.   **YIELD:** 1 serving

VICKEY ABATE • GREEN ISLAND, NEW YORK

Pamper yourself some sunny morning with this scrumptious, single-serving egg dish...you're worth it! I've gotten many compliments on this recipe; basil gives it fresh flavor.

1/4	cup chopped sweet onion
1/4	cup chopped tomato
1/8	tsp. dried basil

Dash salt and pepper

1	egg
1	Tbsp. water
2	Tbsp. shredded reduced-fat cheddar cheese

1. In a small nonstick skillet coated with cooking spray, cook and stir onion over medium heat until tender. Add the tomato, basil, salt and pepper; cook 1 minute longer.

2. In a small bowl, whisk egg and water. Add egg mixture to the pan; cook and stir until the egg is completely set. Remove from the heat. Sprinkle with cheese; cover and let stand until cheese is melted.

Nutrition Facts: 1 serving equals 136 calories, 8 g fat (4 g saturated fat), 222 mg cholesterol, 310 mg sodium, 7 g carbohydrate, 1 g fiber, 11 g protein.

Banana Blueberry Smoothies F S

PREP/TOTAL TIME: 10 min.   **YIELD:** 6 servings

KRISTA FRANK • RHODODENDRON, OREGON

My sons love this smoothie, whether it's served frozen or with a straw. Either way, I feel good giving them this healthy treat.

1	cup fat-free milk
1	cup orange juice
1/2	tsp. vanilla extract
2	medium bananas, halved
1	cup unsweetened applesauce
1	cup frozen unsweetened blueberries

1. In a blender, combine all ingredients; cover and process for 30 seconds or until blended. Pour into chilled glasses; serve immediately.

Nutrition Facts: 3/4 cup equals 99 calories, trace fat (trace saturated fat), 1 mg cholesterol, 19 mg sodium, 23 g carbohydrate, 2 g fiber, 2 g protein. **Diabetic Exchange:** 1-1/2 fruit.

Makeover Breakfast Cake

PREP: 20 min. **BAKE:** 25 min. + cooling
YIELD: 20 servings

NANCY TAYLOR • SEDRO WOOLLEY, WASHINGTON

This yummy morning treat, a family favorite for years, was redone and now has about half the fat and a fourth fewer calories. That's something to crow about!

1	cup buttermilk
3/4	cup sugar
1/2	cup unsweetened applesauce
2	eggs
2	Tbsp. canola oil
1-1/2	cups whole wheat flour
1-1/4	cups all-purpose flour
1/2	cup oat bran
1/2	cup ground flaxseed
2	tsp. ground cinnamon
1-1/4	tsp. baking powder
1	tsp. salt
1/2	tsp. baking soda

TOPPING:

1	cup packed brown sugar
1/4	cup all-purpose flour
2	Tbsp. butter, melted

1. In a large bowl, beat the buttermilk, sugar, applesauce, eggs and oil until well blended. Combine the flours, oat bran, flax, cinnamon, baking powder, salt and baking soda; gradually beat into buttermilk mixture until blended.

2. Coat a 13-in. x 9-in. baking pan with cooking spray and sprinkle with flour; add batter. Combine topping ingredients; sprinkle over batter.

3. Bake at 350° for 25-30 minutes or until a toothpick inserted near the center comes out clean. Cool for 10 minutes on a wire rack. Serve warm.

Nutrition Facts: 1 piece equals 193 calories, 5 g fat (1 g saturated fat), 25 mg cholesterol, 209 mg sodium, 36 g carbohydrate, 3 g fiber, 4 g protein.

Start-Right Strata

PREP: 15 min. + chilling **BAKE:** 35 min. + standing
YIELD: 4 servings

CECILE BROWN • CHILLICOTHE, TEXAS

I reworked this recipe to fit my diet...and my tastes! It's ideal for overnight guests.

4	slices white bread, torn into pieces
4	breakfast turkey sausage links, casings removed, crumbled
1/3	cup chopped onion
1	cup fat-free milk
3/4	cup egg substitute
1/2	cup reduced-fat sour cream
1/4	cup shredded reduced-fat cheddar cheese
1/4	cup salsa

1. Place bread in an 8-in. square baking dish coated with cooking spray; set aside.

2. In a small nonstick skillet, cook the sausage and onion over medium heat until meat is no longer pink; drain. Spoon over bread. In a small bowl, combine milk, egg substitute and sour cream. Stir in cheese. Pour over the meat mixture. Cover baking dish and refrigerate overnight.

3. Remove from the refrigerator 30 minutes before baking. Bake, uncovered, at 325° for 35-40 minutes or until a knife inserted near the center comes out clean. Let stand for 10 minutes before cutting. Serve the strata with salsa.

Nutrition Facts: 1 piece with 1 Tbsp. salsa equals 247 calories, 10 g fat (4 g saturated fat), 39 mg cholesterol, 580 mg sodium, 21 g carbohydrate, 1 g fiber, 17 g protein. **Diabetic Exchanges:** 2 lean meat, 1-1/2 starch, 1 fat.

START-RIGHT STRATA

MAKEOVER BREAKFAST CAKE

Apple Walnut Pancakes ☐M

PREP: 15 min. **COOK:** 5 min./batch **YIELD:** 18 pancakes

KERRY BLONDHEIM • DENMARK, WISCONSIN

The whole wheat flavor really comes through in these hearty pancakes. They taste great with a light touch of maple syrup.

1	cup all-purpose flour
1	cup whole wheat flour
1	Tbsp. brown sugar
2	tsp. baking powder
1	tsp. salt
2	egg whites
1	egg, lightly beaten
2	cups fat-free milk
2	Tbsp. canola oil
1	medium apple, peeled and chopped
1/2	cup chopped walnuts

Maple syrup

1. In a large bowl, combine the flours, brown sugar, baking powder and salt. Combine the egg whites, egg, milk and oil; add to dry ingredients just until moistened. Fold in apple and walnuts.

2. Pour batter by 1/4 cupfuls onto a hot griddle coated with cooking spray; turn when bubbles form on top. Cook until the second side is golden brown. Serve with syrup.

Nutrition Facts: 2 pancakes (calculated without syrup) equals 208 calories, 8 g fat (1 g saturated fat), 25 mg cholesterol, 396 mg sodium, 27 g carbohydrate, 3 g fiber, 8 g protein. **Diabetic Exchanges:** 2 starch, 1 fat.

Berry & Yogurt Phyllo Nests ☐F ☐S ☐C

PREP: 25 min. + cooling **YIELD:** 6 servings

HEALTHY COOKING TEST KITCHEN

This elegant dessert adds a special touch to any meal. Add variety by using your favorite combination of flavored yogurt and fresh fruit.

6	sheets phyllo dough (14 inches x 9 inches)

Butter-flavored cooking spray

2-1/2	tsp. sugar, *divided*
1/3	cup vanilla yogurt
1	tsp. grated orange peel
1	tsp. orange juice
1/2	cup halved fresh strawberries
1/2	cup fresh raspberries
1/2	cup fresh blueberries

Fresh mint leaves, optional

1. Place one sheet of phyllo dough on a work surface; spritz with butter-flavored spray. Top with another sheet of phyllo; spritz with spray. Cut into six squares. (Keep the remaining phyllo covered with plastic wrap to avoid drying out.) Repeat with the remaining phyllo.

2. Stack three squares of layered phyllo in each of six muffin cups coated with cooking spray, rotating squares so corners do not overlap. Sprinkle 1/4 tsp. sugar into each cup. Spritz with cooking spray. Bake at 375° for 6-8 minutes or until golden brown. Cool on a wire rack.

3. Meanwhile, in a small bowl, whisk the yogurt, orange peel and juice, and remaining sugar. Spoon yogurt mixture into cups; top with berries. Garnish with mint if desired.

Nutrition Facts: 1 serving equals 72 calories, 1 g fat (trace saturated fat), 1 mg cholesterol, 54 mg sodium, 14 g carbohydrate, 2 g fiber, 2 g protein. **Diabetic Exchange:** 1 starch.

BERRY & YOGURT PHYLLO NESTS

APPLE WALNUT PANCAKES

VEGGIE BREAKFAST PIZZA

Veggie Breakfast Pizza M

PREP: 50 min. **BAKE:** 15 min. **YIELD:** 8 slices

BEV LEHRMAN • GIJOCA, BRAZIL

This is often our Saturday breakfast. The kids look forward to getting up for it!

1-1/4	tsp. active dry yeast
3/4	cup warm water (110° to 115°)
1	Tbsp. sugar
1	Tbsp. olive oil
1	tsp. salt
2-1/4	cups all-purpose flour

TOPPINGS:

1	cup salsa
2	medium tomatoes, seeded and chopped
1	large onion, chopped
1	small green pepper, chopped
1	Tbsp. olive oil
6	eggs, beaten
1/2	tsp. seasoned salt
1/4	tsp. salt
1/4	tsp. garlic pepper blend
1	cup (4 oz.) shredded part-skim mozzarella cheese

1. In a large bowl, dissolve yeast in warm water. Add the sugar, oil, salt and 1-1/4 cups flour. Beat until smooth. Stir in enough remaining flour to form a soft dough (dough will be sticky). Turn onto a lightly floured surface; knead until smooth and elastic, about 6-8 minutes.

2. Place in a bowl coated with cooking spray, turning once to coat top. Cover and let rise in a warm place for 30 minutes.

3. Punch dough down; roll into a 13-in. circle. Transfer to a 12-in. pizza pan coated with cooking spray. Build up edges slightly. Prick dough thoroughly with a fork. Bake at 425° for 8-10 minutes or until golden brown.

4. Meanwhile, drain salsa, discarding the liquid. In a large skillet over medium heat, cook and stir the tomatoes, onion and green pepper in oil until crisp-tender. Combine eggs and seasonings; add to pan. Cook and stir until eggs are set.

5. Spoon salsa and egg mixture over crust; sprinkle with cheese. Bake for 3-5 minutes or until the cheese is melted.

Nutrition Facts: 1 slice equals 285 calories, 10 g fat (3 g saturated fat), 168 mg cholesterol, 731 mg sodium, 34 g carbohydrate, 2 g fiber, 13 g protein. **Diabetic Exchanges:** 2 starch, 1 lean meat, 1 vegetable, 1 fat.

Nutmeg Waffles F M

PREP/TOTAL TIME: 15 min. **YIELD:** 8 waffles

JAMES CHRISTENSEN • ST. ANTHONY, IDAHO

Bake an extra batch of these tender, golden waffles on the weekend. Eat one, then freeze the other in packages of two, to pop in the toaster and reheat on hurried mornings. Nutmeg adds to their warm, feel-good flavor!

1-1/4 cups all-purpose flour
   1 tsp. baking powder
   1 tsp. ground cinnamon
  1/2 tsp. salt
  1/2 tsp. ground nutmeg
  1/4 tsp. baking soda
   1 egg, lightly beaten
   1 cup fat-free milk
   1 tsp. canola oil
   1 tsp. vanilla extract
Butter and maple syrup, optional

1. In a small bowl, combine the flour, baking powder, cinnamon, salt, nutmeg and baking soda. In another bowl, combine the egg, milk, oil and vanilla; stir into dry ingredients until smooth.

2. Bake in a preheated waffle iron according to manufacturer's directions until golden brown. Serve with butter and syrup if desired.

Nutrition Facts: 2 waffles (calculated without butter and syrup) equal 196 calories, 3 g fat (1 g saturated fat), 54 mg cholesterol, 518 mg sodium, 34 g carbohydrate, 1 g fiber, 8 g protein. **Diabetic Exchanges:** 2 starch, 1 fat.

Spiced Bacon Twists C

PREP: 10 min. **BAKE:** 25 min. **YIELD:** 5 servings

GLENDA EVANS WITTNER • JOPLIN, MISSOURI

A sweet and savory rub makes these tasty twists of bacon deliciously different and worth the extra step to prepare. Cook a bit longer if you want them crispy.

  1/4 cup packed brown sugar
1-1/2 tsp. ground mustard
  1/8 tsp. ground cinnamon
  1/8 tsp. ground nutmeg
Dash cayenne pepper
  10 center-cut bacon strips

1. Combine the first five ingredients; rub over bacon on both sides. Twist bacon; place on a rack in a 15-in. x 10-in. x 1-in. baking pan.

2. Bake at 350° for 25-30 minutes or until firm; bake longer if desired.

Nutrition Facts: 2 bacon twists equals 75 calories, 4 g fat (1 g saturated fat), 15 mg cholesterol, 212 mg sodium, 6 g carbohydrate, trace fiber, 5 g protein. **Diabetic Exchanges:** 1 lean meat, 1/2 starch.

Potato Egg Bake M

PREP: 20 min. **BAKE:** 35 min. **YIELD:** 8 servings

RENA CHARBONEAU • GANSEVOORT, NEW YORK

No one will guess this mouthwatering breakfast bake is lighter than other morning casseroles.

2	lbs. Yukon Gold potatoes (about 6 medium), peeled and diced
1/2	cup water
1	cup frozen chopped broccoli, thawed
6	green onions, thinly sliced
1	small sweet red pepper, chopped
6	eggs
8	egg whites
1	cup (8 oz.) 1% cottage cheese
1	cup (4 oz.) shredded reduced-fat cheddar cheese
1/2	cup grated Parmesan cheese
1/2	cup fat-free milk
2	Tbsp. dried parsley flakes
1/2	tsp. salt
1/4	tsp. pepper

1. Place potatoes and water in a microwave-safe dish. Cover and microwave on high for 7 minutes or until tender; drain.

2. Spread potatoes in a 13-in. x 9-in. baking dish coated with cooking spray. Top with broccoli, onions and red pepper. In a large bowl, whisk the remaining ingredients until blended. Pour over vegetables. Bake, uncovered, at 350° for 35-40 minutes or until center is set.

Nutrition Facts: 1 piece equals 263 calories, 9 g fat (4 g saturated fat), 174 mg cholesterol, 558 mg sodium, 25 g carbohydrate, 2 g fiber, 21 g protein.

Cherry Yogurt F S

PREP: 10 min. + chilling **YIELD:** 3 cups

HEALTHY COOKING TEST KITCHEN

Serve wholesome granola over this thick, rich yogurt for a quick breakfast. Or layer it in parfait glasses with granola and fruit for something special. For a healthy touch, look for 100 percent cherry juice at the store; the cocktail blends have added sugar.

4	cups (32 oz.) reduced-fat plain yogurt
1	cup frozen pitted dark sweet cherries, thawed and quartered
1/2	cup cherry juice
3	Tbsp. confectioners' sugar
1-1/2	tsp. vanilla extract

1. Line a strainer with four layers of cheesecloth or one coffee filter and place over a bowl. Place yogurt in prepared strainer; cover yogurt with edges of cheesecloth. Refrigerate for 8 hours or overnight.

2. Remove yogurt from cheesecloth and discard liquid from bowl. Place the yogurt in a small bowl; stir in the remaining ingredients. Cover and refrigerate until serving.

Nutrition Facts: 1/2 cup equals 147 calories, 3 g fat (2 g saturated fat), 10 mg cholesterol, 115 mg sodium, 22 g carbohydrate, 1 g fiber, 9 g protein. **Diabetic Exchanges:** 1 reduced-fat milk, 1/2 fruit.

CHERRY YOGURT

POTATO EGG BAKE

Hash Brown Breakfast Casserole

PREP: 10 min. **BAKE:** 40 min. **YIELD:** 4 servings

CINDY SCHNEIDER • SARASOTA, FLORIDA

This savory, scrumptious recipe uses egg substitute for lower fat and cholesterol. Serve with fresh fruit for a morning meal that'll keep your family going strong until lunch!

- 4 cups frozen country-style shredded hash brown potatoes, thawed
- 1-1/2 cups egg substitute
- 1 cup finely chopped cooked chicken breast
- 1/2 tsp. garlic powder
- 1/2 tsp. pepper
- 3/4 cup shredded reduced-fat cheddar cheese

1. In a large bowl, combine the hash browns, egg substitute, chicken, garlic powder and pepper. Transfer to an 8-in. square baking dish coated with cooking spray; sprinkle with cheese.

2. Bake, uncovered, at 350° for 40-45 minutes or until set.

Nutrition Facts: 1 piece equals 220 calories, 6 g fat (3 g saturated fat), 42 mg cholesterol, 355 mg sodium, 16 g carbohydrate, 1 g fiber, 26 g protein. **Diabetic Exchanges:** 3 very lean meat, 1 starch.

Spring Brunch Bake

PREP: 15 min. **BAKE:** 35 min. + standing **YIELD:** 6 servings

NANCY ZIMMERMAN • CAPE MAY COURT HOUSE, NEW JERSEY

What a delicious way to use up leftover ham and fresh asparagus! Fluffy and moist, this entree will be welcomed at breakfast or any meal.

SPRING BRUNCH BAKE

- 8 cups cubed French bread
- 2 cups cut fresh asparagus (1-in. pieces)
- 1 cup cubed fully cooked lean ham
- 3/4 cup shredded part-skim mozzarella cheese
- 6 egg whites
- 3 eggs
- 1-1/2 cups fat-free milk
- 2 Tbsp. lemon juice
- 1/4 tsp. garlic powder

1. In a large bowl, combine the bread, asparagus, ham and cheese. Whisk the egg whites, eggs, milk, lemon juice and garlic powder; pour over bread mixture and stir until blended. Transfer to a 13-in. x 9-in. baking dish coated with cooking spray.

2. Cover and bake at 350° for 25 minutes. Uncover and bake 8-10 minutes longer or until a knife inserted near the center comes out clean. Let stand for 10 minutes before serving.

Nutrition Facts: 1 piece equals 224 calories, 6 g fat (3 g saturated fat), 124 mg cholesterol, 640 mg sodium, 20 g carbohydrate, 2 g fiber, 21 g protein.

Makeover Sunday Brunch Casserole C

PREP: 20 min. **BAKE:** 30 min. **YIELD:** 8 servings

ALICE HOFMANN • SUSSEX, WISCONSIN

I found this lovely recipe, but wanted to lighten it up a bit. By decreasing the amount of bacon originally called for, and sauteeing the veggies in canola oil rather than bacon drippings, the fat was greatly reduced.

- 6 bacon strips
- 1 small onion, chopped
- 1 small green pepper, chopped
- 1 tsp. canola oil
- 2 cartons (8 oz. *each*) egg substitute
- 4 eggs
- 1 cup fat-free milk
- 4 cups frozen shredded hash brown potatoes, thawed
- 1 cup (4 oz.) shredded reduced-fat cheddar cheese
- 3/4 tsp. salt
- 1/2 tsp. pepper
- 1/4 tsp. dill weed

1. In a large skillet, cook bacon over medium heat until crisp. Remove to paper towels; drain. Crumble bacon and set aside. In the same skillet, saute onion and green pepper in oil until tender; remove with a slotted spoon.

2. In a large bowl, whisk the egg substitute, eggs and milk. Stir in the hash browns, cheese, salt, pepper, dill, onion mixture and reserved bacon.

3. Transfer to a 13-in. x 9-in. baking dish coated with cooking spray. Bake, uncovered, at 350° for 30-35 minutes or until a knife inserted near the center comes out clean.

Nutrition Facts: 1 piece equals 181 calories, 8 g fat (3 g saturated fat), 122 mg cholesterol, 591 mg sodium, 11 g carbohydrate, 1 g fiber, 16 g protein. **Diabetic Exchanges:** 2 lean meat, 1 starch.

HASH BROWN BREAKFAST CASSEROLE

HONEY MUSTARD PORK

SCALLOPS & SHRIMP WITH YELLOW RICE

GOURMET DELI TURKEY WRAPS

Dinner in 30

When time is tight, don't head for the drive-thru; turn to this chapter instead. Here you'll find slimmed-down entrees that are ready in just 30 minutes--or less! Best of all, these work-week dishes are special enough for weekend guests.

Gourmet Deli Turkey Wraps

PREP/TOTAL TIME: 15 min. **YIELD:** 6 servings

TAMARA HANSON • BIG LAKE, MINNESOTA

These wraps are easy and delicious. They can be served for dinner, lunch or even as appetizers.

- 2 Tbsp. water
- 2 Tbsp. red wine vinegar
- 1 Tbsp. olive oil
- 1/8 tsp. pepper
- 3/4 lb. sliced deli turkey
- 6 flour tortillas (8 in.), room temperature
- 4 cups spring mix salad greens
- 2 medium pears, peeled and sliced
- 6 Tbsp. crumbled blue cheese
- 6 Tbsp. dried cranberries
- 1/4 cup chopped walnuts

1. In a jar with a tight-fitting lid, combine the water, vinegar, oil and pepper; shake well. Divide turkey among tortillas; top with salad greens, pears, cheese, cranberries and walnuts. Drizzle with dressing. Roll up tightly. Secure with toothpicks. Serve immediately.

Nutrition Facts: 1 wrap equals 330 calories, 11 g fat (2 g saturated fat), 25 mg cholesterol, 819 mg sodium, 44 g carbohydrate, 3 g fiber, 17 g protein.

Honey Mustard Pork

PREP/TOTAL TIME: 30 min. **YIELD:** 4 servings

JANET LES • CHILLIWACK, BRITISH COLUMBIA

Dijon mustard and honey create a sweet, tangy sauce that's perfect with pork tenderloin.

- 1 lb. pork tenderloin, cut into thin strips
- 1 Tbsp. canola oil
- 1 cup reduced-sodium beef broth, *divided*
- 1/4 cup honey
- 1 Tbsp. Dijon mustard
- 1 Tbsp. cornstarch
- 2 Tbsp. cold water

Hot cooked long grain and wild rice, optional

1. In a large nonstick skillet, brown pork in oil on all sides. Add 1/2 cup broth. Bring to a boil. Reduce heat; cover and simmer for 10 minutes or until meat is no longer pink. Remove pork with a slotted spoon and keep warm.

2. Stir in the honey, mustard and remaining broth. Combine cornstarch and water until smooth. Gradually stir into the pan. Bring to a boil; cook and stir for 2 minutes or until thickened. Return pork to the pan; heat through. Serve with rice if desired.

Nutrition Facts: 3 oz. cooked pork with 1/4 cup sauce (calculated without rice) equals 242 calories, 7 g fat (2 g saturated fat), 64 mg cholesterol, 246 mg sodium, 20 g carbohydrate, trace fiber, 23 g protein. **Diabetic Exchanges:** 3 lean meat, 1 starch, 1 fat.

Scallops & Shrimp with Yellow Rice

PREP/TOTAL TIME: 30 min. **YIELD:** 4 servings

LILLIAN CHARVES • NEW BERN, NORTH CAROLINA

Bright, colorful and weeknight simple, this seafood entree is even special enough for company.

- 1 large onion, chopped
- 1 garlic clove, minced
- 1 Tbsp. olive oil
- 1 cup uncooked long grain rice
- 1/2 tsp. ground turmeric
- 1 can (14-1/2 oz.) reduced-sodium chicken broth
- 3/4 cup water
- 1/2 lb. uncooked medium shrimp, peeled and deveined
- 1/2 lb. bay scallops
- 1 cup frozen peas
- 1/4 tsp. salt
- 1/8 tsp. pepper

1. In a large nonstick skillet, saute the onion and garlic in oil until tender. Add the rice and turmeric; stir to coat. Stir in broth and water. Bring to a boil. Reduce heat; cover and simmer for 15 minutes or until the rice is tender.

2. Stir in the remaining ingredients; return to a boil. Reduce heat; cover and simmer for 5 minutes or until shrimp turn pink.

Nutrition Facts: 1-1/2 cups equals 349 calories, 5 g fat (1 g saturated fat), 88 mg cholesterol, 646 mg sodium, 48 g carbohydrate, 3 g fiber, 26 g protein.

EASY CHICKEN CHASSEUR

Easy Chicken Chasseur

PREP/TOTAL TIME: 30 min. **YIELD:** 4 servings

LILLIAN CHARVES • NEW BERN, NORTH CAROLINA

Without much fuss, tarragon and sherry dress up this delicious restaurant-style entree in half an hour.

1/2	cup cornstarch
1	lb. boneless skinless chicken breasts, cut into 1-in. strips
4	tsp. olive oil, *divided*
1	cup sliced fresh mushrooms
3	green onions, thinly sliced
1/2	cup reduced-sodium chicken broth
1/2	cup sherry *or* reduced-sodium chicken broth
1/2	tsp. dried tarragon
1/2	tsp. dried thyme
1/4	tsp. salt
1/4	tsp. pepper
2	medium tomatoes, cut into wedges and seeded

Hot cooked rice, optional

1. Place cornstarch in a large resealable plastic bag. Add the chicken, a few pieces at a time, and shake to coat. In a large nonstick skillet coated with cooking spray, brown the chicken in 2 tsp. oil. Remove and set aside.

2. In the same skillet, saute mushrooms and onions in remaining oil until tender. Add the broth, sherry and seasonings; bring to a boil. Carefully return chicken to the pan; simmer, uncovered, for 4-6 minutes or until chicken is no longer pink. Stir in tomatoes; heat through. Serve with rice if desired.

Nutrition Facts: 3/4 cup (calculated without rice) equals 260 calories, 7 g fat (1 g saturated fat), 63 mg cholesterol, 283 mg sodium, 18 g carbohydrate, 2 g fiber, 25 g protein. **Diabetic Exchanges:** 3 very lean meat, 1 starch, 1 vegetable, 1 fat.

Asian Pork Linguine

PREP/TOTAL TIME: 30 min. **YIELD:** 5 servings

LISA VARNER • GREENVILLE, SOUTH CAROLINA

Peanut butter, ginger and honey make a decadent sauce for my noodle toss. If I have fresh ginger on hand, I grate 1/4 tsp. to use in place of the ground ginger.

6	oz. uncooked linguine
2	tsp. cornstarch
1/2	cup water
1/4	cup reduced-fat creamy peanut butter
2	Tbsp. reduced-sodium soy sauce
1	Tbsp. honey
1/2	tsp. garlic powder
1/8	tsp. ground ginger
1	lb. boneless pork loin chops, cubed
3	tsp. sesame oil, *divided*
2	medium carrots, sliced
1	medium onion, halved and sliced

1. Cook linguine according to package directions. For sauce, in a small bowl, combine cornstarch and water until smooth. Whisk in the peanut butter, soy sauce, honey, garlic powder and ginger until blended; set aside.

2. In a large nonstick skillet or wok coated with cooking spray, stir-fry the pork in 2 tsp. oil until no longer pink. Remove and keep warm. Stir-fry carrots and onion in remaining oil until crisp-tender. Stir the sauce and add to the pan. Bring to a boil; cook and stir for 2 minutes or until thickened.

3. Return pork to the pan. Drain linguine; add to the pan and stir to coat.

Nutrition Facts: 1 cup equals 376 calories, 13 g fat (3 g saturated fat), 44 mg cholesterol, 358 mg sodium, 39 g carbohydrate, 3 g fiber, 27 g protein.

Thai Chicken Pasta

PREP/TOTAL TIME: 25 min. **YIELD:** 2 servings

JENI PITTARD • CANON, GEORGIA

I try to buy fresh chicken when it's on sale. I cook a big batch in the slow cooker, then shred it and package it in amounts suitable for recipes like this. When I want it, it just needs to be pulled out of the freezer and defrosted!

3	oz. uncooked whole wheat fettuccine
1/2	cup salsa
2	Tbsp. reduced-fat creamy peanut butter
1	Tbsp. orange juice
1-1/2	tsp. honey
1	tsp. reduced-sodium soy sauce
1	cup cubed cooked chicken breast
1	Tbsp. chopped unsalted peanuts
1	Tbsp. minced fresh cilantro

1. Cook fettuccine according to package directions.

2. Meanwhile, in a microwave-safe dish, combine the salsa, peanut butter, orange juice, honey and soy sauce. Cover and microwave on high for 1 minute; stir. Add the chicken; heat through.

3. Drain fettuccine. Serve with the chicken mixture. Garnish with peanuts and cilantro.

Editor's Note: This recipe was tested in a 1,100-watt microwave.

Nutrition Facts: 1 serving equals 409 calories, 10 g fat (2 g saturated fat), 54 mg cholesterol, 474 mg sodium, 46 g carbohydrate, 6 g fiber, 33 g protein.

ASIAN PORK LINGUINE

THAI CHICKEN PASTA

Hearty Turkey & Rice

PREP/TOTAL TIME: 25 min.   YIELD: 4 servings

JOAN HALLFORD • NORTH RICHLAND HILLS, TEXAS

We love this tasty dinner. It's quick to prepare, making it a great (and yummy!) meal when you're running late.

1-1/2 cups instant brown rice
    1 lb. extra-lean ground turkey
    1 medium onion, chopped
1-1/2 cups salsa
    1 can (8 oz.) no-salt-added tomato sauce
    1 tsp. reduced-sodium chicken bouillon granules
  1/4 tsp. salt
  1/4 cup shredded reduced-fat cheddar cheese
  1/4 cup reduced-fat sour cream
Chopped tomatoes, baked tortilla chip scoops and sliced ripe olives, optional

1. Cook rice according to package directions.

2. Meanwhile, in a large nonstick skillet coated with cooking spray, cook turkey and onion over medium heat until meat is no longer pink. Add the salsa, tomato sauce, bouillon and salt; heat through.

3. Serve with rice; top with cheese and sour cream. Garnish with tomatoes, chips and olives if desired.

Nutrition Facts: 1 cup turkey mixture with 3/4 cup rice (calculated without optional ingredients) equals 354 calories, 5 g fat (2 g saturated fat), 55 mg cholesterol, 732 mg sodium, 40 g carbohydrate, 3 g fiber, 34 g protein. **Diabetic Exchanges:** 4 very lean meat, 2 starch, 2 vegetable, 1/2 fat.

"Little Kick" Jalapeno Burgers

PREP/TOTAL TIME: 20 min.   YIELD: 6 servings

DAWN DHOOGHE • CONCORD, NORTH CAROLINA

I lightened up one of my husband's favorite burgers, and although the original was good, we actually like this better!

HEARTY TURKEY & RICE

---

    2 jalapeno peppers, seeded and finely chopped
    2 Tbsp. minced fresh cilantro
    2 Tbsp. light beer or water
    2 dashes hot pepper sauce
    2 garlic cloves, minced
  1/2 tsp. pepper
  1/4 tsp. salt
  1/4 tsp. cayenne pepper
    1 lb. extra-lean ground turkey
    3 slices pepper Jack cheese, cut in half
    6 dinner rolls, split
    6 Tbsp. salsa
    6 Tbsp. fat-free sour cream
    6 Tbsp. shredded lettuce

1. In a large bowl, combine the first eight ingredients. Crumble turkey over mixture and mix well. Shape into six patties.

2. Coat grill rack with cooking spray before starting the grill. Grill burgers, covered, over medium heat for 2-3 minutes on each side or until no longer pink. Top with cheese; cover and grill 1-2 minutes longer or until cheese is melted. Serve on rolls with salsa, sour cream and lettuce.

Editor's Note: When cutting hot peppers, disposable gloves are recommended. Avoid touching your face.

Nutrition Facts: 1 burger equals 254 calories, 7 g fat (2 g saturated fat), 61 mg cholesterol, 471 mg sodium, 23 g carbohydrate, 2 g fiber, 26 g protein. **Diabetic Exchanges:** 3 very lean meat, 1-1/2 starch, 1/2 fat.

Mustard Turkey Cutlets F

PREP/TOTAL TIME: 25 min.   YIELD: 4 servings

DEBORAH WILLIAMS • PEORIA, ARIZONA

My grilled turkey cutlets are treated with a slightly sweet sauce that mustard-lovers thoroughly enjoy.

    2 tsp. cornstarch
  1/2 tsp. salt, *divided*
  1/8 tsp. plus 1/4 tsp. pepper, *divided*
  1/2 cup thawed apple juice concentrate
  1/4 cup Dijon mustard
1-1/2 Tbsp. minced fresh rosemary *or* 1-1/2 tsp. dried rosemary, crushed
    1 pkg. (17.6 oz.) turkey breast cutlets
    1 tsp. olive oil

1. In a small saucepan, combine the cornstarch, 1/4 tsp. salt and 1/8 tsp. pepper. Gradually whisk in the concentrate, mustard and rosemary until blended. Cook and stir over medium-high heat until thickened and bubbly. Reduce heat; cook and stir 2 minutes longer. Set aside 1/4 cup sauce.

2. Coat grill rack with cooking spray before starting the grill. Brush the turkey with oil; sprinkle with remaining salt and pepper. Grill, covered, over medium heat for 2-3 minutes on each side or until no longer pink, basting occasionally with remaining sauce. Brush with reserved sauce before serving.

Nutrition Facts: 4 oz. cooked turkey equals 230 calories, 2 g fat (trace saturated fat), 77 mg cholesterol, 725 mg sodium, 19 g carbohydrate, trace fiber, 31 g protein. **Diabetic Exchanges:** 4 very lean meat, 1 starch.

CHILI MAC

Chili Mac

PREP/TOTAL TIME: 30 min. **YIELD:** 6 servings

KRISSY BLACK • MT. VERNON, OHIO

Family and friends love this recipe. I use three power foods: tomatoes, black beans and olive oil, plus whole wheat pasta…it's comfort food to feel good about!

2	cups uncooked whole wheat elbow macaroni
1	lb. lean ground turkey
1	small onion, chopped
2 to 3	jalapeno peppers, seeded and chopped
2	garlic cloves, minced
2	tsp. olive oil
1	can (15 oz.) black beans, rinsed and drained
1	can (14-1/2 oz.) diced tomatoes, undrained
1	can (8 oz.) tomato sauce
1 to 2	Tbsp. hot pepper sauce
2 to 3	tsp. chili powder
1	tsp. ground cumin
1/4	tsp. cayenne pepper
1/4	tsp. pepper
3/4	cup shredded reduced-fat cheddar cheese

1. Cook macaroni according to package directions. Meanwhile, in a large nonstick skillet coated with cooking spray, cook the turkey, onion, jalapenos and garlic in oil over medium heat until meat is no longer pink; drain.

2. Add the beans, tomatoes, tomato sauce, pepper sauce and seasonings. Drain macaroni; stir into turkey mixture. Cook over medium-low heat for 5 minutes or until heated through.

3. Sprinkle with cheese. Remove from the heat; cover and let stand until cheese is melted.

Editor's Note: When cutting hot peppers, disposable gloves are recommended. Avoid touching your face.

Nutrition Facts: 1-1/2 cups equals 396 calories, 12 g fat (4 g saturated fat), 70 mg cholesterol, 581 mg sodium, 45 g carbohydrate, 9 g fiber, 28 g protein. **Diabetic Exchanges:** 3 lean meat, 2-1/2 starch, 1 vegetable, 1 fat.

Get creative when preparing the Chili Mac recipe. Chili gives you the chance to add all sorts of healthy items! As the chili simmers, toss in some frozen corn kernels, sliced mushrooms or chopped green pepper.

JERK TURKEY TENDERLOINS

Jerk Turkey Tenderloins ⒞

PREP/TOTAL TIME: 30 min.
YIELD: 5 servings (2 cups salsa)

HOLLY BAUER • WEST BEND, WISCONSIN

This is best with fresh pineapple, however, on particularly busy days, I have used canned pineapple tidbits in an effort to speed preparation even more. My family enjoys this recipe several times a year. It's good on the grill, too.

> 1 pkg. (20 oz.) turkey breast tenderloins
> 1/2 tsp. seasoned salt
> 2 Tbsp. olive oil
> 1 Tbsp. dried rosemary, crushed
> 1 Tbsp. Caribbean jerk seasoning
> 1 Tbsp. brown sugar

SALSA:
> 1-1/2 cups cubed fresh pineapple
> 1 medium sweet red pepper, chopped
> 1/4 cup chopped red onion
> 1/4 cup minced fresh cilantro
> 1 jalapeno pepper, seeded and minced
> 2 Tbsp. lime juice

> 2 garlic cloves, minced
> 1/4 tsp. salt
> 1/8 tsp. pepper

1. Sprinkle tenderloins with seasoned salt. Combine the oil, rosemary, jerk seasoning and brown sugar. Rub over tenderloins. Broil 3-4 in. from the heat for 7-9 minutes on each side or until a meat thermometer reaches 170°.

2. Meanwhile, in a large bowl, combine salsa ingredients. Serve with turkey.

Editor's Note: When cutting hot peppers, disposable gloves are recommended. Avoid touching your face.

Nutrition Facts: 3 oz. cooked turkey with 1/3 cup salsa equals 216 calories, 7 g fat (1 g saturated fat), 56 mg cholesterol, 503 mg sodium, 12 g carbohydrate, 2 g fiber, 27 g protein. **Diabetic Exchanges:** 3 very lean meat, 1 vegetable, 1 fat, 1/2 fruit.

Simple Sausage Pasta Toss

PREP/TOTAL TIME: 30 min. **YIELD:** 5 servings

HEALTHY COOKING TEST KITCHEN

This filling pasta dish is ideal for busy nights when you need a good, quick meal with a healthy touch.

8 oz. uncooked multigrain spaghetti

1/4 cup seasoned bread crumbs

1 tsp. olive oil

3/4 lb. Italian turkey sausage links, cut into 1/2-in. slices

1 garlic clove, minced

2 cans (14-1/2 oz. *each*) no-salt-added diced tomatoes, drained

1 can (2-1/4 oz.) sliced ripe olives, drained

1. Cook spaghetti according to package directions. Meanwhile, in a small skillet, toast bread crumbs in oil over medium heat; remove from the heat and set aside.

2. In a large nonstick skillet, cook sausage over medium heat until no longer pink. Add garlic; cook 1 minute longer. Stir in tomatoes and olives. Cook and stir until heated through. Drain pasta; add to skillet. Sprinkle with bread crumbs.

Nutrition Facts: 1-2/3 cups equals 340 calories, 10 g fat (2 g saturated fat), 41 mg cholesterol, 689 mg sodium, 44 g carbohydrate, 6 g fiber, 21 g protein. **Diabetic Exchanges:** 3 lean meat, 2 starch, 1 vegetable, 1/2 fat.

Turkey Scallopini C

PREP/TOTAL TIME: 25 min. **YIELD:** 4 servings

SUSAN WARREN • NORTH MANCHESTER, INDIANA

This recipe is easy to double for company or family gatherings. It's great served with rice, pasta or veggies. A splash of white wine and spicy mustard add special flavor.

1/3 cup all-purpose flour

1/4 tsp. dried rosemary, crushed

1/4 tsp. dried thyme

1/8 tsp. white pepper

1 pkg. (17.6 oz.) turkey breast cutlets

4 tsp. canola oil

1/4 cup white wine *or* reduced-sodium chicken broth

1/2 tsp. cornstarch

1/3 cup reduced-sodium chicken broth

1/2 cup reduced-fat sour cream

1 tsp. spicy brown mustard

Paprika, optional

1. In a large resealable plastic bag, combine the flour, rosemary, thyme and pepper. Add turkey; seal bag and shake to coat. In a large nonstick skillet coated with cooking spray, cook turkey in oil over medium heat for 2-4 minutes on each side or until juices run clear. Remove and keep warm.

2. Add wine to skillet; cook and stir for 30 seconds, stirring to loosen browned bits from pan. Combine cornstarch and broth until smooth; stir into skillet. Add sour cream and mustard; heat through. Bring to a boil; cook and stir for 2 minutes or until slightly thickened. Pour over turkey; sprinkle with paprika if desired.

Nutrition Facts: 4 oz. cooked turkey with about 2 Tbsp. sauce equals 263 calories, 8 g fat (2 g saturated fat), 88 mg cholesterol, 194 mg sodium, 11 g carbohydrate, trace fiber, 34 g protein. **Diabetic Exchanges:** 4 very lean meat, 1 starch, 1 fat.

Southwestern Chicken Salad

PREP/TOTAL TIME: 30 min. **YIELD:** 6 servings

JEANNE HOLT • MENDOTA HEIGHTS, MINNESOTA

Add some fun and great citrus flavor to your salad. Creative and colorful ingredients make this fresh-tasting dish really stand out.

1/2 cup orange juice

2 Tbsp. olive oil

1 Tbsp. minced fresh cilantro

1 Tbsp. lime juice

1 Tbsp. jalapeno pepper jelly

1 Tbsp. honey

1/4 tsp. ground cumin

2-1/2 cups cubed cooked chicken breast

1 can (15 oz.) black beans, rinsed and drained

1 cup cubed peeled mango

2/3 cup julienned sweet red pepper

2/3 cup julienned peeled jicama

4 green onions, chopped

3 cups fresh baby spinach

3 cups torn mixed salad greens

1/3 cup pepitas or salted pumpkin seeds

1. For dressing, in a small bowl, whisk the first seven ingredients. In a large bowl, combine the chicken, beans, mango, red pepper, jicama and onions. Drizzle with dressing and toss to coat. Refrigerate for at least 10 minutes.

2. Just before serving, toss the chicken mixture with the spinach and salad greens. Sprinkle with the pepitas.

Nutrition Facts: 1-2/3 cups equals 314 calories, 12 g fat (2 g saturated fat), 45 mg cholesterol, 266 mg sodium, 28 g carbohydrate, 6 g fiber, 26 g protein. **Diabetic Exchanges:** 3 very lean meat, 2 fat, 1 starch, 1 vegetable, 1/2 fruit.

SOUTHWESTERN CHICKEN SALAD

Chicken Thighs With Shallots & Spinach c

PREP/TOTAL TIME: 30 min. **YIELD:** 6 servings

GENNA JOHANNES • WRIGHTSTOWN, WISCONSIN

This moist and tender chicken comes complete with its own creamy and flavorful vegetable side! It makes a pretty presentation and goes together in no time flat for a nutritious weeknight meal-in-one.

    6 boneless skinless chicken thighs (about
       1-1/2 lbs.)
  1/2 tsp. seasoned salt
  1/2 tsp. pepper
1-1/2 tsp. olive oil
    4 shallots, thinly sliced
  1/3 cup white wine *or* reduced-sodium chicken
       broth
  1/4 cup fat-free sour cream
  1/4 tsp. salt
    1 pkg. (10 oz.) fresh spinach

1. Sprinkle chicken with seasoned salt and pepper. In a large nonstick skillet coated with cooking spray, cook chicken in oil over medium heat for 6 minutes on each side or until chicken juices run clear. Remove and keep warm.

2. In the same skillet, saute shallots until tender. Add the wine, sour cream and salt. Bring to a boil; cook and stir for 2-3 minutes or until slightly thickened. Add spinach; cook and stir until spinach is wilted. Serve with chicken.

Nutrition Facts: 1 chicken thigh with 1/4 cup spinach mixture equals 225 calories, 10 g fat (2 g saturated fat), 77 mg cholesterol, 338 mg sodium, 8 g carbohydrate, 1 g fiber, 24 g protein. **Diabetic Exchanges:** 3 lean meat, 1-1/2 fat, 1 vegetable.

Buffalo Turkey Burgers

PREP/TOTAL TIME: 25 min. **YIELD:** 4 servings

MARY PAX-SHIPLEY • BEND, OREGON

There's nothing bland about these juicy turkey burgers! Celery and blue cheese salad dressing help tame the hot sauce. For an even "skinnier" version, skip the bun and add sliced onion and chopped tomato.

    2 Tbsp. Louisiana-style hot sauce, *divided*
    2 tsp. ground cumin
    2 tsp. chili powder
    2 garlic cloves, minced
  1/2 tsp. salt
  1/8 tsp. pepper
    1 lb. lean ground turkey
    4 whole wheat hamburger buns, split
    1 cup shredded lettuce
    2 celery ribs, chopped
    2 Tbsp. fat-free blue cheese salad dressing

1. In a large bowl, combine 1 Tbsp. hot sauce, cumin, chili powder, garlic, salt and pepper. Crumble turkey over mixture and mix well. Shape into four patties.

2. In a large nonstick skillet coated with cooking spray, cook patties over medium heat for 4-5 minutes on each side or until a meat thermometer reads 165° and juices run clear.

3. Serve on buns with lettuce, celery, blue cheese dressing and remaining hot sauce.

Nutrition Facts: 1 burger equals 312 calories, 12 g fat (3 g saturated fat), 90 mg cholesterol, 734 mg sodium, 28 g carbohydrate, 5 g fiber, 24 g protein. **Diabetic Exchanges:** 3 lean meat, 2 starch, 1/2 fat.

CHICKEN THIGHS WITH SHALLOTS & SPINACH

BUFFALO TURKEY BURGERS

Zeus Burgers

PREP/TOTAL TIME: 30 min. **YIELD:** 4 servings

LORI ANN PANCHISIN • ORMOND BEACH, FLORIDA

I always eat healthy meals, and I'm not afraid to experiment with food. I put together some common Greek ingredients and really liked the results. These burgers are delicious with roasted-garlic ciabatta rolls.

3	Tbsp. fat-free mayonnaise
2	tsp. lemon juice
1	garlic clove, minced
1/4	tsp. dried oregano
1/8	tsp. salt

BURGERS:

1/4	cup frozen chopped spinach, thawed and squeezed dry
1/4	cup crumbled reduced-fat feta cheese
2	Tbsp. lemon juice
1	Tbsp. pine nuts, finely chopped
1	garlic clove, minced
1	tsp. dried oregano
1/4	tsp. salt
1/4	tsp. pepper
1	lb. lean ground beef
4	hamburger buns, split

1. In a small bowl, combine the mayonnaise, lemon juice, garlic, oregano and salt. Cover and refrigerate until serving.

2. For burgers, coat grill rack with cooking spray before starting the grill. In a large bowl, combine the spinach, cheese, lemon juice, pine nuts, garlic, oregano, salt and pepper. Crumble beef over mixture and mix well. Shape into four patties.

3. Grill, covered, over medium heat for 5-7 minutes on each side or until a meat thermometer reads 160° and juices run clear. Toast buns on grill for 1 minute or until lightly browned. Serve burgers on buns with reserved sauce.

Nutrition Facts: 1 burger equals 335 calories, 13 g fat (5 g saturated fat), 73 mg cholesterol, 669 mg sodium, 26 g carbohydrate, 2 g fiber, 28 g protein.

Looking for a no-fuss dinner addition? Just serve the hearty Zeus Burgers with a small portion of cucumber, pasta or potato salad. The full-flavored burgers are also delicious with a simple side of carrot and celery sticks.

Chicken with Garden Salsa ⓒ

PREP/TOTAL TIME: 30 min. **YIELD:** 4 servings

MARY RELYEA • CANASTOTA, NEW YORK

Fresh chiles vary greatly in taste and price. A fruity serrano gives this dish authentic Mexican flavor, but jalapenos cost less and are more commonly available. To save time, use canned tomatoes and corn in the salsa.

1/2	cup lime juice
1	Tbsp. olive oil
1/2	tsp. garlic salt
1/2	tsp. coarsely ground pepper
4	boneless skinless chicken breast halves (4 oz. *each*)
1	cup frozen corn, thawed
1	medium tomato, chopped
1	serrano pepper, seeded and chopped
1	green onion, cut into 1/2-in. pieces
1/4	tsp. ground cumin
2	slices Monterey Jack *or* pepper Jack cheese, halved

1. In a small bowl, combine the lime juice, oil, garlic salt and pepper. Set aside 5 Tbsp. Pour remaining lime juice mixture into a resealable plastic bag; add chicken. Seal and turn to coat; let stand at room temperature for 10 minutes.

2. Meanwhile, in a small bowl, combine the corn, tomato, pepper, green onion, cumin and 3 Tbsp. reserved lime juice mixture. Cover and refrigerate.

3. If grilling the chicken, coat grill rack with cooking spray before starting the grill. Drain and discard marinade from chicken. Grill, covered, over medium heat or broil 3-4 in. from heat for 5-6 minutes on each side or until juices are almost clear, basting twice with remaining lime juice mixture.

4. Top with cheese; grill or broil 1-2 minutes longer or until cheese is melted and chicken juices run clear. Serve with salsa.

Editor's Note: When cutting or seeding hot peppers, use rubber or plastic gloves to protect your hands. Avoid touching your face.

Nutrition Facts: 1 chicken breast half with 1/3 cup salsa equals 239 calories, 9 g fat (3 g saturated fat), 74 mg cholesterol, 276 mg sodium, 13 g carbohydrate, 2 g fiber, 28 g protein. **Diabetic Exchanges:** 3 very lean meat, 1 starch, 1 fat.

Polynesian Stir-Fry

PREP/TOTAL TIME: 30 min. YIELD: 4 servings

SUSIE VAN ETTEN • CHAPMANSBORO, TENNESSEE

This restaurant-style meal blends the sweet tastes of pineapple and apricot with crunchy veggies and tender pork. Peanuts add a special touch.

1	can (8 oz.) unsweetened pineapple chunks
1	Tbsp. cornstarch
2	Tbsp. cold water
1	Tbsp. reduced-sodium soy sauce
2	Tbsp. reduced-sugar apricot preserves
1	pork tenderloin (1 lb.), thinly sliced
3	tsp. canola oil, *divided*
1	medium onion, halved and sliced
1	small green pepper, cut into 1-in. pieces
1	small sweet red pepper, cut into 1-in. pieces
2	cups hot cooked rice

Chopped unsalted peanuts, optional

1. Drain pineapple, reserving juice; set aside. For sauce, in a small bowl, combine cornstarch and water until smooth. Stir in the soy sauce, preserves and reserved pineapple juice; set aside.

2. In a large nonstick skillet or wok, stir-fry pork in 2 tsp. oil until no longer pink. Remove and keep warm.

3. Stir-fry the onion and peppers in remaining oil for 3 minutes. Add pineapple; stir-fry 2-3 minutes longer or until vegetables are crisp-tender.

4. Stir cornstarch mixture and add to the pan. Bring to a boil; cook and stir for 2 minutes or until thickened. Add pork; heat through. Serve with rice. Just before serving, sprinkle each serving with peanuts if desired.

Nutrition Facts: 1 cup stir-fry with 1/2 cup rice (calculated without peanuts) equals equals 339 calories, 8 g fat (2 g saturated fat), 63 mg cholesterol, 204 mg sodium, 40 g carbohydrate, 2 g fiber, 26 g protein. **Diabetic Exchanges:** 3 lean meat, 1-1/2 starch, 1 vegetable, 1/2 fruit, 1/2 fat.

Santa Fe Chicken Pita Pizzas

PREP/TOTAL TIME: 30 min. YIELD: 4 servings

ATHENA RUSSELL • FLORENCE, SOUTH CAROLINA

Your whole family will enjoy the taste of this fast and versatile main dish.

4	pita breads (6 in.)
1/2	cup refried black beans
1/2	cup salsa
1	cup cubed cooked chicken breast
2	Tbsp. chopped green chilies
2	Tbsp. sliced ripe olives
3/4	cup shredded Colby-Monterey Jack cheese
1/2	cup reduced-fat sour cream
1	green onion, chopped

1. Place pita breads on an ungreased baking sheet; spread with beans. Top with salsa, chicken, chilies, olives and cheese.

2. Bake at 350° for 8-10 minutes or until cheese is melted. Serve with sour cream; sprinkle with onion.

Nutrition Facts: 1 pizza with 2 Tbsp. sour cream equals 380 calories, 11 g fat (7 g saturated fat), 56 mg cholesterol, 796 mg sodium, 43 g carbohydrate, 4 g fiber, 24 g protein. **Diabetic Exchanges:** 3 starch, 2 lean meat, 1 fat.

POLYNESIAN STIR-FRY | SANTA FE CHICKEN PITA PIZZAS

Lactose-Free Potato Soup

PREP/TOTAL TIME: 30 min.   YIELD: 6 servings

LISANNE HEYWARD • RICHMOND, VIRGINIA

This is a great way for my husband and me to have rich, creamy soup without worrying about my lactose intolerance. Try it—you won't believe it's dairy-free!

- 3 medium onions, chopped
- 2 celery ribs, chopped
- 2 Tbsp. canola oil
- 4 cups reduced-sodium chicken broth
- 4 medium potatoes, peeled and cubed

1. In a large saucepan, saute onions and celery in oil until tender. Add broth and potatoes; bring to a boil. Reduce heat; cover and simmer for 15-20 minutes or until potatoes are tender.

2. Cool slightly. In a blender, process half of the soup until smooth. Return to pan; heat through.

Nutrition Facts: 1 cup equals 166 calories, 5 g fat (trace saturated fat), 0 cholesterol, 396 mg sodium, 27 g carbohydrate, 3 g fiber, 5 g protein. **Diabetic Exchanges:** 1 starch, 1 vegetable, 1 fat.

Broiled Apricot Chicken [c]

PREP/TOTAL TIME: 30 min.   YIELD: 6 servings

SUSAN WARREN • NORTH MANCHESTER, INDIANA

What a tasty treatment for lean, tender chicken breasts! A little sweet blends perfectly with the bold taste of horseradish. This works well on the grill, too.

- 1 cup apricot nectar
- 3 Tbsp. brown sugar
- 2 Tbsp. ketchup
- 2 tsp. cornstarch
- 1 tsp. grated orange peel
- 1 tsp. horseradish mustard
- 6 boneless skinless chicken breast halves (6 oz. *each*)

LACTOSE-FREE POTATO SOUP

1. In a small saucepan, combine the first six ingredients. Bring to a boil. Cook and stir for 1 minute or until thickened.

2. Place chicken on a broiler pan coated with cooking spray. Broil 4 in. from the heat for 6-8 minutes on each side or until chicken juices run clear, basting frequently with apricot mixture.

Nutrition Facts: 1 chicken breast half equals 241 calories, 4 g fat (1 g saturated fat), 94 mg cholesterol, 158 mg sodium, 15 g carbohydrate, trace fiber, 34 g protein. **Diabetic Exchanges:** 5 very lean meat, 1 starch.

Easy Chicken Broccoli Pasta

PREP/TOTAL TIME: 25 min.   YIELD: 4 servings

RENEE PAJESTKA • BRUNSWICK, OHIO

This is so easy to throw together in a pinch. It's wonderful served with crusty bread and a nice veggie salad.

- 2 cups uncooked penne pasta
- 2 cups frozen broccoli florets
- 1 lb. boneless skinless chicken breasts, cut into 1-in. cubes
- 1/4 tsp. salt
- 1/4 tsp. pepper
- 1 Tbsp. canola oil
- 1 small sweet red pepper, chopped
- 1/2 cup white wine *or* reduced-sodium chicken broth
- 1 cup reduced-fat Alfredo sauce

1. Cook pasta according to package directions, adding the broccoli during the last 5 minutes of cooking.

2. Meanwhile, sprinkle chicken with salt and pepper. In a large nonstick skillet, saute chicken in oil until lightly browned. Add pepper; saute 3-5 minutes longer or until chicken is no longer pink and pepper is tender.

3. Drain pasta mixture; add to the pan. Reduce heat to low. Stir in wine, then Alfredo sauce; cook and stir until heated through.

Nutrition Facts: 1-1/2 cups equals 400 calories, 13 g fat (5 g saturated fat), 88 mg cholesterol, 654 mg sodium, 33 g carbohydrate, 2 g fiber, 31 g protein.

Spanish Rice Supper

PREP/TOTAL TIME: 30 min.   YIELD: 6 servings

CATHY FLIKKEMA • SALT LAKE CITY, UTAH

Mom made this when I was growing up, and now both of my children love it!

- 1 lb. lean ground beef
- 3 cups instant brown rice
- 1 can (29 oz.) tomato puree
- 1-1/2 cups water
- 1 can (4 oz.) chopped green chilies
- 1 can (2-1/4 oz.) sliced ripe olives, drained
- 1 envelope chili seasoning
- 1/2 cup shredded reduced-fat cheddar cheese

1. In a large skillet, cook beef over medium heat until no longer pink; drain. Stir in the rice, tomato puree, water, chilies, olives and chili seasoning. Bring to a

boil. Reduce the heat; cover and simmer for 10-12 minutes or until rice is tender.

2. Remove from the heat. Sprinkle with cheese; cover and let stand until cheese is melted.

Nutrition Facts: 1-1/3 cups equals 380 calories, 10 g fat (4 g saturated fat), 44 mg cholesterol, 741 mg sodium, 47 g carbohydrate, 4 g fiber, 24 g protein.

Hoisin Shrimp & Broccoli

PREP/TOTAL TIME: 30 min. **YIELD:** 4 servings

MARY KISINGER • CALGARY, ALBERTA

This healthy dish looks impressive and is a snap to prepare. I hope you adore it as much as I do.

1	Tbsp. cornstarch
1/3	cup reduced-sodium chicken broth
4-1/2	tsp. reduced-sodium soy sauce
4-1/2	tsp. hoisin sauce
1	tsp. sesame oil
3	cups fresh broccoli florets
1	Tbsp. canola oil
4	green onions, chopped
3	garlic cloves, minced
1	tsp. minced fresh gingerroot
1	lb. uncooked medium shrimp, peeled and deveined
2	cups hot cooked rice

1. In a small bowl, combine cornstarch and broth until smooth. Stir in the soy sauce, hoisin sauce and sesame oil; set aside.

2. In a large nonstick skillet or wok, stir-fry the broccoli in canola oil until crisp-tender. Add the onions, garlic and ginger; stir-fry for 3-4 minutes or until vegetables are tender. Add the shrimp; stir-fry 4-5 minutes longer or until shrimp turn pink.

3. Stir the cornstarch mixture and add to the pan. Bring to a boil; cook and stir for 2 minutes or until thickened. Serve with rice.

Nutrition Facts: 3/4 cup shrimp mixture with 1/2 cup rice equals 289 calories, 7 g fat (1 g saturated fat), 138 mg cholesterol, 524 mg sodium, 33 g carbohydrate, 2 g fiber, 23 g protein. **Diabetic Exchanges:** 3 very lean meat, 1-1/2 starch, 1 vegetable, 1 fat.

For an easy way to lend Asian flair to dishes without adding a lot of calories, consider a few teaspoons of hoisin sauce. Found in the ethnic or Asian aisle of most grocery stores, the thick sauce is a wonderful way to flavor everything from appetizers to entrees.

EASY CUBAN PICADILLO

ITALIAN POT ROAST

SOUP-BOWL CABBAGE ROLLS

Beef Entrees

Dropping pounds doesn't mean dropping meat from your diet. Let these mouth-watering dishes show you how delicious eating right can be. Bubbling casseroles, savory pot roasts and juicy steaks are just a few of the meaty items found here.

Soup-Bowl Cabbage Rolls

PREP: 15 min. **COOK:** 35 min. **YIELD:** 4 servings

TERRI PEARCE • HOUSTON, TEXAS

This fabulous alternative to traditional stuffed cabbage rolls is simple to assemble, so it's handy for busy weeknights. Best of all, it's very filling and has plenty of fiber from the cabbage.

1	lb. lean ground beef
1	garlic clove, minced
1	small head cabbage, chopped
2-1/2	cups water
2/3	cup uncooked long grain rice
1	Tbsp. Worcestershire sauce
1	tsp. onion powder
1	tsp. dried basil
1/4	tsp. cayenne pepper
1/4	tsp. pepper
1	can (28 oz.) crushed tomatoes
1/2	tsp. salt
2	Tbsp. grated Parmesan cheese, optional

1. In a nonstick Dutch oven, cook beef and garlic over medium heat until meat is no longer pink; drain. Stir in cabbage, water, rice, Worcestershire sauce, onion powder, basil, cayenne and pepper; bring to a boil. Reduce heat; cover and simmer for 25-30 minutes or until rice is tender.

2. Stir in tomatoes and salt; heat through. Sprinkle with cheese if desired.

Nutrition Facts: 2-1/4 cups (calculated without cheese) equals 397 calories, 9 g fat (4 g saturated fat), 56 mg cholesterol, 707 mg sodium, 51 g carbohydrate, 9 g fiber, 30 g protein.

Easy Cuban Picadillo

PREP/TOTAL TIME: 30 min. **YIELD:** 4 servings

MARIE WIELGUS • WAYNE, NEW JERSEY

My girlfriend gave me this delicious recipe years ago. I've made it ever since for family and friends, and they all love it. My daughter says it's the best dish I make and loves to take leftovers to school for lunch the next day.

1	lb. lean ground beef
1	small green pepper, chopped
1/4	cup chopped onion
1	can (8 oz.) tomato sauce
1/2	cup sliced pimiento-stuffed olives
1/4	cup raisins
1	Tbsp. cider vinegar
2	cups hot cooked rice

1. In a large nonstick skillet, cook the beef, pepper and onion over medium heat until meat is no longer pink; drain. Stir in the tomato sauce, olives, raisins and vinegar. Cook for 5-6 minutes or until raisins are plumped. Serve with rice.

Nutrition Facts: 1 cup picadillo with 1/2 cup rice equals 354 calories, 12 g fat (3 g saturated fat), 56 mg cholesterol, 697 mg sodium, 36 g carbohydrate, 2 g fiber, 25 g protein. **Diabetic Exchanges:** 3 lean meat, 1-1/2 starch, 1 vegetable, 1 fat, 1/2 fruit.

Weeknight Beef Skillet

PREP/TOTAL TIME: 30 min. **YIELD:** 4 servings

CLARA COULSTON • WASHINGTON COURT HOUSE, OHIO

This mild but hearty family fare is chock-full of veggies, Italian seasoning and nutrition. It's a quick-and-easy meal that just might become one of your family's favorites!

3	cups uncooked yolk-free whole wheat noodles
1	lb. lean ground beef
1	medium green pepper, finely chopped
1	pkg. (16 oz.) frozen mixed vegetables, thawed and drained
1	can (15 oz.) tomato sauce
1	Tbsp. Worcestershire sauce
1-1/2	tsp. Italian seasoning
2	tsp. sugar
1/4	tsp. salt
1/4	cup minced fresh parsley

1. Cook noodles according to package directions.

2. Meanwhile, in a large nonstick skillet over medium heat, cook beef and pepper until meat is no longer pink; drain. Stir in mixed vegetables, tomato sauce, Worcestershire sauce, Italian seasoning, sugar and salt; heat through. Drain noodles; serve with meat mixture. Sprinkle with parsley.

Nutrition Facts: 1-1/4 cups beef mixture with 3/4 cup noodles equals 389 calories, 9 g fat (3 g saturated fat), 56 mg cholesterol, 800 mg sodium, 49 g carbohydrate, 10 g fiber, 31 g protein.

Stir-Fried Steak & Veggies

PREP/TOTAL TIME: 25 min. **YIELD:** 6 servings

VICKY PRIESTLEY • ALUM CREEK, WEST VIRGINIA

I combine convenience products with simple seasonings for a healthful meal everyone loves. And it can be ready in under 30 minutes tonight!

1-1/2	cups uncooked instant brown rice
1	Tbsp. cornstarch
1	Tbsp. brown sugar
3/4	tsp. ground ginger
1/2	tsp. chili powder
1/4	tsp. garlic powder
1/4	tsp. pepper
1/2	cup cold water
1/4	cup reduced-sodium soy sauce
1	lb. boneless beef sirloin steak, cut into 1/2-in. cubes
2	Tbsp. canola oil, *divided*
1	pkg. (16 oz.) frozen stir-fry vegetable blend, thawed

1. Cook the rice according to package directions. Meanwhile, in a small bowl, combine the cornstarch, brown sugar and seasonings. Stir in water and soy sauce until smooth; set aside.

2. In a large nonstick skillet or wok coated with cooking spray, stir-fry beef in 1 Tbsp. oil until no longer pink. Remove and keep warm. Stir-fry vegetables in remaining oil until crisp-tender.

3. Stir cornstarch mixture and add to the pan. Bring to a boil; cook and stir for 2 minutes or until thickened. Add beef; heat through. Serve with rice.

Nutrition Facts: 3/4 cup stir-fry with 1/2 cup rice equals 304 calories, 8 g fat (2 g saturated fat), 42 mg cholesterol, 470 mg sodium, 37 g carbohydrate, 3 g fiber, 19 g protein. **Diabetic Exchanges:** 2 lean meat, 2 vegetable, 1-1/2 starch, 1 fat.

Makeover Nacho Beef Bake

PREP: 25 min. **BAKE:** 20 min. **YIELD:** 12 servings

CARLA WEEKS • INDEPENDENCE, IOWA

Almost 100 calories and half the fat were removed from my casserole, while its signature nacho chip topping and hearty beefy filling were salvaged. This version incorporates generous amount of veggies. You'll love it!

1-1/2	lbs. lean ground beef
1	can (15 oz.) black beans, rinsed and drained
1/2	cup water
1	envelope reduced-sodium taco seasoning
2	tubes (8 oz. *each*) refrigerated reduced-fat crescent rolls
1	cup (8 oz.) reduced-fat sour cream
1	cup (4 oz.) shredded reduced-fat cheddar cheese
4	oz. baked nacho tortilla chips (about 2 cups), crushed
3	cups shredded lettuce
3	medium tomatoes, chopped

1. In a large skillet, cook beef over medium heat until meat is no longer pink; drain. Add the beans, water and taco seasoning; mash slightly. Cook and stir for 4-5 minutes or until heated through; set aside.

2. Unroll crescent dough and press onto the bottom and up the sides of a 13-in. x 9-in. baking dish coated with cooking spray; seal seams and perforations. Spoon beef mixture over dough. Spread sour cream over beef mixture; sprinkle with cheese and chips.

3. Bake, uncovered, at 375° for 18-22 minutes or until cheese is melted. Top with lettuce and tomatoes. Serve immediately.

Nutrition Facts: 1 piece equals 357 calories, 15 g fat (6 g saturated fat), 41 mg cholesterol, 728 mg sodium, 34 g carbohydrate, 3 g fiber, 20 g protein.

STIR-FRIED STEAK & VEGGIES

MAKEOVER NACHO BEEF BAKE

Italian Pot Roast C

PREP: 30 min. **COOK:** 6 hours **YIELD:** 8 servings

KAREN BURDELL • LAFAYETTE, COLORADO

I'm always collecting recipes from newspapers and magazines, and this one just sounded too good not to try! I love the slow cooker convenience and the blend of healthful ingredients and aromatic spices.

6	whole peppercorns
4	whole cloves
3	whole allspice
1	cinnamon stick (3 in.)
1	boneless beef chuck roast (2 lbs.)
2	tsp. olive oil
2	celery ribs, sliced
2	medium carrots, sliced
1	large onion, chopped
4	garlic cloves, minced
1	cup sherry or reduced-sodium beef broth
1	can (28 oz.) crushed tomatoes
1/4	tsp. salt

Hot cooked egg noodles, optional

1. Place the peppercorns, cloves, allspice and cinnamon stick on a double thickness of cheesecloth; bring up corners of cloth and tie with string to form a bag. Set aside.

2. In a large skillet, brown meat in oil on all sides; transfer to a 4-qt. slow cooker. Top with celery, carrots and spice bag.

3. In the same pan, saute onion in drippings until tender. Add garlic; cook 1 minute longer. Add sherry, stirring to loosen browned bits from pan. Bring to a boil; cook and stir until liquid is reduced to 2/3 cup. Stir in tomatoes and salt; pour over vegetables.

4. Cover and cook on low for 6-7 hours or until meat and vegetables are tender. Remove meat to a serving platter; keep warm. Discard spice bag. Skim fat from vegetable mixture; serve with beef.

Nutrition Facts: 3 oz. cooked meat with 2/3 cup vegetable mixture (calculated without egg noodles) equals 251 calories, 12 g fat (4 g saturated fat), 74 mg cholesterol, 271 mg sodium, 11 g carbohydrate, 3 g fiber, 24 g protein. **Diabetic Exchanges:** 3 lean meat, 2 vegetable, 1/2 fat.

> Tough cuts of beef, such as boneless beef chuck roast, cook best using a **slow cooking method**, often combined with cooking in a liquid. Select roasts with a cherry-red color and without any gray or brown patches.

Hearty Salisbury Steaks C

PREP/TOTAL TIME: 30 min. **YIELD:** 5 servings

DOROTHY BAYES • SARDIS, OHIO

This is great with mashed potatoes and vegetables. With its down-home taste, it always disappears fast!

1/4	cup egg substitute
1	medium onion, finely chopped
1/2	cup crushed saltines (about 15 crackers)
1/2	tsp. pepper
1	lb. lean ground beef
1	Tbsp. canola oil
1	envelope reduced-sodium onion soup mix
2	Tbsp. all-purpose flour
2	cups water

1. In a large bowl, combine the egg substitute, onion, saltines and pepper. Crumble beef over mixture and mix well. Shape into five patties. In a large skillet, cook patties in oil over medium heat for 3 minutes on each side or until lightly browned. Remove patties and keep warm; drain drippings.

2. In a small bowl combine the soup mix, flour and water; stir into skillet. Bring to a boil. Return patties to skillet. Reduce heat; cover and simmer for 5-7 minutes or until meat is no longer pink.

Nutrition Facts: 1 patty with 1/4 cup gravy equals 233 calories, 10 g fat (3 g saturated fat), 45 mg cholesterol, 418 mg sodium, 14 g carbohydrate, 1 g fiber, 20 g protein. **Diabetic Exchanges:** 2 lean meat, 1 starch, 1 fat.

Makeover Tater-Topped Casserole

PREP: 15 min. **BAKE:** 55 min. **YIELD:** 8 servings

SCOTT WOODWARD • ELKHORN, WISCONSIN

I love Tater Tots, and this casserole is a delicious dinner, but I wanted a healthier version. The "Healthy Cooking" experts slashed the fat from my favorite recipe while keeping all the tots!

1	lb. lean ground beef
1/2	lb. extra-lean ground turkey
1	pkg. (16 oz.) frozen mixed vegetables, thawed and drained
3/4	cup French-fried onions
1	can (10-3/4 oz.) reduced-fat reduced-sodium condensed cream of celery soup, undiluted
1	can (10-3/4 oz.) reduced-fat reduced-sodium condensed cream of chicken soup, undiluted
1/2	cup fat-free milk
4	cups frozen Tater Tots, thawed

1. In a large skillet, cook the beef and turkey over medium heat until no longer pink. In a 13-in. x 9-in. baking dish coated with cooking spray, layer the meat mixture, vegetables and onions.

2. In a small bowl, combine soups and milk; spread over onions. Top with Tater Tots. Bake, uncovered, at 350° for 55-60 minutes or until golden brown.

Nutrition Facts: 1 cup equals 340 calories, 14 g fat (4 g saturated fat), 44 mg cholesterol, 657 mg sodium, 33 g carbohydrate, 4 g fiber, 22 g protein.

Hamburger Corn Bread Casserole

PREP: 25 min. **BAKE:** 15 min. **YIELD:** 6 servings

KATHY GARRISON • FORT WORTH, TEXAS

Welcome friends in from the cold with a comforting hot bake that all ages will adore. A layer of corn bread makes this meal-in-one both filling and delicious!

- 1 lb. lean ground beef
- 1 small onion, chopped
- 1 can (15 oz.) ranch-style beans
- 1 can (14-1/2 oz.) diced tomatoes, undrained
- 1 tsp. chili powder
- 1 tsp. Worcestershire sauce

TOPPING:
- 1/2 cup all-purpose flour
- 1/2 cup cornmeal
- 2 Tbsp. sugar
- 2 tsp. baking powder
- 1/4 tsp. salt
- 1 egg, beaten
- 1/2 cup fat-free milk
- 1 Tbsp. canola oil

1. In a large skillet, cook beef and onion over medium heat until meat is no longer pink; drain. Add the beans, tomatoes, chili powder and Worcestershire sauce; bring to a boil. Reduce the heat; simmer, uncovered, for 5 minutes.

2. Transfer to an 11-in. x 7-in. baking dish coated with cooking spray. For topping, in a small bowl, combine the flour, cornmeal, sugar, baking powder and salt. Combine the egg, milk and oil; stir into dry ingredients just until moistened. Spoon over filling; gently spread to cover the top.

3. Bake, uncovered, at 425° for 14-18 minutes or until filling is bubbly and a toothpick inserted into topping comes out clean. Let stand for 5 minutes before cutting.

Nutrition Facts: 1 serving equals 339 calories, 10 g fat (3 g saturated fat), 73 mg cholesterol, 722 mg sodium, 38 g carbohydrate, 6 g fiber, 22 g protein. **Diabetic Exchanges:** 3 lean meat, 2 starch, 1 vegetable.

Family-Favorite Meat Loaf

PREP: 15 min. **BAKE:** 45 min. **YIELD:** 6 servings

COLETTE GEROW • RAYTOWN, MISSOURI

Combining ground beef with ground turkey is the key to this flavorful meat loaf that has become a menu staple. Horseradish adds just the right amount of zip. It has my husband's seal of approval!

- 1/3 cup egg substitute
- 1 can (6 oz.) tomato paste, *divided*
- 2 Tbsp. Dijon mustard
- 2 tsp. prepared horseradish, *divided*
- 1/2 cup quick-cooking oats
- 1 envelope onion soup mix
- 1-1/2 tsp. garlic powder
- 1 tsp. steak seasoning
- 1 lb. lean ground beef
- 1/2 lb. lean ground turkey
- 1 tsp. water
- 1/2 tsp. sugar

1. In a large bowl, combine the egg substitute, 1/2 cup tomato paste, mustard, 1 tsp. horseradish, oats, soup mix, garlic powder and steak seasoning. Crumble beef and turkey over mixture and mix well.

2. Shape into a loaf and place in an 11-in. x 7-in. baking dish coated with cooking spray. Combine the water, sugar, remaining tomato paste and remaining horseradish; spread over meat loaf.

3. Bake, uncovered, at 350° for 45-55 minutes or until a meat thermometer reads 165°. Drain if necessary.

Editor's Note: This recipe was tested with McCormick's Montreal Steak Seasoning. Look for it in the spice aisle.

Nutrition Facts: 1 slice equals 250 calories, 10 g fat (3 g saturated fat), 76 mg cholesterol, 763 mg sodium, 16 g carbohydrate, 3 g fiber, 24 g protein. **Diabetic Exchanges:** 3 lean meat, 1 vegetable, 1 fat, 1/2 starch.

FAMILY-FAVORITE MEAT LOAF

HAMBURGER CORN BREAD CASSEROLE

Red, White and Blue Pita Pockets

PREP: 15 min. + marinating **COOK:** 5 min.
YIELD: 4 servings

CHARLENE CHAMBERS • ORMOND BEACH, FLORIDA

Completely packed with delicious fillings, these pockets get their patriotic name from red peppers, white sour cream and tangy blue cheese. But don't wait for the Fourth of July to serve them; they're fantastic all year!

2	Tbsp. red wine vinegar
4	tsp. olive oil
2	garlic cloves, minced
1	lb. beef top sirloin steak, thinly sliced
1/2	cup fat-free sour cream
1/3	cup crumbled blue cheese
2	whole wheat pita breads (6 in.), halved
2	cups torn red leaf lettuce
1/2	cup roasted sweet red peppers, drained and cut into strips
1/4	cup sliced red onion

1. In a large resealable plastic bag, combine the vinegar, oil and garlic; add the beef. Seal bag and turn to coat; refrigerate for 8 hours or overnight.

2. In a small bowl, combine sour cream and blue cheese; set aside. Drain and discard marinade.

3. In a large nonstick skillet or wok coated with cooking spray, stir-fry beef for 2-3 minutes or until no longer pink. Line pita halves with lettuce, red peppers and onion; fill each with 1/3 cup beef. Serve with sour cream mixture.

Nutrition Facts: 1 filled pita half equals 351 calories, 12 g fat (4 g saturated fat), 59 mg cholesterol, 522 mg sodium, 26 g carbohydrate, 3 g fiber, 32 g protein. **Diabetic Exchanges:** 4 lean meat, 1-1/2 fat, 1 starch, 1 vegetable.

Slow-Cooked Caribbean Pot Roast

PREP: 30 min. **COOK:** 6 hours **YIELD:** 10 servings

JENN TIDWELL • FAIR OAKS, CALIFORNIA

I put this dish together throughout the fall and winter seasons, but considering how simple it is to prepare, anytime is a great time to enjoy it!

2	medium sweet potatoes, cubed
2	large carrots, sliced
1/4	cup chopped celery
1	boneless beef chuck roast (2-1/2 lbs.)
1	Tbsp. canola oil
1	large onion, chopped
2	garlic cloves, minced
1	Tbsp. all-purpose flour
1	Tbsp. sugar
1	Tbsp. brown sugar
1	tsp. ground cumin
3/4	tsp. salt
3/4	tsp. ground coriander
3/4	tsp. chili powder
1/2	tsp. dried oregano
1/8	tsp. ground cinnamon
3/4	tsp. grated orange peel
3/4	tsp. baking cocoa
1	can (15 oz.) tomato sauce

1. Place potatoes, carrots and celery in a 5-qt. slow cooker. In a large skillet, brown the meat in oil on all sides. Transfer meat to slow cooker.

2. In the same skillet, saute onion in drippings until tender. Add garlic; cook 1 minute longer. Combine the flour, sugar, brown sugar, seasonings, orange peel and cocoa. Stir in tomato sauce; add to skillet and heat through. Pour over beef. Cover and cook on low for 6-8 hours or until beef and vegetables are tender.

Nutrition Facts: 3 oz. cooked beef with 1/2 cup vegetable mixture equals 278 calories, 12 g fat (4 g saturated fat), 74 mg cholesterol, 453 mg sodium, 16 g carbohydrate, 3 g fiber, 25 g protein. **Diabetic Exchanges:** 3 lean meat, 1 starch, 1 vegetable, 1/2 fat.

RED, WHITE AND BLUE PITA POCKETS

SLOW-COOKED CARIBBEAN POT ROAST

Family-Favorite Cheeseburger Pasta

PREP/TOTAL TIME: 30 min. **YIELD:** 4 servings

RAQUEL HAGGARD • EDMOND, OKLAHOMA

I created this recipe to satisfy a cheeseburger craving. What a delicious, healthy classic!

1-1/2	cups uncooked whole wheat penne pasta
3/4	lb. lean ground beef
2	Tbsp. finely chopped onion
1	can (14-1/2 oz.) no-salt-added diced tomatoes
2	Tbsp. dill pickle relish
2	Tbsp. prepared mustard
2	Tbsp. ketchup
1	tsp. steak seasoning
1/4	tsp. seasoned salt
3/4	cup shredded reduced-fat cheddar cheese

Chopped green onions, optional

1. Cook the pasta according to package directions. Meanwhile, in a large skillet, cook beef and onion over medium heat until meat is no longer pink; drain. Drain pasta; add to meat mixture.

2. Stir in the tomatoes, relish, mustard, ketchup, steak seasoning and seasoned salt. Bring to a boil. Reduce heat; simmer, uncovered, for 5 minutes.

3. Sprinkle with cheese. Remove from the heat; cover and let stand until cheese is melted. Garnish with green onions if desired.

Editor's Note: This recipe was tested with McCormick's Montreal Steak Seasoning. Look for it in the spice aisle.

Nutrition Facts: 1-1/2 cups equals 391 calories, 12 g fat (6 g saturated fat), 57 mg cholesterol, 759 mg sodium, 43 g carbohydrate, 4 g fiber, 28 g protein. **Diabetic Exchanges:** 3 lean meat, 2 starch, 1 vegetable, 1/2 fat.

Not crazy about pickle relish? Leave it out of the recipe for the cheeseburger pasta. If you like extra onions on your burger, add more to the pasta dish. Switch the cheese with reduced-fat Swiss and add some sliced and sauteed mushrooms for a whole new flavor!

Italian Beef Barley Stew

PREP: 30 min. **COOK:** 1-1/4 hours
YIELD: 10 servings (3-1/2 qt.)

JACQUELINE KLOESS • IOWA CITY, IOWA

With potatoes, carrots, roast beef and barley, this is a hearty meal-in-a-bowl. Best of all, the leftovers freeze extremely well, so you can store some away for busy nights. A healthy meal is always at hand when this stew is in the freezer.

- 1 boneless beef chuck roast (2 lbs.), cut into 3/4-in. cubes
- 3 medium onions, coarsely chopped
- 4 celery ribs, thinly sliced
- 3 medium carrots, halved lengthwise and thinly sliced
- 2 medium potatoes, peeled and cubed
- 2 garlic cloves, minced
- 1 can (46 oz.) tomato juice
- 1 can (28 oz.) diced tomatoes, undrained
- 1 bay leaf
- 1-1/2 tsp. dried marjoram
- 1-1/2 tsp. dried thyme
- 1/2 tsp. salt
- 1/4 tsp. coarsely ground pepper
- 1/2 cup medium pearl barley

1. In a Dutch oven coated with cooking spray, cook beef and onions over medium heat until meat is no longer pink; drain. Stir in the celery, carrots, potatoes and garlic. Cook and stir 5 minutes longer.

2. Stir in the tomato juice, tomatoes, bay leaf and seasonings. Bring to a boil. Stir in barley. Reduce heat; cover and simmer for 1-1/4 to 1-1/2 hours or until meat and barley are tender.

3. Discard bay leaf. Serve desired amount. Cool the remaining soup; transfer to freezer containers. Freeze for up to 3 months.

4. To use frozen soup: Thaw in the refrigerator overnight. Place in a saucepan and heat through.

Nutrition Facts: 1-1/3 cups equals 281 calories, 9 g fat (3 g saturated fat), 59 mg cholesterol, 636 mg sodium, 30 g carbohydrate, 6 g fiber, 22 g protein. **Diabetic Exchanges:** 3 lean meat, 2 starch.

South of the Border Sirloin [C]

PREP: 15 min. + marinating **BROIL:** 5 min.
YIELD: 4 servings

GILDA LESTER • WILMINGTON, NORTH CAROLINA

Marinated in beer and jalapenos, these steaks have a mild kick the whole family will love! They're topped with veggies, bread crumbs and cheese for a fussed-over look and very special flavor. But they're oh-so-easy to prepare!

- 1 bottle (12 oz.) light *or* nonalcoholic beer
- 1 medium onion, chopped
- 3 garlic cloves, minced
- 1 Tbsp. chili powder
- 1 tsp. salt
- 1 tsp. pepper
- 1 beef top sirloin steak (1 lb.)

TOPPING:
- 2 large onions, thinly sliced
- 5 tsp. olive oil, *divided*
- 2 jalapeno peppers, seeded and minced
- 1 medium sweet red pepper, julienned
- 3 garlic cloves, minced
- 3 Tbsp. dry bread crumbs
- 3 Tbsp. shredded reduced-fat cheddar cheese

1. In a large resealable plastic bag, combine the first six ingredients. Cut steak into four serving-size pieces; place in bag. Seal bag and turn to coat; refrigerate for up to 2 hours.

2. Meanwhile, in a large ovenproof skillet, cook the onions in 2 tsp. oil over medium heat for 15-20 minutes or until onions are golden brown, stirring occasionally. Add peppers and garlic; cook 4 minutes longer. Remove and keep warm.

3. Drain and discard the marinade. In the same skillet over medium heat, cook steak in 2 tsp. oil for 3-4 minutes on each side or until the meat reaches desired doneness (for medium-rare, a meat thermometer should read 145°; medium, 160°; well-done, 170°).

4. Spoon the onion mixture over steaks. In a small bowl, combine the bread crumbs, cheese and remaining oil; sprinkle over tops. Broil 3-4 in. from the heat for 2-3 minutes or until golden brown.

Editor's Note: When cutting hot peppers, disposable gloves are recommended. Avoid touching your face.

Nutrition Facts: 1 serving equals 280 calories, 12 g fat (3 g saturated fat), 50 mg cholesterol, 228 mg sodium, 15 g carbohydrate, 3 g fiber, 28 g protein. **Diabetic Exchanges:** 3 lean meat, 2 vegetable, 1 fat.

Hamburger Chop Suey

PREP/TOTAL TIME: 30 min. **YIELD:** 6 servings

BETH PISULA • FREEPORT, ILLINOIS

Fast, hearty and colorful, this chop suey uses up those summer garden peppers and spinach. If you happen to have pea pods, they'd be excellent in this mix. Visit your produce department for fresh baby corn or add the canned variety.

- 1 Tbsp. cornstarch
- 2 tsp. minced fresh gingerroot
- 1 tsp. reduced-sodium beef bouillon granules
- 3/4 cup water
- 1/3 cup reduced-sodium soy sauce

CHOP SUEY:
- 1 lb. lean ground beef
- 2 celery ribs, sliced
- 1 cup sliced fresh mushrooms
- 1 medium green pepper, sliced
- 1 medium sweet red pepper, sliced
- 1 medium onion, halved and thinly sliced
- 1 can (14 oz.) bean sprouts, drained
- 1 can (8 oz.) sliced water chestnuts, drained
- 1 cup fresh spinach, torn
- 3 cups hot cooked rice

1. In a small bowl, combine the cornstarch, ginger and bouillon; stir in the water and soy sauce until blended. Set aside.

2. In a large nonstick skillet or wok, stir-fry the beef, celery, mushrooms, peppers and onion until meat is no longer pink and vegetables are tender. Drain. Stir in the bean sprouts, water chestnuts and spinach.

3. Stir the reserved sauce mixture; add to the pan. Bring to a boil; cook and stir for 1-2 minutes or until thickened. Serve with rice.

Nutrition Facts: 1-1/3 cups chop suey with 1/2 cup rice equals 287 calories, 6 g fat (2 g saturated fat), 37 mg cholesterol, 679 mg sodium, 37 g carbohydrate, 4 g fiber, 20 g protein. **Diabetic Exchanges:** 2 lean meat, 2 vegetable, 1-1/2 starch.

Serving Hamburger Chop Suey tonight? Picking up a tasty **low-fat dessert** on your way home is easier than you might think. Most large grocery chains carry boxed fortune cookies in the ethnic cooking aisle. Or, grab some mint sherbert. Both treats are low in fat and calories.

HAMBURGER CHOP SUEY

Succulent Beef Skewers C

PREP: 15 min. + marinating **GRILL:** 10 min.
YIELD: 6 skewers

AGNES WARD • STRATFORD, ONTARIO

These are no ordinary beef kabobs! They're herb-infused and need to marinate at least 2 hours or overnight for the best flavor. If you feel like splurging, this recipe's also fantastic with beef tenderloin.

2	Tbsp. Dijon mustard
2	Tbsp. balsamic vinegar
1	Tbsp. brown sugar
1	Tbsp. olive oil
1	Tbsp. minced fresh rosemary *or* 1 tsp. dried rosemary, crushed
1-1/2	tsp. minced fresh thyme *or* 1/2 tsp. dried thyme
2	garlic cloves, minced
1/2	tsp. salt
1/2	tsp. pepper
1-1/2	lbs. boneless beef sirloin steak, cut into 1-1/2-in. cubes

1. In a large resealable plastic bag, combine the first nine ingredients. Add the beef; seal bag and turn to coat. Refrigerate for at least 2 hours or overnight, turning occasionally. Drain and discard marinade.

2. Coat grill rack with cooking spray before starting the grill. Thread beef onto six metal or soaked wooden skewers. Grill, covered, over medium-hot heat for 8-10 minutes or until beef reaches desired doneness, turning occasionally.

Nutrition Facts: 1 skewer equals 170 calories, 7 g fat (2 g saturated fat), 64 mg cholesterol, 297 mg sodium, 4 g carbohydrate, trace fiber, 22 g protein. **Diabetic Exchanges:** 3 lean meat, 1 fat.

Makeover Gourmet Enchiladas

PREP: 35 min. **BAKE:** 35 min.
YIELD: 2 dishes (6 servings each)

BETH DAUENHAUER • PUEBLO, COLORADO

I love cheesy entrees but wanted to cut the fat from a favorite of mine. With this better-for-you recipe, now I can enjoy the great flavor of these enchiladas more often!

1	lb. lean ground beef
1	lb. extra-lean ground turkey
1	large onion, chopped
1-1/2	cups (12 oz.) 2% cottage cheese
1-1/2	cups (12 oz.) reduced-fat sour cream
2	cans (4 oz. *each*) chopped green chilies
1/2	tsp. ground cumin
1/2	tsp. ground coriander

SAUCE:

1	medium onion, chopped
2	cans (8 oz. *each*) tomato sauce
1	cup salsa
1	Tbsp. chili powder
1	tsp. dried oregano
1/2	tsp. garlic powder
1/2	tsp. dried thyme
12	whole wheat tortilla (8 in.), warmed
3/4	cup shredded cheddar cheese, divided

1. In a large skillet, cook the beef, turkey and onion over medium heat until meat is no longer pink; drain. Stir in the cottage cheese, sour cream, chilies, cumin and coriander; set aside.

2. For sauce, in a large nonstick skillet coated with cooking spray, saute onion until tender. Stir in the tomato sauce, salsa, chili powder, oregano, garlic powder and thyme. Bring to a boil. Reduce heat; simmer, uncovered, for 15-20 minutes or until slightly thickened.

3. Place a heaping 1/2 cup meat mixture down the center of each tortilla. Roll up and place seam side down in two 13-in. x 9-in. baking dishes coated with cooking spray. Pour sauce over top.

4. Cover and freeze one dish for up to 3 months. Bake the remaining dish, uncovered, at 350° for 30-35 minutes or until heated through. Sprinkle with 6 Tbsp. cheese; bake 5 minutes longer or until cheese is melted.

SUCCULENT BEEF SKEWERS

MAKEOVER GOURMET ENCHILADAS

5. **To use frozen enchiladas:** Thaw in refrigerator overnight. Remove from the refrigerator 30 minutes before baking. Cover and bake as directed.

Nutrition Facts: 1 enchilada equals 358 calories, 12 g fat (5 g saturated fat), 55 mg cholesterol, 715 mg sodium, 33 g carbohydrate, 3 g fiber, 28 g protein. **Diabetic Exchanges:** 3 lean meat, 2 starch, 1 vegetable, 1 fat.

Pizza Joes

PREP/TOTAL TIME: 30 min. **YIELD:** 6 servings

CONNIE PETTIT • LOGAN, OHIO

If you're tired of the same old, boring sloppy joes, here's a tasty twist! These messy, kid-friendly sandwiches have a definite pizza flavor that families will love, but be sure to serve them with a fork!

- 1 lb. lean ground beef
- 1 medium onion, chopped
- 1/4 cup chopped green pepper
- 1 jar (14 oz.) pizza sauce
- 3 oz. sliced turkey pepperoni (about 50 slices), chopped
- 1/2 tsp. dried basil
- 1/4 tsp. dried oregano
- 6 hamburger buns, split
- 6 Tbsp. shredded part-skim mozzarella cheese

1. In a large nonstick skillet, cook the beef, onion and pepper over medium heat until meat is no longer pink. Drain if necessary. Stir in the pizza sauce, pepperoni and herbs. Bring to a boil. Reduce heat; cover and simmer for 10 minutes.

2. Spoon 2/3 cup beef mixture onto each bun; sprinkle with cheese. Place on a baking sheet. Broil

3-4 in. from the heat for 1 minute or until cheese is melted. Replace tops.

Nutrition Facts: 1 sandwich equals 329 calories, 11 g fat (4 g saturated fat), 59 mg cholesterol, 825 mg sodium, 29 g carbohydrate, 3 g fiber, 26 g protein.

Grilled Red Chili Steak C

PREP: 10 min. **GRILL:** 10 min. + standing
YIELD: 4 serving

MARY RELYEA • CANASTOTA, NEW YORK

This super-simple recipe turns regular steak into a mouth-watering entree. I like it best with a little salsa on the side.

- 3 Tbsp. chili powder
- 2 tsp. brown sugar
- 2 tsp. pepper
- 2 garlic cloves, minced
- 1/2 tsp. salt
- 1/2 tsp. dried oregano
- 1/4 tsp. ground cumin
- 1 lb. boneless beef sirloin steak

Salsa

1. Combine the first seven ingredients; rub over the steak.

2. Grill steak, covered, over medium heat for 5-7 minutes on each side or until meat reaches desired doneness (for medium-rare, a meat thermometer should read 145°; medium, 160°; well-done, 170°). Let stand for 10 minutes before slicing. Serve with salsa.

Nutrition Facts: 3 oz. cooked beef (calculated without salsa) equals 160 calories, 6 g fat (2 g saturated fat), 64 mg cholesterol, 269 mg sodium, 4 g carbohydrate, 2 g fiber, 22 g protein. **Diabetic Exchanges:** 3 lean meat, 1/2 fat.

Enchilada Casser-Ole!

PREP: 25 min. **BAKE:** 30 min. **YIELD:** 8 servings

MARSHA WILLS • HOMOSASSA, FLORIDA

Packed with Southwestern flavor, this main course is as simple as it is simply delicious!

1	lb. lean ground beef
1	large onion, chopped
2	cups salsa
1	can (15 oz.) black beans, rinsed and drained
1/4	cup reduced-fat Italian salad dressing
2	Tbsp. reduced-sodium taco seasoning
1/4	tsp. ground cumin
6	flour tortillas (8 in.)
3/4	cup reduced-fat sour cream
1	cup (4 oz.) shredded reduced-fat Mexican cheese blend
1	cup shredded lettuce
1	medium tomato, chopped
1/4	cup minced fresh cilantro

1. In a large skillet, cook beef and onion over medium heat until meat is no longer pink; drain. Stir in the salsa, beans, dressing, taco seasoning and cumin. Place three tortillas in a 2-qt. baking dish coated with cooking spray. Layer with half of the meat mixture, sour cream and cheese. Repeat layers.

2. Cover and bake at 400° for 25 minutes. Uncover; bake 5-10 minutes longer or until heated through. Let stand for 5 minutes before topping with lettuce, tomato and cilantro.

Nutrition Facts: 1 piece equals 357 calories, 12 g fat (5 g saturated fat), 45 mg cholesterol, 864 mg sodium, 37 g carbohydrate, 3 g fiber, 23 g protein

Crab-Stuffed Filet Mignon C

PREP/TOTAL TIME: 30 min. **YIELD:** 2 servings

SHANE HARRIS • ABINGDON, VIRGINIA

Here's a perfectly elegant entree for you and someone special. They'll be impressed with the flavor...you'll love that it's so fast and easy! The filets are ideal for Christmas, New Year's Eve or Valentine's Day.

1/2	cup lump crabmeat, drained
2	Tbsp. shredded Parmesan cheese
1	Tbsp. chopped green onion
1	tsp. butter, melted
2	beef tenderloin steaks (6 oz. *each*)
1/4	tsp. salt
1/8	tsp. pepper

1. In a small bowl, combine the crabmeat, cheese, onion and butter. Sprinkle steaks with salt and pepper. Cut a horizontal slit through each steak to within 1/2 in. of the opposite side, forming a pocket. Fill with 1/2 cup crab mixture. Secure with kitchen string if necessary.

2. Broil 4 in. from the heat for 7-9 minutes on each side or until meat reaches desired doneness (for medium-rare, a meat thermometer should read 145°; medium, 160°; well-done, 170°). Let stand for 5 minutes before serving.

Nutrition Facts: 1 stuffed filet equals 318 calories, 14 g fat (6 g saturated fat), 113 mg cholesterol, 506 mg sodium, trace carbohydrate, trace fiber, 45 g protein.

My Take on Mom's Meat Loaf ⬤

PREP: 20 min. **BAKE:** 35 min. + standing
YIELD: 4 servings

BRENDA MOEHRINGER • GANSEVOORT, NEW YORK

Here's a lower-in-fat-and-salt take on my mother's original recipe. I substituted fresh ingredients like garlic, mushrooms and onions for dried onion soup mix and garlic powder. It's still juicy, hearty and tastes like home.

1	egg white
1	Tbsp. steak sauce
1	Tbsp. Worcestershire sauce
5	medium fresh mushrooms, finely chopped
1/2	cup seasoned bread crumbs
1/3	cup finely chopped sweet onion

2	Tbsp. grated Parmesan cheese
2	garlic cloves, minced
1	tsp. dried sage leaves
1/2	tsp. pepper
1/8	tsp. salt
1	lb. lean ground beef

Barbecue sauce, optional

1. In a large bowl, combine the first 11 ingredients. Crumble beef over mixture and mix well. Shape into a loaf; place in an 11-in. x 7-in. baking dish coated with cooking spray.

2. Bake, uncovered, at 350° for 35-40 minutes or until no pink remains and a meat thermometer reads 160°. Let stand for 10 minutes before slicing. Drizzle with barbecue sauce is desired.

Nutrition Facts: 2 slices (calculated without barbecue sauce) equals 264 calories, 11 g fat (4 g saturated fat), 71 mg cholesterol, 503 mg sodium, 15 g carbohydrate, 1 g fiber, 26 g protein. **Diabetic Exchanges:** 3 lean meat, 1 starch, 1 fat.

The next time you have a hankering for something comforting, consider a hearty meat loaf supper. Stick to lean ground beef and take advantage of herbs and low-salt seasonings. Bake the loaf in baking dish (not a loaf pan), so the fat is able to run off the loaf.

MY TAKE ON MOM'S MEAT LOAF

CRAB-STUFFED FILET MIGNON

ROAST TURKEY BREAST WITH ROSEMARY GRAVY

MEDITERRANEAN CHICKEN WITH SPAGHETTI SQUASH

POTATO-CRUSTED CHICKEN CASSEROLE

Chicken & Turkey

Not only is poultry a quick favorite with today's cooks, but it's low in calories, fat and carbohydrates, making it a perfect fit with health-minded moms. Best of all, chicken and turkey offer all of the comforting flavors families crave.

Mediterranean Chicken With Spaghetti Squash

PREP: 35 min. **COOK:** 35 min. **YIELD:** 6 servings

JAYNE MARTIN • STRATHCLAIR, MANITOBA

Brimming with classic Mediterranean ingredients, this restaurant-quality dish will be an instant dinnertime hit.

1	medium spaghetti squash
1-1/2	lbs. boneless skinless chicken breasts, cut into 1/2-in. cubes
5	center-cut bacon strips, chopped
1	medium leek (white portion only), coarsely chopped
4	garlic cloves, minced
3	Tbsp. all-purpose flour
1	cup reduced-sodium chicken broth
1/2	cup white wine *or* additional reduced-sodium chicken broth
1/3	cup half-and-half cream
2	plum tomatoes, chopped
1	can (2-1/4 oz.) sliced ripe olives, drained
1/3	cup grated Parmesan cheese
1-1/2	tsp. minced fresh sage *or* 1/2 tsp. rubbed sage
1	tsp. minced fresh thyme *or* 1/4 tsp. dried thyme
1/2	tsp. salt
1/8	tsp. pepper

1. Cut squash in half lengthwise; discard seeds. Place squash cut side down on a microwave-safe plate. Microwave, uncovered, on high for 15-18 minutes or until tender.

2. Meanwhile, in a large nonstick skillet coated with cooking spray, cook chicken over medium heat until no longer pink; drain. Remove from the skillet.

3. In the same skillet, cook bacon and leek over medium heat until bacon is crisp. Using a slotted spoon, remove bacon mixture to paper towels. Add garlic; cook for 1 minute. Stir in flour until blended; gradually add the broth, wine and cream. Bring to a boil; cook and stir for 1-2 minutes or until thickened. Stir in remaining ingredients. Add chicken and bacon mixture; heat through.

4. When squash is cool enough to handle, use a fork to separate strands. Serve with chicken mixture.

Nutrition Facts: 3/4 cup chicken mixture with 1 cup squash equals 340 calories, 12 g fat (4 g saturated fat), 82 mg cholesterol, 656 mg sodium, 27 g carbohydrate, 5 g fiber, 30 g protein. **Diabetic Exchanges:** 4 very lean meat, 2 fat, 1-1/2 starch.

Roast Turkey Breast With Rosemary Gravy F S C

PREP: 20 min. **BAKE:** 1-3/4 hours + standing **YIELD:** 18 servings (1-1/3 cups gravy)

REBECCCA CLARK • WARRIOR, ALABAMA

A velvety gravy coats this remarkably tender and juicy turkey breast that's perfect for a special get-together.

2	medium apples, sliced
1-1/2	cups sliced leeks (white portion only)
2-1/4	cups reduced-sodium chicken broth, *divided*
1	bone-in turkey breast (6 lbs.)
1	Tbsp. canola oil
2	tsp. minced fresh rosemary, *divided*
3	Tbsp. reduced-fat butter
1/4	cup all-purpose flour

1. Arrange apples and leeks in a roasting pan; add 1 cup broth. Place turkey breast over apple mixture. In a small bowl, combine oil and 1-1/2 tsp. rosemary. With fingers, carefully loosen skin from the turkey breast; rub rosemary mixture under the skin. Secure skin to underside of breast with toothpicks.

2. Bake, uncovered, at 325° for 1-3/4 to 2-1/4 hours or until a meat thermometer reads 170°, basting every 30 minutes. Cover loosely with foil if turkey browns too quickly. Cover and let stand for 15 minutes before carving, reserving 1/4 cup pan juices. Discard apples and leeks.

3. In a small saucepan, melt butter; add flour and remaining rosemary until blended, stirring constantly. Skim fat from pan juices. Gradually add pan juices and remaining broth to saucepan. Bring to a boil. Cook and stir for 1 minute or until thickened. Serve with turkey.

Editor's Note: This recipe was tested with Land O'Lakes light stick butter.

Nutrition Facts: 4 oz. cooked turkey with 1 Tbsp. gravy equals 151 calories, 3 g fat (1 g saturated fat), 81 mg cholesterol, 136 mg sodium, 2 g carbohydrate, trace fiber, 29 g protein. **Diabetic Exchange:** 4 very lean meat.

Texan Ranch Chicken Casserole

PREP: 25 min. BAKE: 30 min. YIELD: 8 servings

KENDRA DOSS • SMITHVILLE, MISSOURI

Every time I serve this creamy casserole, it gets rave reviews. The recipe was passed down to me and is so good! It's really easy to make, freezes well and has just a touch of heat. If your family likes more spice, add some jalapenos!

- 1 large onion, finely chopped
- 2 celery ribs, finely chopped
- 1 medium green pepper, finely chopped
- 1 medium sweet red pepper, finely chopped
- 1 Tbsp. canola oil
- 1 garlic clove, minced
- 3 cups cubed cooked chicken breast
- 1 can (10-3/4 oz.) reduced-fat reduced-sodium condensed cream of celery soup, undiluted
- 1 can (10-3/4 oz.) reduced-fat reduced-sodium condensed cream of chicken soup, undiluted
- 1 can (10 oz.) diced tomatoes and green chilies, undrained
- 1 Tbsp. chili powder
- 12 corn tortillas (6 in.), cut into 1-in. strips
- 2 cups (8 oz.) shredded reduced-fat cheddar cheese, *divided*

1. In a large nonstick skillet coated with cooking spray, saute the onion, celery and peppers in oil until crisp-tender. Add garlic; cook 1 minute longer. Stir in the chicken, soups, tomatoes and chili powder.

2. Line the bottom of a 3-qt. baking dish with half of the tortilla strips; top with half of the chicken mixture and 1 cup cheese. Repeat layers. Bake, uncovered, at 350° for 30-35 minutes or until bubbly.

Nutrition Facts: 1 cup equals 329 calories, 12 g fat (5 g saturated fat), 65 mg cholesterol, 719 mg sodium, 31 g carbohydrate, 3 g fiber, 26 g protein. **Diabetic Exchanges:** 3 lean meat, 1-1/2 starch, 1 vegetable, 1 fat.

Makeover Cajun Chicken Pasta

PREP: 20 min. COOK: 20 min. YIELD: 6 servings

HEATHER PRIVRATSKY • GREENFIELD, WISCONSIN

This slimmed-down dish has less sodium, calories and saturated fat than my original, but all the same rich creamy flavor!

- 6 boneless skinless chicken breast halves (4 oz. each)
- 2 Tbsp. Cajun seasoning, *divided*
- 2-1/4 cups uncooked penne pasta
- 1 large onion, chopped
- 2 tsp. olive oil
- 2 garlic cloves, minced
- 1 can (28 oz.) crushed tomatoes, drained
- 1/4 tsp. pepper
- 1-1/2 cups half-and-half cream

1. Rub chicken with 1 Tbsp. Cajun seasoning. Coat grill rack with cooking spray before starting the grill. Grill chicken, covered, over medium heat for 4-7 minutes on each side or until juices run clear; keep warm.

2. Meanwhile, in a large saucepan, cook pasta according to package directions. In a Dutch oven coated with cooking spray, saute onion in oil until crisp-tender. Add garlic and remaining Cajun seasoning; saute 1 minute longer. Stir in the tomatoes and pepper.

3. Drain pasta; add to the onion mixture. Stir in cream; heat through (do not boil). Serve chicken with pasta.

Nutrition Facts: 1 chicken breast half with 1 cup pasta equals 421 calories, 12 g fat (5 g saturated fat), 93 mg cholesterol, 803 mg sodium, 45 g carbohydrate, 4 g fiber, 33 g protein.

Indonesian Peanut Chicken

PREP: 15 min. COOK: 4 hours YIELD: 6 servings

SARAH NEWMAN • BROOKLYN CENTER, MINNESOTA

Here's a great make-ahead recipe! I cut up fresh chicken, put it in a bag with the remaining slow-cooker ingredients and freeze.

- 1-1/2 lbs. boneless skinless chicken breasts, cut into 1-in. cubes
- 1/3 cup chopped onion
- 1/3 cup water
- 1/4 cup reduced-fat creamy peanut butter

TEXAN RANCH CHICKEN CASSEROLE

MAKEOVER CAJUN CHICKEN PASTA

3 Tbsp. chili sauce
1/4 tsp. salt
1/4 tsp. cayenne pepper
1/4 tsp. pepper
3 cups cooked brown rice
6 Tbsp. chopped salted peanuts
6 Tbsp. chopped sweet red pepper

1. Place chicken in a 4-qt. slow cooker. In a small bowl, combine the onion, water, peanut butter, chili sauce, salt, cayenne and pepper; pour over chicken. Cover and cook on low for 4-6 hours or until chicken is tender.

2. Shred meat with two forks and return to slow cooker; heat through. Serve with rice. Sprinkle with peanuts and red pepper.

Nutrition Facts: 1/2 cup chicken mixture with 1/2 cup rice equals 353 calories, 12 g fat (2 g saturated fat), 63 mg cholesterol, 370 mg sodium, 31 g carbohydrate, 3 g fiber, 31 g protein. **Diabetic Exchanges:** 3 very lean meat, 2 starch, 2 fat.

Spicy Chicken Breasts With Pepper Peach Relish

PREP: 20 min. **GRILL:** 15 min. **YIELD:** 4 servings

ROXANNE CHAN • ALBANY, CALIFORNIA

This summery entree is simply packed with the good-for-your-eyes vitamins found in both peaches and peppers.

1/2 tsp. salt
1/4 tsp. *each* ground cinnamon, cloves and nutmeg
4 boneless skinless chicken breast halves (6 oz. each)

GLAZE:
1/4 cup peach preserves
2 Tbsp. lemon juice
1/4 tsp. crushed red pepper flakes
RELISH:
2 medium peaches, peeled and finely chopped
1/3 cup finely chopped sweet red pepper
1/3 cup finely chopped green pepper
1 green onion, finely chopped
2 Tbsp. minced fresh mint

1. Combine the salt, cinnamon, cloves and nutmeg; rub over chicken. In a small bowl, combine the glaze ingredients; set aside. In a small bowl, combine the peaches, peppers, onion, mint and 2 Tbsp. glaze; set mixture aside.

2. Coat grill rack with cooking spray before starting the grill. Grill chicken, covered, over medium heat for 6-8 minutes on each side or until juices run clear, basting frequently with reserved glaze. Serve with reserved relish.

Nutrition Facts: 1 chicken breast half with 1/2 cup relish equals 263 calories, 4 g fat (1 g saturated fat), 94 mg cholesterol, 379 mg sodium, 20 g carbohydrate, 2 g fiber, 35 g protein. **Diabetic Exchanges:** 5 very lean meat, 1 starch, 1/2 fruit.

After taking uncooked chicken out to the grill, always **thoroughly clean** the platter. Avoid the temptation to reuse it to bring the cooked chicken back into the house.

CREOLE-POACHED CHICKEN BREASTS

Creole-Poached Chicken Breasts

PREP: 15 min. **COOK:** 30 min. **YIELD:** 4 servings

HEALTHY COOKING TEST KITCHEN

Aside from a little veggie chopping, this one-dish chicken dinner couldn't get much easier! A dash of cayenne adds some Creole-style heat to the hearty weeknight meal.

- 2 medium onions, finely chopped
- 2 celery ribs, finely chopped
- 1 medium green pepper, diced
- 2 tsp. canola oil
- 4 boneless skinless chicken breast halves (4 oz. *each*)
- 1 can (15 oz.) crushed tomatoes
- 1/2 cup reduced-sodium chicken broth
- 1 tsp. dried thyme
- 1/4 tsp. salt
- 1/8 tsp. cayenne pepper

1. In a large nonstick skillet coated with cooking spray, saute the onions, celery and pepper in oil until tender. Add the remaining ingredients. Bring to a boil; reduce heat. Simmer, uncovered, for 10-15 minutes or until a meat thermometer reads 170°. Remove chicken; keep warm.

2. Return cooking juices to a boil. Reduce heat; simmer, uncovered, for 8-10 minutes or until most of the sauce is evaporated. Serve with chicken.

Nutrition Facts: 1 chicken breast half with 3/4 cup sauce equals 220 calories, 5 g fat (1 g saturated fat), 63 mg cholesterol, 432 mg sodium, 18 g carbohydrate, 5 g fiber, 26 g protein. **Diabetic Exchanges:** 3 very lean meat, 1 starch.

Potato-Crusted Chicken Casserole

PREP: 30 min. **BAKE:** 40 min. **YIELD:** 6 servings

BECKY MATHENY • STRASBURG, VIRGINIA

An herby, comforting filling is surrounded by a sliced potato "crust" in this unique casserole. You'd never guess it's healthy!

- 1 large potato, thinly sliced
- 1 Tbsp. olive oil
- 1/2 tsp. salt
- 1/4 tsp. pepper

FILLING:
- 1-1/2 lbs. chicken tenderloins, cut into 1/2-in. cubes
- 2 tsp. olive oil
- 1 medium onion, chopped
- 1 Tbsp. butter
- 2 Tbsp. all-purpose flour
- 1-1/2 cups fat-free milk
- 1/4 cup shredded part-skim mozzarella cheese
- 1/4 cup grated Parmesan cheese
- 2 Tbsp. shredded reduced-fat cheddar cheese
- 2 cups frozen peas and carrots
- 1/2 tsp. salt
- 1/2 tsp. dried thyme
- 1/4 tsp. dried basil

Dash rubbed sage

CRUMB TOPPING:
- 1 cup soft bread crumbs
- 1 Tbsp. butter, melted
- 1/2 tsp. garlic powder

1. In a large bowl, toss potato slices with oil, salt and pepper. Arrange slices onto the bottom and sides of an 11-in. x 7-in. baking dish coated with cooking spray. Bake at 400° for 20-25 minutes or until potato is tender. Reduce heat to 350°.

2. Meanwhile, for filling, in a large skillet over medium heat, cook chicken in oil until no longer pink. Remove from skillet. In the same skillet, saute onion in butter. Stir in flour until blended; gradually add milk. Bring to a boil; cook and stir for 2 minutes or until thickened. Reduce heat; stir in cheeses until melted. Stir in vegetables and seasonings. Spoon into potato crust.

3. Combine topping ingredients; sprinkle over chicken mixture. Bake, uncovered, for 40-45 minutes or until bubbly and topping is golden brown.

Nutrition Facts: 1 serving equals 340 calories, 11 g fat (4 g saturated fat), 85 mg cholesterol, 674 mg sodium, 28 g carbohydrate, 3 g fiber, 35 g protein. **Diabetic Exchanges:** 4 very lean meat, 2 starch, 1 fat.

Creamy Olive-Stuffed Chicken **C**

PREP: 20 min. **BAKE:** 20 min. **YIELD:** 4 servings

HEALTHY COOKING TEST KITCHEN

A creamy olive stuffing turns these breaded chicken breasts into a special weeknight meal.

4	boneless skinless chicken breast halves (6 oz. *each*)
4	oz. fat-free cream cheese
1	can (2-1/4 oz.) sliced ripe olives, drained
1/8	tsp. dried oregano
1/8	tsp. pepper
1/2	cup seasoned bread crumbs
1	Tbsp. olive oil

1. Flatten chicken to 1/4-in. thickness. In a small bowl, combine the cream cheese, olives, oregano and pepper. Spoon 2 Tbsp. down the center of each chicken breast. Fold chicken over filling; secure with toothpicks, then roll in bread crumbs.

2. In a large oven-proof skillet, brown chicken in oil. Bake at 350° for 20-25 minutes or until juices run clear. Discard toothpicks.

Nutrition Facts: 1 stuffed chicken breast half equals 286 calories, 10 g fat (2 g saturated fat), 96 mg cholesterol, 483 mg sodium, 8 g carbohydrate, 1 g fiber, 40 g protein. **Diabetic Exchanges:** 5 very lean meat, 1 fat, 1/2 starch.

Prosciutto Chicken In Wine Sauce **C**

PREP: 25 min. **COOK:** 30 min. **YIELD:** 6 servings

LORRAINE CALAND • THUNDER BAY, ONTARIO

You mention "Italian," and there's no second ringing of the dinner bell at my house! Happily, there's a bit of Italian flavor in this wonderful entree. It's terrific with pasta.

1	broiler/fryer chicken (3 lbs.), cut up and skin removed
1/2	tsp. salt
1/4	tsp. pepper
1	Tbsp. olive oil
1	Tbsp. butter
1	cup white wine or reduced-sodium chicken broth
4	thin slices prosciutto or deli ham, chopped
1	shallot, chopped
1	Tbsp. fresh sage or 1 tsp. dried sage leaves
1	garlic clove, minced

1. Sprinkle chicken with salt and pepper. In a large nonstick skillet coated with cooking spray, brown chicken on all sides in oil and butter.

2. Add the remaining ingredients, stirring to loosen browned bits. Bring to a boil. Reduce heat; cover and simmer for 20-25 minutes or until chicken juices run clear. Remove chicken and keep warm. Bring sauce to a boil; cook for 10-12 minutes or until liquid is reduced to 3/4 cup. Serve with chicken.

Nutrition Facts: 3 oz. cooked chicken with 2 Tbsp. sauce equals 231 calories, 11 g fat (4 g saturated fat), 87 mg cholesterol, 456 mg sodium, 2 g carbohydrate, trace fiber, 27 g protein. **Diabetic Exchanges:** 4 lean meat, 1 fat.

PROSCIUTTO CHICKEN IN WINE SAUCE

POTATO-CRUSTED CHICKEN CASSEROLE

Balsamic Chicken Breasts ⓈⒸ

PREP: 15 min. **COOK:** 20 min. **YIELD:** 4 servings

DENISE JOHANOWICZ • MADISON, WISCONSIN

This quick savory chicken is a family favorite. It's easy, healthy and satisfying. Served with a salad or whole wheat roll, it's a perfect meal that's good enough for company!

- 1/4 cup all-purpose flour
- 1/2 tsp. pepper
- 1/8 tsp. salt
-   4 boneless skinless chicken breast halves (4 oz. *each*)
-   1 Tbsp. canola oil
-   1 small onion, thinly sliced
- 1/4 cup water
-   2 Tbsp. balsamic vinegar
- 1/2 tsp. dried thyme
- 1/8 tsp. dried rosemary, crushed

1. In a large resealable plastic bag, combine the flour, pepper and salt. Add chicken, one piece at a time, and shake to coat.

2. In a large nonstick skillet coated with cooking spray, cook chicken in oil over medium heat for 4-5 minutes on each side or until juices run clear. Remove and keep warm.

3. In the same pan, cook onion until tender. Add water, stirring to loosen browned bits. Add the vinegar, thyme and rosemary; cook and stir for 3-4 minutes or until sauce is slightly thickened. Serve with chicken.

Nutrition Facts: 1 chicken breast half with 2 Tbsp. sauce equals 194 calories, 6 g fat (1 g saturated fat), 63 mg cholesterol, 131 mg sodium, 9 g carbohydrate, 1 g fiber, 24 g protein. **Diabetic Exchanges:** 3 very lean meat, 1 fat, 1/2 starch.

BALSAMIC CHICKEN BREASTS

Quick Turkey Spaghetti

PREP: 15 min. **COOK:** 20 min. **YIELD:** 4 servings

MARY LOU MOELLER • WOOSTER, OHIO

My family never tires of this versatile entree. We can have it once a week, and it's different each time! I sometimes omit the turkey for a meatless meal, change up the veggies or use my own tomato sauce.

-   1 lb. lean ground turkey
-   1 small green pepper, chopped
- 1/2 cup sliced fresh mushrooms
- 1/4 cup chopped onion
-   1 can (15 oz.) tomato sauce
-   6 oz. uncooked multigrain spaghetti, broken into 2-in. pieces
- 3/4 cup water
- 1/4 tsp. garlic salt

Grated Parmesan cheese, optional

1. In a large nonstick skillet coated with cooking spray, cook the turkey, pepper, mushrooms and onion over medium heat until meat is no longer pink and vegetables are crisp-tender.

2. Stir in the tomato sauce, spaghetti, water and garlic salt. Bring to a boil. Reduce heat; cover and simmer for 15-20 minutes or until spaghetti and vegetables are tender. Garnish with cheese if desired.

Nutrition Facts: 1-1/4 cups (calculated without cheese) equals 357 calories, 10 g fat (3 g saturated fat), 90 mg cholesterol, 728 mg sodium, 36 g carbohydrate, 4 g fiber, 30 g protein. **Diabetic Exchanges:** 3 lean meat, 2 starch, 1 vegetable.

Turkey Pasta Toss

PREP: 15 min. **COOK:** 20 min. **YIELD:** 6 servings

HEATHER SAVAGE • CORYDON, INDIANA

This recipe is one of our family's favorites. I served it once for a church supper, and it was a big hit there, too! Make it a complete meal with salad and some Italian bread. It's loaded with fresh flavor and so simple to put together!

-   3 cups uncooked penne pasta
-   2 Italian turkey sausage links, casings removed
-   1 large sweet yellow pepper, cut into 1/2-in. strips
-   1 Tbsp. olive oil

QUICK TURKEY SPAGHETTI

TURKEY PASTA TOSS

6 garlic cloves, minced

4 plum tomatoes, cut into 1-in. chunks

20 pitted ripe olives, halved

1/4 cup minced fresh basil

1/4 tsp. crushed red pepper flakes

1/4 tsp. salt

1/4 cup shredded Romano cheese

1. Cook pasta according to package directions. Meanwhile, crumble sausage into a large skillet. Cook over medium heat until meat is no longer pink; drain and keep warm.

2. In the same skillet, saute the pepper in oil until crisp-tender. Add garlic; cook 1 minute longer. Stir in the tomatoes, olives, basil, pepper flakes, salt and reserved sausage. Drain pasta. Stir into skillet and heat through. Sprinkle with cheese.

Nutrition Facts: 1-3/4 cups equals 323 calories, 9 g fat (2 g saturated fat), 24 mg cholesterol, 481 mg sodium, 47 g carbohydrate, 3 g fiber, 15 g protein.

Pretzel-Crusted Chicken

PREP: 20 min. **BAKE:** 40 min. **YIELD:** 6 servings

EILEEN KORECKO • HOT SPRINGS VILLAGE, ARIZONA

I often double this recipe so we have leftovers the next day. It tastes just as good cold as it does hot!

4 cups miniature pretzels

5 cooked bacon strips, coarsely chopped

1/2 cup grated Parmesan cheese

1 Tbsp. dried parsley flakes

1 egg

1/2 cup light or nonalcoholic beer

1/3 cup all-purpose flour

1 tsp. paprika

1/4 tsp. ground ginger

1/4 tsp. pepper

1 broiler/fryer chicken (3 lbs.), cut up and skin removed

1. Place the pretzels, bacon, cheese and parsley in a food processor; cover and process until coarsely chopped. Transfer to a shallow bowl.

2. In another shallow bowl, whisk the egg, beer, flour and spices. Dip a few pieces of chicken at a time in beer mixture, then pretzel mixture. Place chicken in a 13-in. x 9-in. baking dish coated with cooking spray. Bake at 350° for 40-50 minutes or until chicken juices run clear.

Nutrition Facts: 4 oz. cooked chicken equals 283 calories, 9 g fat (3 g saturated fat), 98 mg cholesterol, 498 mg sodium, 19 g carbohydrate, 1 g fiber, 30 g protein. **Diabetic Exchanges:** 4 lean meat, 1 starch, 1/2 fat.

CITRUS GRILLED TURKEY CUTLETS

Citrus Grilled Turkey Cutlets F C

PREP: 15 min. + marinating **GRILL:** 5 min.
YIELD: 4 servings

JANICE MENTZER • SHARPSBURG, MARYLAND

My family enjoys this turkey recipe year-round, but it's especially nice in the summer as an alternative to grilled chicken.

2	Tbsp. *each* lemon, lime and orange juices
1	Tbsp. minced fresh cilantro
1	Tbsp. canola oil
1	Tbsp. honey
1	small garlic clove, minced
1/2	tsp. salt
1/2	tsp. chili powder
1/4	tsp. ground cumin
1/4	tsp. pepper
1	pkg. (17.6 oz.) turkey breast cutlets

1. In a large resealable plastic bag, combine the juices, cilantro, oil, honey, garlic and seasonings; add the turkey. Seal bag and turn to coat; refrigerate for 2 hours.

2. Coat grill rack with cooking spray before starting the grill. Drain and discard marinade.

3. Grill the turkey, covered, over medium heat for 2-4 minutes on each side or until no longer pink.

Nutrition Facts: about 4 oz. cooked turkey equals 160 calories, 2 g fat (trace saturated fat), 77 mg cholesterol, 173 mg sodium, 3 g carbohydrate, trace fiber, 31 g protein. **Diabetic Exchanges:** 4 very lean meat, 1/2 fat.

Makeover Poppy Seed Chicken

PREP: 10 min. **BAKE :** 30 min. **YIELD:** 6 servings

CAROLYN KEESE • SENECA, SOUTH CAROLINA

This revised recipe is comforting and homey, but with fewer calories and much less fat and cholesterol than my original. And because it only takes 10 minutes to put together, it's great for weeknights.

3	cups cubed cooked chicken breast
2	cans (10-3/4 oz. *each*) reduced-fat reduced-sodium condensed cream of chicken soup, undiluted
1	cup (8 oz.) reduced-fat sour cream
2	tsp. poppy seeds
1	cup crushed reduced-fat butter-flavored crackers (about 25 crackers)
3	Tbsp. reduced-fat butter, melted
1/3	cup grated Parmesan cheese

1. In a large bowl, combine the chicken, soup, sour cream and poppy seeds. In a small bowl, combine cracker crumbs and butter; set aside 1/2 cup for topping. Stir remaining crumbs into chicken mixture.

2. Transfer to an 11-in. x 7-in. baking dish coated with cooking spray. Top with reserved crumbs; sprinkle with cheese. Bake, uncovered, at 350° for 30-35 minutes or until bubbly.

Nutrition Facts: 1 cup equals 332 calories, 13 g fat (6 g saturated fat), 87 mg cholesterol, 705 mg sodium, 23 g carbohydrate, trace fiber, 27 g protein.

Chicken Caesar Deluxe Pizza

PREP: 30 min. + standing **BAKE:** 30 min.
YIELD: 8 pieces

ERIN HAMANN • REESEVILLE, WISCONSIN

Here's my favorite pizza recipe. The tomatoes really add a lovely dash of color!

1	lb. boneless skinless chicken breasts, cubed
1	tsp. dried rosemary, crushed
1	Tbsp. olive oil
1-3/4	cups all-purpose flour
1	cup whole wheat flour
4	tsp. sugar
1	pkg. (1/4 oz.) quick-rise yeast
3/4	tsp. salt
1	tsp. dried basil
1-1/4	cups warm water (120° to 130°)
3/4	cup reduced-fat Caesar vinaigrette
2	cups fresh baby spinach
1	small green pepper, chopped
1/2	cup chopped fresh mushrooms
1/3	cup finely chopped onion
1-3/4	cups shredded part-skim mozzarella cheese
4	plum tomatoes, chopped

1. In a large skillet over medium heat, cook chicken and rosemary in oil until chicken is no longer pink; set aside.

2. In a large bowl, combine 1-1/4 cups all-purpose flour, whole wheat flour, sugar, yeast, salt and basil. Add water; beat just until moistened. Stir in enough remaining all-purpose flour to form a soft dough (dough will be sticky). Turn onto a lightly floured surface; knead until smooth and elastic, about 5 minutes. Cover and rest for 10 minutes.

3. Press the dough onto the bottom and up the sides of a 15-in. x 10-in. x 1-in. baking pan coated with cooking spray. Bake at 400° for 7-9 minutes or until lightly browned.

4. Spread vinaigrette over crust. Layer with spinach, green pepper, mushrooms, onion and chicken. Sprinkle with cheese and tomatoes. Bake for 20-25 minutes or until crust is golden brown and cheese is melted.

Nutrition Facts: 1 piece equals 358 calories, 11 g fat (4 g saturated fat), 47 mg cholesterol, 794 mg sodium, 39 g carbohydrate, 4 g fiber, 24 g protein. **Diabetic Exchanges:** 3 very lean meat, 2-1/2 starch, 2 fat.

Slow-Cooked Southwest Chicken **F**

PREP: 15 min. **COOK:** 6 hours **YIELD:** 6 servings

BRANDI CASTILLO • SANTA MARIA, CALIFORNIA

With just 15-minutes of prep, this dish will have you out of the kitchen in no time. It makes a deliciously low-fat entree that's terrific with reduced-fat sour cream and chopped cilantro.

2	cans (15 oz. *each*) black beans, rinsed and drained
1	can (14-1/2 oz.) reduced-sodium chicken broth
1	can (14-1/2 oz.) diced tomatoes with mild green chilies, undrained
1/2	lb. boneless skinless chicken breast
1	jar (8 oz.) chunky salsa
1	cup frozen corn
1	Tbsp. dried parsley flakes
1	tsp. ground cumin
1/4	tsp. pepper
3	cups hot cooked rice

1. In a 2- or 3-qt. slow cooker, combine the beans, broth, tomatoes, chicken, salsa, corn and seasonings. Cover and cook on low for 6-8 hours or until chicken shreds easily with two forks.

2. Shred chicken and return to the slow cooker; heat through. Serve with rice.

Nutrition Facts: 1 cup chicken mixture with 1/2 cup rice equals 320 calories, 1 g fat (trace saturated fat), 21 mg cholesterol, 873 mg sodium, 56 g carbohydrate, 8 g fiber, 19 g protein.

SLOW-COOKED SOUTHWEST CHICKEN

CHICKEN CAESAR DELUXE PIZZA

Lasagna Deliziosa

PREP: 45 min. **BAKE:** 50 min. + standing
YIELD: 12 servings

HEATHER O'NEILL • TROY, OHIO

Everyone loves this lasagna. It's often served as a birthday treat for guests. I've lightened it up a lot from the original, but no one can tell the difference!

9	uncooked lasagna noodles
1	pkg. (20 oz.) Italian turkey sausage links, casings removed
1/2	lb. lean ground beef
1	large onion, chopped
2	garlic cloves, minced
1	can (28 oz.) diced tomatoes, undrained
1	can (12 oz.) tomato paste
1/4	cup water
2	tsp. sugar
1	tsp. dried basil
1/2	tsp. fennel seed
1/4	tsp. pepper
1	egg, lightly beaten
1	container (15 oz.) reduced-fat ricotta cheese
1	Tbsp. minced fresh parsley
1/2	tsp. salt
2	cups (8 oz.) shredded part-skim mozzarella cheese
3/4	cup grated Parmesan cheese

1. Cook noodles according to package directions. Meanwhile, in a Dutch oven, cook the sausage, beef, onion and garlic over medium heat until meat is no longer pink; drain.

2. Stir in the tomatoes, tomato paste, water, sugar, basil, fennel and pepper. Bring to a boil. Reduce heat; cover and simmer for 15-20 minutes, stirring the sauce occasionally.

3. In a small bowl, combine the egg, ricotta cheese, parsley and salt. Drain noodles and rinse in cold water. Spread 1 cup meat sauce in a 13-in. x 9-in. baking dish coated with cooking spray. Top with three noodles, 2 cups meat sauce, 2/3 cup ricotta cheese mixture, 2/3 cup mozzarella and 1/4 cup Parmesan. Repeat layers twice.

4. Cover and bake at 375° for 40 minutes. Uncover; bake 10-15 minutes longer or until a thermometer reads 160°. Let stand for 10 minutes before cutting.

Nutrition Facts: 1 piece equals 323 calories, 12 g fat (5 g saturated fat), 79 mg cholesterol, 701 mg sodium, 28 g carbohydrate, 4 g fiber, 25 g protein. **Diabetic Exchanges:** 3 lean meat, 2 vegetable, 1 fat, 1 starch.

Aromatic Fennel Chicken C

PREP: 35 min. **COOK:** 50 min. **YIELD:** 6 servings

REBECCA HUNT • SANTA PAULA, CALIFORNIA

Fennel, along with lemon, capers, wine, spices and a bit of bacon, adds to the flavor of this wonderful chicken dish. Serve with a colorful salad and baked potato for a special meal.

4	bacon strips, chopped
1	broiler/fryer chicken (3-1/2 to 4 lbs.), cut up, skin removed
1/2	tsp. salt
1/2	tsp. pepper
2	fennel bulbs, sliced
2	medium onions, chopped
6	garlic cloves, minced
3/4	cup white wine *or* reduced-sodium chicken broth
1/4	cup lemon juice
1	Tbsp. grated lemon peel
2	bay leaves
2	tsp. dried thyme

Pinch cayenne pepper

3	Tbsp. capers, drained

1. In a large nonstick skillet, cook the bacon over medium heat until crisp. Using a slotted spoon, remove to paper towels; drain, reserving 1 Tbsp. drippings.

2. Sprinkle chicken with salt and pepper. Brown chicken on all sides in reserved drippings; remove and keep warm. Add fennel and onions to the pan; cook and stir for 3 minutes. Add garlic; cook 2-3 minutes longer or until onions are tender.

3. Stir in the wine, lemon juice and peel, bay leaves, thyme and cayenne. Return chicken to the pan. Bring to a boil. Reduce heat; cover and simmer for 20-25 minutes or until chicken juices run clear. Remove chicken and keep warm. Cook the fennel mixture, uncovered, for 8-10 minutes or until slightly thickened, stirring occasionally. Stir in capers and reserved bacon. Discard bay leaves. Serve fennel mixture with the chicken.

Nutrition Facts: about 4 oz. cooked chicken with 1/2 cup fennel mixture equals 290 calories, 12 g fat (4 g saturated fat), 92 mg cholesterol, 520 mg sodium, 13 g carbohydrate, 4 g fiber, 31 g protein. **Diabetic Exchanges:** 4 lean meat, 2 vegetable, 1 fat.

LASAGNA DELIZIOSA

Turkey Burritos With Fresh Fruit Salsa

PREP: 30 min. **COOK:** 20 min. **YIELD:** 10 servings

LISA EATON • KENNEBUNK, MAINE

Packed with fruit, veggies, nutrition and flavor, this lighter, whole-grain twist on traditional burritos is sure to be a big hit with your family. Even our pickiest eater loves these with the sweet-spicy fruit salsa. Yum!

  1 pint grape tomatoes, quartered
  1 medium mango, peeled and chopped
  2 medium kiwifruit, peeled and chopped
  3 green onions, thinly sliced
  3 Tbsp. finely chopped red onion
  1 jalapeno pepper, seeded and chopped
  1 Tbsp. lime juice

BURRITOS:
  1 lb. lean ground turkey
  2 garlic cloves, minced
  1/2 tsp. ground turmeric
  1/4 tsp. ground cumin
  1 Tbsp. olive oil
  1/2 cup burgundy wine *or* reduced-sodium beef broth
  1 jar (16 oz.) salsa
  2 cups frozen corn, thawed
  1 can (15 oz.) black beans, rinsed and drained
  10 whole wheat tortilla (8 in.), warmed
  1 cup (4 oz.) shredded reduced-fat cheddar cheese

1. For salsa, combine the first seven ingredients. Chill until serving.

2. In a large nonstick skillet, cook the turkey, garlic, turmeric and cumin in oil over medium heat until turkey is no longer pink; drain. Stir in wine. Bring to a boil. Reduce heat; simmer, uncovered, for 3-5 minutes or until thickened.

3. Stir in the jarred salsa, corn and black beans. Bring to a boil. Reduce heat; simmer, uncovered, for 10-15 minutes or until thickened. Remove from the heat. Spoon about 1/2 cup turkey mixture off center on each tortilla. Sprinkle with cheese. Fold sides and ends over filling and roll up. Serve with salsa.

Editor's Note: When cutting hot peppers, disposable gloves are recommended. Avoid touching your face.

Nutrition Facts: 1 burrito with 1/3 cup salsa equals 371 calories, 11 g fat (3 g saturated fat), 44 mg cholesterol, 553 mg sodium, 47 g carbohydrate, 6 g fiber, 18 g protein.

The wonderful thing about Southwestern foods is that they are full of flavor but don't necessary pack on the pounds. Pair the enchiladas with a **light side dish** such as red beans and rice, fat-free refried beans or even something as simple as baked tortilla chips and salsa.

Makeover Greek Chicken Penne

PREP: 20 min. **COOK:** 20 min. **YIELD:** 6 servings

HEALTHY COOKING TEST KITCHEN

You'll love the big flavors in this hearty pasta dish that's been lightened up. It's perfect paired with a salad.

- 2 cups uncooked penne pasta
- 1/2 cup sun-dried tomatoes (not packed in oil)
- 1-1/2 cups boiling water
- 1 large onion, chopped
- 3 Tbsp. reduced-fat butter
- 1/4 cup all-purpose flour
- 1 can (14-1/2 oz.) reduced-sodium chicken broth
- 3 cups cubed cooked chicken breast
- 1 cup (4 oz.) crumbled feta cheese
- 1 cup water-packed artichoke hearts, rinsed, drained and chopped
- 1/3 cup Greek olives, sliced
- 2 Tbsp. minced fresh parsley
- 1/4 tsp. Greek seasoning

1. Cook pasta according to package directions. Meanwhile, place tomatoes in a small bowl; add boiling water. Cover and let stand for 5 minutes.

2. In a Dutch oven, saute onion in butter until tender. Stir in flour until blended; gradually add broth. Bring to a boil; cook and stir for 2 minutes or until thickened. Drain and chop tomatoes; add to the pan. Stir in remaining ingredients. Drain pasta; add to the pan and heat through.

Editor's Note: This recipe was tested with Land O'Lakes light stick butter.

Nutrition Facts: 1-1/3 cups equals 343 calories, 11 g fat (5 g saturated fat), 71 mg cholesterol, 813 mg sodium, 31 g carbohydrate, 3 g fiber, 30 g protein.

Chicken Noodle Casserole

PREP: 20 min. **BAKE:** 40 min. **YIELD:** 8 servings

SYLVIA MCCRONE • DANVILLE, ILLINOIS

This rich casserole is ideal comfort food for your family on a chilly spring night. Round out the menu with a favorite steamed vegetable for a hearty meal that will please everyone at the table.

- 5 cups uncooked egg noodles
- 1 cup frozen peas
- 1 celery rib, chopped
- 1 medium carrot, chopped
- 4 cups cubed cooked chicken breast
- 1 can (14-3/4 oz.) cream-style corn
- 1 can (10-3/4 oz.) reduced-fat reduced-sodium condensed cream of chicken soup, undiluted
- 2 cups (8 oz.) shredded reduced-fat Colby-Monterey Jack cheese, *divided*
- 1 small onion, chopped
- 1/4 cup chopped green pepper
- 1/4 cup chopped sweet red pepper
- 1/4 tsp. pepper

1. In a large saucepan, cook noodles according to package directions, adding the peas, celery and carrot during the last 5 minutes of cooking. Drain.

2. Stir in the chicken, corn, soup, 1 cup cheese, onion, green and red peppers and pepper. Transfer to a 13-in. x 9-in. baking dish coated with cooking spray. Cover and bake at 350° for 30 minutes.

3. Sprinkle with remaining cheese; bake 10 minutes longer or until cheese is melted.

Nutrition Facts: 1-1/2 cups equals 367 calories, 9 g fat (5 g saturated fat), 92 mg cholesterol, 606 mg sodium, 37 g carbohydrate, 3 g fiber, 34 g protein. **Diabetic Exchanges:** 4 lean meat, 2 starch, 1 vegetable.

Almond Chicken & Strawberry-Balsamic Sauce

PREP: 20 min. **COOK:** 20 min. **YIELD:** 4 servings

VIRGINIA ANTHONY • JACKSONVILLE, FLORIDA

Crispy chicken with a sweet-tart sauce is served alongside wilted spinach for this special meal. I created the recipe many years ago for a contest, and it won the grand prize! It's easy to make and comes off as very elegant.

1/2	cup panko (Japanese) bread crumbs
1/3	cup unblanched almonds, coarsely ground
1/2	tsp. salt
1/4	tsp. pepper
4	boneless skinless chicken breast halves (4 oz. each)

Butter-flavored cooking spray

3	tsp. canola oil, *divided*
1/4	cup chopped shallots
1/3	cup reduced-sodium chicken broth
1/3	cup strawberry preserves
3	Tbsp. balsamic vinegar
1	Tbsp. minced fresh rosemary *or* 1 tsp. dried rosemary, crushed
1	pkg. (9 oz.) fresh baby spinach

1. In a large resealable plastic bag, combine the bread crumbs, almonds, salt and pepper. Add chicken, one piece at a time, and shake to coat.

2. In a large nonstick skillet coated with butter-flavored spray, cook chicken in 2 tsp. oil over medium heat for 4-5 minutes on each side or until juices run clear. Remove and keep warm.

3. In the same pan, cook shallots in remaining oil until tender. Stir in the broth, preserves, vinegar and rosemary. Bring to a boil. Reduce heat; simmer for 5-6 minutes or until thickened.

4. Meanwhile, in a large saucepan, bring 1/2 in. of water to a boil. Add spinach; cover and boil for 3-5 minutes or until wilted. Drain; serve with chicken and sauce.

Nutrition Facts: 1 chicken breast half with 1/4 cup spinach and 2 Tbsp. sauce equals 349 calories, 13 g fat (2 g saturated fat), 63 mg cholesterol, 476 mg sodium, 31 g carbohydrate, 3 g fiber, 29 g protein.

Coconut Curry Chicken

PREP: 20 min. **COOK:** 5 hours **YIELD:** 4 servings

ANDI KAUFFMAN • BEAVERCREEK, OREGON

My husband and I love this yummy dish! It's a breeze to prepare in the slow cooker, and it tastes just like a meal you'd have at your favorite Indian or Thai restaurant.

2	medium potatoes, peeled and cubed
1	small onion, chopped
4	boneless skinless chicken breast halves (4 oz. each)
1	cup light coconut milk
4	tsp. curry powder
1	garlic clove, minced
1	tsp. reduced-sodium chicken bouillon granules
1/4	tsp. salt
1/4	tsp. pepper
2	cups hot cooked rice
1/4	cup thinly sliced green onions

Raisins, flaked coconut and chopped unsalted peanuts, optional

1. Place potatoes and onion in a 3- or 4-qt. slow cooker. In a large nonstick skillet coated with cooking spray, brown chicken on both sides. Transfer to slow cooker.

2. In a small bowl, combine the coconut milk, curry, garlic, bouillon, salt and pepper; pour over chicken. Cover and cook on low for 5 hours or until chicken is tender.

3. Serve chicken and sauce with rice; sprinkle with green onions. Garnish with raisins, coconut and peanuts if desired.

Nutrition Facts: 1 serving (calculated without optional ingredients) equals 396 calories, 11 g fat (7 g saturated fat), 63 mg cholesterol, 309 mg sodium, 43 g carbohydrate, 3 g fiber, 27 g protein. **Diabetic Exchanges:** 3 very lean meat, 2-1/2 starch, 2 fat.

ALMOND CHICKEN & STRAWBERRY-BALSAMIC SAUCE

COCONUT CURRY CHICKEN

Chicken with Artichokes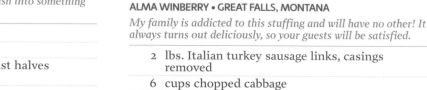

PREP: 10 min. **COOK:** 35 min. **YIELD:** 4 servings

HEALTHY COOKING TEST KITCHEN

Artichokes and a splash of white wine lend distinctive flavors to chicken, and turn this quick-and-easy dish into something quite special.

1/2	tsp. salt
1/8	tsp. pepper
4	boneless skinless chicken breast halves (4 oz. *each*)
3	tsp. canola oil, *divided*
1	medium onion, thinly sliced
3	garlic cloves, minced
1/2	cup white wine *or* reduced-sodium chicken broth
1/2	cup reduced-sodium chicken broth
1	can (14 oz.) water-packed artichoke hearts, rinsed, drained and coarsely chopped

1. Combine salt and pepper; sprinkle over chicken. In a large nonstick skillet coated with cooking spray, cook chicken in 2 tsp. oil for 4-5 minutes on each side or until lightly browned. Remove and keep warm.

2. In the same skillet, cook onion and garlic in remaining oil for 3-4 minutes or until onions are tender. Stir in wine and chicken broth, stirring to loosen any browned bits from pan. Bring to a boil. Add the chicken. Reduce heat; simmer, uncovered, for 10-15 minutes or until chicken juices run clear. Remove chicken; keep warm.

3. Add artichokes to pan. Return to a boil. Reduce heat; simmer, uncovered, for 8-12 minutes or until liquid is reduced by half. Serve with chicken.

Nutrition Facts: 1 chicken breast half with 1/3 cup artichoke mixture equals 230 calories, 6 g fat (1 g saturated fat), 63 mg cholesterol, 678 mg sodium, 11 g carbohydrate, 1 g fiber, 26 g protein. **Diabetic Exchanges:** 3 very lean meat, 2 vegetable, 1 fat.

Turkey with Sausage Stuffing

PREP: 30 min. **BAKE:** 3 hours + standing **YIELD:** 24 servings (12 cups)

ALMA WINBERRY • GREAT FALLS, MONTANA

My family is addicted to this stuffing and will have no other! It always turns out deliciously, so your guests will be satisfied.

2	lbs. Italian turkey sausage links, casings removed
6	cups chopped cabbage
3	medium carrots, shredded
2	celery ribs, chopped
1/3	cup chopped onion
3	cups stuffing mix
3	cups seasoned stuffing cubes
1	cup reduced-sodium chicken broth
6	Tbsp. egg substitute
1/4	cup half-and-half cream
1/2	tsp. poultry seasoning
1/2	tsp. pepper
1/8	tsp. salt
1	turkey (12 lbs.)

1. In a large nonstick skillet coated with cooking spray, cook the sausage, cabbage, carrots, celery and onion over medium heat until meat is no longer pink and vegetables are tender. Transfer to a large bowl; stir in the stuffing mix, stuffing cubes, broth, egg substitute, cream, poultry seasoning, pepper and salt.

2. Just before baking, loosely stuff the turkey with 4 cups of stuffing. Place the remaining stuffing in a 13-in. x 9-in. baking dish coated with cooking spray; refrigerate until ready to bake. Skewer turkey openings; tie drumsticks together. Place breast side up on a rack in a roasting pan. Bake, uncovered, at 325° for 3 to 3-1/2 hours or until a meat thermometer inserted in the thigh reads 180° for the turkey and 165° for the stuffing, basting occasionally with pan drippings. Cover loosely with foil if turkey browns too quickly.

3. Cover and bake additional stuffing for 25-30 minutes. Uncover; bake 10 minutes longer or until lightly browned. Cover turkey and let stand for 20 minutes before removing stuffing and carving turkey.

TURKEY WITH SAUSAGE STUFFING

CHICKEN WITH ARTICHOKES

ZESTY MEXICAN CHICKEN

Nutrition Facts: 4 oz. cooked turkey (calculated without skin) with 1/2 cup stuffing equals 317 calories, 10 g fat (3 g saturated fat), 109 mg cholesterol, 568 mg sodium, 12 g carbohydrate, 1 g fiber, 41 g protein. **Diabetic Exchanges:** 5 lean meat, 1 starch.

Zesty Mexican Chicken ꘘ

PREP: 15 min. **COOK:** 3-1/2 hours **YIELD:** 6 servings

MICHELLE SHELDON • MIDDLETOWN, DELEWARE

A hint of lime juice helps tame the heat in this zesty, tender chicken with crunchy vegetables. And because it's all prepared in the slow cooker, you and your kitchen will stay cool, too!

6	boneless skinless chicken breast halves (4 oz. each)
1	can (14-1/2 oz.) diced tomatoes
1	large onion, chopped
1	medium green pepper, chopped
3	garlic cloves, minced
2	Tbsp. lime juice
1	Tbsp. hot pepper sauce
1/4	tsp. salt
1/4	tsp. pepper
3	cups hot cooked rice

1. Place chicken in a 3- or 4-qt. slow cooker coated with cooking spray. In a large bowl, combine the tomatoes, onion, green pepper, garlic, lime juice, pepper sauce, salt and pepper. Pour over chicken.

2. Cover and cook on low for 3-1/2 to 4 hours or until a meat thermometer reads 170°. Serve with rice.

Nutrition Facts: 1 chicken breast half with 1/2 cup rice and 1/2 cup tomato mixture equals 256 calories, 3 g fat (1 g saturated fat), 63 mg cholesterol, 257 mg sodium, 30 g carbohydrate, 2 g fiber, 26 g protein. **Diabetic Exchanges:** 3 very lean meat, 1-1/2 starch, 1 vegetable.

Keep you cabinet stocked with a few items, and you'll never have trouble **punching up flavor** in you light dishes. Extra-virgin olive oil, minced garlic, onion powder, lemon and lime juices, hot pepper sauce and dried red pepper flakes are great staples.

GINGERED CHICKEN THIGHS

Gingered Chicken Thighs C

PREP: 20 min + marinating **BAKE:** 20 min.
YIELD: 6 servings

DEBBIE FLEENOR •MONTEREY, TENNESSEE

Pantry staples like peanut butter, honey and soy sauce help create bold ethnic flavors for these delectable and juicy chicken thighs.

- 2 Tbsp. ground ginger
- 2 Tbsp. orange juice
- 2 Tbsp. honey
- 2 Tbsp. reduced-sodium soy sauce
- 2 tsp. curry powder
- 2 garlic cloves, minced
- 1/2 tsp. crushed red pepper flakes
- 6 boneless skinless chicken thighs (about 1-1/2 lbs.)

PEANUT SAUCE:
- 2 Tbsp. chicken broth
- 2 Tbsp. orange juice
- 1 Tbsp. reduced-fat creamy peanut butter
- 1/2 tsp. ground ginger

1. In a large resealable plastic bag, combine the first seven ingredients; add the chicken. Seal bag and turn to coat; refrigerate for up to 4 hours.

2. Drain and discard marinade. In a large skillet coated with cooking spray, brown chicken on each side. Transfer to an 11-in. x 7-in. baking dish coated with cooking spray. In a small bowl, whisk sauce ingredients; pour over chicken. Bake, uncovered, at 350° for 20-25 minutes or until no longer pink.

Nutrition Facts: 1 chicken thigh with about 1 Tbsp. sauce equals 199 calories, 9 g fat (2 g saturated fat), 76 mg cholesterol, 200 mg sodium, 6 g carbohydrate, trace fiber, 22 g protein. **Diabetic Exchanges:** 3 lean meat, 1/2 starch.

Lemony Spinach-Stuffed Chicken Breasts C

PREP: 30 min. **COOK:** 20 min. **YIELD:** 4 servings

PAM NELSON • BEAVERTON, OREGON

These chicken breasts are flattened and rolled with a flavorful combo of feta, caramelized onions and spinach. While they're very elegant, they're also very easy.

- 1/2 cup chopped sweet onion
- 3 tsp. olive oil, *divided*
- 6-1/2 cups fresh baby spinach, chopped
- 1 garlic clove, minced
- 1 Tbsp. balsamic vinegar
- 1/4 cup crumbled feta cheese
- 1/2 tsp. grated lemon peel
- 1/4 tsp. salt
- 1/4 tsp. pepper
- 4 boneless skinless chicken breast halves (6 oz. *each*)

1. In a large skillet, cook onion in 2 tsp. oil over medium heat for 15-20 minutes or until onion is golden brown, stirring frequently. Add the spinach, garlic and vinegar; cook 1 minute longer. Remove from the heat; cool for 5 minutes. Stir in the cheese, lemon peel, salt and pepper.

2. Flatten the chicken to 1/4-in. thickness. Spread spinach mixture over chicken. Roll up and secure the seams with toothpicks.

3. In a large skillet over medium heat, cook chicken in remaining oil for 8-10 minutes on each side or until chicken juices run clear. Discard toothpicks.

Nutrition Facts: 1 stuffed chicken breast half equals 253 calories, 9 g fat (2 g saturated fat), 98 mg cholesterol, 337 mg sodium, 5 g carbohydrate, 2 g fiber, 37 g protein. **Diabetic Exchanges:** 5 very lean meat, 1 vegetable, 1 fat.

Chicken Saltimbocca with Mushroom Sauce 🄲

PREP: 20 min **COOK:** 45 min. **YIELD:** 8 servings

VIRGINIA ANTHONY • JACKSONVILLE, FLORIDA

I created this recipe to capture the flavors of saltimbocca, but without all the fat and sodium. With the addition of beans, it becomes a one-dish meal. We really enjoy it.

1/2	cup all-purpose flour
1/4	tsp. salt
1/2	tsp. pepper, *divided*
8	boneless skinless chicken thighs (2 lbs.)
2	Tbsp. olive oil, *divided*
2	cups sliced fresh mushrooms
2	thin slices prosciutto *or* deli ham
1/2	cup chopped shallots
2	garlic cloves, minced
1	cup white wine *or* reduced-sodium chicken broth
1	can (15 oz.) white kidney *or* cannellini beans, rinsed and drained, *divided*
1/4	cup water
3	Tbsp. fresh sage *or* 3 tsp. dried sage leaves, *divided*
1	cup reduced-sodium chicken broth
1/3	cup half-and-half cream

1. In a large resealable plastic bag, combine the flour, salt and 1/4 tsp. pepper. Add chicken, a few pieces at a time, and shake to coat. In a large skillet over medium heat, cook chicken in 1 Tbsp. oil for 8-10 minutes on each side or until chicken juices run clear. Remove and keep warm.

2. In the same skillet, saute the mushrooms, prosciutto, shallots and garlic in remaining oil until tender. Stir in wine. Bring to a boil; cook until liquid is reduced to about 1/3 cup, about 10 minutes.

3. Meanwhile, in a small saucepan, lightly mash 1/2 cup beans; add the water, 1 Tbsp. sage and remaining pepper and beans; cook and stir until heated through. Set aside and keep warm.

4. Add chicken broth to the mushroom mixture. Bring to a boil. Reduce heat; simmer, uncovered, for 5 minutes or until slightly reduced. Stir in cream and remaining sage; heat through (do not boil). Return chicken to skillet; cook for 2 minutes. Serve with bean mixture.

Nutrition Facts: 1 serving equals 290 calories, 13 g fat (4 g saturated fat), 84 mg cholesterol, 371 mg sodium, 14 g carbohydrate, 3 g fiber, 26 g protein.

> Saltimbocca is a popular dish in many Italian restaurants. Ingredients and cooking methods vary, but most versions include chicken, pork or veal, and involve prosciutto or ham. The result is a **delightfully impressive** entree that's perfect for special occasions.

CHICKEN SALTIMBOCCA WITH MUSHROOM SAUCE

LEMONY SPINACH-STUFFED CHICKEN BREASTS

Chevre-Stuffed Chicken With Apricot Glaze

PREP: 20 min. **COOK:** 20 min. **YIELD:** 2 servings

DAVID DAHLMAN • CHATSWORTH, CALIFORNIA

My original version of this recipe used several tablespoons of butter versus the single teaspoon of olive oil and more cheese. This light version tastes just as good.

2	boneless skinless chicken breast halves (6 oz. *each*)
1/4	tsp. salt
1/4	tsp. pepper
2	Tbsp. goat cheese
2	Tbsp. part-skim ricotta cheese
4	Tbsp. chopped shallots, *divided*
1	tsp. olive oil
2/3	cup reduced-sodium chicken broth
2	Tbsp. apricot spreadable fruit
1	Tbsp. lemon juice
1	tsp. spicy brown mustard
1	tsp. minced fresh parsley

1. Flatten chicken to 1/4-in. thickness; sprinkle with salt and pepper. In a small bowl, combine the goat cheese, ricotta and 1 Tbsp. shallots; spread over chicken. Roll up and secure with toothpicks.

2. In a small nonstick skillet, brown chicken in oil on all sides. Remove and keep warm. In the same skillet, saute remaining shallots until tender; stir in the broth, spreadable fruit, lemon juice and mustard. Bring to a boil. Cook until liquid is reduced by half.

3. Return the chicken to the pan; cover and cook for 6-7 minutes or until a meat thermometer reads 170°. Discard toothpicks. Serve with cooking liquid. Sprinkle with parsley.

Nutrition Facts: 1 serving equals 340 calories, 12 g fat (5 g saturated fat), 110 mg cholesterol, 695 mg sodium, 16 g carbohydrate, trace fiber, 41 g protein. **Diabetic Exchanges:** 5 very lean meat, 2 fat, 1 starch.

Chicken Shrimp Creole

PREP: 20 min. **COOK:** 35 min. **YIELD:** 6 servings

BONNIE ROHER • WRANGELL, ARKANSAS

Living in coastal Alaska, we put out our own shrimp pots. I am always looking for ways to prepare our fresh catches. This is an easy recipe, and my family really enjoys it.

2	bacon strips
1/2	lb. boneless skinless chicken breasts, cut into 1-in. cubes
1	medium onion, chopped
1	small green pepper, chopped
1	celery rib, chopped
1	garlic clove, minced
1	can (14-1/2 oz.) diced tomatoes, undrained
1	bay leaf
1/2	tsp. salt
1/4	tsp. pepper
1/4	tsp. Worcestershire sauce
1/4	tsp. hot pepper sauce
1	lb. uncooked medium shrimp, peeled and deveined
3	cups cooked brown rice

1. In a large skillet, cook bacon over medium heat until crisp. Remove to paper towels; drain, reserving 1 Tbsp. drippings. Crumble bacon and set aside. Saute the chicken, onion, green pepper and celery in drippings for 5-6 minutes or until chicken is no longer pink. Add garlic; cook 1 minute longer.

2. Stir in the tomatoes, bay leaf, salt, pepper, Worcestershire sauce and pepper sauce. Bring to a boil. Reduce heat; cover and simmer for 20 minutes. Add the shrimp and reserved bacon; return to a boil. Reduce heat; cover and simmer for 5 minutes or until shrimp turn pink. Discard bay leaf. Serve with rice.

Nutrition Facts: 2/3 cup shrimp mixture with 1/2 cup rice equals 272 calories, 6 g fat (2 g saturated fat), 117 mg cholesterol, 458 mg sodium, 30 g carbohydrate, 4 g fiber, 24 g protein. **Diabetic Exchanges:** 3 very lean meat, 1-1/2 starch, 1 vegetable.

CHEVRE-STUFFED CHICKEN WITH APRICOT GLAZE

CHICKEN SHRIMP CREOLE

Chicken Orzo Skillet

PREP: 15 min. **COOK:** 20 min. **YIELD:** 4 servings

KELLIE MULLEAVY • LAMBERTVILLE, MICHIGAN

Here's a great one-skillet supper that's colorful, healthy, filling and definitely special! I just love the blend of spices, the touch of heat and the sophisticated flavor that make this dish a must-try.

- 1 lb. boneless skinless chicken breasts, cut into 1/2-in. strips
- 2 tsp. salt-free garlic seasoning blend
- 1 small onion, chopped
- 1 Tbsp. olive oil
- 1 garlic clove, minced
- 1 can (14-1/2 oz.) diced tomatoes, undrained
- 1 pkg. (10 oz.) frozen chopped spinach, thawed and squeezed dry
- 1 cup reduced-sodium chicken broth
- 3/4 cup uncooked orzo pasta
- 1 tsp. Italian seasoning
- 1/8 tsp. crushed red pepper flakes, optional
- 1/4 cup grated Parmesan cheese, optional

1. Sprinkle chicken with garlic seasoning blend. In a large skillet, saute chicken and onion in oil for 5-6 minutes or until chicken is no longer pink. Add garlic; cook 1 minute longer.

2. Stir in the tomatoes, spinach, broth, orzo, Italian seasoning and pepper flakes if desired. Bring to a boil; reduce heat. Cover and simmer for 15-20 minutes or until orzo is tender and liquid is absorbed. Garnish with cheese if desired.

Nutrition Facts: 1-1/4 cups (calculated without cheese) equals 339 calories, 7 g fat (1 g saturated fat), 63 mg cholesterol, 384 mg sodium, 38 g carbohydrate, 5 g fiber, 32 g protein. **Diabetic Exchanges:** 3 very lean meat, 2 starch, 2 vegetable, 1/2 fat.

Sausage & Rice Stew

PREP: 20 min. **COOK:** 30 min. **YIELD:** 6 servings

KELLY YOUNG • COCOA, FLORIDA

My husband loves sausage, so I find ways to serve it with healthy ingredients, like beans and spinach. This hearty recipe will have your taste buds begging for more. Add a no-fuss green salad or a simple loaf of bread for a complete meal.

- 1 pkg. (16 oz.) smoked turkey kielbasa, halved lengthwise and sliced
- 1 large sweet onion, chopped
- 2 shallots, chopped
- 1 Tbsp. chopped pickled jalapeno slices
- 3 garlic cloves, minced
- 1 Tbsp. canola oil
- 2 cups water
- 1 can (14-1/2 oz.) reduced-sodium chicken broth
- 2 cans (15 oz. *each*) white kidney or cannellini beans, rinsed and drained
- 1 cup uncooked long grain rice
- 1 tsp. dried oregano
- 1 tsp. dried thyme
- 1/2 tsp. pepper
- 2 cups fresh baby spinach

1. In a Dutch oven, saute the kielbasa, onion, shallots, jalapeno and garlic in oil until onion is tender. Add the water, broth, beans, rice and seasonings. Bring to a boil.

2. Reduce heat; cover and simmer for 15-20 minutes or until rice is tender. Stir in spinach. Cook 5 minutes longer or until spinach is wilted.

Nutrition Facts: 1-2/3 cups equals 369 calories, 7 g fat (2 g saturated fat), 47 mg cholesterol, 1,162 mg sodium, 52 g carbohydrate, 7 g fiber, 22 g protein.

Grilled Chicken with Barley

PREP: 20 min. + marinating **COOK:** 50 min.
YIELD: 4 servings

HEALTHY COOKING TEST KITCHEN

With this meal's delicious, fresh flavors, perfect portion size and balance of nutrition, you'll get a big reward for just a little effort. What a great dish for summer.

1/4	cup lemon juice
1	Tbsp. plus 1 tsp. canola oil, *divided*
2	garlic cloves, minced
1	tsp. dried oregano
1/2	tsp. dried basil
4	boneless skinless chicken breast halves (4 oz. *each*)
1	can (14-1/2 oz.) reduced-sodium chicken broth
1/2	cup medium pearl barley
1/4	tsp. salt
1	medium carrot, chopped
1	small sweet red pepper, chopped
3	green onions, thinly sliced
1/4	tsp. pepper

1. In a small bowl, combine the lemon juice, 1 Tbsp. oil, garlic, oregano and basil. Pour 2 Tbsp. marinade into a large resealable plastic bag; add the chicken. Seal bag and turn to coat; refrigerate for 1 hour. Cover and refrigerate remaining marinade.

2. In a large saucepan, bring broth to a boil. Stir in barley and salt. Reduce heat; cover and simmer for 45-50 minutes or until tender. In a small nonstick skillet, saute carrot and red pepper in remaining oil until crisp-tender. Add the onions and pepper; saute 2-3 minutes longer or until tender. Stir vegetables and reserved marinade into cooked barley.

3. Coat grill rack with cooking spray before starting the grill. Drain and discard marinade. Grill chicken, covered, over medium heat for 4-7 minutes on each side or until juices run clear. Serve chicken with the barley mixture.

Nutrition Facts: 1 chicken breast half with 3/4 cup barley equals 270 calories, 7 g fat (1 g saturated fat), 63 mg cholesterol, 514 mg sodium, 25 g carbohydrate, 5 g fiber, 28 g protein. **Diabetic Exchanges:** 3 very lean meat, 1-1/2 starch, 1 fat.

Spinach-Walnut Stuffed Chicken **C**

PREP: 20 min. **BAKE:** 25 min. **YIELD:** 4 servings

KERI CAPUANO • NARRAGANSETT, RHODE ISLAND

For just 300 calories, this hearty yet elegant chicken entree, stuffed with healthy spinach, is one you can savor. The walnut coating is a delicious bonus, because walnuts, in small amounts, are super-healthy, too.

1/2	cup finely chopped onion
1/2	cup finely chopped fresh mushrooms
1/4	cup finely chopped celery
2	garlic cloves, minced
2-1/2	tsp. olive oil
1	pkg. (10 oz.) frozen chopped spinach, thawed and squeezed dry

1/4   cup crumbled Gorgonzola cheese

4   boneless skinless chicken breast halves
(6 oz. *each*)

1/4   tsp. salt

1/4   tsp. pepper

1   egg white

1/4   cup ground walnuts

1. In a small skillet, saute onion, mushrooms, celery and garlic in oil until tender. Stir in spinach and cheese; remove from the heat.

2. Cut a lengthwise slit through the thickest part of each chicken breast; fill with spinach mixture. Sprinkle with salt and pepper. Place egg white and walnuts in separate shallow bowls. Dip one side of chicken in egg white, then in walnuts.

3. Place in an 11-in. x 7-in. baking dish coated with cooking spray. Bake, uncovered, at 350° for 25-30 minutes or until chicken juices run clear.

Nutrition Facts: 1 stuffed chicken breast half equals 300 calories, 12 g fat (3 g saturated fat), 100 mg cholesterol, 398 mg sodium, 7 g carbohydrate, 3 g fiber, 40 g protein. **Diabetic Exchanges:** 5 very lean meat, 2 fat, 1 vegetable.

Turkey Spaghetti Sauce F C

PREP: 25 min. **COOK:** 40 min. **YIELD:** 7-1/2 cups

JENNIFER KOLB • OVERLAND PARK, KANSAS

This is rich, homey and flavorful, but lower in sodium than jarred meat sauce.

1   lb. Italian turkey sausage links, casings removed

1/2   lb. extra-lean ground turkey

1-3/4   cups sliced fresh mushrooms

1   medium green pepper, chopped

1   medium onion, chopped

1   can (29 oz.) tomato puree

1   can (14-1/2 oz.) diced tomatoes, undrained

1   can (6 oz.) tomato paste

2   bay leaves

1   Tbsp. dried oregano

1   tsp. garlic powder

1   tsp. dried basil

1/2   tsp. salt

1/4   tsp. pepper

Hot cooked multigrain spaghetti

1. Crumble sausage and turkey into a large nonstick skillet coated with cooking spray. Add the mushrooms, green pepper and onion. Cook and stir over medium heat until meat is no longer pink; drain. Stir in the puree, tomatoes, tomato paste, bay leaves and seasonings. Bring to a boil. Reduce heat; simmer, uncovered, for 30 minutes.

2. Discard bay leaves. Serve desired amount with spaghetti. Cool remaining sauce; transfer to freezer containers. Freeze for up to 3 months.

3. To use frozen sauce: Thaw in the refrigerator overnight. Place in a saucepan and heat through.

Nutrition Facts: 1/2 cup (calculated without spaghetti) equals 103 calories, 3 g fat (1 g saturated fat), 24 mg cholesterol, 325 mg sodium, 9 g carbohydrate, 2 g fiber, 10 g protein. **Diabetic Exchanges:** 2 vegetable, 1 lean meat.

Italian Chicken and Peppers

PREP: 20 min. **COOK:** 4 hours **YIELD:** 6 servings

BRENDA NOLEN • SIMPSONVILLE, SOUTH CAROLINA

I put this recipe together one day when I had leftover peppers and wanted something easy with tomatoes. To my delight, the flavor reminds me of pizza—something I love but can no longer eat! It's great with steamed broccoli.

6   boneless skinless chicken breast halves
(4 oz. *each*)

1   jar (26 oz.) garden-style spaghetti sauce

1   medium onion, sliced

1/2   *each* small green, sweet yellow and red peppers, julienned

1/4   cup grated Parmesan cheese

2   garlic cloves, minced

1   tsp. dried oregano

1   tsp. dried basil

1/2   tsp. salt

1/4   tsp. pepper

4-1/2   cups uncooked spiral pasta

1. Place chicken in a 3-qt. slow cooker. In a large bowl, combine the spaghetti sauce, onion, peppers, cheese, garlic, oregano, basil, salt and pepper. Pour over chicken.

2. Cover and cook on low for 4-5 hours or until a meat thermometer reads 170°. Meanwhile, cook pasta according to package directions; drain. Serve chicken with pasta and sauce.

Nutrition Facts: 1 chicken breast half with 3/4 cup pasta and 2/3 cup sauce equals 396 calories, 7 g fat (2 g saturated fat), 70 mg cholesterol, 770 mg sodium, 50 g carbohydrate, 5 g fiber, 32 g protein.

ITALIAN CHICKEN AND PEPPERS

Refreshing Grilled Chicken Salad

PREP: 20 min. + marinating **GRILL:** 10 min.
YIELD: 4 servings

DENISE RASMUSSEN • SALINA, KANSAS

This recipe is unique, light, zippy and flavorful. It's a nice, healthy salad that's great for a casual luncheon with friends. And with blueberries, walnuts and olive oil, it's nutritionally exceptional as well.

1/2	cup lime juice
2	Tbsp. honey
4	tsp. olive oil
1/2	tsp. salt
1/2	tsp. pepper
4	boneless skinless chicken breast halves (4 oz. *each*)
6	cups spring mix salad greens
2	cups cubed seedless watermelon
1	cup fresh blueberries
1	medium sweet yellow pepper, cut into 1-in. pieces
1/3	cup chopped walnuts, toasted

1. In a small bowl, combine the lime juice, honey, oil, salt and pepper. Pour 1/3 cup into a large resealable plastic bag; add the chicken. Seal bag and turn to coat; refrigerate for at least 1 hour. Cover and refrigerate remaining lime juice mixture for dressing.

2. Coat grill rack with cooking spray before starting the grill. Drain and discard marinade. Grill chicken, covered, over medium heat for 4-7 minutes on each side or until juices run clear.

3. In a large bowl, combine the salad greens, watermelon, blueberries and yellow pepper; add reserved dressing and toss to coat. Divide among four serving plates. Slice chicken; serve with salads. Sprinkle each serving with 4 tsp. walnuts.

Nutrition Facts: 1 serving equals 300 calories, 12 g fat (2 g saturated fat), 63 mg cholesterol, 257 mg sodium, 25 g carbohydrate, 4 g fiber, 28 g protein. **Diabetic Exchanges:** 3 very lean meat, 2 fat, 1 vegetable, 1 fruit, 1/2 starch.

Chicken & Spinach Pasta

PREP/TOTAL TIME: 30 min. **YIELD:** 4 servings

PAMELA ZIEMER • HUTCHINSON, MINNESOTA

One of my favorites! I can't remember where I got this recipe, but I make it often. You can also double the amounts and freeze the leftovers. I enjoy it because it's tasty enough to eat even without the pasta!

1-1/2	cups uncooked medium pasta shells
1	medium onion, chopped
1	large portobello mushroom, chopped
2	garlic cloves, minced
1	tsp. olive oil
1	Tbsp. all-purpose flour
1	cup fat-free milk
1/2	cup reduced-sodium chicken broth
2-1/2	cups cubed cooked chicken breast
1	pkg. (10 oz.) frozen chopped spinach, thawed and squeezed dry
6	Tbsp. shredded Parmesan cheese, *divided*
1	tsp. lemon juice
1/4	tsp. pepper
1/4	tsp. crushed red pepper flakes

1. Cook pasta according to package directions. Meanwhile, in a large saucepan, saute the onion, mushroom and garlic in oil until tender. Stir in flour until blended; gradually add milk and broth. Bring to a boil; cook and stir for 2 minutes or until thickened.

2. Add the chicken, spinach, 3 Tbsp. cheese, lemon juice, pepper and pepper flakes; heat through.

3. Drain pasta; toss with chicken mixture. Sprinkle with remaining cheese.

Nutrition Facts: 1-1/2 cups equals 396 calories, 7 g fat (2 g saturated fat), 74 mg cholesterol, 337 mg sodium, 44 g carbohydrate, 5 g fiber, 40 g protein. **Diabetic Exchanges:** 5 very lean meat, 2 starch, 1 vegetable, 1 fat.

REFRESHING GRILLED CHICKEN SALAD

CHICKEN & SPINACH PASTA

Makeover Creamy Macaroni and Cheese

PREP: 20 min. **BAKE:** 35 min. **YIELD:** 7 servings

DARCIE ZERNIAK • ONTARIO, NEW YORK

With its creamy consistency and two different cheeses, this entree captures the essence of comfort food. But here's the kicker—it's been slimmed down for you so you can enjoy it without overindulging.

2	cups uncooked elbow macaroni
1/4	cup butter, cubed
1/3	cup all-purpose flour
1-1/2	cups fat-free milk
1/4	cup reduced-sodium chicken broth
1	cup (8 oz.) fat-free sour cream
1/2	lb. reduced-fat process cheese (Velveeta), cubed
1/4	cup grated Parmesan cheese
1/2	tsp. ground mustard
1/2	tsp. pepper
2	cups (8 oz.) shredded reduced-fat cheddar cheese

Minced chives, optional

1. Cook macaroni according to package directions. Meanwhile, in a large saucepan, melt the butter. Stir in flour until smooth. Gradually add the milk and broth. Bring to a boil; cook and stir for 2 minutes or until thickened.

2. Reduce heat; stir in the sour cream, process cheese, Parmesan, mustard and pepper until smooth.

3. Drain macaroni; stir in cheddar cheese. Transfer to a 13-in. x 9-in. baking dish coated with cooking spray. Add cream sauce and mix well. Bake, uncovered, at 350° for 35-40 minutes or until bubbly. Sprinkle with chives if desired.

Nutrition Facts: 1 cup equals 394 calories, 18 g fat (11 g saturated fat), 61 mg cholesterol, 842 mg sodium, 37 g carbohydrate, 1 g fiber, 23 g protein.

Get more vegetables into your diet by stirring any of the following into **mac and cheese**: cooked peas, salsa, diced mushrooms, chopped spinach or sauteed onions.

Bow Ties with Chicken & Shrimp

PREP: 20 min. **COOK:** 15 min. **YIELD:** 7 servings

JAN ARCHER • KANSAS CITY, MISSOURI

What a nourishing stovetop supper to keep your family warm and satisfied in cold weather! It's also simple, savory and special enough for company.

5-1/4 cups uncooked bow tie pasta
  3/4 lb. boneless skinless chicken breasts, cubed
    1 Tbsp. butter
    1 Tbsp. olive oil
    2 green onions, chopped
    2 garlic cloves, minced
    2 cans (14-1/2 oz. *each*) Italian diced tomatoes, undrained
    2 Tbsp. minced fresh parsley, *divided*
    1 Tbsp. *each* minced fresh basil, thyme and oregano *or* 1 tsp. *each* dried basil, thyme and oregano
  1/4 tsp. pepper
    2 tsp. cornstarch
  1/2 cup reduced-sodium chicken broth
  3/4 lb. cooked large shrimp, peeled and deveined
    3 plum tomatoes, diced
   10 large pitted ripe olives, sliced
Minced fresh parsley, optional

1. Cook pasta according to package directions. Meanwhile, in a large nonstick skillet, saute chicken in butter and oil until no longer pink. Add onions and garlic; cook 1 minute longer. Stir in the canned tomatoes, parsley, basil, thyme, oregano and pepper.

2. Combine cornstarch and broth until smooth; stir into the pan. Bring to a boil; cook and stir for 2 minutes or until thickened. Add the shrimp, plum tomatoes and olives; heat through. Drain pasta; serve with chicken mixture. Sprinkle with the parsley if desired.

Nutrition Facts: 1 cup pasta with 1 cup sauce equals 399 calories, 8 g fat (2 g saturated fat), 105 mg cholesterol, 661 mg sodium, 54 g carbohydrate, 3 g fiber, 29 g protein.

Stuffed Chicken Breasts C

PREP: 35 min. **BAKE:** 35 min. **YIELD:** 8 servings

CAROL MEAD • LOS ALAMOS, NEW MEXICO

I usually cut this recipe in half to satisfy my appetite for roast chicken without buying more meat than I could ever eat. But it makes a nice, easy company dish, too.

    1 small onion, chopped
    1 celery rib, chopped
    1 garlic clove, minced
    2 Tbsp. butter, *divided*
    1 tsp. reduced-sodium chicken bouillon granules
  1/4 cup boiling water

3 cups soft bread crumbs
3 Tbsp. fat-free milk
1/2 tsp. dried parsley flakes
1/2 tsp. dried rosemary, crushed
1/2 tsp. dried thyme
8 boneless skinless chicken breast halves (4 oz. *each*)
1/2 tsp. salt
1/4 tsp. pepper

1. In a small nonstick skillet, saute the onion, celery and garlic in 1 Tbsp. butter until tender. In a large bowl, dissolve bouillon in boiling water. Stir in bread crumbs, milk, herbs and celery mixture. Set aside.

2. Flatten chicken to 1/4-in. thickness. Sprinkle with salt and pepper. Spread bread crumb mixture over chicken; roll up. Secure with toothpicks.

3. Place in a 13-in. x 9-in. baking dish coated with cooking spray. Bake, uncovered, at 350° for 25 minutes. Melt remaining butter and brush over chicken. Bake 10-15 minutes longer or until a meat thermometer reads 170°. Discard toothpicks.

Nutrition Facts: 1 stuffed chicken breast half equals 200 calories, 6 g fat (3 g saturated fat), 71 mg cholesterol, 368 mg sodium, 10 g carbohydrate, 1 g fiber, 25 g protein. **Diabetic Exchanges:** 3 very lean meat, 1/2 starch, 1/2 fat.

Enchilada Lasagna

PREP: 25 min. **BAKE:** 20 min. + standing
YIELD: 8 servings

JULIE CACKLER • DES MOINES, IOWA

The whole family will love the familar Southwestern flavors in this tasty casserole.

1 lb. lean ground turkey
1 large onion, chopped
1 large green pepper, chopped
1 small sweet red pepper, chopped
1 pkg. (8 oz.) fat-free cream cheese
1 tsp. chili powder
1 can (10 oz.) enchilada sauce
6 whole wheat flour tortillas (8 in.)
1 cup (4 oz.) shredded reduced-fat Mexican cheese blend
Salsa and sour cream, optional

1. In a large skillet, cook the turkey, onion and peppers over medium heat until meat is no longer pink; drain. Stir in cream cheese and chili powder.

2. Pour the enchilada sauce in a shallow bowl. Dip the tortillas in sauce to coat. Place two tortillas in a 13-in. x 9-in. baking dish coated with cooking spray; spread with half of the turkey mixture. Sprinkle with 1/3 cup cheese. Repeat layers. Top with the remaining tortillas and cheese.

3. Cover and freeze for up to 3 months or bake, uncovered, at 400° for 20-25 minutes or until heated through and cheese is melted. Let stand 10 minutes before serving. Serve with the salsa and sour cream if desired.

4. To use frozen lasagna: Thaw in the refrigerator overnight. Remove from the refrigerator 30 minutes before baking. Bake as directed.

Nutrition Facts: 1 piece (calculated without salsa and sour cream) equals 282 calories, 11 g fat (3 g saturated fat), 57 mg cholesterol, 697 mg sodium, 27 g carbohydrate, 2 g fiber, 22 g protein. **Diabetic Exchanges:** 2 lean meat, 1-1/2 starch, 1 fat.

Effortless Alfredo Pizza

PREP/TOTAL TIME: 20 min. **YIELD:** 6 slices

BRITTNEY HOUSE • LOCKPORT, ILLINOIS

Here's a lighter, scrumptious twist for pizza night. It makes great use of convenience products, boosting flavor and zip with turkey, nutty fontina cheese and red pepper flakes.

1 pkg. (10 oz.) frozen chopped spinach, thawed and squeezed dry
1 cup shredded cooked turkey breast
2 tsp. lemon juice
1/4 tsp. salt
1/4 tsp. pepper
1 prebaked Italian bread shell crust (14 oz.)
1 garlic clove, peeled and halved
1/2 cup reduced-fat Alfredo sauce
3/4 cup shredded fontina cheese
1/2 tsp. crushed red pepper flakes

1. In a large bowl, combine the spinach, turkey, lemon juice, salt and pepper; set aside.

2. Place crust on an ungreased 12-in. pizza pan; rub with cut sides of garlic. Discard garlic. Spread Alfredo sauce over crust. Top with spinach mixture, cheese and pepper flakes. Bake at 450° for 8-12 minutes or until crust is lightly browned.

Nutrition Facts: 1 slice equals 302 calories, 10 g fat (4 g saturated fat), 45 mg cholesterol, 756 mg sodium, 33 g carbohydrate, 1 g fiber, 20 g protein. **Diabetic Exchanges:** 2 starch, 2 lean meat, 1/2 fat.

EFFORTLESS ALFREDO PIZZA

MEAT LOAF FROM THE SLOW COOKER

IRISH STEW

CANADIAN PORK ROAST WITH GRAVY

Pork, Ham & More

Setting healthy meals on the table? Don't forget about pork. After all, pork is one of the leanest (and tastiest) sources of protein around. Here, you'll find recipes for pork chops, tenderloin and roast, as well as ham, lamb and sausage.

Meat Loaf from The Slow Cooker

PREP: 25 min. **COOK:** 3 hours **YIELD:** 8 servings

LAURA BURGESS • MT. VERNON, SOUTH DAKOTA

This is one of my personal favorites. I'm often asked for the recipe. This dinnertime classic is lightened up and made easier, but keeps its tried-and-true flavor.

1/2	cup tomato sauce
1/2	cup egg substitute
1/4	cup ketchup
1	tsp. Worcestershire sauce
1	small onion, chopped
1/3	cup crushed saltines (about 10 crackers)
3/4	tsp. minced garlic
1/2	tsp. seasoned salt
1/8	tsp. seasoned pepper
1/2	lb. reduced-fat bulk pork sausage
1-1/2	lbs. lean ground beef

SAUCE:

1/2	cup ketchup
3	Tbsp. brown sugar
3/4	tsp. ground mustard
1/4	tsp. ground nutmeg

1. Cut three long narrow strips of heavy-duty foil; crisscross so they resemble spokes of a wheel. Place strips on the bottom and up the sides of a 4- or 5-qt. slow cooker. Coat strips with cooking spray.

2. In a large bowl, combine the first nine ingredients. Crumble sausage and beef over mixture and mix well (mixture will be moist). Shape into a loaf. Place meat loaf in the center of the strips.

3. In a small bowl, combine sauce ingredients. Spoon over meat loaf. Cover and cook on low 3-4 hours or until a meat thermometer reads 160°. Using foil strips as handles, remove the meat loaf to a platter.

Nutrition Facts: 1 slice equals 267 calories, 12 g fat (5 g saturated fat), 72 mg cholesterol, 740 mg sodium, 16 g carbohydrate, trace fiber, 23 g protein. **Diabetic Exchanges:** 3 lean meat, 1 starch, 1/2 fat.

Canadian Pork Roast With Gravy ⑤ ⓒ

PREP: 20 min. **COOK:** 5 hours **YIELD:** 10 servings

MARILYN MCCRORY • CRESTON, BRITISH COLUMBIA

I came up with this quick recipe for my son to prepare for his second date with a new girlfriend. With just a handful of ingredients, it's a simple way to make a big impression on anyone.

1	boneless whole pork loin roast (3 lbs.)
1/3	cup maple syrup
1	Tbsp. lemon juice
1	Tbsp. Dijon mustard
1	garlic clove, minced
2	Tbsp. cornstarch
1/4	cup cold water

1. Cut roast in half. Transfer to a 5-qt. slow cooker. Combine the syrup, lemon juice, mustard and garlic; pour over pork. Cover and cook on low for 5-6 hours or until a meat thermometer reads 160° and the pork roast is tender.

2. Remove meat to a serving platter; keep warm. Strain cooking juices; transfer 1 cup to a small saucepan. Combine cornstarch and water until smooth; stir into cooking juices. Bring to a boil; cook and stir for 2 minutes or until thickened. Slice roast; serve with gravy.

Nutrition Facts: about 4 oz. cooked pork with 2 Tbsp. gravy equals 205 calories, 6 g fat (2 g saturated fat), 68 mg cholesterol, 76 mg sodium, 9 g carbohydrate, trace fiber, 26 g protein. **Diabetic Exchanges:** 4 lean meat, 1/2 starch.

Ounce for ounce, pork tenderloin is almost as lean as boneless skinless chicken breasts. Some of the **leanest cuts of pork** are boneless loin roasts or chops, boneless sirloin roasts or chops and bone-in pork loin chops.

Ham & Asparagus Casserole

PREP: 25 min. **BAKE:** 25 min. **YIELD:** 4 servings

RACHEL KOWASIC • CONNELLSVILLE, PENNSYLVANIA

I'm always looking for ways to add veggies to main dishes, and this comforting casserole was a success!

3-3/4   cups uncooked yolk-free whole wheat noodles
2-1/2   cups cut fresh asparagus (1-in. pieces)
   1   medium onion, chopped
   1   Tbsp. reduced-fat butter
 1/4   cup all-purpose flour
 1/2   tsp. dried thyme
 1/8   tsp. pepper
   1   cup fat-free milk
   1   cup reduced-sodium chicken broth
   1   Tbsp. lemon juice
1-1/2   cups cubed fully cooked lean ham
 1/4   cup minced fresh parsley
 1/3   cup french-fried onions
   2   Tbsp. shredded Parmesan cheese

1. Cook noodles according to package directions. Meanwhile, in a large saucepan, bring 2 cups of water to a boil. Add asparagus. Cover and cook for 3-5 minutes or until crisp-tender; drain and set aside.

2. In a large skillet, saute the chopped onion in butter until tender. Combine the flour, thyme and pepper; gradually whisk in milk and broth until smooth. Add milk mixture to the skillet. Bring to a boil; cook and stir for 1-2 minutes or until thickened. Remove from the heat; stir in lemon juice.

3. Drain noodles; add the ham, parsley, sauce and asparagus. Transfer to a 13-in. x 9-in. baking dish coated with cooking spray. Top with the fried onions and cheese.

4. Cover and bake at 350° for 20 minutes or until bubbly. Uncover and bake 5-10 minutes longer or until golden brown.

Editor's Note: This recipe was tested with Land O'Lakes light stick butter.

Nutrition Facts: 1-1/2 cups equals 343 calories, 8 g fat (3 g saturated fat), 27 mg cholesterol, 946 mg sodium, 50 g carbohydrate, 7 g fiber, 22 g protein.

Cajun Herb Mix F S C

PREP/TOTAL TIME: 5 min. **YIELD:** about 2/3 cup

HEALTHY COOKING TEST KITCHEN

Low-salt foods can help to derease your risk for high blood pressure. Try this spicy salt-free rub on pork to boost flavor, not sodium. It's also great on chicken.

   5   Tbsp. paprika
   2   Tbsp. dried minced onion
   2   Tbsp. dried minced garlic
   1   Tbsp. cayenne pepper
1-1/2   tsp. dried oregano
1-1/2   tsp. dried basil
1-1/2   tsp. white pepper

1. In a small bowl, combine all ingredients. Store mixture in an airtight container for up to six months. Rub over meat before cooking.

Nutrition Facts: 1 tsp. equals 6 calories, trace fat (trace saturated fat), 0 cholesterol, 1 mg sodium, 1 g carbohydrate, trace fiber, trace protein. **Diabetic Exchange:** Free food.

CAJUN HERB MIX

HAM & ASPARAGUS CASSROLE

Southwestern Pasta & Cheese

PREP: 30 min. **BAKE:** 20 min. **YIELD:** 8 servings

NAOMI REED • MCMINNVILLE, OREGON

I gave mac 'n' cheese a twist by adding some favorite ingredients. My family absolutely loves this side dish!

3-1/3	cups uncooked bow tie pasta
1	medium sweet red pepper, chopped
8	green onions, chopped
1	Tbsp. olive oil
1/4	cup all-purpose flour
1	tsp. chili powder
1	tsp. minced chipotle pepper in adobo sauce
1/2	tsp. salt
1/2	tsp. ground cumin
2-1/4	cups fat-free milk
1	cup (4 oz.) shredded sharp cheddar cheese, *divided*
4	center-cut bacon strips, cooked and crumbled
2	Tbsp. minced fresh cilantro

1. Cook pasta according to package directions.

2. Meanwhile, in a large skillet, saute pepper and onions in oil until tender. Stir in the flour, chili powder, chipotle pepper, salt and cumin until blended. Gradually stir in milk. Bring to a boil; cook and stir for 2 minutes or until thickened. Stir in 1/4 cup cheese until melted.

3. Drain pasta; toss with sauce. Stir in bacon and cilantro. Transfer to a 2-qt. baking dish coated with cooking spray. Sprinkle with remaining cheese. Bake, uncovered, at 400° for 20-25 minutes or until bubbly.

Nutrition Facts: 3/4 cup equals 240 calories, 8 g fat (4 g saturated fat), 20 mg cholesterol, 327 mg sodium, 32 g carbohydrate, 2 g fiber, 12 g protein. **Diabetic Exchanges:** 2 starch, 1 lean meat, 1 fat.

Ham & Spinach Couscous

PREP/TOTAL TIME: 20 min. **YIELD:** 4 servings

LISA SHANNON • CULLMAN, ALABAMA

A simple way to dress up couscous, this colorful, foolproof dish makes a lovely one-pot meal when time's tight. For extra flair, toss in some sliced mushrooms, peas, chopped onion, diced carrot or even some chopped broccoli.

2	cups water
1	cup chopped fully cooked ham
1	cup chopped fresh spinach
1/2	tsp. garlic salt
1	cup uncooked couscous
1/4	cup shredded cheddar cheese

1. In a large saucepan, combine the water, ham, spinach and garlic salt. Bring to a boil. Stir in couscous. Remove from the heat; cover and let stand for 5-10 minutes or until water is absorbed. Fluff with a fork. Sprinkle with cheese.

Nutrition Facts: 1 cup equals 248 calories, 6 g fat (3 g saturated fat), 26 mg cholesterol, 727 mg sodium, 36 g carbohydrate, 2 g fiber, 14 g protein. **Diabetic Exchanges:** 2 starch, 1 lean meat, 1 fat.

Irish Stew

PREP: 15 min. **COOK:** 1-1/2 hours
YIELD: 8 servings (2-1/2 qt.)

HEALTHY COOKING TEST KITCHEN

Lamb, a great protein source, adds delicious flavor to this classic stew. Can't find it at the grocery store? Use beef stew meat instead.

- 1/3 cup plus 1 Tbsp. all-purpose flour, *divided*
- 1-1/2 lbs. lamb stew meat, cut into 1-in. cubes
- 3 Tbsp. olive oil, *divided*
- 3 medium onions, chopped
- 3 garlic cloves, minced
- 4 cups reduced-sodium beef broth
- 2 medium potatoes, peeled and cubed
- 4 medium carrots, cut into 1-in. pieces
- 1 cup frozen peas
- 1 tsp. salt
- 1 tsp. dried thyme
- 1/2 tsp. pepper
- 1/2 tsp. Worcestershire sauce
- 2 Tbsp. water

1. Place 1/3 cup flour in a large resealable plastic bag. Add lamb, a few pieces at a time, and shake to coat. In a Dutch oven, brown lamb in batches in 2 Tbsp. oil. Remove and set aside.

2. In the same pan, saute onions and garlic in remaining oil until tender. Add broth, stirring to loosen browned bits from pan. Add meat. Bring to a boil. Reduce heat; cover and simmer for 1 hour or until meat is tender.

3. Add potatoes and carrots; cover and cook for 20 minutes. Stir in peas; cook 5-10 minutes longer or until vegetables are tender. Add seasonings and Worcestershire sauce. Combine remaining flour with water until smooth. Stir into the pan. Bring to a boil; cook and stir for 2 minutes or until thickened.

Nutrition Facts: 1-1/4 cups equals 271 calories, 10 g fat (2 g saturated fat), 58 mg cholesterol, 618 mg sodium, 24 g carbohydrate, 4 g fiber, 22 g protein. **Diabetic Exchanges:** 2 lean meat, 1 starch, 1 vegetable, 1 fat.

Spicy Sausage and Penne

PREP: 10 min. **COOK:** 25 min. **YIELD:** 4 servings

BRIAN ALBRIGHT • SEWARD, NEBRASKA

I got the inspiration for this recipe from a dish at a local restaurant. It's a quick meal-in-one that I fix often. You can also substitute whatever pasta or veggies you have on hand for this versatile skillet supper.

- 1 cup uncooked penne pasta
- 1 cup frozen mixed vegetables
- 1/2 lb. smoked turkey sausage, cut into 1/4-in. slices
- 2 Tbsp. all-purpose flour
- 1/4 tsp. garlic powder
- 1/4 tsp. ground mustard
- 1/4 tsp. crushed red pepper flakes
- 1-1/4 cups fat-free milk
- 1/3 cup shredded part-skim mozzarella cheese

1. In a large saucepan, cook pasta according to package directions, adding the vegetables during the last 6 minutes of cooking.

2. Meanwhile, in a large nonstick skillet coated with cooking spray, brown sausage; remove from skillet and keep warm.

3. In a small bowl, combine the flour, garlic powder, mustard and pepper flakes; gradually whisk in milk until smooth. Add milk mixture to the skillet; stirring to loosen browned bits from pan. Bring to a boil; cook and stir for 1-2 minutes or until thickened.

4. Drain pasta and vegetables; stir into the pan. Add cheese and reserved sausage; cook and stir until cheese is melted.

Nutrition Facts: 1 cup equals 228 calories, 5 g fat (2 g saturated fat), 42 mg cholesterol, 650 mg sodium, 27 g carbohydrate, 3 g fiber, 18 g protein. **Diabetic Exchanges:** 2 lean meat, 1-1/2 starch.

Best-Ever Lamb Chops C

PREP: 10 min. + chilling **BROIL:** 10 min.
YIELD: 4 servings

KIM MUNDY • VISALIA, CALIFORNIA

My mom just loved a good lamb chop, and this easy recipe was her favorite way to have them. I've also grilled these chops with great results.

- 1 tsp. *each* dried basil, marjoram and thyme
- 1/2 tsp. salt
- 8 lamb loin chops (3 oz. *each*)
Mint jelly, optional

1. Combine herbs and salt; rub over lamb chops. Cover and refrigerate for 1 hour.

2. Broil 4-6 in. from the heat for 5-8 minutes on each side or until meat reaches desired doneness (for medium-rare, a meat thermometer should read 145°; medium, 160°; well-done, 170°). Serve chops with jelly if desired.

Nutrition Facts: 2 lamb chops (calculated without jelly) equals 157 calories, 7 g fat (2 g saturated fat), 68 mg cholesterol, 355 mg sodium, trace carbohydrate, trace fiber, 22 g protein. **Diabetic Exchanges:** 3 lean meat, 1/2 fat.

Pork Tenderloin With Cherry Relish S C

PREP: 10 min. + chilling **COOK:** 2 min.
YIELD: 8 servings (1 cup relish)

HEALTHY COOKING TEST KITCHEN

We gave pork tenderloin an herb rub to keep flavor high and sodium low, then paired it with a dried-cherry relish, rich in antioxidants, for a tasty meal.

- 1 tsp. garlic powder
- 1 tsp. *each* dried oregano, tarragon and rosemary, crushed
- 2 pork tenderloins (1 lb. *each*), trimmed

RELISH:
- 1 large red onion, sliced
- 2 Tbsp. olive oil
- 3 Tbsp. sugar
- 1/2 cup dried cherries
- 1/4 cup red wine vinegar
- 1/4 tsp. dried rosemary, crushed

1. In a small bowl, combine garlic powder and herbs; rub over pork. Cover and refrigerate for 30 minutes.

2. For relish, in a large saucepan, saute onion in oil until tender. Add sugar; cook and stir over medium heat for 10 minutes or until onion is browned. Add the cherries, vinegar and rosemary. Bring to a boil. Reduce heat; cover and simmer for 10 minutes. Cool to room temperature.

3. Place pork on a rack in a shallow roasting pan lined with foil. Bake at 425° for 25-30 minutes or until a meat thermometer reads 160°. Let stand for 10 minutes before slicing. Serve with relish.

Nutrition Facts: 3 oz. cooked pork with 2 Tbsp. relish equals 217 calories, 7 g fat (2 g saturated fat), 63 mg cholesterol, 46 mg sodium, 14 g carbohydrate, 1 g fiber, 23 g protein. **Diabetic Exchanges:** 3 lean meat, 1/2 starch, 1/2 fruit, 1/2 fat.

PORK TENDERLOIN WITH CHERRY RELISH

BEST-EVER LAMB CHOPS

Chinese Spinach-Almond Salad [C]

PREP/TOTAL TIME: 10 min. **YIELD:** 4 servings

MARY ANN KIEFFER • LAWRENCE, KANSAS

This recipe combines power-packed spinach, a good source of vitamins A and K, with other veggies, lean meat and crunchy, heart-healthy almonds. Reduced-fat dressing adds a light Asian flavor to each serving.

1	pkg. (6 oz.) fresh baby spinach
2	cups cubed cooked pork
1	cup fresh bean sprouts
2	medium carrots, thinly sliced
1/2	cup sliced fresh mushrooms
1/4	cup sliced almonds, toasted
1/2	cup reduced-fat sesame ginger salad dressing

1. In a large bowl, combine the first six ingredients. Divide among four salad plates; drizzle each serving with 2 Tbsp. of dressing. Serve immediately.

Nutrition Facts: 1 serving equals 244 calories, 11 g fat (3 g saturated fat), 63 mg cholesterol, 500 mg sodium, 12 g carbohydrate, 3 g fiber, 24 g protein. **Diabetic Exchanges:** 3 lean meat, 1 vegetable, 1 fat, 1/2 starch.

Glazed Pork Chops [C]

PREP: 10 min. + marinating **GRILL:** 10 min.
YIELD: 8 servings

LOUISE GILBERT • QUESNEL, BRITISH COLUMBIA

Rosemary adds a special touch to these beautifully glazed chops that are just right for any weeknight meal.

1/2	cup ketchup
1/4	cup packed brown sugar
1/4	cup white vinegar
1/4	cup orange juice
1/4	cup Worcestershire sauce
2	garlic cloves, minced
1/2	tsp. dried rosemary, crushed
8	bone-in pork loin chops (1/2 in. thick and 7 oz. *each*)

CHINESE SPINACH-ALMOND SALAD

1. In a small bowl, combine the first seven ingredients. Pour 3/4 cup into a large resealable plastic bag; add the pork chops. Seal bag and turn to coat; refrigerate for 8 hours or overnight. Cover and refrigerate remaining marinade for basting.

2. Coat grill rack with cooking spray before starting the grill. Drain and discard marinade. Grill pork, covered, over medium heat for 4-6 minutes on each side or until a meat thermometer reads 160°, basting occasionally with reserved marinade.

Nutrition Facts: 1 pork chop equals 246 calories, 8 g fat (3 g saturated fat), 86 mg cholesterol, 284 mg sodium, 11 g carbohydrate, trace fiber, 30 g protein. **Diabetic Exchanges:** 4 lean meat, 1 starch.

Pork Medallions In Mustard Sauce [C]

PREP/TOTAL TIME: 30 min. **YIELD:** 4 servings

TAHNIA FOX • TRENTON, MICHIGAN

Mustard and apple juice liven up lean pork tenderloin, creating a dish that's ideal for family and special guests alike.

1/2	cup reduced-sodium chicken broth
2	Tbsp. apple juice concentrate
4-1/2	tsp. whole grain mustard
1	lb. pork tenderloin, cut into 1/2-in. slices
1/4	tsp. salt
1/4	tsp. pepper
1	Tbsp. olive oil
2	garlic cloves, minced
1	tsp. cornstarch
2	Tbsp. cold water
1	Tbsp. minced fresh parsley

1. In a small bowl, combine the broth, juice concentrate and mustard; set aside.

2. Sprinkle pork with salt and pepper. In a large nonstick skillet, brown pork in oil. Remove pork and set aside.

3. Add garlic to the pan; saute for 1 minute. Add reserved broth mixture, stirring to loosen browned bits from pan. Bring to a boil. Reduce heat; simmer, uncovered, for 6-8 minutes or until liquid is reduced to about 1/3 cup.

4. Return pork to the pan; cover and cook over low heat for 3-4 minutes or until meat is no longer pink. Combine cornstarch and water until smooth; add to the pan. Bring to a boil; cook and stir for 2 minutes or until thickened. Sprinkle with parsley.

Nutrition Facts: 3 oz. cooked pork equals 193 calories, 7 g fat (2 g saturated fat), 63 mg cholesterol, 356 mg sodium, 6 g carbohydrate, 1 g fiber, 23 g protein. **Diabetic Exchanges:** 3 lean meat, 1/2 starch, 1/2 fat.

Tangy Pork Chops [C]

PREP: 30 min. **BAKE:** 20 min. **YIELD:** 6 servings

MRS. TOM MAUST • BERLIN, PENNSYLVANIA

I've used this recipe for many years and always get compliments when I serve it. The tender chops pair well with the saucy onion-and-pepper topping. This would also be fantastic served with mashed potatoes.

6 bone-in pork loin chops (7 oz. *each*)
2 tsp. canola oil
2 celery ribs, finely chopped
1 small onion, finely chopped
1 Tbsp. butter
1/2 cup ketchup
1/4 cup water
2 Tbsp. cider vinegar
1 Tbsp. brown sugar
1 Tbsp. lemon juice
1 Tbsp. Worcestershire sauce
1/4 tsp. salt
1/8 tsp. pepper
1 small onion, thinly sliced
1 large green pepper, cut into rings

1. In a large nonstick skillet coated with cooking spray, brown chops in oil in batches. Transfer to a 13-in. x. 9-in. baking dish coated with cooking spray.

2. In the same pan, saute celery and chopped onion in butter until tender. Stir in the ketchup, water, vinegar, brown sugar, lemon juice, Worcestershire sauce, salt and pepper. Bring to a boil. Reduce heat; cover and simmer for 15-20 minutes or until liquid is slightly reduced.

3. Pour sauce over chops. Top with sliced onion and pepper rings. Cover and bake at 350° for 20-25 minutes or until a meat thermometer reads 160°.

Nutrition Facts: 1 serving equals 284 calories, 12 g fat (4 g saturated fat), 91 mg cholesterol, 469 mg sodium, 12 g carbohydrate, 1 g fiber, 31 g protein. **Diabetic Exchanges:** 4 lean meat, 1 starch, 1/2 fat.

Grilled Pork Tenderloin Satay

PREP: 25 min. **GRILL:** 10 min.
YIELD: 8 skewers (1/2 cup sauce)

GAYLE JEFFERSON • LAS VEGAS, NEVADA

My dad made this often when grilling for the family. I love this served on roasted veggies and yellow rice. Peanut butter and soy sauce come together for a great Asian flavor.

1 small onion, chopped
1/4 cup packed brown sugar
1/4 cup water
3 Tbsp. reduced-sodium soy sauce
2 Tbsp. reduced-fat creamy peanut butter
4-1/2 tsp. canola oil
2 garlic cloves, minced
1/4 tsp. ground ginger
1 pork tenderloin (1 lb.)

1. In a small saucepan, bring the first eight ingredients to a boil. Reduce heat; simmer, uncovered, for 10-12 minutes or until thickened. Set aside 1/2 cup mixture for sauce.

2. Cut pork in half widthwise; cut each half into thin strips. Thread pork strips onto eight metal or soaked wooden skewers. Grill, uncovered, over medium-hot heat for 2-3 minutes on each side or until no longer pink, basting occasionally with remaining mixture. Serve with reserved sauce.

Nutrition Facts: 2 skewers with 2 Tbsp. sauce equals 287 calories, 12 g fat (2 g saturated fat), 63 mg cholesterol, 549 mg sodium, 19 g carbohydrate, 1 g fiber, 26 g protein. **Diabetic Exchanges:** 3 lean meat, 1-1/2 fat, 1 starch.

Pork Chop Skillet

PREP: 15 min. **COOK:** 30 min. **YIELD:** 4 servings

SUSAN BLAIR • STERLING, MICHIGAN

My husband and I enjoy this quick supper on busy days when there's little time to cook. It satisfies our meat-and-potato cravings and goes together in a snap, and leftovers (if there are any) taste even better the next day!

4	medium red potatoes, cubed
1/2	cup water
1-1/4	cups fresh baby carrots
2	celery ribs, coarsely chopped
1	medium onion, cut into wedges
4	boneless pork loin chops (4 oz. *each*)
1	Tbsp. canola oil

SAUCE:

1	can (10-3/4 oz.) condensed tomato soup, undiluted
1/2	cup water
1	tsp. dried thyme
1	tsp. Worcestershire sauce
1/4	tsp. pepper
1-1/2	tsp. all-purpose flour
2	Tbsp. cold water

1. Place potatoes and water in a microwave-safe dish; cover and microwave on high for 3 minutes. Add the carrots, celery and onion; cook 4-6 minutes longer or until crisp-tender. Drain. In a large skillet over medium heat, brown pork chops in oil on both sides. Top with vegetables.

2. Combine the soup, water, thyme, Worcestershire sauce and pepper; pour over the top. Bring to a boil. Reduce heat; cover and simmer for 20-25 minutes or until meat and vegetables are tender. Remove chops and vegetables; keep warm.

3. Combine flour and cold water until smooth; gradually stir into the sauce. Bring to a boil; cook and stir for 2 minutes or until thickened. Serve with chops and vegetables.

Editor's Note: This recipe was tested in a 1,100-watt microwave.

Nutrition Facts: 1 pork chop with 1-1/2 cups vegetables and 1/4 cup sauce equals 360 calories, 10 g fat (3 g saturated fat), 55 mg cholesterol, 548 mg sodium, 40 g carbohydrate, 5 g fiber, 26 g protein. **Diabetic Exchanges:** 3 lean meat, 2 starch, 1 vegetable, 1/2 fat.

Cranberry-Glazed Pork Roast C

PREP: 10 min. **COOK:** 2-1/4 hours +standing **YIELD:** 16 servings

BETH BRANDENBURGER • ROCHESTER, MINNESOTA

This recipe is so easy. It's a favorite! Cranberries lend a subtle sweet-tart undertone to this elegant and tender entree.

1	cup whole-berry cranberry sauce
3/4	cup unsweetened apple juice

3/4	cup barbecue sauce	
1	tsp. salt	
1	Tbsp. cornstarch	
2	Tbsp. cold water	
1	boneless rolled pork loin roast (4 lbs.)	

1. In a small saucepan, combine the cranberry sauce, apple juice, barbecue sauce and salt. Bring to a boil. Reduce heat; simmer, uncovered, for 10 minutes. Combine the cornstarch and water until smooth; stir into cranberry mixture. Bring to a boil; cook and stir for 2 minutes or until sauce is thickened. Set aside 1 cup sauce.

2. Place roast in a shallow roasting pan. Bake, uncovered, at 350° for 1-3/4 hours. Spoon a third of the remaining glaze over pork. Bake 30 minutes longer or until a meat thermometer reads 160°, basting twice. Let stand for 10 minutes before slicing. Serve with reserved sauce.

Nutrition Facts: 3 oz. cooked pork with 1 Tbsp. reserved sauce equals 181 calories, 5 g fat (2 g saturated fat), 56 mg cholesterol, 280 mg sodium, 10 g carbohydrate, trace fiber, 22 g protein. **Diabetic Exchanges:** 3 lean meat, 1/2 starch.

Glazed Pork Chops With Corn Bread Dressing

PREP: 10 min. **BAKE:** 25 min. **YIELD:** 6 servings

DAWN ZUBKE • WATERTOWN, WISCONSIN

A subtle glaze coats delicious pork chops in this no-fuss meal-in-one staple.

1-1/4	cups reduced-sodium chicken broth	
3/4	cup chopped onion	
3/4	cup frozen corn	
1	celery rib, chopped	
Dash cayenne pepper		
3	cups crushed corn bread stuffing	
6	boneless pork loin chops (6 oz. *each*)	
2	Tbsp. brown sugar	
2	tsp. spicy brown mustard	

1. In a large saucepan, bring the broth, onion, corn, celery and cayenne to a boil. Remove from the heat; stir in stuffing. Transfer to a 13-in. x 9-in. baking dish coated with cooking spray. Top with pork chops. Combine the brown sugar and the mustard; spread over chops.

2. Bake, uncovered, at 400° for 25-30 minutes or until a meat thermometer reads 160°.

Nutrition Facts: 1 pork chop with 2/3 cup dressing equals 389 calories, 11 g fat (4 g saturated fat), 82 mg cholesterol, 516 mg sodium, 33 g carbohydrate, 2 g fiber, 37 g protein. **Diabetic Exchanges:** 5 lean meat, 2 starch.

Elegant Pork Marsala ⒸC

PREP/TOTAL TIME: 30 min. **YIELD:** 6 servings

KIM GILLIS • HIGH FALLS, NEW YORK

Wine and fresh mushrooms lend elegance to this oh-so-simple pork dish. Use presliced mushrooms and jarred minced garlic rather than fresh to shave even more time off preparation. Cleanup is one-pan easy!

5	tsp. cornstarch	
2/3	cup reduced-sodium chicken broth	
1/3	cup whole wheat flour	
1/2	tsp. pepper	
6	boneless pork loin chops (4 oz. *each*)	
1	Tbsp. olive oil	
2	cups sliced fresh mushrooms	
1/3	cup chopped onion	
2	turkey bacon strips, diced	
1/4	tsp. minced garlic	
1	cup marsala wine *or* additional reduced-sodium chicken broth	

1. In a small bowl, combine cornstarch and broth until smooth; set aside.

2. Place flour and pepper in a large resealable plastic bag. Add pork, a few pieces at a time, and shake to coat. In a large nonstick skillet coated with cooking spray, cook chops in oil for 4-5 minutes on each side or until a meat thermometer reads 160°. Remove and keep warm.

3. In the same skillet, saute the mushrooms, onion and bacon in drippings for 3 minutes or until bacon is crisp-tender. Add garlic; cook 1 minute longer. Add wine, stirring to loosen browned bits from pan. Stir cornstarch mixture; add to pan. Bring to a boil; cook and stir for 2 minutes or until slightly thickened. Serve with pork.

Editor's Note: When cutting or seeding hot peppers, use rubber or plastic gloves to protect your hands. Avoid touching your face.

Nutrition Facts: 1 pork chop with 1/3 cup sauce equals 232 calories, 10 g fat (3 g saturated fat), 60 mg cholesterol, 161 mg sodium, 7 g carbohydrate, 1 g fiber, 24 g protein. **Diabetic Exchanges:** 3 lean meat, 1/2 starch, 1/2 fat.

ELEGANT PORK MARSALA

Pork Burritos

PREP: 20 min.　**COOK:** 8 hours　**YIELD:** 14 servings

SHARON BELMONT • LINCOLN, NEBRASKA

These slow cooked burritos are easy, delicious and feed a crowd. I've been making the recipe for 20 years, changing it here and there, until I created this favorite version.

- 1 boneless pork sirloin roast (3 lbs.)
- 1/4 cup reduced-sodium chicken broth
- 1 envelope reduced-sodium taco seasoning
- 1 Tbsp. dried parsley flakes
- 2 garlic cloves, minced
- 1/2 tsp. pepper
- 1/4 tsp. salt
- 1 can (16 oz.) refried beans
- 1 can (4 oz.) chopped green chilies
- 14 flour tortillas (8 in.), warmed

Optional toppings: shredded lettuce, chopped tomatoes, chopped green pepper, guacamole, reduced-fat sour cream and shredded reduced-fat cheddar cheese

1. Cut roast in half; place in a 4- or 5-qt. slow cooker. In a small bowl, combine the broth, taco seasoning, parsley, garlic, pepper and salt. Pour mixture over roast. Cover and cook on low for 8-10 hours or until meat is very tender.

2. Remove pork from the slow cooker; cool slightly. Shred with two forks; set aside. Skim fat from the liquid; stir in beans and chilies. Return pork to the slow cooker; heat through. Spoon 1/2 cup pork mixture down the center of each tortilla; add toppings of your choice. Fold sides and ends over the filling and roll up.

Nutrition Facts: 1 burrito (calculated without optional toppings) equals 320 calories, 9 g fat (3 g saturated fat), 61 mg cholesterol, 606 mg sodium, 33 g carbohydrate, 2 g fiber, 26 g protein. **Diabetic Exchanges:** 2 starch, 2 lean meat, 1 fat.

Chipotle Mustard Pork Tenderloin c

PREP: 15 min. + marinating　**GRILL:** 25 min.
YIELD: 4 servings

LINDA FOREMAN • • LOCUST GROVE, OKLAHOMA

Here's one flavorful entree with a lot of kick! The chipotle's heat really comes through, and mustard lovers will savor this fun, fast meal. Serve with plenty of ice-cold lemonade or iced tea.

- 1/2 cup honey Dijon mustard
- 1/3 cup minced fresh cilantro
- 1/4 cup lime juice
- 1 Tbsp. minced chipotle pepper in adobo sauce
- 2 garlic cloves, minced
- 1/2 tsp. ground cumin
- 1/4 tsp. salt
- 1/8 tsp. ground cinnamon
- 1 pork tenderloin (1 lb.)

Chopped honey-roasted peanuts, optional

1. In a small bowl, combine the first eight ingredients. Pour 1/2 cup marinade into a large resealable plastic bag; add the pork. Seal bag and turn to coat; refrigerate for 8 hours or overnight. Cover and refrigerate remaining mustard mixture.

2. Coat grill rack with cooking spray before starting the grill. Drain pork and discard marinade. Grill pork, covered, over indirect medium-hot heat for 25-40 minutes or until a meat thermometer reads 160°. Let stand for 5 minutes before slicing.

3. Heat reserved mustard mixture; brush over pork before serving. Sprinkle with peanuts if desired.

Nutrition Facts: 3 oz. cooked pork (calculated without peanuts) equals 191 calories, 6 g fat (2 g saturated fat), 64 mg cholesterol, 366 mg sodium, 13 g carbohydrate, 1 g fiber, 24 g protein. **Diabetic Exchanges:** 3 lean meat, 1 starch.

Teriyaki Pork Kabobs

PREP: 20 min.　**GRILL:** 15 min.　**YIELD:** 4 servings

EDIE DESPAIN • LOGAN, UTAH

Soy sauce, garlic and ginger add Asian flavor to this quick dish, and help to make it delicious without a lot of added fat. More flavor and less fat is something I strive for in my cooking, and this recipe is a staple.

PORK BURRITOS

TERIYAKI PORK KABOBS

4-1/2 tsp. cornstarch
1 Tbsp. brown sugar
1 can (14-1/2 oz.) reduced-sodium beef broth
2 Tbsp. reduced-sodium soy sauce
2 garlic cloves, minced
1/4 tsp. ground ginger
1 pork tenderloin (1 lb.), cut into 1-in. cubes
16 medium fresh mushrooms
1 large red onion, cut into wedges
8 cherry tomatoes
Hot cooked rice, optional

1. In a small saucepan, combine cornstarch and brown sugar. Stir in the broth, soy sauce, garlic and ginger until blended. Bring to a boil; cook and stir for 2 minutes or until thickened. Set aside half of the sauce for serving; keep warm.

2. On eight metal or soaked wooden skewers, alternately thread the pork, mushrooms and onion. Grill, covered, over medium heat for 10-15 minutes or until meat is no longer pink, basting frequently with remaining sauce and turning once.

3. Place a tomato on the end of each kabob. Grill 1-2 minutes longer or until tomatoes are heated through, turning occasionally. Serve with reserved sauce and rice if desired.

Nutrition Facts: 2 kabobs with 3 Tbsp. sauce (calculated without rice) equals 210 calories, 4 g fat (1 g saturated fat), 65 mg cholesterol, 539 mg sodium, 16 g carbohydrate, 2 g fiber, 27 g protein. **Diabetic Exchanges:** 3 lean meat, 2 vegetable, 1/2 starch.

Cajun Orange Pork Chops S C

PREP: 15 min. + marinating **GRILL:** 10 min.
YIELD: 4 servings

PATRICIA HARMON • BADEN, PENNSYLVANIA

My husband and I are busy and calorie-conscious. This dish is quick, delicious and easy on the waistline.

1/2 cup orange juice
2 green onions, chopped
2 Tbsp. orange marmalade
2 garlic cloves, minced
1 tsp. Cajun seasoning
4 boneless pork loin chops (4 oz. each)

1. In a small bowl, combine the first five ingredients. Pour 1/3 cup marinade into a large resealable bag; add the pork. Seal bag and turn to coat; refrigerate for 8 hours or overnight. Cover and refrigerate remaining marinade for sauce.

2. In a small saucepan, bring reserved marinade to a boil. Reduce heat; simmer, uncovered, for 5-7 minutes or until thickened. Keep warm.

3. Coat grill rack with cooking spray before starting the grill. Drain pork chops and discard marinade. Grill, covered, over medium heat for 4-5 minutes on each side or until a meat thermometer reads 160°. Brush with sauce.

Nutrition Facts: 1 pork chop equals 183 calories, 6 g fat (2 g saturated fat), 55 mg cholesterol, 138 mg sodium, 8 g carbohydrate, trace fiber, 22 g protein. **Diabetic Exchanges:** 3 lean meat, 1/2 starch.

TILAPIA & LEMON SAUCE

SALMON IN DILL SAUCE

SHRIMP PICCATA PASTA

Fish & Seafood

Health-minded cooks are making fish and seafood a regular part of mealtime. Not only is seafood a fast and delicious dinner option, but it's often low in calories and keeps carbs at bay as well. Dig into one of these fresh favorites tonight!

Shrimp Piccata Pasta

PREP/TOTAL TIME: 20 min. **YIELD:** 4 servings

CAROLE BESS WHITE • PORTLAND, OREGON

This dish is quick, simple and flavorful and a terrific way to introduce shrimp and capers to your menu. The light sauce really enhances the wonderful flavor of shrimp.

- 6 oz. uncooked spaghetti
- 2 shallots, chopped
- 1 Tbsp. olive oil
- 1 lb. uncooked medium shrimp, peeled and deveined
- 1 jar (3 oz.) capers, drained
- 3 Tbsp. lemon juice
- 1/2 tsp. garlic powder

1. Cook spaghetti according to package directions. Meanwhile, in a large nonstick skillet, saute shallots in oil until tender. Add the shrimp, capers, lemon juice and garlic powder; cook and stir for 5-6 minutes or until shrimp turn pink.

2. Drain spaghetti; toss with shrimp mixture.

Nutrition Facts: 1-1/4 cups equals 293 calories, 5 g fat (1 g saturated fat), 168 mg cholesterol, 453 mg sodium, 37 g carbohydrate, 2 g fiber, 24 g protein. **Diabetic Exchanges:** 3 very lean meat, 2 starch, 1/2 fat.

Tilapia & Lemon Sauce

PREP/TOTAL TIME: 30 min. **YIELD:** 4 servings

SUSAN TAUL • BIRMINGHAM, ALABAMA

Serve this main course with any tossed salad, your favorite vegetables and lightly buttered bread.

- 1/4 cup plus 1 Tbsp. all-purpose flour, *divided*
- 1 tsp. salt
- 4 tilapia fillets (4 oz. *each*)
- 2 Tbsp. plus 2 tsp. butter, *divided*
- 1/3 cup reduced-sodium chicken broth
- 2 Tbsp. white wine or additional reduced-sodium chicken broth
- 1-1/2 tsp. lemon juice
- 1-1/2 tsp. minced fresh parsley
- 1/4 cup sliced almonds, toasted
- 2 cups hot cooked rice

1. In a shallow bowl, combine 1/4 cup flour and salt. Dip fillets in flour mixture. In a large nonstick skillet coated with cooking spray, cook fillets in 2 Tbsp. butter over medium-high heat for 4-5 minutes on each side or until fish flakes easily with a fork. Remove and keep warm.

2. In the same skillet, melt remaining butter. Stir in remaining flour until smooth; gradually add the broth, wine and lemon juice. Bring to a boil; cook and stir for 2 minutes or until thickened. Stir in parsley. Spoon sauce over fish; sprinkle with almonds. Serve with rice.

Nutrition Facts: 1 fillet with 1/2 cup rice and 4 tsp. sauce equals 334 calories, 12 g fat (6 g saturated fat), 75 mg cholesterol, 586 mg sodium, 30 g carbohydrate, 1 g fiber, 26 g protein. **Diabetic Exchanges:** 3 very lean meat, 2 starch, 2 fat.

Salmon with Dill Sauce [C]

PREP/TOTAL TIME: 20 min. **YIELD:** 6 servings

MARY RELYEA • CANASTOTA, NEW YORK

This lovely moist salmon topped with a mild and creamy dill sauce can be ready in minutes.

- 6 salmon fillets (4 oz. *each*)
- 1/2 tsp. plus 2 Tbsp. snipped fresh dill, *divided*
- 1/4 tsp. pepper
- 4 tsp. cornstarch
- 2/3 cup reduced-sodium chicken broth
- 1/3 cup evaporated milk
- 1 Tbsp. Dijon mustard
- 2 tsp. lemon juice

1. Place each salmon fillet on a double thickness of heavy-duty foil (about 12 in. square). Sprinkle with 1/2 tsp. dill and pepper. Fold foil around salmon and seal tightly. Grill, covered, over high heat for 5-10 minutes or until fish flakes easily with a fork.

2. In a small saucepan, combine the cornstarch, broth, milk, mustard, lemon juice and remaining dill. Bring to a boil over medium heat; cook and stir for 1-2 minutes or until thickened.

3. Open foil packets carefully to allow steam to escape. Serve salmon with dill sauce.

Nutrition Facts: 1 fillet with about 3 Tbsp. sauce equals 238 calories, 13 g fat (3 g saturated fat), 71 mg cholesterol, 213 mg sodium, 4 g carbohydrate, trace fiber, 24 g protein. **Diabetic Exchanges:** 3 lean meat, 1 fat.

Red Clam Sauce

PREP: 25 min. **COOK:** 3 hours **YIELD:** 4 servings

JOANN BROWN • LATROBE, PENNSYLVANIA

This recipe tastes like it's been slaved over all day. Instead, it cooks while you do other things. What a great way to jazz up pasta sauce!

1	medium onion, chopped
2	garlic cloves, minced
1	Tbsp. canola oil
2	cans (6-1/2 oz. *each*) chopped clams, undrained
1	can (14-1/2 oz.) diced tomatoes, undrained
1	can (6 oz.) tomato paste
1/4	cup minced fresh parsley
1	bay leaf
1	tsp. sugar
1	tsp. dried basil
1/2	tsp. dried thyme
6	oz. linguine, cooked and drained

1. In a small skillet, saute onion and garlic in oil until tender. Transfer to a 1-1/2- or 2-qt. slow cooker. Stir in the clams, tomatoes, tomato paste, parsley, bay leaf, sugar, basil and thyme. Cover and cook on low for 3-4 hours or until heated through. Discard bay leaf. Serve with linguine.

Nutrition Facts: 1 cup sauce with 3/4 cup cooked linguine equals 305 calories, 5 g fat (trace saturated fat), 15 mg cholesterol, 553 mg sodium, 53 g carbohydrate, 7 g fiber, 15 g protein.

Mini Scallop Casseroles

PREP: 30 min. **BAKE:** 20 min. **YIELD:** 4 servings

VIVIAN MANARY • NEPEAN, ONTARIO

Tiny and tender bay scallops take center stage in these cute individual dishes. They're reminiscent of potpies, very creamy and packed with flavorful veggies in every bite.

3	celery ribs, chopped
1	cup sliced fresh mushrooms
1	medium green pepper, chopped
1	small onion, chopped
2	Tbsp. butter
1/3	cup all-purpose flour
1/4	tsp. salt
1/4	tsp. pepper
2	cups fat-free milk
1	lb. bay scallops

TOPPING:
1	cup soft bread crumbs
1	Tbsp. butter, melted
1/4	cup shredded cheddar cheese

1. In a large skillet, saute the celery, mushrooms, green pepper and onion in butter until tender. Stir in the flour, salt and pepper until blended; gradually add milk. Bring to a boil; cook and stir for 2 minutes or until thickened.

2. Reduce heat; add scallops. Cook, stirring occasionally, for 3-4 minutes or until scallops are firm and opaque.

3. Divide mixture among four 10-oz. ramekins or custard cups. In a small bowl, combine crumbs and butter; sprinkle over scallop mixture. Bake, uncovered, at 350° for 15-20 minutes or until bubbly. Sprinkle with cheese; bake 5 minutes longer or until the cheese is melted.

Nutrition Facts: 1 serving equals 332 calories, 12 g fat (7 g saturated fat), 70 mg cholesterol, 588 mg sodium, 27 g carbohydrate, 2 g fiber, 28 g protein. **Diabetic Exchanges:** 3 very lean meat, 2 fat, 1 starch, 1 vegetable, 1/2 fat-free milk.

Grilled Tilapia with Mango C

PREP/TOTAL TIME: 20 min. **YIELD:** 4 servings

GREGG MAY • COLUMBUS, OHIO

This is a different twist on tilapia that I created for my wife. She enjoyed the combination of mango with the Parmesan. There's nothing like eating this out on the deck with a cold glass of iced tea.

4	tilapia fillets (6 oz. *each*)
1	Tbsp. olive oil
1/2	tsp. salt
1/2	tsp. dill weed

RED CLAM SAUCE

GRILLED TILAPIA WITH MANGO

1/4 tsp. pepper

1 Tbsp. grated Parmesan cheese

1 medium lemon sliced

1 medium mango, peeled and thinly sliced

1. Coat grill rack with cooking spray before starting the grill. Brush fillets with oil; sprinkle with salt, dill and pepper.

2. Grill tilapia, covered, over medium heat for 5 minutes. Turn tilapia; top with cheese, lemon and mango. Grill 4-6 minutes longer or until fish flakes easily with a fork.

Nutrition Facts: 1 serving equals 213 calories, 5 g fat (1 g saturated fat), 84 mg cholesterol, 377 mg sodium, 10 g carbohydrate, 1 g fiber, 32 g protein. **Diabetic Exchanges:** 5 very lean meat, 1/2 fruit, 1/2 fat.

Company-Ready Crusted Salmon

PREP: 20 min. **BAKE:** 20 min. **YIELD:** 6 servings

SUSAN ROBENSON • HOT SPRINGS, ARKANSAS

My husband had high cholesterol, so I created this heart-healthy entree. Now I serve it to guests all the time...even those who don't like fish rave and ask for the recipe! Best of all it's a tasty meal-in-one. All I have to do is add a salad and dinner is ready.

2 pkg. (6 oz. *each*) fresh baby spinach

1 salmon fillet (1-1/2 lbs.)

1 tsp. olive oil

3 Tbsp. honey

3 Tbsp. Dijon mustard

1/4 cup cornflakes

2 Tbsp. sliced almonds

2 Tbsp. chopped pecans

1/4 cup fat-free mayonnaise

Hot cooked couscous, optional

1. Place spinach in a 13-in. x 9-in. baking dish coated with cooking spray; top with salmon. Drizzle oil over spinach.

2. Combine honey and mustard. Remove 2 Tbsp. mixture; brush over salmon. Place the cornflakes, almonds and pecans in a small food processor; cover and process until ground. Press onto salmon. Stir mayonnaise into remaining honey mixture; refrigerate until serving.

3. Bake, uncovered, at 450° for 18-22 minutes or until fish flakes easily with a fork. Drizzle with reserved sauce. Serve with couscous if desired.

Nutrition Facts: about 3 oz. cooked salmon with 1/4 cup spinach and 1 Tbsp. sauce equals 296 calories, 15 g fat (3 g saturated fat), 68 mg cholesterol, 381 mg sodium, 15 g carbohydrate, 2 g fiber, 25 g protein.

Walnut Ginger Salmon C

PREP: 10 min. + marinating **BROIL:** 10 min.
YIELD: 4 servings

BECKY WALCH • MANTECA, CALIFORNIA

Pantry ingredients combine for a delightful marinade that lightly glazes this tender, moist salmon.

1	Tbsp. brown sugar
1	Tbsp. Dijon mustard
1	Tbsp. soy sauce
1	tsp. ground ginger
4	skinless salmon fillets (4 oz. *each*)
1/4	cup chopped walnuts

1. In a large resealable plastic bag, combine the brown sugar, mustard, soy sauce and ginger; add the salmon. Seal bag and turn to coat; refrigerate for 30 minutes, turning occasionally.

2. Drain and discard marinade. Place salmon on a foil-lined baking sheet coated with cooking spray. Broil 4-6 in. from the heat for 7-9 minutes or until fish flakes easily with a fork, sprinkling with walnuts during the last 2 minutes of cooking.

Nutrition Facts: 1 fillet equals 270 calories, 17 g fat (3 g saturated fat), 67 mg cholesterol, 292 mg sodium, 4 g carbohydrate, trace fiber, 25 g protein.**Diabetic Exchanges:** 3 medium-fat meat, 1 fat.

Pan-Seared Shrimp

PREP/TOTAL TIME: 30 min. **YIELD:** 4 servings

PATRICIA ZARTMAN • YORK, PENNSYLVANIA

Garlic, parsley and wine punch up the buttery flavor of this simple shrimp recipe, giving it a decadent and special feel. Best of all it comes together in just half an hour, so it's perfect for company and for hectic weeknights alike. Serve it with steamed spinach for a fabulous meal.

1	lb. uncooked medium shrimp, peeled and deveined
2	garlic cloves, minced
2	Tbsp. olive oil
1/3	cup white wine *or* reduced-sodium chicken broth
1/2	tsp. seafood seasoning
2	cups hot cooked rice
2	Tbsp. minced fresh parsley

1. In a large skillet, saute shrimp and garlic in oil for 3 minutes. Add wine and seasoning; cook and stir 3-5 minutes longer or until shrimp turn pink. Serve with rice; sprinkle with parsley.

Nutrition Facts: 1/2 cup shrimp with 1/2 cup rice equals 262 calories, 9 g fat (1 g saturated fat), 138 mg cholesterol, 238 mg sodium, 24 g carbohydrate, trace fiber, 21 g protein. **Diabetic Exchanges:** 3 very lean meat, 1-1/2 starch, 1 fat.

Shrimp Curry

PREP/TOTAL TIME: 30 min. **YIELD:** 4 servings

AGNES WARD • STRATFORD, ONTARIO

Here's a tasty way to add seafood to your diet. It's great with chicken, too. Either way, your family will request this satisfying supper again and again!

1/4	cup finely chopped onion	
1-1/2	tsp. curry powder	
2	Tbsp. butter	
3	Tbsp. all-purpose flour	
1	cup reduced-sodium chicken broth	
1	cup fat-free milk	
1	lb. uncooked medium shrimp, peeled and deveined	
3/4	tsp. sugar	
1/2	tsp. salt	
1/8	tsp. ground ginger	
1/2	tsp. lemon juice	
2	cups hot cooked rice	

1. In a large skillet, saute onion and curry in butter until tender. Stir in the flour until blended; gradually add broth and milk. Bring to a boil; cook and stir for 2 minutes or until thickened.

2. Reduce heat; add the shrimp, sugar, salt and ginger. Cook and stir over medium heat until shrimp turn pink. Remove from the heat; stir in lemon juice. Serve with rice.

Nutrition Facts: 3/4 cup shrimp mixture with 1/2 cup rice equals 305 calories, 8 g fat (4 g saturated fat), 154 mg cholesterol, 640 mg sodium, 33 g carbohydrate, 1 g fiber, 24 g protein.

Pistachio-Crusted Fish Fillets C

PREP/TOTAL TIME: 25 min. **YIELD:** 4 servings

MARIE STUPIN • ROANOKE, VIRGINA

What a fresh, fun, absolutely delicious way to fix orange roughy in a hurry! I really adore the nutty crunch of the pistachio and parsley crust.

1	egg white, beaten
1/2	cup pistachios, finely chopped
1/3	cup dry bread crumbs
1/4	cup minced fresh parsley
1/2	tsp. pepper
1/4	tsp. salt
4	orange roughy fillets (6 oz. *each*)
4	tsp. butter, melted

1. Place egg white in a shallow bowl. In another shallow bowl, combine the pistachios, bread crumbs, parsley, pepper and salt. Dip fillets in egg white, then pistachio mixture.

2. Place fish on a baking sheet coated with cooking spray. Drizzle with butter. Bake at 450° for 8-10 minutes or until fish flakes easily with a fork.

Nutrition Facts: 1 fillet equals 295 calories, 13 g fat (3 g saturated fat), 112 mg cholesterol, 444 mg sodium, 11 g carbohydrate, 2 g fiber, 34 g protein.

Light-but-Hearty Tuna Casserole

PREP: 20 min. **BAKE:** 25 min. **YIELD:** 4 servings

HEIDI CAROFANO • BROOKLYN, NEW YORK

My boyfriend grew up loving his mom's tuna casserole and says he can't tell this is light!

3	cups uncooked yolk-free noodles
1	can (10-3/4 oz.) reduced-fat reduced-sodium condensed cream of mushroom soup, undiluted
1/2	cup fat-free milk
2	Tbsp. reduced-fat mayonnaise
1/2	tsp. ground mustard
1	can (6 oz.) solid white tuna, drained
1	jar (6 oz.) sliced mushrooms, drained
1/4	cup chopped roasted sweet red pepper

TOPPING:

1/4	cup dry bread crumbs
1	Tbsp. butter, melted
1/2	tsp. paprika
1/4	tsp. Italian seasoning
1/4	tsp. pepper

1. Cook noodles according to package directions.

2. In a large bowl, combine the soup, milk, mayonnaise and mustard. Stir in the tuna, mushrooms and red pepper. Drain noodles; add to soup mixture and stir until blended. Transfer to an 8-in. square baking dish coated with cooking spray. Combine topping ingredients; sprinkle over casserole. Bake at 400° for 25-30 minutes or until bubbly.

Nutrition Facts: 1-1/2 cups equals 322 calories, 9 g fat (3 g saturated fat), 32 mg cholesterol, 843 mg sodium, 39 g carbohydrate, 4 g fiber, 18 g protein.

LIGHT-BUT-HEARTY TUNA CASSEROLE

Salmon Grilled in Foil [C]

PREP/TOTAL TIME: 20 min. **YIELD:** 4 servings

MERIDETH BERKOVICH • THE DALLES, OREGON

Steamed in its own juices, this salmon is incredibly tender. Curry adds a punch of flavor that's perfectly balanced by onion and tomato.

4	salmon fillets (4 oz. *each*)
1	tsp. garlic powder
1	tsp. lemon-pepper seasoning
1	tsp. curry powder
1/2	tsp. salt
1	small onion, cut into rings
2	medium tomatoes, seeded and chopped

1. Place salmon, skin side down, on a double thickness of heavy-duty foil (about 18 in. x 12 in.). Combine the garlic powder, lemon-pepper, curry and salt; sprinkle over salmon. Top with onion and tomatoes. Fold foil over fish and seal tightly.

2. Grill, covered, over medium heat for 10-15 minutes or until fish flakes easily with a fork. Open foil carefully to allow steam to escape.

Nutrition Facts: 1 serving equals 232 calories, 13 g fat (3 g saturated fat), 67 mg cholesterol, 482 mg sodium, 5 g carbohydrate, 1 g fiber, 24 g protein.

Tangy Shrimp Kabobs [F]

PREP: 25 min. + marinating
GRILL: 15 min. **YIELD:** 6 servings

PAT WAYMIRE • YELLOW SPRINGS, OHIO

You'd never guess that a pair of these colorful kabobs has only 2 g of fat total! An easy tomato-based mixture is used as a marinade and basting sauce to add just the right amount of sweet-sour taste to the shrimp, pineapple and veggies.

1	can (20 oz.) unsweetened pineapple chunks
1	can (8 oz.) tomato sauce
1/2	cup fat-free Italian salad dressing
4-1/2	tsp. brown sugar
1	tsp. prepared mustard
1-1/2	lbs. uncooked large shrimp, peeled and deveined
12	pearl onions
1	large sweet red pepper, cut into 1-in. pieces
1	large green pepper, cut into 1-in. pieces

Hot cooked rice, optional

1. Drain pineapple, reserving 1/4 cup juice; set aside. In a bowl, combine the tomato sauce, Italian dressing, brown sugar, mustard and reserved pineapple juice. Pour 3/4 cup marinade into a large resealable plastic bag; add the shrimp. Seal bag and turn to coat; refrigerate for 3 hours, turning occasionally. Cover and refrigerate remaining mixture for sauce.

2. In a Dutch oven, bring 6 cups water to a boil. Add onions; boil for 2 minutes. Add peppers and boil 2 minutes longer. Drain and rinse in cold water; peel onions. Refrigerate vegetables until ready to grill.

3. In a small saucepan, bring 3/4 cup of reserved tomato sauce mixture to a boil. Reduce heat; simmer, uncovered, for 5 minutes or until slightly thickened. Keep warm.

4. Coat grill rack with cooking spray before starting the grill. Drain shrimp and discard marinade. On 12 metal or soaked wooden skewers, alternately thread shrimp and vegetables.

5. Grill the kabobs, covered, over medium heat for 3-5 minutes on each side or until shrimp turn pink, basting occasionally with remaining tomato sauce mixture. Drizzle kabobs with warm sauce. Serve with rice if desired.

Nutrition Facts: 2 kabobs with about 2 Tbsp. sauce (calculated without rice) equals 194 calories, 2 g fat (trace saturated fat), 138 mg cholesterol, 474 mg sodium, 24 g carbohydrate, 3 g fiber, 20 g protein. **Diabetic Exchanges:** 3 very lean meat, 2 vegetable, 1 fruit.

Salmon Supreme With Ginger Soy Sauce [C]

PREP/TOTAL TIME: 25 min. **YIELD:** 4 servings

AGNES WARD • STRATFORD, ONTARIO

This salmon has an excellent delicate flavor. I like to prepare this dish on Friday nights; it's very fast and easy. It's also light in calories and delicious, too.

2	Tbsp. all-purpose flour
1	Tbsp. cornstarch
4	salmon fillets (4 oz. *each*)
1	Tbsp. canola oil
1/3	cup sherry *or* unsweetened apple juice
2	green onions, chopped
1/4	cup minced fresh gingerroot
3	Tbsp. reduced-sodium soy sauce
2	Tbsp. honey
1	Tbsp. balsamic vinegar
1/2	tsp. garlic powder

1. In a shallow bowl, combine flour and cornstarch. Dip fillets in flour mixture. In a large nonstick skillet coated with cooking spray, cook salmon in oil over medium-high heat for 4-6 minutes on each side or until fish flakes easily with a fork. Remove and keep warm.

2. Add sherry, stirring to loosen browned bits from the pan. Stir in the remaining ingredients; cook, stirring occasionally, for 2 minutes to allow flavors to blend. Serve with salmon.

Nutrition Facts: 1 fillet with 2 Tbsp. sauce equals 319 calories, 16 g fat (3 g saturated fat), 67 mg cholesterol, 526 mg sodium, 15 g carbohydrate, trace fiber, 24 g protein.

SALMON GRILLED IN FOIL

TANGY SHRIMP KABOBS

THAI SHRIMP SALAD

Thai Shrimp Salad c

PREP: 25 min. **GRILL:** 10 min. **YIELD:** 4 servings

ANNETTE TRAVERSO • SAN RAFAEL, CALIFORNIA

Here's a deliciously different salad that blends grilled shrimp, a lean source of protein, with the low-calorie crunch of cucumber and onion. It's tossed and dressed with Thai flavors of sesame, cilantro, lime and refreshing mint.

1/4	cup lime juice
2	Tbsp. sesame oil
2	Tbsp. reduced-sodium soy sauce
1	Tbsp. sesame seeds, toasted
1	Tbsp. minced fresh mint
1	Tbsp. minced fresh cilantro
1/8	tsp. crushed red pepper flakes
1	lb. uncooked large shrimp, peeled and deveined
1/4	tsp. salt
1/4	tsp. pepper
1	sweet onion, sliced
1	medium cucumber, peeled and sliced
4	cups torn leaf lettuce

1. In a large bowl, combine the first seven ingredients; set aside.

2. Coat grill rack with cooking spray before starting the grill. Sprinkle shrimp with salt and pepper; thread onto four metal or soaked wooden skewers. Grill, covered, over medium heat for 2-4 minutes on each side or until shrimp turn pink.

3. Stir the reserved dressing; add the shrimp, onion and cucumber. Toss to coat. Divide lettuce among four salad plates; top with shrimp mixture and serve immediately.

Nutrition Facts: 1 cup shrimp mixture with 1 cup lettuce equals 202 calories, 9 g fat (1 g saturated fat), 168 mg cholesterol, 661 mg sodium, 10 g carbohydrate, 3 g fiber, 21 g protein. **Diabetic Exchanges:** 3 very lean meat, 2 vegetable, 1-1/2 fat.

Poached Salmon With Dill Sauce c

PREP: 25 min. **COOK:** 10 min. **YIELD:** 4 servings

PATTI SHERMAN • SCHENECTADY, NEW YORK

Known for its omega-3 fatty acids, tender salmon is treated to a classic dill sauce in this recipe.

2	cups water
1	cup white wine *or* reduced-sodium chicken broth

1 medium onion, chopped
1/4 cup chopped celery
4 salmon fillets (4 oz. *each*)
SAUCE:
1/4 cup reduced-fat sour cream
1/4 cup plain yogurt
2 tsp. snipped fresh dill
1-1/2 tsp. Dijon mustard
1/4 tsp. salt
Dash hot pepper sauce

1. In a large nonstick skillet, combine the water, wine, onion and celery. Bring to a boil. Reduce heat; add salmon and poach, uncovered, for 5-10 minutes or until fish is firm and flakes easily with a fork.

2. Meanwhile, in a small bowl, combine the sauce ingredients. Serve with salmon.

Nutrition Facts: 1 fillet with 2 Tbsp. sauce equals 239 calories, 14 g fat (4 g saturated fat), 74 mg cholesterol, 277 mg sodium, 2 g carbohydrate, trace fiber, 24 g protein.

Makeover Shrimp and Grits

PREP: 30 min. **COOK:** 15 min. **YIELD:** 4 servings

LIZABETH ELVINGTON • DILLON, SOUTH CAROLINA

Shrimp and grits is an iconic comfort dish in most parts of the South. This version has a creamy richness that is so critical to the essence of good shrimp and grits.

1 can (14-1/2 oz.) plus 1/2 cup reduced-sodium chicken broth, *divided*
2 cups water
3/4 cup fat-free half-and-half
1 cup uncooked old-fashioned grits
2 center-cut bacon strips
1/4 cup all-purpose flour
1/4 tsp. pepper
1 lb. uncooked medium shrimp, peeled and deveined
1 cup sliced fresh mushrooms
4 green onions, chopped
2 garlic cloves, minced
2 Tbsp. lemon juice
3/4 tsp. hot pepper sauce, *divided*
1/3 cup shredded sharp cheddar cheese
1/4 cup grated Parmesan cheese
2 Tbsp. reduced-fat butter
1/4 tsp. white pepper

1. In a large heavy saucepan, bring the can of broth, water and half-and-half to a boil. Slowly whisk in grits. Reduce heat; cover and simmer for 15-20 minutes or until thickened, stirring occasionally.

2. Meanwhile, in a large nonstick skillet, cook bacon over medium heat until crisp. Remove to paper towels; drain, reserving drippings. Crumble bacon and set aside.

3. In a large resealable plastic bag, combine flour and pepper. Add shrimp, a few at a time, and shake to coat; set aside.

4. Saute mushrooms in the bacon drippings until tender. Add the onions, garlic and shrimp; cook and

stir until shrimp turn pink. Stir in the lemon juice, 1/4 tsp. pepper sauce and remaining broth.

5. Stir the cheeses, butter, white pepper and remaining pepper sauce into the grits. Serve with shrimp mixture. Top with reserved bacon.

Editor's Note: This recipe was tested with Land O'Lakes light stick butter.

Nutrition Facts: 1-1/4 cups grits with 1/2 cup shrimp mixture equals 423 calories, 12 g fat (6 g saturated fat), 165 mg cholesterol, 784 mg sodium, 46 g carbohydrate, 2 g fiber, 32 g protein.

Dilly Salmon Patties C

PREP/TOTAL TIME: 25 min. **YIELD:** 4 servings

AERIAL RYAN • ACRA, NEW YORK

Here's a quick and easy recipe that's also a great way to use up leftover salmon. I like to serve it with a vegetable or crisp side salad. The patties have a great herb flavor!

2 eggs
1 medium onion, finely chopped
1/4 cup mashed potato flakes
1/4 cup seasoned bread crumbs
1 garlic clove, minced
1/4 tsp. dill weed
1/4 tsp. pepper
1/8 tsp. celery salt
1 can (14-3/4 oz.) salmon, drained, bones and skin removed
1 tsp. olive oil

1. In a small bowl, combine the first eight ingredients. Add salmon; mix well. Shape into four patties. In a large nonstick skillet coated with cooking spray, cook patties in oil over medium heat for 5 minutes on each side or until browned.

Nutrition Facts: 1 patty equals 265 calories, 12 g fat (3 g saturated fat), 152 mg cholesterol, 761 mg sodium, 12 g carbohydrate, 1 g fiber, 27 g protein.

DILLY SALMON PATTIES

Scallop Kabobs C

PREP: 30 min. + marinating GRILL: 10 min.
YIELD: 4 servings

EDIE DESPAIN • LOGAN, UTAH

I like recipes that are lower in fat and heart-healthy. These kabobs fill the bill. I serve them with a simple fruit salad and a light dessert.

3	Tbsp. lemon juice
3	Tbsp. reduced-sodium soy sauce
2	Tbsp. canola oil
Dash garlic powder	
Dash pepper	
1-1/2	lbs. sea scallops
3	medium green peppers, cut into 1-1/2-in. pieces
2	cups cherry tomatoes

1. In a small bowl, combine the first five ingredients. Pour 1/4 cup into a large resealable plastic bag; add scallops. Seal bag and turn to coat; refrigerate for 20 minutes. Cover and refrigerate remaining marinade for basting.

> Uncooked fish freezes quite well. Wrap the fish in freezer paper, heavy-duty foil or heavy-duty plastic bags if you're considering **longterm storage**. Freeze fatty fish (7% to 50% fat content) for up to 3 months, and freeze lean fish (2.5% to 6% fat content) for up 6 months. Buy frozen fish in packages that are solidly frozen and free of odor.

SCALLOP KABOBS

2. Meanwhile, in a large saucepan, bring 3 cups water to a boil. Add peppers; cover and boil for 2 minutes. Drain and immediately place peppers in ice water. Drain and pat dry.

3. Coat grill rack with cooking spray before starting the grill. Drain and discard marinade. On eight metal or soaked wooden skewers, alternately thread the tomatoes, scallops and peppers.

4. Grill, covered, over medium heat for 3-5 minutes on each side or until scallops are firm and opaque, basting occasionally with reserved marinade.

Nutrition Facts: 2 kabobs equals 238 calories, 7 g fat (1 g saturated fat), 56 mg cholesterol, 624 mg sodium, 13 g carbohydrate, 2 g fiber, 31 g protein. **Diabetic Exchanges:** 4 very lean meat, 2 vegetable, 1 fat.

Mediterranean Shrimp Couscous

PREP: 20 min. COOK: 25 min. YIELD: 6 servings

HEATHER CARROLL • COLORADO SPRINGS, COLORADO

This is a lower-fat, flavorful recipe that my family loves! It's light and elegant. You'll be proud to serve this dish.

1-1/2	lbs. uncooked medium shrimp, peeled and deveined
1	Tbsp. chopped shallot
2	garlic cloves, minced
3	Tbsp. olive oil, *divided*
1	cup chopped zucchini
1/2	cup white wine *or* reduced-sodium chicken broth
1/4	cup chopped sun-dried tomatoes (not packed in oil)
2	Tbsp. capers, drained
3	cups fresh baby spinach
1-1/2	cups reduced-sodium chicken broth
1-1/2	cups uncooked couscous
2	Tbsp. lemon juice
2	Tbsp. balsamic vinegar
1/2	cup crumbled feta cheese, *divided*
1/2	tsp. dried oregano
1/4	tsp. salt
1/4	tsp. pepper

1. In a large skillet, saute the shrimp, shallot and garlic in 1 Tbsp. oil until shrimp turn pink. Remove and keep warm.

2. In the same skillet, cook and stir the zucchini, wine, tomatoes and capers until zucchini is tender. Add spinach; cook just until wilted. Add broth and bring to a boil. Stir in couscous. Cover and remove from the heat; let stand for 5 minutes or until liquid is absorbed. Fluff with a fork.

3. Whisk the lemon juice, vinegar and remaining oil; add to the pan. Stir in 1/4 cup of the cheese, the seasonings and reserved shrimp mixture; cook and stir over low heat until mixture is heated through. Sprinkle with the remaining cheese.

Nutrition Facts: 1 cup equals 385 calories, 11 g fat (2 g saturated fat), 143 mg cholesterol, 619 mg sodium, 41 g carbohydrate, 3 g fiber, 28 g protein. **Diabetic Exchanges:** 3 very lean meat, 2-1/2 starch, 2 fat.

MEDITERRANEAN SHRIMP COUSCOUS

Apricot-Glazed Salmon With Herb Rice

PREP: 25 min. **COOK:** 20 min. **YIELD:** 6 servings

CHARLENE CHAMBERS • ORMOND BEACH, FLORIDA

Salmon lovers will really enjoy this nice, fruity-tasting fish with just the right amount of sweetness. If salmon is new to your family, this is a great way to introduce it to them.

6	salmon fillets (4 oz. *each*)
1/4	tsp. salt
1/8	tsp. pepper
1/3	cup white wine *or* reduced-sodium chicken broth
1/3	cup apricot spreadable fruit
1/2	tsp. grated fresh gingerroot
2	cups reduced-sodium chicken broth
1	cup uncooked long grain rice
2	tsp. butter
2	Tbsp. chopped dried apricots
2	Tbsp. minced fresh parsley
1	Tbsp. minced fresh chives
1	tsp. minced fresh thyme *or* 1/4 tsp. dried thyme
3	Tbsp. sliced almonds, toasted

1. Place salmon in a 13-in. x 9-in. baking dish coated with cooking spray. Sprinkle with salt and pepper. In a small bowl, combine the wine, spreadable fruit and ginger; spoon over salmon. Bake at 375° for 15-20 minutes or until fish flakes easily with a fork.

2. Meanwhile, in a small saucepan, bring the broth, rice and butter to a boil. Reduce heat; cover and simmer for 10 minutes. Add apricots; cover and cook 5-8 minutes longer or until liquid is absorbed and rice is tender. Stir in the parsley, chives and thyme. Serve with salmon. Sprinkle each serving with almonds.

Nutrition Facts: 1 salmon fillet with 1/2 cup rice and 1-1/2 tsp. almonds equals 408 calories, 15 g fat (3 g saturated fat), 70 mg cholesterol, 369 mg sodium, 37 g carbohydrate, 1 g fiber, 27 g protein.

Creamy Tuna-Noodle Casserole

PREP: 25 min. **BAKE:** 25 min. **YIELD:** 6 servings

EDIE DESPAIN • LOGAN, UTAH

Tuna fish is always an excellent standby when you need supper on the table in a hurry. You'll love this main-dish casserole packed with peas, peppers and onions. Not fond of tuna? Simply substitute chicken instead!

- 5 cups uncooked egg noodles
- 1 can (10-3/4 oz.) reduced-fat reduced-sodium condensed cream of mushroom soup, undiluted
- 1 cup (8 oz.) fat-free sour cream
- 2/3 cup grated Parmesan cheese
- 1/3 cup 2% milk
- 1/4 tsp. salt
- 2 cans (5 oz. *each*) light water-packed tuna, drained and flaked
- 1 cup frozen peas, thawed
- 1/4 cup finely chopped onion
- 1/4 cup finely chopped green pepper

TOPPING:
- 1/2 cup soft bread crumbs
- 1 Tbsp. butter, melted

1. Cook noodles according to package directions.

2. Meanwhile, in a large bowl, combine the soup, sour cream, cheese, milk and salt. Stir in the tuna, peas, onion and pepper. Drain noodles; add to soup mixture.

3. Transfer to an 11-in. x 7-in. baking dish coated with cooking spray. Combine topping ingredients; sprinkle over the top. Bake, uncovered, at 350° for 25-30 minutes or until bubbly.

Nutrition Facts: 1-1/3 cups equals 340 calories, 8 g fat (4 g saturated fat), 63 mg cholesterol, 699 mg sodium, 41 g carbohydrate, 3 g fiber, 25 g protein. **Diabetic Exchanges:** 3 starch, 2 very lean meat, 1 fat.

Balsamic-Glazed Salmon C

PREP: 20 min. **BAKE:** 15 min. **YIELD:** 6 servings

MARY LOU TIMPSON • COLORADO CITY, ARIZONA

Rich in omega-3s, this tender salmon boasts a delicious blend of flavors with just a touch of balsamic vinegar.

- 4 garlic cloves, minced
- 1 tsp. olive oil
- 1/3 cup balsamic vinegar
- 4 tsp. Dijon mustard
- 1 Tbsp. white wine *or* water
- 1 Tbsp. honey
- 1/4 tsp. salt
- 1/4 tsp. pepper
- 6 salmon fillets (4 oz. *each*)
- 1 Tbsp. minced fresh oregano *or* 1 tsp. dried oregano

1. Line a 15-in. x 10-in. x 1-in. baking pan with foil; coat foil with cooking spray. Set aside.

2. In a small saucepan, saute garlic in oil until tender. Stir in the vinegar, mustard, wine, honey, salt and pepper. Bring to a boil. Reduce heat; simmer, uncovered, for 3-5 minutes or until slightly thickened. Set aside 2 Tbsp. for basting.

3. Place fillets on prepared pan. Brush with sauce and sprinkle with oregano. Bake, uncovered, at 425° for 15-18 minutes or until salmon flakes easily with a fork. Brush with reserved sauce before serving.

Nutrition Facts: 1 fillet equals 243 calories, 13 g fat (3 g saturated fat), 67 mg cholesterol, 249 mg sodium, 7 g carbohydrate, trace fiber, 23 g protein.

BALSAMIC-GLAZED SALMON

CREAMY TUNA-NOODLE CASSEROLE

PUMPKIN LASAGNA

BLACK BEAN TACO PIZZA

ZESTY LIGHT TACOS

Meatless Mains

For many, going meatless is a way of life. For others, it's simply an occasional change-of-pace dinner option. Regardless of your eating habits, the recipes that follow are sure to brighten up your meal lineup and lighten up your waistline.

Zesty Light Tacos M

PREP: 15 min. **COOK:** 50 min. **YIELD:** 8 servings

MAUREEN MACK • MILWAUKEE, WISCONSIN

This colorful main dish is very high in fiber. A complete protein with black beans and brown rice, it's perfect for vegetarians. If you need to cut down on sodium, use reduced-sodium beans and tomatoes.

- 1 cup uncooked brown rice
- 1 medium red onion, halved and sliced
- 1 medium green pepper, thinly sliced
- 1 Tbsp. canola oil
- 1 can (15 oz.) black beans, rinsed and drained
- 1 can (14-1/2 oz.) diced tomatoes with mild green chilies, undrained
- 1/2 cup frozen corn
- 1/3 cup taco sauce
- 1 tsp. chili powder
- 3/4 tsp. cayenne pepper
- 8 whole wheat tortillas (8 in.), warmed

Optional toppings: shredded lettuce, chopped tomatoes, pickled jalapeno slices, shredded reduced-fat cheddar cheese and reduced-fat sour cream

1. Cook rice according to the package directions. Meanwhile, in a large nonstick skillet, saute onion and pepper in oil until tender. Stir in the beans, tomatoes, corn, taco sauce, chili powder and cayenne; heat through. Stir in cooked rice. Spoon 3/4 cup mixture down the center of each tortilla. Add toppings if desired.

Nutrition Facts: 1 taco (calculated without toppings) equals 326 calories, 6 g fat (trace saturated fat), 0 cholesterol, 565 mg sodium, 57 carbohydrate, 7 g fiber, 10 g protein.

Pumpkin Lasagna M

PREP: 25 min. **BAKE:** 55 min. + standing
YIELD: 6 servings

TAMARA HURON • COLORADO SPRINGS, COLORADO

I especially like this comforting fall dish because it's vegetarian. Even friends who aren't big fans of pumpkin are surprised by this delectable lasagna! Canned pumpkin and no-cook noodles make it a cinch to prepare.

- 1/2 lb. sliced fresh mushrooms
- 1 small onion, chopped
- 1/2 tsp. salt, *divided*
- 2 tsp. olive oil
- 1 can (15 oz.) solid-pack pumpkin
- 1/2 cup half-and-half cream
- 1 tsp. dried sage leaves
Dash pepper
- 9 no-cook lasagna noodles
- 1 cup reduced-fat ricotta cheese
- 1 cup (4 oz.) shredded part-skim mozzarella cheese
- 3/4 cup shredded Parmesan cheese

1. In a small skillet, saute the mushrooms, onion and 1/4 tsp. salt in oil until tender; set aside. In a small bowl, combine the pumpkin, cream, sage, pepper and remaining salt.

2. Spread 1/2 cup pumpkin sauce in an 11-in. x 7-in. baking dish coated with cooking spray. Top with three noodles (noodles will overlap slightly). Spread 1/2 cup pumpkin sauce to edges of noodles. Top with half of mushroom mixture, 1/2 cup ricotta, 1/2 cup mozzarella and 1/4 cup Parmesan cheese. Repeat layers. Top with remaining noodles and sauce.

3. Cover and bake at 375° for 45 minutes. Uncover; sprinkle with remaining Parmesan cheese. Bake 10-15 minutes longer or until cheese is melted. Let stand for 10 minutes before cutting.

Nutrition Facts: 1 piece equals 310 calories, 12 g fat (6 g saturated fat), 36 mg cholesterol, 497 mg sodium, 32 g carbohydrate, 5 g fiber, 17 g protein. **Diabetic Exchanges:** 2 starch, 2 fat, 1 lean meat.

You'll love the unique flavor and comforting goodness of **Pumpkin Lasagna**. For convenience, assemble the hearty casserole on Sunday and keep it in the fridge to bake later during the busy week.

Black Bean Taco Pizza M

PREP: 25 min. **BAKE:** 10 min. **YIELD:** 6 servings

SHERIE NELSON • DULUTH, MINNESOTA

My husband absolutely loves this pizza. I make it several times a month for family and friends.

1	Tbsp. cornmeal
1	pkg. (6-1/2 oz.) pizza crust mix
1	bottle (8 oz.) taco sauce
2	medium tomatoes, seeded and chopped
3/4	cup canned black beans
1/2	cup frozen corn
1	can (4 oz.) chopped green chilies
2	green onions, chopped
1-1/2	cups (6 oz.) shredded reduced-fat Colby-Monterey Jack cheese

Reduced-fat sour cream, optional

1. Coat a 12-in. pizza pan with cooking spray; sprinkle with cornmeal. Prepare pizza dough according to package directions. With floured hands, press dough onto pan. Bake at 450° for 7 minutes or until lightly browned.

2. Spread with taco sauce. Top with tomatoes, beans, corn, chilies, onions and cheese. Bake for 10 minutes or until cheese is melted and crust is golden. Serve with sour cream if desired.

Nutrition Facts: 1 slice (calculated without sour cream) equals 264 calories, 6 g fat (4 g saturated fat), 15 mg cholesterol, 783 mg sodium, 38 g carbohydrate, 4 g fiber, 14 g protein. **Diabetic Exchanges:** 2-1/2 starch, 1 lean meat, 1/2 fat.

Vegetarian Tex-Mex Peppers M

PREP: 20 min. **BAKE:** 45 min. **YIELD:** 4 servings

CELE KNIGHT • NACOGDOCHES, TEXAS

Folks who enjoy stuffed peppers will love this delightfully delicious Tex-Mex twist on their old favorite. A bonus? The veggie filling is hearty enough to satisfy meat eaters!

4	large green peppers
2	eggs, beaten

VEGETARIAN TEX-MEX PEPPERS

2	cups cooked brown rice
1	cup frozen vegetarian meat crumbles
1	cup canned black beans, rinsed and drained
1/2	tsp. pepper
1/4	tsp. hot pepper sauce
1/4	tsp. ground cardamom, optional
1	can (14-1/2 oz.) diced tomatoes, drained
1	can (10 oz.) diced tomatoes and green chilies
1	can (8 oz.) no-salt-added tomato sauce
1/2	cup shredded Colby cheese

1. Cut peppers in half lengthwise and remove seeds. Discard stems. In a large kettle, cook peppers in boiling water for 3-5 minutes. Drain and rinse in cold water; set aside.

2. In a large bowl, combine the eggs, rice, meat crumbles, beans, pepper, pepper sauce and cardamom if desired. Spoon into peppers. Place in a 13-in. x 9-in. baking dish coated with cooking spray.

3. In a small bowl, combine the diced tomatoes, tomatoes and green chilies, and tomato sauce. Spoon over peppers. Cover and bake at 350° for 40-45 minutes or until a thermometer reads 160°. Sprinkle with cheese; bake 5 minutes longer or until the cheese is melted.

Nutrition Facts: 2 stuffed pepper halves equals 364 calories, 9 g fat (4 g saturated fat), 119 mg cholesterol, 769 mg sodium, 53 g carbohydrate, 11 g fiber, 19 g protein.

Skillet Pasta Florentine M

PREP: 20 min. **COOK:** 30 min. **YIELD:** 6 servings

KELLY TURNBULL • JUPITER, FLORIDA

Here's a great weeknight supper that's budget-friendly, healthy and liked by children. And with such a thick, cheesy topping, who'd ever guess that it's light?

3	cups uncooked spiral pasta
1	egg, beaten
2	cups (16 oz.) 2% cottage cheese
1-1/2	cups reduced-fat ricotta cheese
1	pkg. (10 oz.) frozen chopped spinach, thawed and squeezed dry
1	cup (4 oz.) shredded part-skim mozzarella cheese, *divided*
1	tsp. *each* dried parsley flakes, oregano and basil
1	jar (14 oz.) meatless spaghetti sauce
2	Tbsp. grated Parmesan cheese

1. Cook pasta according to package directions. Meanwhile, in a large bowl, combine the egg, cottage cheese, ricotta, spinach, 1/2 cup mozzarella and herbs.

2. Drain pasta. Place half of sauce in a large skillet; layer with pasta and remaining sauce. Top with the cheese mixture.

3. Bring to a boil. Reduce heat; cover and cook for 25-30 minutes or until a thermometer reads 160°. Sprinkle with Parmesan and remaining mozzarella; cover and cook 5 minutes longer or until cheese is melted. Let stand for 5 minutes before serving.

Nutrition Facts: 1 serving equals 383 calories, 9 g fat (5 g saturated fat), 73 mg cholesterol, 775 mg sodium, 47 g carbohydrate, 4 g fiber, 27 g protein.

SKILLET PASTA FLORENTINE

Cheese Tortellini With Tomatoes and Corn M

PREP/TOTAL TIME: 25 min. **YIELD:** 4 servings

SALLY MALONEY • DALLAS, GEORGIA

Garden-fresh flavors make this dish a delight! Plus, it's as light and easy as it is special.

- 1 pkg. (9 oz.) refrigerated cheese tortellini
- 1 pkg. (16 oz.) frozen corn, thawed *or* 3-1/3 cups fresh corn
- 2 cups cherry tomatoes, quartered
- 1/4 cup thinly sliced green onions
- 1/4 cup minced fresh basil
- 2 Tbsp. grated Parmesan cheese
- 4 tsp. olive oil
- 1/4 tsp. garlic powder
- 1/8 tsp. pepper

1. In a Dutch oven, cook tortellini according to package directions, adding the corn during the last 5 minutes of cooking. Drain and rinse in cold water.

2. In a large serving bowl, combine tortellini mixture and remaining ingredients; toss to coat.

Nutrition Facts: 1-3/4 cups equals 366 calories, 12 g fat (4 g saturated fat), 30 mg cholesterol, 286 mg sodium, 57 g carbohydrate, 5 g fiber, 14 g protein.

Slow-Cooked Stuffed Peppers M

PREP: 15 min. **COOK:** 3 hours **YIELD:** 4 servings

MICHELLE GURNSEY • LINCOLN, NEBRASKA

What an easy way to fix stuffed peppers without parboiling! Using the slow cooker makes dinner a snap. Light and packed with Southwest flavor, they also come with 8 g of fiber per serving.

4 medium sweet red peppers
1 can (15 oz.) black beans, rinsed and drained
1 cup (4 oz.) shredded pepper Jack cheese
3/4 cup salsa
1 small onion, chopped
1/2 cup frozen corn
1/3 cup uncooked converted long grain rice
1-1/4 tsp. chili powder
1/2 tsp. ground cumin
Reduced-fat sour cream, optional

1. Cut tops off peppers and remove seeds; set aside. In a large bowl, combine the beans, cheese, salsa, onion, corn, rice, chili powder and cumin; spoon into peppers. Place in a 5-qt. slow cooker coated with cooking spray.

2. Cover and cook on low for 3-4 hours or until peppers are tender and filling is heated through. Serve with sour cream if desired.

Nutrition Facts: 1 stuffed pepper (without sour cream) equals 317 calories, 10 g fat (5 g saturated fat), 30 mg cholesterol, 565 mg sodium, 43 g carbohydrate, 8 g fiber, 15 g protein. **Diabetic Exchanges:** 2 starch, 2 lean meat, 2 vegetable, 1 fat.

Lactose-Free Veggie-Stuffed Shells Ⓜ

PREP: 30 min. **BAKE:** 35 min. **YIELD:** 12 servings

KIMBERLY HAMMOND • KINGWOOD, TEXAS

I wanted my family to get the benefits of soy, so I tweaked a traditional recipe. This is a low-fat, great tasting dish that everyone enjoys.

1 pkg. (12 oz.) jumbo pasta shells
1/2 lb. sliced fresh mushrooms
1 medium onion, chopped
1 Tbsp. olive oil
4 garlic cloves, minced
1 pkg. (12.3 oz.) silken extra-firm tofu
3 Tbsp. lemon juice
1 pkg. (10 oz.) frozen chopped spinach, thawed and squeezed dry
1 can (3.8 oz.) sliced ripe olives, drained
3 Tbsp. minced fresh basil

1/2 tsp. salt
1/8 tsp. pepper
1 jar (26 oz.) meatless spaghetti sauce
1/4 cup pine nuts

1. Cook pasta according to package directions; drain. Meanwhile, in a large skillet, saute mushrooms and onion in oil until tender. Add garlic; cook 1 minute longer.

2. In a large bowl, mash tofu with lemon juice. Stir in the spinach, olives, basil, salt and pepper. Add to mushroom mixture; heat through. Spoon into shells.

3. Spread 1 cup spaghetti sauce in a 13-in. x 9-in. baking dish coated with cooking spray. Arrange shells over sauce; top with remaining sauce. Sprinkle with pine nuts. Cover and bake at 375° for 30 minutes. Uncover; bake 5-10 minutes longer or until bubbly.

Nutrition Facts: 3 stuffed shells equals 198 calories, 5 g fat (1 g saturated fat), trace cholesterol, 485 mg sodium, 32 g carbohydrate, 4 g fiber, 9 g protein. **Diabetic Exchanges:** 1-1/2 starch, 1 lean meat, 1 vegetable, 1 fat.

Some with lactose intolerance are actually able to tolerate **some products** containing lactose. Certain people are able to handle small amounts of milk and ice cream, especially when consumed with a meal.

SLOW-COOKED STUFFED PEPPERS

LACTOSE-FREE VEGGIE-STUFFED SHELLS

Vegetarian Stuffed Peppers M

PREP: 20 min. **BAKE:** 25 min. **YIELD:** 3 servings

LISA DEMARSH • MT. SOLON, VIRGINIA

No one will even miss the meat in this hearty, cheesy vegetarian meal. Brown rice helps make the tender peppers surprisingly filling, and the seasonings add lots of flavor.

- 3 large green peppers
- 2 cups frozen vegetarian meat crumbles
- 1 cup cooked brown rice
- 1 small onion, finely chopped
- 1 can (8 oz.) no-salt-added tomato sauce
- 1/3 cup grated Parmesan cheese
- 1/4 tsp. onion powder
- 1/4 tsp. garlic powder
- 1/4 tsp. dried parsley flakes
- 1/4 tsp. dried thyme
- 1/4 tsp. dried oregano
- 1/4 tsp. pepper
- 3/4 cup shredded part-skim mozzarella cheese

1. Cut peppers in half lengthwise and remove seeds. Discard stems. In a large kettle, cook peppers in boiling water for 3-5 minutes. Drain and rinse in cold water; set aside.

2. In a large bowl, combine the meat crumbles, rice, onion, tomato sauce, Parmesan cheese and the seasonings. Spoon into pepper halves. Place in a 13-in. x 9-in. baking dish coated with cooking spray.

3. Bake, uncovered, at 325° for 20-25 minutes or until heated through and peppers are tender. Sprinkle with mozzarella cheese; bake 5 minutes longer or until cheese is melted.

Nutrition Facts: 2 stuffed pepper halves equals 364 calories, 11 g fat (5 g saturated fat), 24 mg cholesterol, 605 mg sodium, 38 g carbohydrate, 8 g fiber, 28 g protein. **Diabetic Exchanges:** 3 very lean meat, 3 vegetable, 1-1/2 starch, 1-1/2 fat.

Penne with Kale and Onion M

PREP: 15 min. **COOK:** 20 min. **YIELD:** 6 servings

KIMBERLY HAMMOND • KINGWOOD, TEXAS

I love kale; my husband hates it. But when I swapped it into this recipe, it was so delicious, he asked for seconds!

PENNE WITH KALE AND ONION

- 1 medium onion, sliced
- 2 Tbsp. olive oil, *divided*
- 8 garlic cloves, thinly sliced
- 3 cups uncooked penne pasta
- 6 cups chopped fresh kale
- 1/2 tsp. salt

1. In a large skillet, cook onion in 1 Tbsp. oil over medium heat for 15-20 minutes or until onion is golden brown, stirring frequently and adding the garlic during the last 2 minutes of cooking time.

2. Meanwhile, in a large saucepan, cook penne according to package directions.

3. In a Dutch oven, bring 1 in. of water to a boil. Add kale; cover and cook for 10-15 minutes or until tender; drain.

4. Drain penne; drizzle with remaining oil. Stir the salt, penne and kale into the onion mixture; heat through.

Nutrition Facts: 3/4 cup equals 191 calories, 5 g fat (1 g saturated fat), 0 cholesterol, 206 mg sodium, 31 g carbohydrate, 2 g fiber, 6 g protein. **Diabetic Exchanges:** 1-1/2 starch, 1 vegetable, 1 fat.

Freezer Veggie Burgers F M

PREP: 25 min. + freezing **BAKE:** 30 min.
YIELD: 6 servings

ELAINE SOLOCHIER • CONCORD, NORTH CAROLINA

My family enjoys these veggie burgers. Make them at your convenience, then cook frozen for a fast bite when needed!

- 1 can (16 oz.) kidney beans, rinsed and drained
- 1/2 cup old-fashioned oats
- 2 Tbsp. ketchup
- 1/2 cup finely chopped fresh mushrooms
- 1 medium onion, finely chopped
- 1 medium carrot, shredded
- 1 small sweet red pepper, finely chopped
- 2 garlic cloves, minced
- 1/2 tsp. salt
- 1/8 tsp. white pepper
- 6 hamburger buns, split
- 6 lettuce leaves
- 6 slices tomato

1. Place the beans, oats and ketchup in a food processor; cover and pulse until blended. Transfer to a small bowl; stir in the vegetables, garlic and seasonings. Shape into six 3-in. patties; wrap each in plastic wrap and freeze.

2. When ready to use, unwrap burgers and place on a baking sheet coated with cooking spray. Bake at 350° for 30 minutes or until heated through, turning once. Serve on buns with lettuce and tomato.

Nutrition Facts: 1 burger equals 241 calories, 3 g fat (1 g saturated fat), 0 cholesterol, 601 mg sodium, 45 g carbohydrate, 7 g fiber, 11 g protein. **Diabetic Exchanges:** 2-1/2 starch, 1 very lean meat, 1 vegetable.

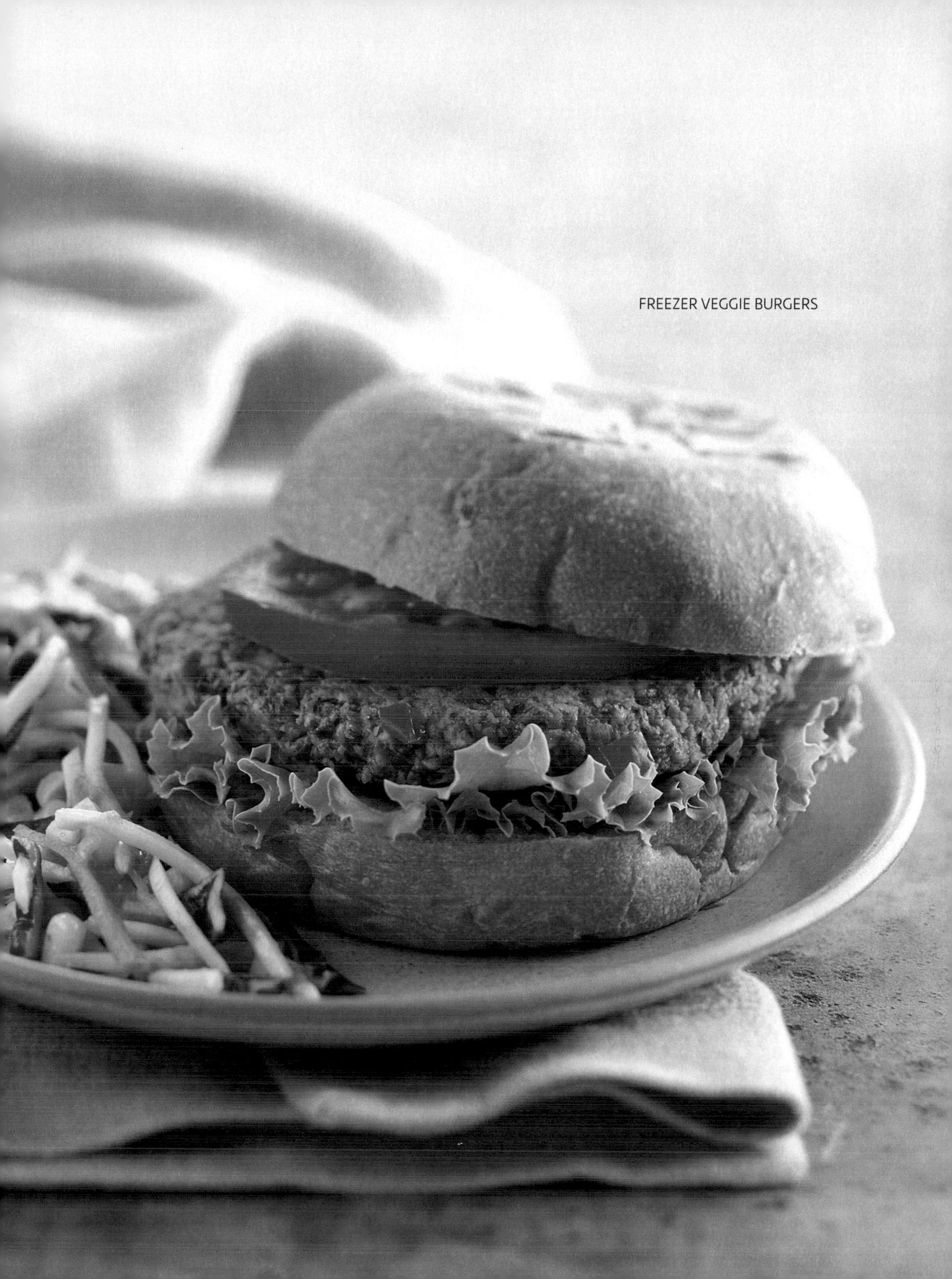
FREEZER VEGGIE BURGERS

HEARTY BEAN BURRITOS

Hearty Bean Burritos M

PREP/TOTAL TIME: 30 min. **YIELD:** 6 servings

HEALTHY COOKING TEST KITCHEN

This super-easy entree bursts with flavor, thanks to flavorful spices, tomatoes and a cream-cheese filling.

1/2	cup instant brown rice
1	small green pepper, chopped
2	tsp. canola oil
1	can (15 oz.) pinto beans, rinsed and drained
1	cup no-salt-added diced tomatoes
4	oz. fat-free cream cheese, cubed
1/2	tsp. chili powder
1/4	tsp. ground cumin
1/8	tsp. ground coriander
1/8	tsp. dried oregano
6	whole wheat tortillas (8 in.), warmed
3/4	cup shredded reduced-fat cheddar cheese

1. Cook rice according to package directions. Meanwhile, in a large nonstick skillet, saute pepper in oil until tender. In a large bowl, coarsely mash beans. Add the beans, tomatoes, cream cheese and seasonings to the skillet. Cook and stir until heated through; stir in rice.

2. Spoon scant 1/2 cup filling off center on each tortilla. Sprinkle with 2 Tbsp. cheese. Fold sides and ends over filling and roll up. Serve immediately.

Nutrition Facts: 1 burrito equals 314 calories, 8 g fat (2 g saturated fat), 12 mg cholesterol, 479 mg sodium, 43 g carbohydrate, 6 g fiber, 15 g protein. **Diabetic Exchanges:** 3 starch, 1 lean meat, 1 fat.

Spinach Quesadillas M

PREP/TOTAL TIME: 20 min. **YIELD:** 6 servings

PAM KAISER • MANSFIELD, MISSOURI

I adapted this recipe, using reduced-fat ingredients. I often use non-dairy alternatives in this family favorite. They make a great casual dinner, light lunch or hearty snack.

4 cups fresh baby spinach

4 green onions, chopped

1 small tomato, chopped

2 Tbsp. lemon juice

1 tsp. ground cumin

1/4 tsp. garlic powder

1 cup (4 oz.) shredded reduced-fat Monterey Jack cheese *or* Mexican cheese blend

1/4 cup reduced-fat ricotta cheese

6 flour tortillas (6 in.)

1/4 cup fat-free sour cream

1. In a large nonstick skillet, cook the spinach, onions, tomato, lemon juice, cumin and garlic powder over medium heat until spinach is wilted. Remove from the heat; stir in cheeses.

2. Divide spinach mixture evenly among three tortillas. Top with remaining tortillas. Cook in a large skillet coated with cooking spray over low heat for 1-2 minutes on each side or until heated through. Cut each quesadilla into four wedges. Serve with sour cream.

Nutrition Facts: 2 wedges with 2 tsp. sour cream equals 178 calories, 8 g fat (3 g saturated fat), 18 mg cholesterol, 422 mg sodium, 19 g carbohydrate, 1 g fiber, 10 g protein. **Diabetic Exchanges:** 1 starch, 1 lean meat, 1 fat.

Bean & Pineapple Soft Tacos Ⓜ

PREP/TOTAL TIME: 30 min. YIELD: 10 servings

TRISHA KRUSE • EAGLE, IDAHO

The sweet and spicy filling in these delicious, colorful soft tacos is a refreshing change from basic ground beef or chicken.

1 can (15 oz.) black beans, rinsed and drained

1 large onion, chopped

1 medium sweet red pepper, chopped

1 Tbsp. olive oil

1 can (20 oz.) unsweetened pineapple tidbits, drained

1 jar (16 oz.) salsa

1 can (4 oz.) chopped green chilies

1/4 cup minced fresh cilantro

10 whole wheat tortillas (8 in.), warmed

Sliced avocado, shredded lettuce, chopped tomatoes, shredded reduced-fat cheddar cheese and reduced-fat sour cream, optional

1. Mash half of the beans; set aside. In a large skillet, saute onion and red pepper in oil until tender. Add the pineapple, salsa, chilies, mashed beans and remaining beans; heat through. Stir in cilantro.

2. Place 1/2 cup filling on one side of each tortilla. Add toppings of your choice; fold in half. Serve immediately.

Nutrition Facts: 1 taco (calculated without optional toppings) equals 236 calories, 4 g fat (trace saturated fat), 0 cholesterol, 479 mg sodium, 40 g carbohydrate, 5 g fiber, 7 g protein. **Diabetic Exchanges:** 1-1/2 starch, 1 very lean meat, 1 vegetable, 1/2 fruit, 1/2 fat.

If you're interested in finding a low-fat side dish to go with a **Southwestern entree**, consider a can of refried beans. Canned varieties are available in vegetarian and fat-free versions. Or, mix last night's rice with a little salsa and some kidney beans. Baked tortilla chips and salsa make a no-fuss option as well.

BEAN & PINEAPPLE SOFT TACOS

SPINACH QUESADILLAS

MAKEOVER APPLE BREAD

CHOCOLATE DUNK-SHOT BISCOTTI

MAKEOVER LEMON STREUSEL MUFFINS

The Bread Basket

Even if you're counting carbohydrates, you can still enjoy the goodness of freshly baked breads, sweet muffins, golden scones and scores of other heart-warming specialties. Let this delightful chapter show you how!

Makeover Lemon Streusel Muffins

PREP: 20 min. **BAKE:** 15 min. **YIELD:** 1 dozen

CALVIN HWANG • LA MESA, CALIFORNIA

These delightful muffins mimic the great coffee shop treats, but because they use reduced-fat lemon yogurt and egg whites instead of whole eggs, they're much, much lighter.

1/4	cup butter, softened
3/4	cup sugar
2	egg yolks
1	tsp. grated lemon peel
1	cup cake flour
1	cup all-purpose flour
1	tsp. baking powder
1/2	tsp. salt
1/4	tsp. baking soda
1/2	cup lemon juice
1/2	cup reduced-fat lemon yogurt
4	egg whites

STREUSEL:
2	Tbsp. all-purpose flour
2	Tbsp. brown sugar
1/4	tsp. ground nutmeg
1	Tbsp. cold butter
1/4	cup chopped walnuts

1. In a large bowl, beat butter and sugar until crumbly. Beat in egg yolks and lemon peel. Combine the flours, baking powder, salt and baking soda; add to the butter mixture alternately with lemon juice and yogurt.

2. In a small bowl with clean beaters, beat egg whites until stiff peaks form. Fold into batter. Coat muffin cups with cooking spray or use paper liners; fill two-thirds full with batter.

3. For streusel, combine the flour, brown sugar and nutmeg; cut in butter until crumbly. Stir in walnuts. Sprinkle over muffins. Bake at 375° for 15-20 minutes or until a toothpick comes out clean. Cool for 5 minutes before removing from pan to a wire rack.

Nutrition Facts: 1 muffin equals 226 calories, 7 g fat (3 g saturated fat), 47 mg cholesterol, 218 mg sodium, 36 g carbohydrate, 1 g fiber, 5 g protein.

Chocolate Dunk-Shot Biscotti **F** **S** **C**

PREP: 30 min. **BAKE:** 25 min. + cooling
YIELD: 4-1/2 dozen

NANCY WHITFORD • EDWARDS, NEW YORK

These crunchy bites are great with a hot beverage! I think they're perfect with after-dinner coffee or as a morning treat.

2	cups all-purpose flour
1/2	cup sugar blend
1/3	cup baking cocoa
1/2	tsp. salt
1/2	tsp. baking soda
2	eggs
3	egg whites, *divided*
1	tsp. vanilla extract
1	tsp. instant coffee granules
1	Tbsp. grated orange peel
1/2	cup chopped almonds, toasted
1/4	cup miniature semisweet chocolate chips
1	tsp. water

1. In a large bowl, combine the flour, sugar blend, cocoa, salt and baking soda. In a small bowl, whisk the eggs, 2 egg whites, vanilla and coffee granules; let stand for 3-4 minutes or until granules are dissolved. Stir in orange peel. Stir into flour mixture; mix well. Stir in almonds and chocolate chips.

2. Divide dough in half. On a baking sheet coated with cooking spray, shape each half into a 14-in. x 1-3/4-in. rectangle. Combine water and remaining egg white; brush over rectangles. Bake at 350° for 20-25 minutes or until cracked and firm to the touch. Carefully remove to wire racks; cool for 5 minutes.

3. Transfer to a cutting board; cut diagonally with a serrated knife into 1/2-in. slices. Place cut side down on ungreased baking sheets. Bake for 5-7 minutes on each side or until firm. Remove to wire racks to cool. Store in an airtight container.

Editor's Note: This recipe was tested with Splenda sugar blend.

Nutrition Facts: 1 cookie equals 40 calories, 1 g fat (trace saturated fat), 8 mg cholesterol, 39 mg sodium, 6 g carbohydrate, trace fiber, 1 g protein. **Diabetic Exchange:** 1/2 starch.

Gluten-Free Banana Bread **S**

PREP: 20 min. **BAKE:** 45 min. + cooling
YIELD: 2 loaves (12 slices each)

GLADYS ARNOLD • PITTSBURGH, PENNSYLVANIA

A lot of gluten-free baked goods are dry and crumbly, but this one tastes like the real thing. I hope you try it!

2	cups gluten-free all-purpose baking flour
1	tsp. baking soda
1/4	tsp. salt
4	eggs
2	cups mashed ripe bananas (4-5 medium)
1	cup sugar
1/2	cup unsweetened applesauce
1/3	cup canola oil
1	tsp. vanilla extract
1/2	cup chopped walnuts

1. In a large bowl, combine the flour, baking soda and salt. In a small bowl, whisk the eggs, bananas, sugar, applesauce, oil and vanilla. Stir into dry ingredients just until moistened.

2. Transfer to two 8-in. x 4-in. loaf pans coated with cooking spray. Sprinkle with walnuts. Bake at 350° for 45-55 minutes or until a toothpick inserted near the center comes out clean. Cool for 10 minutes before removing from pans to wire racks.

Nutrition Facts: 1 slice equals 140 calories, 6 g fat (1 g saturated fat), 35 mg cholesterol, 89 mg sodium, 21 g carbohydrate, 2 g fiber, 3 g protein. **Diabetic Exchanges:** 1 starch, 1 fat.

Amish Potato Bread **M**

PREP: 30 min. + rising **BAKE:** 40 min. + cooling
YIELD: 1 loaf (16 slices)

SUE VIOLETTE • NEILLSVILLE, WISCONSIN

A tasty mix of whole wheat and all-purpose flour, plus a small amount of mashed potatoes, give this golden bread its wonderful texture. The loaf is very moist and stays that way even days after making it.

1	pkg. (1/4 oz.) active dry yeast
1/4	cup warm water (110° to 115°)
1-3/4	cups warm fat-free milk (110° to 115°)
1/3	cup butter, softened
1/4	cup mashed potatoes (without added milk and butter)
3	Tbsp. sugar
1-1/2	tsp. salt
1-1/2	cups whole wheat flour
3-1/2	to 4 cups all-purpose flour

1. In a large bowl, dissolve yeast in warm water. Add the milk, butter, potatoes, sugar, salt, whole wheat flour and 1/2 cup all-purpose flour. Beat until smooth. Stir in enough remaining flour to form a firm dough.

2. Turn onto a lightly floured surface; knead until smooth and elastic, about 6-8 minutes. Place in a bowl coated with cooking spray, turning once to coat the top. Cover and let rise in a warm place until doubled, about 1 hour.

3. Punch dough down and turn onto a floured surface; shape into a loaf. Place in a 9-in. x 5-in. loaf pan coated with cooking spay. Cover and let rise until doubled, about 30 minutes.

4. Bake at 350° for 40-45 minutes or until golden brown. Remove from pan to wire rack to cool.

Nutrition Facts: 1 slice equals 193 calories, 4 g fat (2 g saturated fat), 11 mg cholesterol, 276 mg sodium, 33 g carbohydrate, 2 g fiber, 6 g protein. **Diabetic Exchanges:** 2 starch, 1 fat.

Peachy Pecan Bread

PREP: 15 min. **BAKE:** 45 min. + cooling
YIELD: 1 loaf (12 slices)

KATHY FLEMING • LISLE, ILLINOIS

This hearty sweet bread will hit the spot any time of day! Enjoy it with coffee in the morning or with milk for a late-night snack. Hearty loaves also make great gifts.

1-1/2	cups all-purpose flour
1/2	cup uncooked oat bran cereal
2/3	cup packed brown sugar
1-1/2	tsp. baking powder
1/2	tsp. baking soda
1/4	tsp. salt
1/4	cup water
1/2	cup orange juice
1/2	cup egg substitute
1/4	cup canola oil
1	tsp. vanilla extract
1/2	cup dried peaches or apricots, finely chopped
1/4	cup chopped pecans

1. In a large bowl, combine the first six ingredients. In a small bowl, combine the water, orange juice, egg substitute, oil and vanilla. Stir into dry ingredients just until moistened. Fold in peaches and pecans.

2. Transfer to an 8-in. x 4-in. loaf pan coated with cooking spray. Bake at 350° for 45-55 minutes or until a toothpick inserted near the center comes out clean. Cool for 10 minutes before removing from pan to a wire rack.

Editor's Note: Look for oat bran cereal near the hot cereals or in the natural foods section.

Nutrition Facts: 1 slice equals 200 calories, 7 g fat (1 g saturated fat), 0 cholesterol, 178 mg sodium, 32 g carbohydrate, 2 g fiber, 4 g protein.

GLUTEN-FREE BANANA BREAD

Chocolate Ribbon Banana Loaf

PREP: 20 min. **BAKE:** 40 min. + cooling
YIELD: 1 loaf (12 slices)

SHARON GILJUM • SAN DIEGO, CALIFORNIA

With chocolate, bananas and peanut butter, this bread has it all. At less than 275 calories per slice, it's perfect for breakfast, dessert or an afternoon snack.

1/4	cup butter, softened
1	cup sugar
2	eggs
1	cup mashed ripe bananas (about 2 medium)
1/3	cup fat-free plain yogurt
1	tsp. vanilla extract
1-1/2	cups all-purpose flour
1/2	cup whole wheat pastry flour
3/4	tsp. baking soda
1/2	tsp. salt
1/2	tsp. ground cinnamon
1/2	cup peanut butter chips
1/2	cup semisweet chocolate chips, melted

1. In a large bowl, beat butter and sugar until crumbly, about 2 minutes. Add eggs, one at a time, beating well after each addition. Beat in the bananas, yogurt and vanilla. Combine the flours, baking soda, salt and cinnamon; gradually beat into the butter mixture. Stir in peanut butter chips.

2. Remove 1 cup batter to a small bowl; stir in chocolate until well blended. Pour half of the remaining plain batter into a 9-in. x 5-in. loaf pan coated with cooking spray; top with half of the chocolate batter. Repeat layers. Cut through batter with a knife to swirl.

3. Bake at 350° for 40-50 minutes or until a toothpick inserted near the center comes out clean. Cool for 10 minutes before removing from pan to a wire rack.

Nutrition Facts: 1 slice equals 272 calories, 9 g fat (5 g saturated fat), 45 mg cholesterol, 238 mg sodium, 44 g carbohydrate, 2 g fiber, 5 g protein.

Wheat Germ Streusel Banana Muffins

PREP: 20 min. **BAKE:** 20 min. **YIELD:** 10 muffins

TRISHA KRUSE • EAGLE, IDAHO

Using a mild oil like canola adds moisture and tenderness without changing flavor. You'll love the good, healthy feeling and great taste these muffins provide!

- 1 cup all-purpose flour
- 1/2 cup whole wheat flour
- 1/3 cup packed brown sugar
- 1 tsp. baking powder
- 1/2 tsp. baking soda
- 1/2 tsp. salt
- 1-1/3 cups mashed ripe bananas (about 3 medium)
- 1 egg
- 2 Tbsp. canola oil
- 2 Tbsp. unsweetened applesauce

STREUSEL:
- 1/4 cup packed brown sugar
- 2 Tbsp. toasted wheat germ
- 1/8 tsp. ground cinnamon
- 1 Tbsp. cold butter
- 2 Tbsp. finely chopped walnuts

1. In a large bowl, combine the flours, brown sugar, baking powder, baking soda and salt. In another bowl, beat the bananas, egg, oil and applesauce until well blended. Stir into dry ingredients just until moistened.

2. Coat muffin cups with cooking spray or use paper liners; fill two-thirds full with batter. For streusel, combine the brown sugar, wheat germ and cinnamon; cut in butter until crumbly. Stir in walnuts. Sprinkle over batter.

3. Bake at 375° for 18-22 minutes or until a toothpick inserted near the center comes out clean. Cool for 5 minutes before removing from pan to a wire rack.

Nutrition Facts: 1 muffin equals 203 calories, 6 g fat (1 g saturated fat), 24 mg cholesterol, 242 mg sodium, 36 g carbohydrate, 2 g fiber, 4 g protein.

Steamed Hawaiian Bread ⑤

PREP: 20 min. **COOK:** 45 min. + standing
YIELD: 1 loaf (6 wedges)

ROXANNE CHAN • ALBANY, CALIFORNIA

For a moist and flavorful loaf of bread that won't overheat your kitchen, try this unique steaming method. You'll love the subtle sweetness of banana and coconut.

- 3/4 cup all-purpose flour
- 1/2 cup ground almonds, toasted
- 1/4 cup flaked coconut
- 1 tsp. baking powder
- 1/4 tsp. baking soda
- 1/3 cup coconut milk
- 1/4 cup honey
- 3 Tbsp. mashed ripe banana
- 1/4 tsp. coconut extract

1. In a large bowl, combine the first five ingredients. Combine the coconut milk, honey, banana and extract; stir into dry ingredients just until moistened. Pour into a 2-cup stoneware dish or bowl coated with cooking spray; cover with foil.

2. Place on a rack in a deep kettle; add 1 in. of hot water to the kettle. Bring to a gentle boil; cover and steam for 45-50 minutes or until a toothpick inserted near the center comes out clean, adding more water as needed.

3. Remove dish from kettle; let stand for 15 minutes before removing bread from dish.

Nutrition Facts: 1 wedge equals 197 calories, 8 g fat (4 g saturated fat), 0 cholesterol, 132 mg sodium, 29 g carbohydrate, 2 g fiber, 4 g protein.

STEAMED HAWAIIAN BREAD

WHEAT GERM STREUSEL BANANA MUFFINS

Gluten-Free Pizza Crust F

PREP: 20 min. + standing **BAKE:** 20 min.
YIELD: 6 servings

SYLVIA GIRMUS • TORRINGTON, WYOMING

With this inventive crust, gluten-intolerant kids and adults alike can cure those pizza cravings. To keep calories down, I top my pizza with jarred pizza sauce and veggies that have been sauteed with a touch of olive oil.

1	Tbsp. active dry yeast
2/3	cup warm water (110° to 115°)
1/2	cup tapioca flour
2	Tbsp. nonfat dry milk powder
2	tsp. xanthan gum
1	tsp. unflavored gelatin
1	tsp. Italian seasoning
1	tsp. cider vinegar
1	tsp. olive oil
1/2	tsp. salt
1/2	tsp. sugar
1	to 1-1/3 cups brown rice flour

Pizza toppings of your choice

1. In a small bowl, dissolve yeast in warm water. Add the tapioca flour, milk powder, xanthan gum, gelatin, Italian seasoning, vinegar, oil, salt, sugar and 2/3 cup brown rice flour. Beat until smooth. Stir in enough remaining brown rice flour to form a soft dough (dough will be sticky).

2. On a floured surface, roll dough into a 13-in. circle. Transfer to a 12-in. pizza pan coated with cooking spray; build up edges slightly. Cover and let rest for 10 minutes.

3. Bake at 425° for 10-12 minutes or until golden brown. Add toppings of your choice. Bake 10-15 minutes longer or until crust is golden brown and toppings are lightly browned and heated through.

Nutrition Facts: 1/6 of crust (calculated without toppings) equals 142 calories, 2 g fat (trace saturated fat), 1 mg cholesterol, 223 mg sodium, 30 g carbohydrate, 3 g fiber, 4 g protein. **Diabetic Exchange:** 2 starch.

> Keep in mind that ingredient formulas and production facilties vary **among brands**. If you're concerned that a branded ingredient you're using in a recipe contains gluten, you should contact the manufacturer directly.

GLUTEN-FREE PIZZA CRUST

Double-Chip Pumpkin Cinnamon Muffins

PREP: 20 min. **BAKE:** 15 min. + cooling **YIELD:** 2 dozen

VERA DECKER • WINDSOR, NEW YORK

I was searching for a pumpkin muffin recipe for a lady in our church. The one I found used a large amount of eggs, sugar, oil and chocolate chips. This lightened version makes moist, delicious muffins that taste just as good a day or two later... if they last that long!

1	can (15 oz.) solid-pack pumpkin
1	cup sugar
1/2	cup buttermilk
1/3	cup canola oil
2	eggs
2	egg whites
1	tsp. vanilla extract
2	cups all-purpose flour
1/2	cup oat flour
2	tsp. baking powder
1	tsp. baking soda
1	tsp. ground cinnamon
1/2	tsp. salt
1/4	tsp. ground nutmeg
1/2	cup cinnamon baking chips, chopped
1/2	cup miniature semisweet chocolate chips

TOPPING:

1/4	cup sugar
3	tsp. ground cinnamon

1. In a large bowl, beat the first seven ingredients until well blended. Combine the flours, baking powder, baking soda, cinnamon, salt and nutmeg; gradually beat into pumpkin mixture until blended. Stir in chips.

2. Coat muffin cups with cooking spray or use foil liners; fill two-thirds full with batter. Combine topping ingredients; sprinkle over batter.

3. Bake at 400° for 12-15 minutes or until a toothpick comes out clean. Cool for 5 minutes before removing from pans to wire racks.

Nutrition Facts: 1 muffin equals 174 calories, 6 g fat (2 g saturated fat), 18 mg cholesterol, 164 mg sodium, 27 g carbohydrate, 2 g fiber, 3 g protein. **Diabetic Exchanges:** 2 starch, 1 fat.

DOUBLE-CHIP PUMPKIN
CINNAMON MUFFINS

Cheese Flatbread C M

PREP: 5 min. + rising **BAKE:** 20 min. **YIELD:** 16 servings

SHARON DELANEY-CHRONIS • SOUTH MILWAUKEE, WISCONSIN

The convenience of frozen bread dough and dried herbs makes this treat about as easy as it gets. To boost fiber, you can also use frozen whole wheat bread dough.

1	loaf (1 lb.) frozen bread dough, thawed
2	Tbsp. butter, softened
2	tsp. paprika
1/2	tsp. garlic powder
1/2	tsp. dried oregano
1/2	tsp. dried basil
1	cup (4 oz.) shredded part-skim mozzarella cheese

1. On a lightly floured surface, roll dough into a 16-in. x 11-in. rectangle. Transfer to a 15-in. x 10-in. x 1-in. baking pan coated with cooking spray; build up edges slightly. Spread with butter. Sprinkle with paprika, garlic powder, oregano and basil. Prick the dough several times with a fork; sprinkle with cheese. Cover and let rise for 30 minutes.

2. Bake at 375° for 20-25 minutes or until crust is golden brown and cheese is melted. Serve warm.

Nutrition Facts: 1 piece equals 111 calories, 4 g fat (2 g saturated fat), 8 mg cholesterol, 202 mg sodium, 14 g carbohydrate, 1 g fiber, 5 g protein. **Diabetic Exchanges:** 1 starch, 1/2 fat.

Banana Date-Nut Mini Muffins F S C

PREP: 15 min. **BAKE:** 15 min./batch **YIELD:** 4 dozen

LILLIAN JULOW • GAINESVILLE, FLORIDA

These little muffins have so much flavor, they don't need butter or jam to make them complete. Keep some in the freezer for fast snacks. Be sure to not overmix the wet and dry ingredients, so the muffins stay tender.

1	cup mashed ripe bananas (about 2 medium)
3/4	cup sugar
1/3	cup unsweetened applesauce
3	Tbsp. canola oil
1	egg
3/4	cup all-purpose flour
3/4	cup whole wheat flour
1/2	cup quick-cooking oats
1-1/2	tsp. baking powder
1/2	tsp. baking soda
1/3	cup chopped dates
1/4	cup finely chopped walnuts
1	tsp. grated lemon peel

1. In a large bowl, beat bananas, sugar, applesauce, oil and egg until well blended. Combine the flours, oats, baking powder and baking soda; gradually beat into banana mixture until blended. Stir in the dates, walnuts and lemon peel.

2. Coat miniature muffin cups with cooking spray or use paper liners; fill half full with batter. Bake at 350° for 12-14 minutes or until a toothpick comes out clean. Cool for 5 minutes before removing from pans to wire racks.

Nutrition Facts: 1 muffin equals 49 calories, 1 g fat (trace saturated fat), 4 mg cholesterol, 27 mg sodium, 9 g carbohydrate, 1 g fiber, 1 g protein. **Diabetic Exchange:** 1/2 starch.

Cranberry-Pecan Corn Muffins

PREP: 15 min. **COOK:** 20 min. **YIELD:** 1 dozen

LISA VARNER • GREENVILLE, SOUTH CAROLINA

I found a low-fat recipe for corn muffins and added cranberries and pecans to make a wonderful new dish. They have just the right flavor for the holidays or any time .

1-3/4	cups yellow cornmeal
3/4	cup all-purpose flour
1-1/4	tsp. baking soda
1/2	tsp. salt
1-1/2	cups (12 oz.) fat-free plain yogurt
1	egg
1/4	cup canola oil
1/4	cup honey
1/2	cup dried cranberries
1/4	cup chopped pecans

1. In a large bowl, combine the cornmeal, flour, baking soda and salt. In another bowl, combine the yogurt, egg, oil and honey. Stir into dry ingredients just until moistened. Fold in cranberries and pecans. Coat muffin cups with cooking spray; fill three-fourths full with batter.

2. Bake at 375° for 18-20 minutes or until a toothpick inserted near the center comes out clean. Cool for 5 minutes before removing from pans to wire racks. Serve warm.

Nutrition Facts: 1 muffin equals 185 calories, 6 g fat (1 g saturated fat), 16 mg cholesterol, 217 mg sodium, 29 g carbohydrate, 2 g fiber, 4 g protein. **Diabetic Exchanges:** 2 starch, 1 fat.

Candy Cane Chocolate Loaves ⓢ

PREP: 25 min. **BAKE:** 50 min. + cooling
YIELD: 3 loaves (12 slices each)

SHELLY PLATTEN • AMHERST, WISCONSIN

Leftover candy canes after Christmas inspired me to combine them with a favorite chocolate bread recipe.

1/4	cup butter, softened
1-2/3	cups packed brown sugar
4	egg whites
2	eggs
3/4	cup strong brewed coffee
1/2	cup reduced-fat vanilla yogurt
1/4	cup canola oil
1	Tbsp. vanilla extract
1/4	tsp. peppermint extract
3-1/2	cups all-purpose flour
3/4	cup baking cocoa
1-1/2	tsp. baking soda
1/2	tsp. salt
1-1/2	cups buttermilk
1	cup (6 oz.) miniature semisweet chocolate chips

TOPPING:

1/3	cup vanilla or white chips
3	Tbsp. crushed candy canes

1. In a large bowl, beat butter and brown sugar until crumbly, about 2 minutes. Add the egg whites, eggs, coffee, yogurt, oil and extracts until blended.

2. Combine the flour, cocoa, baking soda and salt; add to the butter mixture alternately with buttermilk, beating well after each addition. Fold in chocolate chips.

3. Transfer to three 8-in x 4-in. loaf pans coated with cooking spray. Bake at 350° for 50-55 minutes or until a toothpick inserted near the center comes out clean. Cool for 10 minutes before removing from pans to wire racks to cool completely.

4. For topping, in a microwave, melt vanilla chips; stir until smooth. Drizzle over loaves. Sprinkle with crushed candies.

Nutrition Facts: 1 slice equals 162 calories, 5 g fat (2 g saturated fat), 16 mg cholesterol, 124 mg sodium, 26 g carbohydrate, 1 g fiber, 3 g protein. **Diabetic Exchanges:** 1-1/2 starch, 1 fat.

CRANBERRY-PECAN CORN MUFFINS

Blueberry Orange Scones

PREP/TOTAL TIME: 30 min. **YIELD:** 8 scones

KATY RADTKE • APPLETON, WISCONSIN

Tender, flaky and moist, these buttery scones are studded with juicy blueberries.

2	cups all-purpose flour
3	Tbsp. sugar
2	tsp. baking powder
2	tsp. grated orange peel
1	tsp. salt
1/4	tsp. baking soda
1/4	tsp. ground cloves
1/4	cup cold butter
1/2	cup buttermilk
1/4	cup orange juice
1/2	cup fresh *or* frozen unsweetened blueberries

1. In a large bowl, combine the first seven ingredients. Cut in butter until mixture resembles coarse crumbs. Stir in buttermilk and orange juice just until moistened. Gently fold in blueberries.

2. Turn onto a floured surface; gently knead 10 times. Pat into an 8-in. circle. Cut into eight wedges. Separate wedges and place on a baking sheet coated with cooking spray. Bake at 425° for 10-12 minutes or until golden brown. Serve warm.

Editor's Note: If using frozen blueberries, do not thaw before adding to batter.

Nutrition Facts: 1 scone equals 198 calories, 6 g fat (4 g saturated fat), 16 mg cholesterol, 509 mg sodium, 32 g carbohydrate, 1 g fiber, 4 g protein. **Diabetic Exchanges:** 2 starch, 1 fat.

Pumpkin Nut Bread ⓢ

PREP: 20 min. **BAKE:** 1 hour + cooling
YIELD: 2 loaves (16 slices each)

CONNIE THOMAS • JENSEN, UTAH

Classic fall flavors of pumpkin and pecans make this bread perfect for the season. It's delicious when still warm from the oven, but it makes for a nice gift, too.

1	can (15 oz.) solid-pack pumpkin
1-1/2	cups sugar
1/2	cup fat-free milk
4	egg whites
1/3	cup canola oil
1/3	cup unsweetened applesauce
3-1/3	cups whole wheat flour
2	tsp. baking soda
2	tsp. ground cinnamon
1	tsp. baking powder
3/4	tsp. ground allspice
1/2	tsp. salt
1	cup chopped pecans

1. In a large bowl, beat the pumpkin, sugar, milk, egg whites, oil and applesauce until well blended. In a small bowl, combine the flour, baking soda, cinnamon, baking powder, allspice and salt; gradually beat into the pumpkin mixture until blended. Stir in the pecans.

2. Transfer to two 9-in. x 5-in. loaf pans coated with cooking spray. Bake at 350° for 1 hour or until a toothpick inserted near the center comes out clean. Cool for 10 minutes before removing from pans to wire racks.

Nutrition Facts: 1 slice equals 135 calories, 5 g fat (trace saturated fat), trace cholesterol, 138 mg sodium, 21 g carbohydrate, 3 g fiber, 3 g protein. **Diabetic Exchanges:** 1-1/2 starch, 1 fat.

BLUEBERRY ORANGE SCONES

PUMPKIN NUT BREAD

Makeover Apple Bread

PREP: 25 min. **BAKE:** 45 min. + cooling
YIELD: 2 loaves (12 slices each)

LIZ TITLER • MADISON, OHIO

We're confident that anyone who tries this will be thrilled. The bread has a hearty texture and sweet, home-baked flavor, but none of the fat and calories.

 3 cups all-purpose flour
1-1/2 cups sugar
 1 tsp. baking powder
 1 tsp. salt
 1 tsp. baking soda
 1 tsp. ground cinnamon
 2 eggs
 1/2 cup unsweetened applesauce
 1/3 cup canola oil
 1 tsp. vanilla extract
 3 cups chopped peeled tart apples

TOPPING:
 1/2 cup all-purpose flour
 1/2 cup sugar
 2 Tbsp. chopped walnuts
 1/3 cup cold butter

1. In a large bowl, combine the first six ingredients. In another bowl, whisk the eggs, applesauce, oil and vanilla. Stir into dry ingredients just until moistened. Fold in apples. Transfer to two 8-in. x 4-in. loaf pans coated with cooking spray.

2. For topping, combine the flour, sugar and walnuts; cut in butter until crumbly. Sprinkle over batter.

3. Bake at 350° for 45-55 minutes or until a toothpick inserted near the center comes out clean. Cool for 10 minutes before removing from pans to wire racks.

Nutrition Facts: 1 slice equals 200 calories, 7 g fat (2 g saturated fat), 24 mg cholesterol, 192 mg sodium, 33 g carbohydrate, 1 g fiber, 3 g protein.

Many old-fashioned quick breads are high in sugar. To cut calories, you can usually **decrease the sugar** from such recipes by 1/4 to 1/3 without a noticeable change in the item's overall sweetness.

ROASTED PEPPER, BACON & EGG MUFFINS

BROILED COD

SESAME CHICKEN SALAD

It doesn't matter if you're a newlywed or an empty nester, it's a snap to trim down recipes for a pair...and trim down calories as well. When you don't want to face leftovers for days on end, consider these lightened-up specialties.

Sesame Chicken Salad C

PREP/TOTAL TIME: 15 min. **YIELD:** 2 servings

HEALTHY COOKING TEST KITCHEN

The home economists in our Test Kitchen tossed together this fresh, flavorful Asian salad that's brimming with color and crunch. It's ready in no time and perfectly portioned for two.

1/3	cup fat-free mayonnaise
1	Tbsp. reduced-sodium soy sauce
1/8	tsp. ground ginger
1-1/3	cups cubed cooked chicken breast
1/2	cup chopped fresh snow peas
1	small sweet red pepper, chopped
1	Tbsp. sesame seeds, toasted
4	lettuce leaves
1	Tbsp. chopped cashews

1. In a small bowl, combine the mayonnaise, soy sauce and ginger. Stir in the chicken, peas, pepper and sesame seeds. Serve over lettuce leaves; sprinkle with the cashews.

Nutrition Facts: 1 cup salad with 1-1/2 tsp. cashews equals 254 calories, 8 g fat (2 g saturated fat), 76 mg cholesterol, 736 mg sodium, 14 g carbohydrate, 4 g fiber, 31 g protein. **Diabetic Exchanges:** 4 very lean meat, 1 vegetable, 1 fat, 1/2 starch.

Pumpkin Pie Oatmeal S M

PREP/TOTAL TIME: 15 min. **YIELD:** 2 servings

AMBER RIFF • COLUMBUS, OHIO

I made this oatmeal because I love pumpkin pie and wanted it for breakfast. It's smooth, creamy and wonderful!

1	cup water
1	cup vanilla soy milk
1	cup old-fashioned oats
1/2	cup canned pumpkin
1/4	tsp. pumpkin pie spice
2	Tbsp. sugar
1/4	tsp. vanilla extract

Dried cranberries, optional

1. In a small saucepan, combine the water, soy milk, oats, pumpkin and pie spice. Bring to a boil; cook and stir for 5 minutes.

2. Remove from the heat; stir in sugar and vanilla. Sprinkle with cranberries if desired.

Nutrition Facts: 1 cup (calculated without cranberries) equals 268 calories, 5 g fat (trace saturated fat), 0 cholesterol, 51 mg sodium, 49 g carbohydrate, 6 g fiber, 10 g protein.

Roasted Pepper, Bacon & Egg Muffins

PREP: 20 min. + standing **COOK:** 10 min.
YIELD: 2 servings

LOUISE GILBERT • QUESNEL, BRITISH COLUMBIA

This fun and filling sandwich is just as great for lunch, dinner or a quick snack as it is for breakfast.

1/2	medium sweet red pepper
1/2	cup coarsely chopped sweet onion
1	tsp. butter
4	egg whites
2	eggs
1	Tbsp. fat-free milk
1/4	tsp. pepper
2	center-cut bacon strips, cooked and crumbled
2	Tbsp. shredded reduced-fat cheddar cheese
2	whole wheat English muffins, split and toasted

1. Remove and discard seeds from the pepper half. Place cut side down on a baking sheet. Broil 4 in. from the heat until the skin blisters, about 6 minutes. Immediately place pepper half in a small bowl; cover and let stand for 15-20 minutes. Peel off and discard charred skin; chop pepper.

2. In a small nonstick skillet coated with cooking spray, saute onion in butter until tender. In a large bowl, whisk the egg whites, eggs, milk and pepper. Pour into the pan. Add bacon and chopped pepper; cook and stir over medium heat until eggs are completely set.

3. Remove from the heat. Sprinkle with cheese; cover and let stand until cheese is melted. Spoon onto English muffins. Serve immediately.

Nutrition Facts: 1 serving equals 329 calories, 12 g fat (5 g saturated fat), 229 mg cholesterol, 662 mg sodium, 34 g carbohydrate, 6 g fiber, 25 g protein.

Homemade Fish Sticks

PREP/TOTAL TIME: 25 min. **YIELD:** 2 servings

JENNIFER ROWLAND • ELIZABETHTOWN, KENTUCKY

I'm a nutritionist and needed a healthy fish fix. Moist inside and crunchy outside, these are great with oven fries or roasted veggies and low-fat homemade tartar sauce.

- 1/2 cup all-purpose flour
- 1 egg, beaten
- 1/2 cup dry bread crumbs
- 1/2 tsp. salt
- 1/2 tsp. paprika
- 1/2 tsp. lemon-pepper seasoning
- 3/4 lb. cod fillets, cut into 1-in. strips

Butter-flavored cooking spray

1. Place flour and egg in separate shallow bowls. In another shallow bowl, combine bread crumbs and seasonings. Dip fish in the flour, then egg, then roll in the crumb mixture.

2. Place on a baking sheet coated with cooking spray. Spritz fish sticks with butter-flavored spray. Bake at 400° for 10-12 minutes or until fish flakes easily with a fork, turning once.

Nutrition Facts: 1 serving equals 278 calories, 4 g fat (1 g saturated fat), 129 mg cholesterol, 718 mg sodium, 25 g carbohydrate, 1 g fiber, 33 g protein.

If you'd like to remove 472 mg sodium from the Homemade Fish Sticks, simply **omit the salt** and use salt-free lemon-pepper seasoning instead. A crispy green side salad makes a fine addition to the low-sodium meal.

HOMEMADE FISH STICKS

Grilled Pepper Jack Chicken Sandwiches

PREP/TOTAL TIME: 25 min. **YIELD:** 2 servings

LINDA FOREMAN • LOCUST GROVE, OKLAHOMA

Basic, yet packed with flavor, this sandwich gets a kick from zesty pepper Jack and savory bacon.

- 2 boneless skinless chicken breast halves (4 oz. *each*)
- 1 tsp. poultry seasoning
- 2 center-cut bacon strips, cooked and halved
- 2 slices (1/2 oz. *each*) pepper Jack cheese
- 2 hamburger buns, split
- 2 lettuce leaves
- 1 slice onion, separated into rings
- 2 slices tomato

Dill pickle slices, optional

1. Sprinkle chicken with poultry seasoning. Coat grill rack with cooking spray before starting the grill. Grill chicken, covered, over medium heat for 4-7 minutes on each side or until juices run clear. Top with bacon and cheese; cover and grill 1-2 minutes longer or until cheese is melted.

2. Serve on buns with lettuce, onion, tomato and pickles if desired.

Nutrition Facts: 1 sandwich (calculated without pickles) equals 335 calories, 11 g fat (4 g saturated fat), 85 mg cholesterol, 456 mg sodium, 25 g carbohydrate, 2 g fiber, 33 g protein. **Diabetic Exchanges:** 4 very lean meat, 1-1/2 starch, 1 fat.

Italian Baked Chicken Breasts Ⓒ

PREP: 15 min. **BAKE:** 20 min. **YIELD:** 2 servings

SHIRL PARSONS • CAPE CARTERET, NORTH CAROLINA

Tender and juicy, this chicken is lightly breaded on the outside, moist on the inside...and delicious!

- 2 egg whites
- 2 tsp. balsamic vinegar
- 1/3 cup dry bread crumbs
- 1/2 tsp. dried parsley flakes
- 1/4 tsp. garlic powder
- 1/4 tsp. garlic salt
- 2 boneless skinless chicken breast halves (4 oz. *each*)

Butter-flavored cooking spray

- 1/8 tsp. salt
- 1/8 tsp. pepper

1. In a shallow bowl, beat egg whites and vinegar. In another shallow bowl, combine the bread crumbs, parsley, garlic powder and garlic salt. Dip chicken in egg mixture, then coat with crumb mixture.

2. Place in an 8-in. square baking dish coated with cooking spray; lightly coat chicken with butter-flavored spray. Sprinkle with salt and pepper. Bake, uncovered, at 375° for 20-25 minutes or until a meat thermometer reads 170°.

Nutrition Facts: 1 chicken breast half equals 191 calories, 4 g fat (1 g saturated fat), 63 mg cholesterol, 560 mg sodium, 9 g carbohydrate, 1 g fiber, 28 g protein. **Diabetic Exchanges:** 3 very lean meat, 1 fat, 1/2 starch.

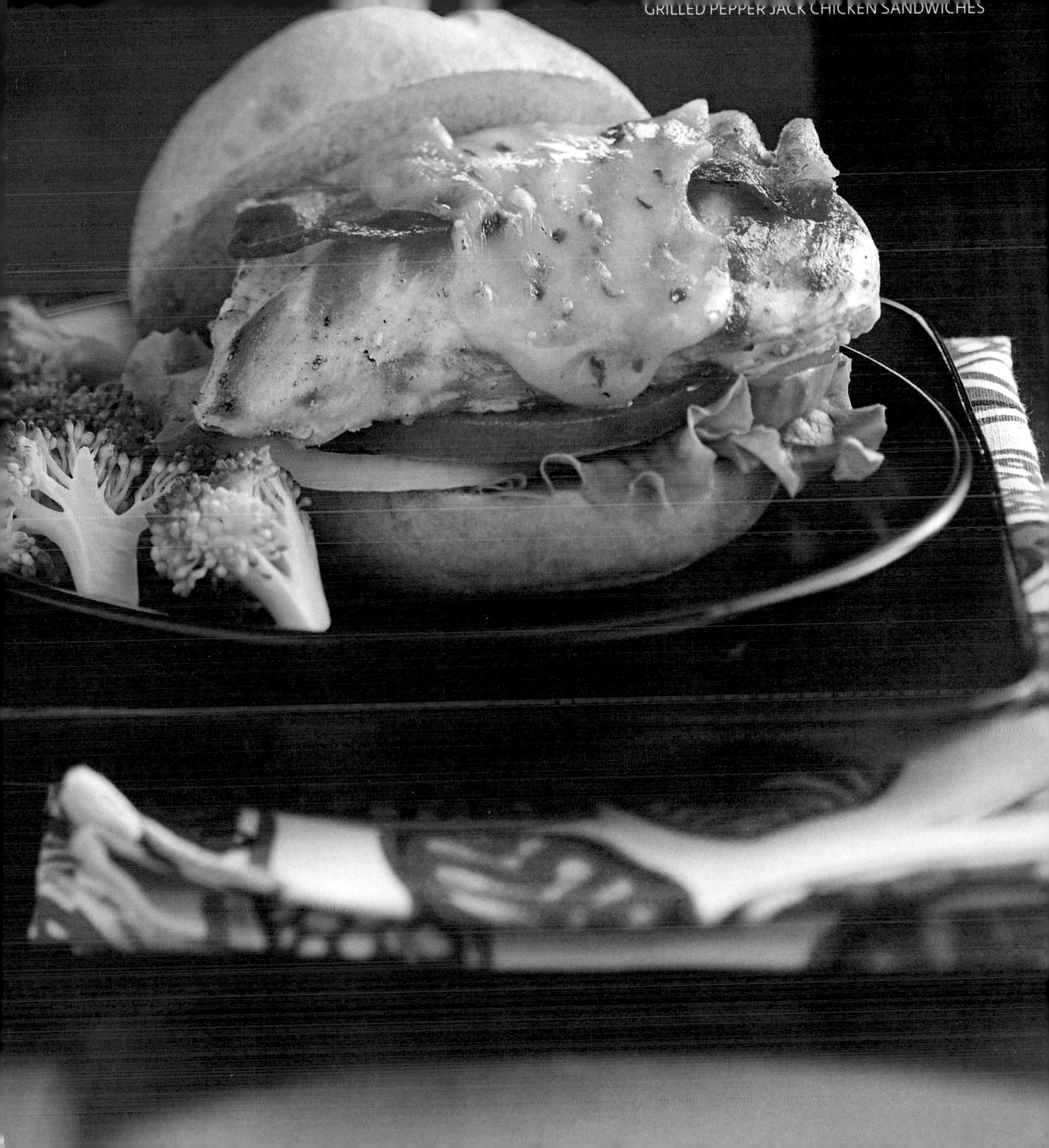
GRILLED PEPPER JACK CHICKEN SANDWICHES

Cranberry-Apple Pork Chops

PREP: 15 min. **COOK:** 15 min. + marinating
YIELD: 2 servings

KATIE SHIREMAN • PHILADELPHIA, PENNSYLVANIA

These colorful, sweet-tart chops deliver seasonal flavors in each bite!

3	tsp. ground cinnamon
1-1/2	tsp. ground nutmeg
1/2	tsp. pumpkin pie spice
2	boneless pork loin chops (4 oz. *each*)
1/2	cup plus 2 Tbsp. unsweetened apple juice, *divided*
1/2	cup plus 2 Tbsp. cranberry juice, *divided*
1	tsp. canola oil
1	medium apple, peeled and finely chopped
1	cup chopped fresh cranberries
1/8	tsp. salt

1. Combine the cinnamon, nutmeg and pie spice; rub over chops. Pour 1/2 cup apple juice and 1/2 cup cranberry juice into a large resealable plastic bag; add the pork chops. Seal bag and turn to coat; refrigerate for 8 hours or overnight.

2. Drain chops and discard marinade. In a large nonstick skillet coated with cooking spray, brown chops in oil over medium heat for 3-4 minutes on each side.

3. Add the apple, cranberries, salt and remaining juices. Bring to a boil. Reduce heat; cover and cook for 10-12 minutes or until chops and apple are tender, turning once.

Nutrition Facts: 1 pork chop with 3/4 cup sauce equals 254 calories, 9 g fat (3 g saturated fat), 55 mg cholesterol, 181 mg sodium, 21 g carbohydrate, 4 g fiber, 22 g protein. **Diabetic Exchanges:** 3 lean meat, 1-1/2 fruit.

Tuna and Tomato Kabobs [c]

PREP: 20 min. + marinating **GRILL:** 10 min.
YIELD: 2 servings

EDRIE O'BRIEN • DENVER, COLORADO

A lime-herb marinade adds great taste to the tuna and vegetables on these attractive skewers. I lightened this up by using tuna in place of the beef. Halibut and swordfish work well, too.

- 2 Tbsp. lime juice
- 1 Tbsp. canola oil
- 1 Tbsp. reduced-sodium soy sauce
- 3/4 tsp. grated lime peel
- 1 small garlic clove, minced
- 1/2 tsp. salt
- 1/2 tsp. dried parsley flakes
- 1/8 tsp. ground cumin
- 1/8 tsp. pepper
- Dash cayenne pepper
- 1/2 lb. tuna steak, cut into 1-in. cubes
- 6 cherry tomatoes
- 6 medium fresh mushrooms

1. In a large resealable plastic bag, combine the first 10 ingredients; add the tuna. Seal bag and turn to coat; refrigerate for 30 minutes.

2. Coat grill rack with cooking spray before starting the grill. Drain and discard marinade. On two metal or soaked wooden skewers, alternately thread tuna and vegetables. For medium-rare tuna, grill, covered, for 6-8 minutes or until slightly pink in the center, turning once.

Nutrition Facts: 1 kabob equals 183 calories, 5 g fat (1 g saturated fat), 51 mg cholesterol, 460 mg sodium, 6 g carbohydrate, 1 g fiber, 29 g protein. **Diabetic Exchanges:** 4 very lean meat, 1 vegetable, 1/2 fat.

Moroccan Chicken Thighs

PREP: 25 min. **COOK:** 40 min. **YIELD:** 2 servings

SUSAN MILLS • THREE RIVERS, CALIFORNIA

My husband and I love Middle Eastern and Mediterranean food. This recipe is one of our favorites.

- 1/2 tsp. brown sugar
- 1/2 tsp. ground coriander
- 1/2 tsp. ground cumin
- 1/2 tsp. paprika
- 1/4 tsp. ground cinnamon
- 1/8 tsp. garlic powder
- 1/8 tsp. salt
- 1/8 tsp. pepper
- 2 tsp. all-purpose flour
- 4 bone-in chicken thighs (about 1 lb.), skin removed
- 1-1/2 tsp. olive oil
- SAUCE:
- 3 shallots, chopped
- 1/2 cup plus 2 Tbsp. reduced-sodium chicken broth, *divided*
- 4 pitted dates, chopped
- 1 tsp. all-purpose flour
- 1-1/2 tsp. minced fresh cilantro
- COUSCOUS:
- 1/4 cup water
- 3 Tbsp. reduced-sodium chicken broth
- 1/8 tsp. salt
- Dash ground cumin
- 1/3 cup uncooked couscous
- 1-1/2 tsp. slivered almonds, toasted

1. In a small bowl, combine the first eight ingredients. Set aside 1 tsp. spice mixture; add flour to remaining mixture and sprinkle over chicken.

2. In a large nonstick skillet coated with cooking spray, brown chicken in oil on both sides. Remove and keep warm. Add shallots to pan; cook and stir over medium heat for 3 minutes. Stir in 1/2 cup broth and dates. Bring to a boil. Reduce the heat; return chicken to pan.

3. Cover and simmer for 20-25 minutes or until chicken juices run clear. Remove chicken and keep warm. Combine flour with reserved spice mixture and remaining broth until smooth; gradually stir into pan. Bring to a boil; cook and stir for 2 minutes or until thickened. Stir in cilantro.

4. For couscous, in a small saucepan, bring the water, broth, salt and cumin to a boil. Stir in couscous. Cover and remove from the heat; let stand for 5-10 minutes or until water is absorbed. Fluff with a fork; stir in almonds. Serve with chicken and sauce.

Nutrition Facts: 2 chicken thighs with 1/2 cup couscous and 1/3 cup sauce equals 381 calories, 15 g fat (4 g saturated fat), 113 mg cholesterol, 364 mg sodium, 26 g carbohydrate, 2 g fiber, 36 g protein.

MOROCCAN CHICKEN THIGHS

Apricot Turkey Sandwiches

PREP/TOTAL TIME: 15 min. **YIELD:** 2 servings

CHARLOTTE GEHLE • BROWNSTOWN, MICHIGAN

Apricot jam and Dijon mustard come together for a wonderful spread on this sandwich with Swiss cheese, turkey bacon and peppered turkey slices.

- 2 turkey bacon strips
- 4 pieces multigrain bread, toasted
- 2 Tbsp. apricot jam
- 3 oz. thinly sliced deli peppered turkey
- 2 slices tomato
- 2 slices red onion
- 2 pieces leaf lettuce
- 2 slices reduced-fat Swiss cheese
- 4 tsp. Dijon mustard

1. In a small skillet, cook bacon over medium heat until crisp. Remove to paper towels to drain; set aside.

2. Spread two toast slices with jam. Layer with turkey, reserved bacon, tomato, onion, lettuce and cheese. Spread remaining toast with mustard; place on top.

Nutrition Facts: 1 sandwich equals 338 calories, 10 g fat (3 g saturated fat), 40 mg cholesterol, 1,109 mg sodium, 43 g carbohydrate, 4 g fiber, 23 g protein.

Chocolate Peanut Parfaits

PREP: 15 min. + chilling **YIELD:** 2 servings

LISA VARNER • GREENVILLE, SOUTH CAROLINA

This lower-in-fat-and-calories version of a pie recipe I dearly love still tastes great and looks richer than it really is. It's make-ahead handy!

CHOCOLATE PEANUT PARFAITS

- 2 chocolate wafers, crushed
- 1/4 cup fat-free sweetened condensed milk
- 2 oz. fat-free cream cheese
- 2 Tbsp. reduced-fat creamy peanut butter
- 3/4 tsp. lemon juice
- 1/2 tsp. vanilla extract
- 1/4 cup reduced-fat whipped topping
- 1 tsp. chocolate syrup
- 1 tsp. chopped dry roasted peanuts

1. Divide crushed wafers between two parfait glasses. In a small bowl, beat the milk, cream cheese, peanut butter, lemon juice and vanilla. Fold in whipped topping. Spoon over crushed wafers. Cover and refrigerate for at least 1 hour. Just before serving, drizzle with syrup and sprinkle with peanuts.

Nutrition Facts: 1 parfait equals 285 calories, 8 g fat (3 g saturated fat), 7 mg cholesterol, 332 mg sodium, 41 g carbohydrate, 1 g fiber, 12 g protein.

Broiled Cod c

PREP: 10 min. + marinating **BROIL:** 10 min.
YIELD: 2 servings

KIM RUSSELL • NORTH WALES, PENNSYLVANIA

This is the easiest and tastiest fish you'll serve. Even finicky eaters who think they don't like fish will love it because it lacks a fishy taste and is beautiful and flakey.

- 1/4 cup fat-free Italian salad dressing
- 1/2 tsp. sugar
- 1/8 tsp. *each* salt, garlic powder, curry powder, paprika and pepper
- 2 cod fillets (6 oz. *each*)
- 2 tsp. butter

1. In a large resealable plastic bag, combine the dressing, sugar and seasonings. Add the fish; seal bag and turn to coat. Refrigerate for 10-30 minutes.

2. Drain and discard marinade; place fillets on a broiler pan coated with cooking spray. Broil 3-4 in. from the heat for 10-12 minutes or until fish flakes easily with a fork. Place 1 tsp. butter on each fillet; let stand until melted.

Nutrition Facts: 1 cod fillet equals 170 calories, 5 g fat (3 g saturated fat), 75 mg cholesterol, 407 mg sodium, 2 g carbohydrate, trace fiber, 27 g protein. **Diabetic Exchange:** 4 very lean meat, 1/2 fat.

BROILED COD

CHICKEN WITH VEGGIES

Chicken with Veggies ⓒ

PREP/TOTAL TIME: 30 min. **YIELD:** 2 servings

NIKKI ADAMS · CHERRY VALLEY, CALIFORNIA

Colorful, nutritious veggies and Italian seasoning make something special of this chicken in minutes!

2	boneless skinless chicken breast halves (6 oz. *each*)
1/4	tsp. salt
1/4	tsp. pepper
2	Tbsp. dry bread crumbs
2	tsp. grated Parmesan cheese
2	tsp. Italian seasoning
3	tsp. olive oil, *divided*
3	cups fresh baby spinach
2	plum tomatoes, chopped
2	garlic cloves, minced

1. Flatten chicken to 1/4-in. thickness; sprinkle with salt and pepper. In a shallow bowl, combine the bread crumbs, cheese and Italian seasoning. Coat chicken in bread crumb mixture.

2. In a large nonstick skillet coated with cooking spray, cook chicken in 2 tsp. oil over medium heat for 3-4 minutes on each side or until no longer pink. Remove and keep warm.

3. Saute spinach in remaining oil just until wilted. Stir in tomatoes and garlic; cook 3 minutes longer. Serve with chicken.

Nutrition Facts: 1 chicken breast half with 1 cup vegetables equals 302 calories, 12 g fat (2 g saturated fat), 95 mg cholesterol, 484 mg sodium, 10 g carbohydrate, 2 g fiber, 38 g protein. **Diabetic Exchanges:** 5 very lean meat, 2 fat, 1 vegetable.

When you're out of **Italian seasoning**, it's a snap to mix up your own! Simply combine a 1/4 teaspoon each of basil, thyme, rosemary and oregano for each teaspoon called for in a recipe.

POACHED PEARS WITH ORANGE CREAM

Poached Pears with Orange Cream F S

PREP: 10 min. **COOK:** 45 min. + cooling **YIELD:** 2 servings

HEALTHY COOKING TEST KITCHEN

This elegant dessert with a hint of sweetness offers just the right ending to any meal.

2	medium firm pears
1-1/2	cups water
1	cup dry red wine *or* red grape juice
1/2	cup sugar
2	tsp. vanilla extract
1/4	cup reduced-fat sour cream
2	tsp. confectioners' sugar
1/2	tsp. grated orange peel
1/8	tsp. orange extract

Additional grated orange peel, optional

1. Core pears from bottom, leaving stems intact. Peel pears; cut a small slice from the bottom of each to level if necessary. Place pears on their sides in a large saucepan. Add water, wine, sugar and vanilla. Bring to a boil. Reduce heat; cover and simmer for 35-40 minutes or until pears are almost tender, turning once.

2. Meanwhile, combine the sour cream, confectioners' sugar, orange peel and extract. Refrigerate until serving.

3. Remove pears with a slotted spoon; cool to room temperature. Discard cooking liquid. Place pears on dessert plates. Serve with orange cream. Garnish with additional grated orange peel if desired.

Nutrition Facts: 1 pear with 2 Tbsp. cream equals 239 calories, 3 g fat (2 g saturated fat), 10 mg cholesterol, 23 mg sodium, 46 g carbohydrate, 5 g fiber, 3 g protein.

Easy Salmon Packets C

PREP: 15 min. **BAKE:** 20 min. **YIELD:** 2 servings

ROCHELLE GEYER • HANNIBAL, MISSOURI

What a delicious way to get omega-3 fatty acids. We enjoy this over pasta for a heart-healthy midweek meal.

2	salmon fillets (4 oz. *each*)
2-1/2	cups sliced fresh mushrooms
1	medium tomato, chopped
1	garlic clove, minced
1/2	tsp. dried basil
1/4	tsp. salt
1/4	tsp. pepper
1/4	cup shredded Parmesan cheese

1. Place each fillet on a double thickness of heavy-duty foil (about 12 in. square). Top with mushrooms, tomato, garlic, basil, salt and pepper. Fold foil around salmon and seal tightly. Place on a baking sheet.

2. Bake at 400° for 15-20 minutes or until fish flakes easily with a fork. Open foil carefully; sprinkle with cheese. Bake, uncovered, 5 minutes longer or until cheese is melted.

Nutrition Facts: 1 packet equals 288 calories, 15 g fat (4 g saturated fat), 74 mg cholesterol, 539 mg sodium, 8 g carbohydrate, 2 g fiber, 30 g protein.

Grandma's French Tuna Salad Wraps

PREP/TOTAL TIME: 15 min. **YIELD:** 2 servings

JENNIFER MAGREY • STERLING, CONNECTICUT

My French Canadian grandmother always made tuna salad with chopped egg in it. I tried a version, added veggies for complete nutrition and turned it into a wrap.

1	can (6 oz.) light water-packed tuna, drained and flaked
1	celery rib, finely chopped
1/4	cup fat-free mayonnaise
1/4	tsp. pepper
2	whole wheat tortillas (8 in.), room temperature
1/2	cup shredded lettuce
1	small carrot, shredded
4	slices tomato
2	slices red onion, separated into rings
1	hard-cooked egg, sliced

1. In a small bowl, combine the tuna, celery, mayonnaise and pepper. Spoon tuna mixture down the center of each tortilla. Top with the lettuce, carrot, tomato, onion and egg. Roll up tightly; secure with toothpicks.

Nutrition Facts: 1 wrap equals 328 calories, 7 g fat (1 g saturated fat), 135 mg cholesterol, 770 mg sodium, 32 g carbohydrate, 4 g fiber, 30 g protein.

When you feel like getting creative in the kitchen, whip up a fun **tuna salad** by starting with the recipe above. Toss in a handful of peas or a dash of hot pepper sauce.

GRANDMA'S FRENCH TUNA SALAD WRAPS

My Healthy Life

Meeting the challenge of cooking light is a snap with a little help from those who do it regularly. Page through this chapter to see how other family cooks make eating right a priority...even on their busiest weeknights.

Family-Friendly Fare

When she became a registered dietitian, Jackie Termont found that lightening up
her favorite dishes was a snap. Here, she shares a no-fuss menu that's perfect
for casual meals at home as well as entertaining weekend guests.

When work began invading Jackie Termont's personal life, it turned out to be a good thing. "I went back to school and became a registered dietitian," says the Richmond, Virginia cook.

"I started lightening recipes and wanted to eat healthier and lose a few pounds. It was a gradual change, but I've been doing it for so long that it just comes naturally now," Jackie explains.

Though she doesn't follow a special diet, Jackie does pay attention to what she eats. "It's more fun for me when I don't have to worry if the food is potentially unhealthy," she says. "But I love food, and I think everything can be worked into a diet if you're careful about how much and how often you eat."

She has a balanced approach when it comes to exercise, too—working out 4 days a week with weights, elliptical trainers and the treadmill.

She also does yoga twice a week and tries to walk or ride her bike on other days. "I just feel better after working out, like I've accomplished something good for myself," she says.

When not at the gym, Jackie can often be found at home...baking. To keep things lighter, she opts for reduced-fat and low-sugar ingredients. "However, I don't generally use totally fat-free dairy because I think you need some fat to make it palatable."

Jackie's menu is the perfect example of her eating philosophy—it relies on lean, nutritious ingredients, but has the slightest touch of indulgence. Just dig into her heavenly Strawberry-Banana Graham Pudding to see what we mean!

Roasted Veggie Orzo **F** **M**

PREP: 25 min. **BAKE:** 20 min. **YIELD:** 8 servings

My sister inspired this recipe. I added a few more spices, but it's her concept. It's easy to vary, is a great way to add veggies to your diet and the olive oil is heart healthy.

1-1/2	cups fresh mushrooms, halved
1	medium zucchini, chopped
1	medium sweet yellow pepper, chopped
1	medium sweet red pepper, chopped
1	small red onion, cut into wedges
1	cup cut fresh asparagus (1-in. pieces)
1	Tbsp. olive oil
1	tsp. *each* dried oregano, thyme and rosemary, crushed
1/2	tsp. salt
1-1/4	cups uncooked orzo pasta
1/4	cup crumbled feta cheese

1. Place vegetables in a 15-in. x 10-in. x 1-in. baking pan coated with cooking spray. Drizzle with oil and sprinkle with seasonings; toss to coat. Bake at 400° for 20-25 minutes or until tender, stirring occasionally.

2. Meanwhile, cook orzo according to package directions. Drain; transfer to a serving bowl. Stir in roasted vegetables. Sprinkle with cheese.

Nutrition Facts: 3/4 cup equals 164 calories, 3 g fat (1 g saturated fat), 2 mg cholesterol, 188 mg sodium, 28 g carbohydrate, 3 g fiber, 6 g protein. **Diabetic Exchanges:** 1-1/2 starch, 1 vegetable, 1/2 fat.

Strawberry-Banana Graham Pudding **F**

PREP: 20 min. + chilling **YIELD:** 12 servings

I mix in additional fruit to get a little closer to all those servings you need every day. You can also try using different flavored puddings and fruit to switch up the recipe.

9	whole reduced-fat cinnamon graham crackers
1-3/4	cups cold fat-free milk
1	pkg. (1 oz.) sugar-free instant cheesecake or vanilla pudding mix
1	large firm banana, sliced
1/2	tsp. lemon juice
2	cups sliced fresh strawberries, *divided*
2-1/2	cups reduced-fat whipped topping, *divided*
	Mint sprigs, optional

1. Line the bottom of a 9-in. square pan with 4-1/2 graham crackers; set aside.

2. In a small bowl, whisk milk and pudding mix for 2 minutes. Let stand for 2 minutes or until soft-set. Place banana slices in another small bowl; toss with lemon juice. Stir bananas and 1 cup strawberries into the pudding. Fold in 1-3/4 cups whipped topping.

3. Spread half of pudding over the graham crackers; repeat layers. Cover and refrigerate overnight. Refrigerate remaining berries and whipped topping.

4. Just before serving, top with remaining berries and topping. Garnish with mint if desired.

Nutrition Facts: 1 piece equals 117 calories, 2 g fat (2 g saturated fat), 1 mg cholesterol, 171 mg sodium, 23 g carbohydrate, 1 g fiber, 2 g protein. **Diabetic Exchanges:** 1 starch, 1/2 fruit.

Zesty Marinated
Pork Chops S C

PREP: 15 min. + marinating **COOK:** 10 min.
YIELD: 6 servings

My husband loves pork chops. They're a good source of lean protein and it's easy to change their flavor. I created this marinade based on a few I saw in "Healthy Cooking" magazine.

1/4	cup balsamic vinegar
2	Tbsp. white wine *or* reduced-sodium chicken broth
4	tsp. olive oil, *divided*
1	tsp. chili powder
1/2	tsp. prepared horseradish
1/4	tsp. dill weed
1/4	tsp. garlic powder
1/4	tsp. salt
6	boneless pork loin chops (4 oz. *each*)

1. In a large resealable plastic bag, combine the vinegar, wine, 1 tsp. oil, chili powder, horseradish, dill, garlic powder and salt. Add the pork chops; seal bag and turn to coat. Refrigerate for 8 hours or overnight, turning occasionally.

2. Drain and discard marinade. In a large nonstick skillet over medium heat, cook chops in remaining oil for 4-5 minutes on each side or until a meat thermometer reads 160°.

Nutrition Facts: 1 pork chop equals 183 calories, 10 g fat (3 g saturated fat), 55 mg cholesterol, 61 mg sodium, 1 g carbohydrate, trace fiber, 22 g protein. **Diabetic Exchanges:** 3 lean meat, 1/2 fat.

> Jackie says that when it comes to **low-fat cooking**, she loves using her rice steamer for vegetables, as well as her grill pan and indoor grill. The microwave comes in handy for getting frozen veggies on the table quickly.

Enticing Extras

For busy TV news reporter Caroline Shively, taking advantage of leftovers is a must. Here, she shares a favorite entree and then explains how she uses the extras in two incredible dishes later in the week.

Eating well and exercising can be daunting, but imagine if you had to do it while capturing the effects of a hurricane or as one of the few Westerners at the voting polls during Iraq's first election. Welcome to the life of Caroline Shively, a correspondent for FOX News. Her work places her in the middle of historic events—including covering the 2008 election—but Caroline's home life in Alexandria, Virginia includes more typical things, such as cooking, spending time with her husband and playing tennis.

"I cook a lot when I'm home," Caroline says. "Kitchen time is fun for my husband, Robb, and me. Our schedules don't always allow us to see each other during the week, so we talk and catch up while cooking." The Kentucky native turns to the recipes she grew up with for inspiration. "A lot of my cooking comes from my mom," she says. "My husband jokes that I can't make a meal without calling her!"

In addition to spending time in the kitchen, the couple enjoys exercising together, too, but learning to mesh eating habits didn't come as naturally at the start. "My husband loves to grill," says Caroline. "At first, he tended to cook fattier things, and I joked I was going to weigh too much if he kept feeding me cheeseburgers. Since then, we've learned to compromise—he still grills but now picks leaner meats." The dishes she offers here feature grilled steak and an easy leftover plan they both appreciate.

Southwest Steak Quesadillas

PREP/TOTAL TIME: 30 min. **YIELD:** 4 servings

Colorful peppers and onions make this fantastic dish look as great as it tastes. As an added bonus, folding over one larger tortilla (instead of using two smaller ones) saves you a few grams of fat.

- 1 *each* small green, sweet red and yellow peppers, finely chopped
- 1 small red onion, finely chopped
- 4 fat-free flour tortillas (10 in.)
- 1/2 cup shredded reduced-fat cheddar cheese
- 1 cooked Southwest Steak (see opposite page), chopped
- 1/4 cup minced fresh cilantro
- 2 Tbsp. chopped seeded jalapeno pepper

Salsa, guacamole and reduced-fat sour cream, optional

1. In a large nonstick skillet coated with cooking spray, cook and stir peppers and onion over medium-high heat until tender. Transfer to a small bowl.

2. Coat the same skillet with cooking spray; add one tortilla. Sprinkle 2 Tbsp. cheese over half of tortilla. Top with a fourth of the steak, 1/3 cup pepper mixture, 1 Tbsp. cilantro and 1-1/2 tsp. jalapeno.

3. Fold over and cook over low heat for 1-2 minutes on each side or until cheese is melted; remove. Repeat for remaining quesadillas, spraying pan as needed. Cut into wedges; serve with salsa, guacamole and sour cream if desired.

Editor's Note: When cutting hot peppers, disposable gloves are recommended. Avoid touching your face.

Nutrition Facts: 1 quesadilla (calculated without optional ingredients) equals 379 calories, 13 g fat (6 g saturated fat), 64 mg cholesterol, 772 mg sodium, 35 g carbohydrate, 3 g fiber, 30 g protein.

Southwest Steak Salad c

PREP/TOTAL TIME: 15 min. **YIELD:** 4 servings

With its tangy combination of lemon juice and balsamic vinegar dressing, this hearty dish perks up dinnertime and fills you up fast.

- 1/4 cup minced fresh cilantro
- 3 Tbsp. balsamic vinegar
- 2 Tbsp. water
- 1 Tbsp. lemon juice
- 1 Tbsp. olive oil
- 1 pkg. (5 oz.) spring mix salad greens
- 1 small red onion, chopped

1 *each* small green, sweet red and yellow peppers, chopped

1 cooked Southwest Steak (see below), thinly sliced

1. In a small bowl, whisk the first five ingredients; set aside. In a large bowl, combine salad greens, onion and peppers. Drizzle with dressing; toss to coat. Divide among four plates. Heat steak if desired; place over salads.

Nutrition Facts: 1 serving equals 252 calories, 13 g fat (4 g saturated fat), 54 mg cholesterol, 274 mg sodium, 9 g carbohydrate, 3 g fiber, 24 g protein.

Southwest Steak

PREP: 15 min. + marinating **GRILL:** 10 min.
YIELD: 8 servings

Lime juice tenderizes the steak while garlic, chili powder and red pepper flakes kick things up. My husband and I came up with this together as something lighter to make on the grill.

1/4 cup lime juice

6 garlic cloves, minced

4 tsp. chili powder

4 tsp. canola oil

1 tsp. salt

1 tsp. crushed red pepper flakes

1 tsp. pepper

2 beef flank steaks (1 lb. *each*)

1. In a large resealable plastic bag, combine the first seven ingredients; add the beef. Seal bag and turn to coat; refrigerate for 4 hours or overnight.

2. Drain and discard marinade. Coat grill rack with cooking spray before starting the grill. Grill beef, covered, over medium heat for 5-7 minutes on each side or until meat reaches desired doneness (for medium-rare, a meat thermometer should read 145°; medium, 160°; well-done, 170°).

3. Let stand for 5 minutes; thinly slice across the grain.

Nutrition Facts: 3 oz. cooked beef equals 187 calories, 10 g fat (4 g saturated fat), 54 mg cholesterol, 259 mg sodium, 2 g carbohydrate, trace fiber, 22 g protein. **Diabetic Exchanges:** 3 lean meat, 1 fat.

"It's great to cook once and end up with several different meals," Caroline says. She and husband Robb created delicious Southwest Steak, which can be turned into a dinner or lunch the next day. Southwest Steak Quesadillas are a tasty handheld treat, and Southwest Steak Salad is filling yet refreshing.

Satisfying Supper

Crusty loaves of bread, hearty pasta entrees...you can enjoy these all-time favorites and still keep your commitment to eating healthy. From Fruita, Colorado, home cook Evelyn Slade explains how she does just that!

Sometimes transitioning into a healthy lifestyle is as easy as taking a few steps in the right direction. "I don't have a set fitness routine," says Evelyn Slade of Fruita, Colorado. "I just strive to get in 10,000 steps each day and ride a bike or do yard work."

That keep-it-simple attitude carries into her cooking, as Evelyn, a school administrator, opts for fast meals low in sodium and calories. "I began cooking healthy several years ago to maintain my weight, keep my blood pressure in check and help my husband, Norm, lose weight. It was a gradual process, and friends and family responded well. I often make meals for the teachers at work, and I never get complaints!"

Along with keeping menus light, Evelyn also adds as many fruits and veggies as possible. "I purchase locally grown produce in the summer and fall—I think it tastes better—and work it into sides and main courses." With its garden-fresh goodness and easy preparation, the dinner Evelyn shares here is reason enough to take a healthy step toward the supper table tonight!

Whole Wheat Bread ⒻⓂ

PREP: 10 min. **BAKE:** 3 hours 35 min. + cooling
YIELD: 1 loaf (2 lbs., 16 slices)

I tweaked an old recipe to create this bread by changing ingredient amounts, adding healthy items and incorporating whole wheat flour into it. The results are tender and delicious!

1-1/2	cups water
1	egg
2	Tbsp. canola oil
2-1/2	cups bread flour
1-1/2	cups whole wheat flour
1/2	cup oat flour
1/2	cup nonfat dry milk powder
3	Tbsp. sugar
1-1/2	tsp. salt
1	pkg. (1/4 oz.) active dry yeast

1. In bread machine pan, place all ingredients in order suggested by manufacturer. Select basic bread setting. Choose crust color and loaf size if available. Bake according to bread machine directions (check dough after 5 minutes of mixing; add 1 to 2 Tbsp. of water or flour if needed).

Nutrition Facts: 1 slice equals 156 calories, 3 g fat (trace saturated fat), 14 mg cholesterol, 246 mg sodium, 28 g carbohydrate, 2 g fiber, 6 g protein. **Diabetic Exchange:** 2 starch.

Veggie Tossed Salad C M

PREP/TOTAL TIME: 10 min. **YIELD:** 4 servings

This 10-minute side salad delivers a dose of veggies and great fresh flavors. Feel free to try it with your favorite dressing.

1-1/2 cups torn romaine
1-1/2 cups fresh baby spinach
3/4 cup sliced fresh mushrooms
3/4 cup grape tomatoes
1/2 cup sliced cucumber
1/3 cup sliced ripe olives
1 Tbsp. grated Parmesan cheese
1/4 cup reduced-fat Italian salad dressing

1. In a large bowl, combine the first seven ingredients. Add salad dressing; toss to coat.

Nutrition Facts: 1 cup equals 62 calories, 4 g fat (1 g saturated fat), 1 mg cholesterol, 245 mg sodium, 5 g carbohydrate, 2 g fiber, 2 g protein. **Diabetic Exchanges:** 1 vegetable, 1 fat.

Shrimp Fettuccine Alfredo

PREP/TOTAL TIME: 30 min. **YIELD:** 4 servings

This has always been a favorite, so when I started cooking healthier, I tried different ways to lighten it. Less butter and fat-free half-and-half worked well, along with using a little flour to thicken the sauce.

6 oz. uncooked fettuccine
2 Tbsp. butter
4-1/2 tsp. all-purpose flour
1 cup fat-free half-and-half
1 lb. cooked medium shrimp, peeled and deveined
1/3 cup grated Parmesan cheese
1/2 tsp. salt
2 Tbsp. minced fresh parsley

1. Cook fettuccine according to package directions. Meanwhile, in a large saucepan, melt butter. Stir in flour until smooth; gradually add half-and-half. Bring to a boil; cook and stir for 1 minute or until thickened. Drain fettuccine; stir into pan. Stir in the shrimp, cheese and salt; heat through. Sprinkle with parsley before serving.

Nutrition Facts: 1 cup equals 397 calories, 11 g fat (5 g saturated fat), 193 mg cholesterol, 670 mg sodium, 39 g carbohydrate, 2 g fiber, 34 g protein.

"When eating away from home, be mindful of what you're ordering," Evelyn suggests. "If I indulge one day, I cut back at home the next."

Comfort Made Light

The next time the weather turns chilly, consider this heartwarming menu from Nancy Zimmerman. Her satisfying chili, crusty oat bread and must-try Black Forest Cake are sure to warm you up from the inside out!

They say being active keeps you healthy, and Nancy Zimmerman proves it's true. Between her job, pets (including 18 ducks!) and hobbies, this Cape May Court House, New Jersey resident keeps busy. "I work part-time helping Christian radio stations, volunteer at the local rescue mission, farm and play volleyball and softball with my husband, Ken," she writes. "I also enjoy photography and chatting with friends on tasteofhome.com."

To fit a workout into her hectic schedule, Nancy begins her day by running or weight training, a routine she started 16 years ago. "I exercise first thing in the morning, so I don't get sidetracked." She attributes exercising and eating right to improving her sports performance and keeping trim.

Her vegetarian diet and Ken's garden ensure she gets plenty of fruits and vegetables. "I freeze and can some for winter and make reduced-sugar preserves," Nancy says. She rounds out meals with whole grains and protein from milk, yogurt and eggs (from her ducks, of course). As you'll see, the following recipes capture Nancy's love for fresh flavors, home-cooked specialties and smart, tasty eating.

Black Forest Cake F

PREP: 40 min. **BAKE:** 35 min. + cooling **YIELD:** 24 servings

Applesauce is used to keep this light version of Black Forest Cake healthy. Now, even people who are on a diet can enjoy a slice of rich chocolate cake!

- 2 cups cherry juice
- 1-3/4 cups sugar
- 1/2 cup unsweetened applesauce
- 1/4 cup canola oil
- 2 eggs
- 2 Tbsp. cider vinegar
- 3 tsp. vanilla extract
- 3 cups all-purpose flour
- 1/3 cup baking cocoa
- 2 tsp. baking soda
- 1 tsp. salt
- 1-1/2 cups cold fat-free milk
- 1 pkg. (1.4 oz.) sugar-free instant chocolate pudding mix
- 1 can (20 oz.) reduced-sugar cherry pie filling
- 1-1/2 cups frozen fat-free whipped topping, thawed

1. In a large bowl, beat the cherry juice, sugar, applesauce, oil, eggs, vinegar and vanilla until well blended. In a large bowl, combine the flour, cocoa, baking soda and salt; gradually beat into cherry juice mixture until blended.

2. Pour into a 13-in. x 9-in. baking pan coated with cooking spray. Bake at 350° for 35-40 minutes or until a toothpick inserted near the center comes out clean. Cool completely on a wire rack.

3. In a small bowl, whisk milk and pudding mix for 2 minutes. Let stand for 2 minutes or until soft-set. Frost top of cake with pudding. Cover and refrigerate for 15 minutes. Top with pie filling. Chill until serving. Serve with whipped topping.

Nutrition Facts: 1 piece with 1 Tbsp. whipped topping equals 186 calories, 3 g fat (trace saturated fat), 18 mg cholesterol, 272 mg sodium, 36 g carbohydrate, 1 g fiber, 3 g protein.

Rustic Oat Bran Bread F

PREP: 30 min. + rising **BAKE:** 20 min. + cooling
YIELD: 1 loaf (12 wedges)

This moist bread is the perfect complement to soups, stews, chili and even crisp salad.

- 2-1/4 to 2-3/4 cups all-purpose flour
- 1/3 cup oat bran
- 1 pkg. (1/4 oz.) active dry yeast

1-1/4 tsp. salt
1 cup water
2 Tbsp. honey
1 Tbsp. cornmeal

1. In a large bowl, combine 1 cup flour, oat bran, yeast and salt. In a small saucepan, heat water and honey to 120°-130°. Add to dry ingredients; beat just until moistened. Stir in enough remaining flour to form a stiff dough (dough will be sticky).

2. Turn onto a lightly floured surface; knead until smooth and elastic, about 6-8 minutes. Place in a bowl coated with cooking spray, turning once to coat the top. Cover and let rise in a warm place until doubled, about 30 minutes.

3. Punch down dough. Turn onto lightly floured surface. Shape into a round loaf. Place on a baking sheet coated with cooking spray and sprinkled with cornmeal. Cover and let rise until nearly doubled, about 30 minutes. With a sharp knife, make three diagonal slashes across the top loaf.

4. Bake at 400° for 20-25 minutes or until golden brown. Remove from baking sheet to wire rack to cool.

Nutrition Facts: 1 wedge equals 107 calories, trace fat (trace saturated fat), 0 cholesterol, 247 mg sodium, 23 g carbohydrate, 1 g fiber, 3 g protein. **Diabetic Exchange:** 1-1/2 starch.

Spicy Vegetable Chili F M

PREP: 25 min. **COOK:** 35 min. **YIELD:** 8 servings (2 qt.)

This chili makes a great comforting meal on cool autumn nights. I love dipping the oat bran bread into it.

1 medium onion, chopped
1 medium carrot, thinly sliced
1 medium green pepper, chopped
1/2 lb. sliced fresh mushrooms
1 small zucchini, sliced
1 Tbsp. olive oil
4 garlic cloves, minced
1 can (28 oz.) diced tomatoes, undrained
2 cans (16 oz. *each*) kidney beans, rinsed and drained
2 cans (8 oz. *each*) no-salt-added tomato sauce
1 can (4 oz.) chopped green chilies
3 Tbsp. chili powder
3 tsp. dried oregano
2 tsp. ground cumin
2 tsp. paprika
1/4 tsp. crushed red pepper flakes
1 Tbsp. white wine vinegar
Minced fresh cilantro and fat-free sour cream, optional

1. In a Dutch oven, saute the onion, carrot, pepper, mushrooms and zucchini in oil until tender. Add garlic; cook 1 minute longer. Add the tomatoes, beans, tomato sauce, green chilies and seasonings. Bring to a boil. Reduce heat; simmer, uncovered, for 35 minutes, stirring occasionally.

2. Stir in vinegar. Serve in soup bowls; garnish each with cilantro and sour cream if desired.

Nutrition Facts: 1 cup (calculated without sour cream) equals 195 calories, 3 g fat (trace saturated fat), 0 cholesterol, 423 mg sodium, 35 g carbohydrate, 11 g fiber, 10 g protein. **Diabetic Exchanges:** 2 starch, 1 very lean meat.

Enjoy Seasonal Flavors

Looking for a satisfying supper tonight? Dig into this delightful pasta dinner from Katie Wollgast. She relies on pumpkin, cranberries, nutmeg, pecans and a little prepared eggnog for her full-flavored feast.

Getting healthy and staying that way doesn't have to be hard. All it takes is smart choices in the kitchen and daily exercise. For Katie Wollgast of Florissant, Missouri, this means growing her own produce, choosing healthy foods and staying in shape with daily exercise. "This definitely involves sticking to an exercise plan," she notes.

"My routine started in high school. I alternate stretching and strength training six mornings a week, and I take a 3-mile walk every evening. I love walking by myself or with my parents, who are walkers, too. It's a pleasant way to spend time with them at the end of each day."

Along with exercise, Katie also has a history of lightening dishes. "My mom was a good cook, who used lots of garden foods and fresh fruits. When I 'took over the kitchen,' I continued much of what she had done. I found that, in general, many recipes called for ingredients that weren't really needed, so I started lightening them right away."

Between Katie's fabulous meal shown here and daily exercise, you, too, can create a balance within your own healthy life.

Sausage and Pumpkin Pasta

PREP: 20 min. **COOK:** 15 min. **YIELD:** 4 servings

Cubed leftover turkey may be substituted for sausage. Just add it to the skillet with the cooked pasta for a fast meal.

- 2 cups uncooked multigrain bow tie pasta
- 1/2 lb. Italian turkey sausage links, casings removed
- 1/2 lb. sliced fresh mushrooms
- 1 medium onion, chopped
- 4 garlic cloves, minced
- 1 cup reduced-sodium chicken broth
- 1 cup canned pumpkin
- 1/2 cup white wine *or* additional reduced-sodium chicken broth
- 1/2 tsp. rubbed sage
- 1/4 tsp. salt
- 1/4 tsp. garlic powder
- 1/4 tsp. pepper
- 1/4 cup grated Parmesan cheese
- 1 Tbsp. dried parsley flakes

1. Cook pasta according to package directions.

2. Meanwhile, in a large nonstick skillet coated with cooking spray, cook the sausage, mushrooms, onion and garlic over medium heat until meat is no longer pink; drain. Stir in the chicken broth, pumpkin, wine, sage, salt, garlic powder and pepper. Bring to a boil. Reduce heat; simmer, uncovered, for 5-6 minutes or until slightly thickened.

3. Drain pasta; add to the skillet and heat through. Just before serving, sprinkle with cheese and parsley.

Nutrition Facts: 1-3/4 cups equals 348 calories, 9 g fat (2 g saturated fat), 38 mg cholesterol, 733 mg sodium, 42 g carbohydrate, 7 g fiber, 23 g protein.

Easy Tossed Salad Ⓢ Ⓜ

PREP/TOTAL TIME: 10 min. **YIELD:** 4 servings

Apples, almonds and cranberries provide powerfoods galore in my easy five-ingredient salad.

- 8 cups torn mixed salad greens
- 1 large apple, sliced
- 1/2 cup sliced almonds, toasted
- 1/2 cup dried cranberries
- 1/2 cup fat-free poppy seed salad dressing

1. In a large bowl, combine the salad greens, apple, almonds and cranberries. Drizzle with dressing; toss to coat. Serve immediately.

Nutrition Facts: 2-1/2 cups equals 210 calories, 6 g fat (1 g saturated fat), 5 mg cholesterol, 109 mg sodium, 36 g carbohydrate, 6 g fiber, 5 g protein.

Eggnog Cake

PREP: 25 min. **BAKE:** 20 min. + cooling **YIELD:** 8 servings

We enjoy this cake so much! During the holidays, I actually buy eggnog to freeze so I can make the dessert year-round.

3/4	cup reduced-fat eggnog
1/4	cup sugar
2	Tbsp. canola oil
2	Tbsp. unsweetened applesauce
1	egg
1-1/2	cups all-purpose flour
2	tsp. baking powder
1/2	tsp. salt
1/4	tsp. ground nutmeg
1/4	cup golden raisins
2	Tbsp. chopped pecans

TOPPING:

1/4	cup packed brown sugar
2	Tbsp. all-purpose flour
1/2	tsp. ground nutmeg
1	Tbsp. cold butter
2	Tbsp. chopped pecans
2	cups reduced-fat vanilla ice cream, optional

1. In a large bowl, beat the eggnog, sugar, oil, applesauce and egg until well blended. In a small bowl, combine the flour, baking powder, salt and nutmeg; gradually beat into eggnog mixture until blended. Stir in raisins and pecans. Pour into a 9-in. round baking pan coated with cooking spray.

2. For topping, in a small bowl, combine the brown sugar, flour and nutmeg. Cut in butter until crumbly. Stir in pecans; sprinkle over batter.

3. Bake at 350° for 20-25 minutes or until a toothpick inserted near the center comes out clean. Cool for 10 minutes before removing from pan to a wire rack to cool completely. Serve with the ice cream if desired.

Editor's Note: This recipe was tested with commercially prepared eggnog.

Nutrition Facts: 1 slice (calculated without ice cream) equals 255 calories, 9 g fat (2 g saturated fat), 48 mg cholesterol, 285 mg sodium, 39 g carbohydrate, 1 g fiber, 5 g protein.

> "I always like to plan my entrees and side dishes around **in-season vegetables** instead of planning menus the other way around," shares Katie. "This way, I seem to eat far more vegetables."

SPICED SWEET POTATO PIE

MOCHA CHEESECAKE BARS

PUMPKIN SPICE CAKE

Cakes, Pies & More

What would a cookbook be without a luscious assortment of cakes, pies, brownies and bars? Just because you're counting calories doesn't mean you can't satisfy your sweet tooth. The 38 recipes in this chapter keep dessert light.

Pumpkin Spice Cake

PREP: 25 min. **COOK:** 50 min. + cooling
YIELD: 16 servings

KATIE WOLLGAST • FLORISSANT, MISSOURI

This spice cake is a little different because of the hint of chocolate. So moist and tender, it'll have guests hoping for seconds!

1	can (15 oz.) solid-pack pumpkin
1-1/2	cups sugar
1/2	cup buttermilk
1/3	cup canola oil
1/3	cup water
2	eggs
2	egg whites
1	tsp. vanilla extract
2	cups all-purpose flour
1	Tbsp. baking cocoa
1-1/2	tsp. ground cinnamon
1	tsp. baking soda
1	tsp. baking powder
1/2	tsp. salt
1/2	tsp. *each* ground nutmeg, allspice and cloves
1/2	cup raisins
1/4	cup miniature semisweet chocolate chips

Confectioners' sugar
Reduced-fat vanilla ice cream, optional

1. In a large bowl, beat the pumpkin, sugar, buttermilk, oil, water, eggs, egg whites and vanilla until well blended. In a small bowl, combine the flour, cocoa, cinnamon, baking soda, baking power, salt, nutmeg, allspice and cloves; gradually beat into pumpkin mixture until blended. Stir in raisins and chocolate chips.

2. Transfer to a 10-in. fluted tube pan coated with cooking spray. Bake at 350° for 50-60 minutes or until a toothpick inserted near the center comes out clean. Cool for 10 minutes before removing from pan to a wire rack to cool completely. Sprinkle with confectioners' sugar. Serve with ice cream if desired.

Nutrition Facts: 1 slice (calculated without ice cream) equals 223 calories, 7 g fat (1 g saturated fat), 27 mg cholesterol, 204 mg sodium, 39 g carbohydrate, 2 g fiber, 4 g protein.

Mocha Cheesecake Bars

PREP: 30 min. + chilling **YIELD:** 24 servings

MARY WILHELM • SPARTA, WISCONSIN

The creamy filling in these bars will surely please! So many cheesecake recipes are hard to make, but this recipe is easy and doesn't require too many ingredients.

25	reduced-fat cream-filled chocolate sandwich cookies
3	Tbsp. fat-free hot fudge ice cream topping
3	Tbsp. butter, melted

FILLING:

1	envelope unflavored gelatin
1/2	cup cold strong brewed coffee
2	pkg. (8 oz. *each*) reduced-fat cream cheese
3/4	cup sugar
1	cup (8 oz.) reduced-fat sour cream
3	squares (1 oz. *each*) bittersweet chocolate, melted and cooled
24	chocolate-covered coffee beans, optional

1. Place cookies in a food processor. Cover and pulse until fine crumbs. Add fudge topping and butter; pulse just until blended. Press onto the bottom of a 13-in. x 9-in. dish coated with cooking spray. Refrigerate for 10 minutes.

2. Meanwhile, for filling, in a small saucepan, sprinkle gelatin over coffee; let stand for 1 minute. Heat over low heat, stirring until gelatin is completely dissolved. Remove from the heat; set aside.

3. In a large bowl, beat cream cheese and sugar until smooth. Beat in the sour cream, chocolate and reserved coffee mixture until blended. Pour over crust. Cover and refrigerate for at least 4 hours or until firm.

4. Cut into bars. Garnish with coffee beans if desired. Refrigerate leftovers.

Nutrition Facts: 1 piece equals 166 calories, 9 g fat (5 g saturated fat), 20 mg cholesterol, 167 mg sodium, 20 g carbohydrate, 1 g fiber, 4 g protein. **Diabetic Exchanges:** 2 fat, 1 starch.

Makeover Two-Tone Spice Cake

PREP: 25 min. **BAKE:** 20 min. + cooling **YIELD:** 16 servings

MICHELE WEDIGE • SHULLSBURG, WISCONSIN

This is a delicious and decadent cake with half the fat and a third less calories than the over-the-top original. Enjoy it with a cup of coffee or a cold glass of milk.

- 1/4 cup butter, softened
- 2/3 cup packed brown sugar
- 2 eggs
- 1/2 cup unsweetened applesauce
- 1-3/4 cups cake flour
- 1-1/2 tsp. baking powder
- 1-1/4 tsp. ground cinnamon
- 1/2 tsp. salt
- 1/2 tsp. baking soda
- 1/2 tsp. ground allspice
- 1/8 tsp. ground nutmeg
- 3/4 cup reduced-fat sour cream
- 1/4 cup finely chopped walnuts

SOUR CREAM FROSTING:
- 1/3 cup butter, softened
- 3 cups confectioners' sugar
- 3 Tbsp. reduced-fat sour cream
- 1-1/2 tsp. vanilla extract
- 2 squares (1 oz. *each*) semisweet chocolate, chopped
- 1 Tbsp. butter

1. Line two 9-in. round baking pans with waxed paper. Coat pans with cooking spray and sprinkle with flour; set aside.

2. In a large bowl, beat butter and brown sugar until crumbly, about 2 minutes. Add eggs, one at a time, beating well after each addition. Beat in applesauce.

3. Combine the flour, baking powder, cinnamon, salt, baking soda, allspice and nutmeg. Add to the butter mixture alternately with sour cream, beating well after each addition. Stir in the nuts. Spread into prepared pans.

4. Bake at 350° for 18-22 minutes or until a toothpick inserted near the center comes out clean. Cool for 10 minutes before removing from pans to wire racks to cool completely.

5. For frosting, in a large bowl, cream butter and confectioners' sugar. Beat in sour cream and vanilla. Place one cake layer on a serving platter; top with half of the frosting. Repeat layers.

6. In a microwave, melt chocolate and butter; stir until smooth. Cool for 2 minutes; drizzle over cake. Refrigerate leftovers.

Nutrition Facts: 1 piece equals 303 calories, 12 g fat (6 g saturated fat), 51 mg cholesterol, 225 mg sodium, 47 g carbohydrate, 1 g fiber, 4 g protein.

Makeover Coconut Cream Pie

PREP: 35 min. **BAKE:** 15 min. + chilling **YIELD:** 8 servings

DIDI DESJARDINS • DARTMOUTH, MASSACHUSETTS

Here's a wonderfully creamy and rich version of an impressive classic that was lightened up. It now has less than half the fat of the original recipe...but every bit of sweet, old-fashioned coconut flavor!

- 1 cup sugar, *divided*
- 1/3 cup all-purpose flour
- Dash salt
- 3 cups fat-free milk
- 2 egg yolks, lightly beaten
- 1-1/4 cups flaked coconut, *divided*
- 1 tsp. vanilla extract
- 1/2 tsp. coconut extract
- 1 reduced-fat graham cracker crust (8 in.)
- 1 Tbsp. cornstarch
- 1/2 cup water
- 3 egg whites

1. In a large saucepan, combine 2/3 cup sugar, flour and salt. Stir in milk until smooth. Cook and stir over medium-high heat until thickened and bubbly. Remove from the heat. Stir a small amount of hot filling into egg yolks; return all to the pan, stirring constantly. Bring to a gentle boil; cook and stir for 2 minutes. Remove from the heat; stir in 3/4 cup coconut and extracts.

2. Place the crust on a baking sheet; add the filling and set aside.

3. For meringue, combine cornstarch and remaining sugar in a small saucepan. Stir in water until smooth. Bring to a boil over medium heat, stirring constantly. Cook and stir for 2 minutes or until thickened and clear. In a bowl, beat egg whites until soft peaks form. Pour hot sugar mixture in a slow, steady stream into egg whites, beating constantly until stiff peaks form.

4. Spread meringue over hot filling, sealing edges to crust. Sprinkle with remaining coconut. Bake at 350° for 15-20 minutes or until meringue is golden brown. Cool on a wire rack. Refrigerate until chilled.

MAKEOVER TWO-TONE SPICE CAKE

Nutrition Facts: 1 piece equals 350 calories, 9 g fat (6 g saturated fat), 53 mg cholesterol, 213 mg sodium, 59 g carbohydrate, 1 g fiber, 7 g protein.

Spiced Sweet Potato Pie

PREP: 15 min. **COOK:** 45 min. + cooling **YIELD:** 8 servings

DIANA RIOS • LYTLE, TEXAS

I wanted to create a lightened version of this traditional pie, so I cut back on the sugar and added vanilla to increase the flavor without adding fat.

- 2 egg whites
- 1 egg
- 1-3/4 cups mashed sweet potatoes
- 1/2 cup 2% milk
- 1/4 cup reduced-fat butter, melted
- 1 Tbsp. bourbon
- 1-1/2 tsp. vanilla extract
- 2/3 cup packed brown sugar
- 1 Tbsp. all-purpose flour
- 1 tsp. ground cinnamon
- 1/2 tsp. salt
- 1/2 tsp. ground nutmeg
- 1/4 tsp. ground cloves
- 1 reduced-fat graham cracker crust (8 in.)
- 1/2 cup fat-free whipped topping

1. In a large bowl, whisk the the first seven ingredients until blended. In another bowl, combine the brown sugar, flour, cinnamon, salt, nutmeg and cloves; gradually beat into pumpkin mixture until blended. Pour into crust.

2. Bake at 350° for 45-55 minutes or until a knife inserted near the center comes out clean. Cool completely on a wire rack. Garnish with whipped topping. Refrigerate leftovers.

Editor's Note: This recipe was tested with Land O'Lakes light stick butter.

Nutrition Facts: 1 piece equals 285 calories, 7 g fat (3 g saturated fat), 35 mg cholesterol, 350 mg sodium, 51 g carbohydrate, 2 g fiber, 4 g protein.

Ready to make Spiced Sweet Potato Pie? Start by preparing the **sweet potatoes for mashing.** Place whole scrubbed sweet potatoes in a large kettle; cover with water. Cover and boil gently for 30 to 45 minutes or until potatoes can be pierced with the tip of a knife. Drain. When cool enough to handle, peel and mash.

Old-Fashioned Strawberry Pie

PREP: 30 min. **COOK:** 10 min. + chilling
YIELD: 8 servings

ERICA COOPER • ELK RIVER, MINNESOTA

This wonderful dessert is a must when fresh berries are in season! It comes together easily with several convenience items you likely already have on hand. Best of all, you can make it ahead of time, storing it in the refrigerator.

1	sheet refrigerated pie pastry
1	pkg. (3 oz.) cook-and-serve vanilla pudding mix
1-1/2	cups water
1	tsp. lemon juice
1	pkg. (.3 oz.) sugar-free strawberry gelatin
1/2	cup boiling water
4	cups sliced fresh strawberries
3	oz. reduced-fat cream cheese
2	cups reduced-fat whipped topping, *divided*
1	tsp. vanilla extract
8	fresh strawberries

1. On a lightly floured surface, unroll pastry. Transfer to a 9-in. pie plate. Trim pastry to 1/2 in. beyond edge of plate; flute edges. Line unpricked pastry with a double thickness of heavy-duty foil. Bake at 450° for 8 minutes. Remove foil; bake 5-7 minutes longer or until lightly browned. Cool on a wire rack.

2. In a small saucepan, combine pudding mix, water and lemon juice. Cook and stir over medium heat until mixture comes to a boil. Cook and stir 1-2 minutes longer or until thickened. Remove from the heat; set aside.

3. In a large bowl, dissolve gelatin in boiling water. Gradually stir in pudding. Cover and refrigerate for 30 minutes or until thickened. Fold in the sliced strawberries. Transfer to crust.

4. For topping, in another bowl, beat the cream cheese, 1/2 cup whipped topping and vanilla until smooth. Fold in remaining whipped topping. Cut a small hole in the corner of a pastry or plastic bag; insert a medium star tip. Fill with topping. Pipe topping around edges of pie; garnish with whole strawberries. Refrigerate for at least 1 hour.

Nutrition Facts: 1 piece equals 259 calories, 12 g fat (7 g saturated fat), 13 mg cholesterol, 220 mg sodium, 37 g carbohydrate, 2 g fiber, 3 g protein.

Peanut Butter Pies

PREP: 15 min. + freezing **YIELD:** 2 pies (8 servings each)

LISA VARNER • GREENVILLE, SOUTH CAROLINA

I absolutely love peanut butter, and peanut butter pie is one of my favorites. But I'm a registered dietitian, so I knew just how high my original recipe was in fat and calories.

1	pkg. (8 oz.) fat-free cream cheese
3/4	cup reduced-fat creamy peanut butter
1	can (14 oz.) fat-free sweetened condensed milk
1	tsp. vanilla extract
1	carton (12 oz.) frozen fat-free whipped topping, thawed
2	reduced-fat graham cracker crusts (8 in.)
1/4	cup chocolate syrup
1/4	cup finely chopped unsalted peanuts

1. In a large bowl, beat cream cheese and peanut butter until smooth. Beat in milk and vanilla until blended. Fold in whipped topping. Pour into crusts. Cover and freeze for 8 hours or overnight.

2. Remove from the freezer 10 minutes before serving. Drizzle with syrup and sprinkle with peanuts. Store leftovers in the freezer.

Nutrition Facts: 1 piece equals 305 calories, 8 g fat (2 g saturated fat), 4 mg cholesterol, 285 mg sodium, 47 g carbohydrate, 1 g fiber, 9 g protein.

Makeover Oatmeal Bars **S**

PREP: 10 min. **BAKE:** 15 min. + cooling
YIELD: 20 servings

CLYDE WILLIAMS • CHAMBERSBURG, PENNSYLVANIA

These delicious bars are even more moist and chewy than my original recipe, but with all the old-fashioned oatmeal flavor and only half the fat!

2/3	cup sugar
1/2	cup unsweetened applesauce
1/3	cup canola oil
1	Tbsp. maple syrup
2	cups quick-cooking oats
1	cup all-purpose flour
1	tsp. baking soda
1/2	tsp. salt
1/2	tsp. ground allspice
1/2	cup raisins

1. In a large bowl, beat sugar, applesauce, oil and syrup until well blended. In a small bowl, combine oats, flour, baking soda, salt and allspice; gradually beat into applesauce mixture until blended. Stir in raisins.

2. Spread the batter into a 13-in. x 9-in. baking pan coated with cooking spray. Bake at 350° for 15-20 minutes or until edges begin to brown. Cool completely on a wire rack. Cut into bars.

Nutrition Facts: 1 bar equals 127 calories, 4 g fat (trace saturated fat), 0 cholesterol, 123 mg sodium, 21 g carbohydrate, 1 g fiber, 2 g protein. **Diabetic Exchanges:** 1 starch, 1 fat.

Makeover Cherry Almond Mousse Pie

PREP: 25 min. + chilling **YIELD:** 8 servings

JULIE HIEGGELKE • GRAYSLAKE, ILLINOIS

With about two-thirds less fat than my favorite recipe, this makeover is decadently rewarding! You'll love the chocolate, cherries and almonds, but never miss the fat!

1	can (14 oz.) fat-free sweetened condensed milk, *divided*
1	square (1 oz.) unsweetened chocolate, chopped
1/2	tsp. almond extract, *divided*
1	frozen pie shell, baked
1	jar (10 oz.) maraschino cherries, drained
1	pkg. (8 oz.) fat-free cream cheese
3/4	cup cold water
1	pkg. (1 oz.) sugar-free instant vanilla pudding mix
2	cups reduced-fat whipped topping
1/4	cup chopped almonds, toasted

Chocolate curls, optional

1. In a small saucepan over low heat, cook and stir 1/2 cup milk and chocolate for 4-5 minutes or until the chocolate is melted. Stir in 1/4 tsp. extract. Pour into pie shell; set aside.

2. Set aside eight whole cherries for garnish. Chop the remaining cherries; set aside. In a large bowl, beat cream cheese until smooth. Gradually beat in water and remaining milk. Add pudding mix and remaining extract; mix well. Fold in whipped topping. Stir in almonds and reserved chopped cherries.

3. Pour over the pie. Refrigerate for 4 hours or until set. Garnish with whole cherries and chocolate curls if desired.

Nutrition Facts: 1 piece (calculated without chocolate curls) equals 426 calories, 13 g fat (7 g saturated fat), 14 mg cholesterol, 453 mg sodium, 69 g carbohydrate, 1 g fiber, 10 g protein.

MAKEOVER CHERRY ALMOND MOUSSE PIE

Makeover Chocolate-Caramel Nut Cake

PREP: 1 hour + chilling **BAKE:** 30 min. + cooling
YIELD: 20 servings

LOIS JOHNSON • BAYFIELD, WISCONSIN

With layers of caramel and marshmallow frosting, this sweet treat really takes the cake! Serve this lightened-up version for special occasions and just wait for the praises!

1/4	cup butter, softened
1-1/2	cups sugar
2	eggs
1/4	cup unsweetened applesauce
1	tsp. vanilla extract
3	cups cake flour
1/3	cup baking cocoa
1-1/2	tsp. baking soda
1/2	tsp. salt
2	cups buttermilk

CARAMEL TOPPING:

1/2	cup packed brown sugar
4-1/2	tsp. all-purpose flour
1/2	cup fat-free milk
1	egg yolk, lightly beaten
1	Tbsp. butter
1/2	cup chopped walnuts, toasted

MARSHMALLOW FROSTING:

2/3	cup sugar
1/3	cup light corn syrup
3	Tbsp. water
2	egg whites
1/4	tsp. cream of tartar
1	tsp. vanilla extract
1	square (1 oz.) semisweet chocolate

1. In a large bowl, beat butter and sugar until crumbly, about 2 minutes. Add eggs, one at a time, beating well after each addition. Beat in applesauce and vanilla. Combine the flour, cocoa, baking soda and salt; add to butter mixture alternately with buttermilk, beating well after each addition.

2. Pour into a 13-in. x 9-in. baking pan coated with cooking spray. Bake at 350° for 30-35 minutes or until a toothpick inserted near the center comes out clean. Cool completely on a wire rack.

3. For caramel topping, in a small saucepan, combine the brown sugar and flour. Stir in the milk until smooth. Cook and stir over medium-high heat until thickened and bubbly. Reduce heat; cook and stir for 2 minutes. Remove from the heat. Stir a small amount of the hot topping into egg yolk; return all to pan, stirring constantly. Bring to a gentle boil; cook and stir for 2 minutes.

4. Remove from the heat. Gently stir in butter. Cool to room temperature without stirring. Spread over cake to within 1/2 in. of edges; sprinkle with walnuts. Refrigerate for 30 minutes or until set.

5. For frosting, in a small heavy saucepan, combine the sugar, corn syrup, water, egg whites and cream of tartar over low heat. With a hand mixer, beat on low speed for 1 minute. Continue beating on low over low heat until frosting reaches 160°, about 8-10 minutes. Pour into a large bowl; add vanilla. Beat on high until frosting forms stiff peaks, about 7 minutes. Spread over the cake.

6. In a microwave, melt chocolate; stir until smooth. Drizzle over frosting. Chill until serving.

Nutrition Facts: 1 piece equals 278 calories, 6 g fat (3 g saturated fat), 40 mg cholesterol, 221 mg sodium, 52 g carbohydrate, 1 g fiber, 5 g protein.

Chocolate Chip Cream Cheese Bars

PREP: 20 min. **BAKE:** 20 min. + cooling
YIELD: 2 dozen

JENNIFER RAFFERTY • MILFORD, OHIO

Lower in fat and calories than you might ever guess, these sweet bars couldn't be easier to whip up. They also boast great chocolaty flavor and make a quick dessert to bring to parties or serve at casual get-togethers.

1	pkg. (18-1/4 oz.) German chocolate cake mix
1/3	cup canola oil
1	egg

FILLING:

1	pkg. (8 oz.) reduced-fat cream cheese
1/3	cup sugar
1	egg
1	cup miniature semisweet chocolate chips

1. In a large bowl, combine cake mix, oil and egg. Set aside 1 cup for topping. Press remaining crumb mixture into a 13-in. x 9-in. baking pan coated with cooking spray. Bake at 350° for 10-12 minutes or until set.

2. For filling, in a large bowl, beat cream cheese and sugar until smooth. Add egg; beat well. Spread over crust. Sprinkle with chocolate chips and reserved crumb mixture.

3. Bake for 18-20 minutes or until set. Cool on a wire rack. Cut into bars. Store in the refrigerator.

Nutrition Facts: 1 bar equals 187 calories, 9 g fat (3 g saturated fat), 24 mg cholesterol, 207 mg sodium, 25 g carbohydrate, trace fiber, 3 g protein. **Diabetic Exchanges:** 1-1/2 starch, 1-1/2 fat.

MAKEOVER CHOCOLATE-CARAMEL NUT CAKE

CHOCOLATE CHIP CREAM CHEESE BARS

Makeover Caramel-Pecan Apple Pie

PREP: 45 min. **BAKE:** 55 min. + cooling **YIELD:** 8 servings

RONDA DAVIS • KING, NORTH CAROLINA

I lost 120 pounds and want my favorite pie to fit my new eating habits. The Healthy Cooking Test Kitchen created a version that better suits my healthy lifestyle and delivers the out-of-this-world taste I love.

7	cups sliced peeled tart apples
1	tsp. lemon juice
1	tsp. vanilla extract
1/4	cup finely chopped pecans
1/4	cup packed brown sugar
2	Tbsp. sugar
4-1/2	tsp. ground cinnamon
1	Tbsp. cornstarch
1	unbaked pastry shell (9 in.)

TOPPING:

2	Tbsp. all-purpose flour
2	Tbsp. sugar
2	Tbsp. cold butter
1/4	cup finely chopped pecans
1/4	cup caramel ice cream topping, room temperature

1. In a large bowl, toss apples with lemon juice and vanilla. Combine the pecans, sugars, cinnamon and cornstarch; add to apple mixture and toss to coat. Transfer to pastry shell.

2. In a small bowl, combine flour and sugar. Cut in butter until mixture resembles coarse crumbs. Stir in pecans. Sprinkle over filling.

3. Bake at 350° for 55-60 minutes or until filling is bubbly and topping is browned. Immediately drizzle with caramel topping. Cool on a wire rack.

Nutrition Facts: 1 piece equals 334 calories, 15 g fat (5 g saturated fat), 13 mg cholesterol, 159 mg sodium, 50 g carbohydrate, 3 g fiber, 2 g protein.

Fruit & Carrot Cake

PREP: 35 min. **BAKE:** 40 min. + cooling **YIELD:** 16 servings

ELLIE RAUSCH • GOODSOIL, SASKATCHEWAN

This is the best carrot cake I've ever made. It has all of the texture, taste and density of regular carrot cake, but is so much lower in fat.

2/3	cup sugar
2/3	cup packed brown sugar
2	eggs
1/3	cup unsweetened applesauce
1/4	cup canola oil
3	tsp. vanilla extract
3	cups all-purpose flour
3	tsp. baking powder
1-1/2	tsp. ground cinnamon
1/2	tsp. salt
3	cups shredded carrots
1/3	cup finely chopped dried apricots

1/3 cup dried currants

3 Tbsp. chopped crystallized ginger

GLAZE:

1 can (6 oz.) unsweetened pineapple juice

1/2 cup orange juice

2 Tbsp. honey

2 Tbsp. finely chopped dried apricots

1 Tbsp. dried currants

4 tsp. chopped pecans, toasted

1. In a large bowl, beat the first six ingredients until well blended. Combine the flour, baking powder, cinnamon and salt; gradually beat into sugar mixture until blended (batter will be thick). Stir in the carrots, apricots, currants and ginger.

2. Coat a 10-in. fluted tube pan with cooking spray and sprinkle with flour; add batter. Bake at 350° for 40-50 minutes or until a toothpick inserted near the center comes out clean. Cool for 10 minutes before removing from pan to a wire rack.

3. Meanwhile, for glaze, in a small saucepan, combine pineapple juice, orange juice and honey. Bring to a boil. Reduce heat; simmer, uncovered, for 25-30 minutes or until mixture is reduced to 1/3 cup. Remove from heat; cool for 15 minutes. Stir in apricots and currants. Spoon over cake. Sprinkle with pecans.

Nutrition Facts: 1 slice equals 256 calories, 5 g fat (1 g saturated fat), 27 mg cholesterol, 173 mg sodium, 50 g carbohydrate, 2 g fiber, 4 g protein.

Makeover Almond Poppy Seed Cake

PREP: 20 min. **BAKE:** 50 min. + cooling **YIELD:** 16 servings

SHIRLEY DURBIN • HUTCHINSON, KANSAS

The mildly sweet flavor and fluffy texture make this cake easy to enjoy. No one will ever suspect that it's lighter than most cakes.

1-3/4 cups sugar

2 eggs

1/2 cup unsweetened applesauce

1/3 cup canola oil

1-1/2 cups fat-free milk

1-1/2 tsp. almond extract

1-1/2 tsp. vanilla extract

1 tsp. butter flavoring

1-1/2 cups cake flour

1-1/2 cups all-purpose flour

3-1/2 tsp. baking powder

1/2 tsp. salt

2 Tbsp. poppy seeds

GLAZE:

3/4 cup confectioners' sugar

1 Tbsp. orange juice

1/2 tsp. almond extract

1/2 tsp. vanilla extract

1/2 tsp. butter flavoring

1. In a large bowl, beat the sugar, eggs, applesauce and oil until well blended. Beat in the milk, extracts and butter flavoring. Combine the flours, baking

powder and salt; gradually beat into sugar mixture until blended. Stir in poppy seeds.

2. Transfer to a 10-in. fluted tube pan coated with cooking spray. Bake at 350° for 50-60 minutes or until a toothpick inserted near the center comes out clean. Cool for 10 minutes before removing from pan to a wire rack to cool completely.

3. In a small bowl, combine glaze ingredients until smooth. Drizzle over cake.

Nutrition Facts: 1 slice equals 269 calories, 6 g fat (1 g saturated fat), 27 mg cholesterol, 181 mg sodium, 49 g carbohydrate, 1 g fiber, 4 g protein.

Peanut Butter Granola Mini Bars S C

PREP: 20 min. **BAKE:** 15 min. + cooling **YIELD:** 3 dozen

VIVIAN LEVINE • SUMMERFIELD, FLORIDA

Kids will flip over this deliciously oaty sweet snack! With honey, peanut butter, brown sugar and two types of chips, what's not to love? And at less than 100 calories per bar, you can afford to have seconds.

1/2 cup reduced-fat creamy peanut butter

1/3 cup honey

1 egg

2 Tbsp. canola oil

1 tsp. vanilla extract

3-1/2 cups old-fashioned oats

1/2 cup packed brown sugar

3/4 tsp. salt

1/3 cup peanut butter chips

1/3 cup miniature semisweet chocolate chips

1. In a large bowl, beat the peanut butter, honey, egg, oil and vanilla until blended. Combine the oats, brown sugar and salt; add to the peanut butter mixture and mix well. Stir in chips. (Batter will be sticky.)

2. Transfer to a 13-in. x 9-in. baking dish coated with cooking spray. Bake at 350° for 12-15 minutes or until set and edges are lightly browned. Cool on a wire rack. Cut into bars.

Nutrition Facts: 1 piece equals 93 calories, 4 g fat (1 g saturated fat), 6 mg cholesterol, 76 mg sodium, 14 g carbohydrate, 1 g fiber, 3 g protein. **Diabetic Exchanges:** 1 starch, 1 fat.

PEANUT BUTTER GRANOLA MINI BARS

Makeover Ricotta Nut Torte

PREP: 35 min. **BAKE:** 20 min. + cooling
YIELD: 16 servings

SUZANNE RUNTZ • MOUNT PLEASANT, SOUTH CAROLINA

Looking for a special, lightened-up treat? "Healthy Cooking" magazine trimmed over half the fat from this incredible cake but kept all of the amazing flavor intact.

>   2 cartons (15 oz. *each*) reduced-fat ricotta cheese
>   1 cup sugar
>   1 tsp. vanilla extract
>   1/3 cup chopped pecans, toasted
>   3 milk chocolate candy bars (1.55 oz. *each*), grated

BATTER:
>   1/4 cup shortening
> 1-1/4 cups sugar
>   2 eggs
>   1/2 cup unsweetened applesauce
> 1-1/2 tsp. vanilla extract
> 2-1/2 cups all-purpose flour
> 2-1/2 tsp. baking powder
>   1 tsp. salt
> 1-1/4 cups fat-free milk
>   1 carton (8 oz.) frozen reduced-fat whipped topping, thawed

Whole hazelnuts and shaved chocolate, optional

1. Line three 9-in. round baking pans with waxed paper. Coat pans with cooking spray and sprinkle with flour; set aside.

2. For filling, in a small bowl, beat ricotta cheese and sugar until smooth; beat in vanilla. Fold in pecans and grated chocolate. Cover and chill.

3. Meanwhile, in a large bowl, beat the shortening and sugar until crumbly, about 2 minutes. Add the eggs, one at a time, beating well after each addition. Beat in applesauce and vanilla until well blended. Combine the flour, baking powder and salt; add to the creamed mixture alternately with milk, beating well after each addition.

4. Pour into prepared pans. Bake at 350° for 20-25 minutes or until a toothpick inserted near the center comes out clean. Cool for 10 minutes before removing from pans to wire racks to cool completely.

5. Cut each cake horizontally into two layers. Place bottom layer on a serving plate; spread with 1 cup filling. Repeat layers four times. Top with remaining cake layer.

6. Spread whipped topping over top and sides of cake. Garnish with hazelnuts and shaved chocolate if desired. Chill until serving. Refrigerate leftovers.

Nutrition Facts: 1 slice (calculated without optional ingredients) equals 372 calories, 12 g fat (5 g saturated fat), 42 mg cholesterol, 281 mg sodium, 57 g carbohydrate, 1 g fiber, 9 g protein.

Gluten-Free Fig Cookies F S

PREP: 30 min. **BAKE:** 15 min. + cooling **YIELD:** 3 dozen

TWINKLE30 • TASTEOFHOME.COM COMMUNITY

These special cookies definitely don't taste gluten-free. For added appeal, soak the figs overnight in a mixture of port and pomegranate juice.

>   1/2 lb. dried figs, quartered
>   1 cup pomegranate juice
>   1/4 cup lemon juice
>   1/2 cup unsalted butter, softened
>   1/2 cup *each* sugar and packed brown sugar
>   1 egg
>   2 Tbsp. molasses
>   1 tsp. vanilla extract
>   1 cup sorghum flour
>   1 cup brown rice flour
>   1/2 cup tapioca flour
>   1 tsp. baking powder
>   1 tsp. ground nutmeg
>   3/4 tsp. salt
>   1/2 tsp. baking soda
>   1/2 tsp. xanthan gum

1. Place the first three ingredients in a bowl; toss. Refrigerate overnight. Drain, reserving 1/4 cup juice. Transfer the figs and reserved juice to a small food processor; cover and process until a thick paste forms. Set aside.

2. Cream butter and sugars until light and fluffy. Beat in egg, molasses and vanilla. Combine the remaining ingredients except fig mixture. Gradually add to creamed mixture; mix well. Divide dough into four portions; cover and refrigerate 1 hour.

3. Between two sheets of waxed paper, roll each portion into a 9-in. x 4-in. rectangle. Transfer two rectangles to a parchment paper-lined baking sheet; remove waxed paper. Spread reserved fig mixture evenly over both rectangles to within 1/2 in. of edges.

MAKEOVER RICOTTA NUT TORTE

GLUTEN-FREE FIG COOKIES

GLUTEN-FREE PEANUT
BUTTER KISS COOKIES

Top with remaining dough; remove waxed paper.
Using a fork, crimp edges to seal.

4. Bake at 350° for 15-18 minutes or until edges are golden. Cool 10 minutes; remove from pan to a wire rack. Cool completely. Cut each in half lengthwise; cut widthwise into slices. Store in an airtight container.

Nutrition Facts: 1 cookie equals 105 calories, 3 g fat (2 g saturated fat), 13 mg cholesterol, 83 mg sodium, 19 g carbohydrate, 1 g fiber, 1 g protein. **Diabetic Exchanges:** 1 starch, 1/2 fat.

Gluten-Free Peanut Butter Kiss Cookies S C

PREP: 20 min. + chilling **BAKE:** 10 min./batch
YIELD: 4 dozen

CANADA60 • TASTEOFHOME.COM COMMUNITY

Guests will stand in line to kiss the cook when these treats are served! For a change of pace, try them with chunky peanut butter, too.

1/4	cup butter-flavored shortening
1-1/4	cups packed brown sugar
3/4	cup creamy peanut butter
1	egg
1/4	cup unsweetened applesauce
3	tsp. vanilla extract
1	cup white rice flour
1/2	cup potato starch
1/4	cup tapioca flour
1	tsp. baking powder
3/4	tsp. baking soda
1/4	tsp. salt
48	milk chocolate kisses

1. In a large bowl, cream the shortening, brown sugar and peanut butter until light and fluffy. Beat in egg, applesauce and vanilla (mixture will appear curdled). Combine the rice flour, potato starch, tapioca flour, baking powder, baking soda and salt; gradually add to creamed mixture and mix well. Cover and refrigerate for 1 hour.

2. Roll into 1-in. balls. Place 2 in. apart on ungreased baking sheets. Bake at 375° for 9-11 minutes or until slightly cracked. Immediately press a chocolate kiss into the center of each cookie. Cool for 2 minutes before removing from pans to wire racks.

Nutrition Facts: 1 cookie equals 98 calories, 5 g fat (2 g saturated fat), 5 mg cholesterol, 67 mg sodium, 13 g carbohydrate, trace fiber, 2 g protein. **Diabetic Exchanges:** 1 starch, 1 fat.

Lightened-Up Holiday Cookie Dough F S C

PREP: 15 min. + chilling **BAKE:** 10 min./batch
YIELD: 4 portions (1-1/4 cups each)

HEALTHY COOKING TEST KITCHEN

This versatile recipe is the base for the other three cookie and bar recipes on these pages.

1	cup butter, softened
1-1/2	cups sugar
1-1/2	cups packed brown sugar
3	eggs
1/3	cup canola oil
1-1/2	tsp. vanilla extract
4	cups all-purpose flour
1	tsp. salt
1/2	tsp. baking soda

1. In a large bowl, cream butter and sugars until light and fluffy. Beat in the eggs, oil and vanilla. Combine the flour, salt and baking soda; gradually add to creamed mixture and mix well.

2. Divide dough into four 1-1/4-cup portions. Shape each into a disk; wrap individually in plastic wrap. Refrigerate for 1 hour or until easy to handle, or freeze for up to 3 months.

3. To use refrigerated dough: Divide each portion into two balls; roll each ball directly on an ungreased baking sheet to 1/4-in. thickness. Cut with a floured 3-in. cookie cutter, leaving at least 1 in. between cookies. Remove the excess dough and reroll scraps if desired.

4. Bake at 350° for 6-7 minutes or until bottoms are lightly browned. Cool for 2 minutes before removing to wire racks to cool completely. Decorate as desired.

5. Or, bake according to individual directions for Chocolate Swirled Bars, Wreath Cookies and Drizzled Cherry Cookie Cups.

6. To use frozen dough: Thaw in the refrigerator overnight. Bake according to recipe directions.

Nutrition Facts: 1 cookie equals 56 calories, 2 g fat (1 g saturated fat), 9 mg cholesterol, 39 mg sodium, 8 g carbohydrate, trace fiber, 1 g protein. **Diabetic Exchanges:** 1/2 starch, 1/2 fat.

Chocolate Swirled Bars S C

PREP: 5 min. **BAKE:** 15 min. + standing
YIELD: about 3 dozen

HEALTHY COOKING TEST KITCHEN

These swirly chocolaty bars make a crunchy and elegant addition to any cookie tray—and couldn't be easier!

1-1/4	cups refrigerated Lightened-Up Holiday Cookie Dough (at left)
1	cup (6 oz.) dark chocolate chips
1/4	cup vanilla or white chips, melted

1. Press the dough onto the bottom of an ungreased 13-in. x 9-in. baking pan (dough will be thin). Bake at 350° for 11-13 minutes or until the edges of the bars begin to brown.

2. Immediately sprinkle with chocolate chips. Allow chips to soften for a few minutes, then spread over bars. Drop spoonfuls of melted vanilla chips over top; cut through chocolate with a knife to swirl. Let stand until set. Cut into bars.

Nutrition Facts: 1 bar equals 82 calories, 4 g fat (2 g saturated fat), 7 mg cholesterol, 31 mg sodium, 11 g carbohydrate, trace fiber, 1 g protein. **Diabetic Exchanges:** 1 fat, 1/2 starch.

Wreath Cookies F S C

PREP: 30 min. **BAKE:** 10 min./batch + cooling
YIELD: 30 cookies

HEALTHY COOKING TEST KITCHEN

Pretty and whimsical, these tiny, tender wreaths will definitely be favorites!

1-1/4	cups refrigerated Lightened-Up Holiday Cookie Dough (see opposite page)
2	Tbsp. all-purpose flour

Green food coloring, optional

2	Tbsp. water
2	Tbsp. coarse sugar
2	Tbsp. M&M's miniature baking bits
2	Tbsp. vanilla frosting

1. Let cookie dough stand at room temperature for 5-10 minutes to soften. In a large bowl, combine the dough and flour; mix until blended. Tint green with food coloring if desired.

2. Shape 1 tsp. dough into a 4-in. rope. Repeat. Place two ropes side by side; press together lightly and twist. Shape into a circle pinching ends to seal. Place 2 in. apart on ungreased baking sheets. Repeat with remaining dough. Brush lightly with water; sprinkle with sugar.

3. Bake at 350° for 7-8 minutes or until set and bottoms are lightly browned. Cool for 2 minutes before removing from pans to wire racks to cool completely. Attach baking bits onto wreaths with frosting.

Nutrition Facts: 1 cookie equals 67 calories, 3 g fat (1 g saturated fat), 9 mg cholesterol, 41 mg sodium, 10 g carbohydrate, trace fiber, 1 g protein. **Diabetic Exchanges:** 1/2 starch, 1/2 fat.

Drizzled Cherry Cookie Cups S

PREP: 15 min. **BAKE:** 10 min. + cooling
YIELD: 22 cookies

HEALTHY COOKING TEST KITCHEN

No one will ever guess these cute cookies drizzled with chocolate are lighter!

1-1/4	cups refrigerated Lightened-Up Holiday Cookie Dough (see opposite page)
22	maraschino cherries with stems, well drained
2	squares (1 oz. *each*) semisweet chocolate, melted

1. Roll dough into 1-in. balls; press onto the bottoms and up the sides of miniature muffin cups coated with cooking spray. Place a cherry into each cup.

2. Bake at 350° for 12-14 minutes or until lightly browned. Cool for 5 minutes before removing from pans to wire racks to cool completely. Drizzle with melted chocolate.

Nutrition Facts: 1 cookie equals 99 calories, 4 g fat (2 g saturated fat), 13 mg cholesterol, 52 mg sodium, 16 g carbohydrate, trace fiber, 1 g protein. **Diabetic Exchanges:** 1 starch, 1/2 fat.

> When making any type of cookies, do your best to avoid **overmixing the dough**. Doing so can result in cookies that are too tough.

WREATH COOKIES

DRIZZLED CHERRY COOKIE CUPS

True Love Chocolate Cake

PREP: 35 min. **BAKE:** 35 min. + cooling **YIELD:** 24 servings

STEPHANIE BASKER • CALDWELL, IDAHO

A college roommate gave me this amazing recipe, and it's been a favorite ever since. For other holidays, replace the hearts with appropriately colored hard candies.

1/4	cup butter, softened
1-2/3	cups sugar
2	eggs
1/2	cup unsweetened applesauce
2-1/4	cups all-purpose flour
2/3	cup baking cocoa
1-1/4	tsp. baking powder
1	tsp. salt
1/4	tsp. baking soda
1-1/4	cups water
1	cup (6 oz.) semisweet chocolate chips

FROSTING:

1	pkg. (8 oz.) reduced-fat cream cheese
1/3	cup confectioners' sugar
1	tsp. vanilla extract
1	carton (8 oz.) frozen reduced-fat whipped topping, thawed

TOPPING:

3/4	cup flaked coconut
1/2	cup candy hearts

1. In a large bowl, beat butter and sugar until crumbly, about 2 minutes. Add eggs, one at a time, beating well after each addition. Beat in applesauce.

2. Combine the flour, cocoa, baking powder, salt and baking soda. Add to the butter mixture alternately with water, beating well after each addition. Fold in chips. Pour into a 13-in. x 9-in. baking pan coated with cooking spray.

3. Bake at 350° for 35-40 minutes or until a toothpick inserted near the center comes out clean. Cool on a wire rack.

4. For frosting, in a mixing bowl, beat cream cheese and confectioners' sugar until smooth. Beat in vanilla. Fold in whipped topping. Frost cake. Refrigerate until

serving. Just before serving, sprinkle with coconut and candy.

Nutrition Facts: 1 piece equals 238 calories, 9 g fat (6 g saturated fat), 29 mg cholesterol, 201 mg sodium, 39 g carbohydrate, 1 g fiber, 4 g protein.

Makeover Chocolate Mint Layer Cake

PREP: 30 min. **BAKE:** 20 min. + chilling
YIELD: 16 servings

MELISSA GLEASON • SUGAR GROVE, ILLINOIS

With its minty, chocolate flavor and rich frosting, this cake tastes decadent, but it's really light!

1/4	cup butter, softened
1-1/4	cups sugar
2	eggs
1	container (2-1/4 oz.) prune baby food
1	tsp. vanilla extract
1	cup all-purpose flour
3/4	cup cake flour
1/2	cup baking cocoa
1	tsp. baking soda
1/2	tsp. salt
1-1/4	cups buttermilk

FILLING:

1	cup heavy whipping cream
3	Tbsp. confectioners' sugar
1/8	tsp. mint extract
3	to 4 drops green food coloring, optional

ICING:

1	cup (6 oz.) semisweet chocolate chips, melted and cooled
2/3	cup fat-free sour cream
1	tsp. vanilla extract

1. Line two 9-in. round baking pans with waxed paper. Coat the pans with cooking spray and sprinkle with flour; set aside.

2. In a large bowl, beat the butter and sugar until crumbly, about 2 minutes. Add the eggs, one at a time, beating well after each addition. Beat in baby food and vanilla. Combine the flours, cocoa, baking soda and salt; add to the butter mixture alternately with buttermilk.

3. Pour into prepared pans. Bake at 350° for 20-25 minutes or until a toothpick comes out clean. Cool for 10 minutes before removing from pans to wire racks to cool completely.

4. For filling, in a small bowl, beat the cream until it begins to thicken. Add confectioners' sugar and extract; beat until stiff peaks form. Beat in food coloring if desired. Place one cake layer on a serving plate; spread with filling. Top with second cake layer.

5. For the icing, in a small bowl, combine the cooled chocolate, sour cream and vanilla. Spread over the top and sides of cake. Refrigerate for at least 2 hours before serving.

Nutrition Facts: 1 slice equals 283 calories, 13 g fat (7 g saturated fat), 57 mg cholesterol, 217 mg sodium, 40 g carbohydrate, 2 g fiber, 5 g protein.

TRUE LOVE CHOCOLATE CAKE

Makeover Peanut Butter Bars

PREP: 20 min. + chilling **BAKE:** 20 min. + cooling
YIELD: 3 dozen

LORI STEVENS • RIVERTON, UTAH

Lighter in calories and fat, this ooey-gooey dessert is still a family favorite. Try it and you'll see why! Using applesauce to replace some of the butter really cuts back on fat without altering flavor.

1-3/4 cups reduced-fat creamy peanut butter, *divided*
1/3 cup butter, softened
1 cup packed brown sugar
3/4 cup sugar
2 eggs
1/2 cup unsweetened applesauce
1 tsp. vanilla extract
2 cups all-purpose flour
2 cups quick-cooking oats
1 tsp. baking soda
FROSTING:
4-1/2 cups confectioners' sugar
1/3 cup fat-free milk
1/4 cup baking cocoa
1/4 cup butter, softened
1 tsp. vanilla extract
1/2 tsp. salt

1. In a large bowl, cream 1 cup peanut butter, the butter, brown sugar and sugar until light and fluffy. Add eggs, one at a time, beating well after each addition. Beat in applesauce and vanilla. Combine the flour, oats and baking soda; gradually add to creamed mixture and mix well (batter will be thick).

2. Spread into a 15-in. x 10-in. x 1-in. baking pan coated with cooking spray. Bake at 350° for 18-22 minutes or until lightly browned. Cool on a wire rack for 10 minutes; spread with the remaining peanut butter. Cool to room temperature, then refrigerate for 30 minutes.

3. In a large bowl, beat frosting ingredients until light and fluffy. Spread over the peanut butter layer. Cut into bars.

Nutrition Facts: 1 bar equals 237 calories, 8 g fat (3 g saturated fat), 20 mg cholesterol, 165 mg sodium, 38 g carbohydrate, 2 g fiber, 5 g protein.

> Use applesauce to lighten up baked goods. It can replace some of the oil or butter in **your recipes.** Remember that you may need to decrease the sugar as well.

Makeover Pumpkin Gooey Butter Cake

PREP: 20 min. **BAKE:** 45 min. + cooling
YIELD: 24 servings

APRIL TAYLOR • FORT RILEY, KANSAS

With all of the original's decadence, this ooey-gooey dessert trims 64 calories and 5 grams fat from my original, making it a guilt-free holiday treat!

>   1 pkg. (18-1/4 oz.) yellow cake mix
>   1 egg
> 1/2 cup reduced-fat butter, melted

FILLING:

>   1 pkg. (8 oz.) reduced-fat cream cheese
>   1 cup canned pumpkin
> 1/2 cup reduced-fat butter, melted
>   2 eggs, lightly beaten
>   2 egg whites
>   1 tsp. vanilla extract
> 2-3/4 cups confectioners' sugar
>   1 tsp. ground cinnamon
>   1 tsp. ground nutmeg

Additional confectioners' sugar, optional

1. In a large bowl, beat the cake mix, egg and butter on low speed until combined. Press into a 13-in. x 9-in. baking pan coated with cooking spray.

2. In a another large bowl, beat cream cheese and pumpkin until smooth. Add the butter, eggs, egg whites and vanilla; beat on low until combined. Add the confectioners' sugar, cinnamon and nutmeg; mix well. Pour over crust.

3. Bake at 350° for 45-50 minutes or until edges are golden brown. Cool completely on a wire rack. Chill until serving. Sprinkle with additional confectioners' sugar if desired. Refrigerate leftovers.

Nutrition Facts: 1 piece equals 210 calories, 8 g fat (5 g saturated fat), 43 mg cholesterol, 258 mg sodium, 33 g carbohydrate, trace fiber, 3 g protein. **Diabetic Exchanges:** 2 starch, 1 fat.

Wonderful Carrot Cake

PREP: 25 min. **BAKE:** 40 min. + cooling
YIELD: 24 servings

BRENDA RANKHORN • NEW MARKET, ALABAMA

I used less sugar, substituted some applesauce for the oil and some wheat flour for the white. The result? A cake that's moist, tender and delectable! Kids will love it because it's sweet, and you'll love that it's packed with good-for-you carrots.

3/4 cup sugar

3/4 cup packed brown sugar

3 eggs

1/2 cup canola oil

1/2 cup unsweetened applesauce

1 tsp. vanilla extract

1-1/2 cups all-purpose flour

1/2 cup whole wheat flour

2 tsp. baking powder

1 tsp. salt

1 tsp. ground cinnamon

1/2 tsp. ground allspice

1/4 tsp. baking soda

3 cups finely shredded carrots

1/2 cup chopped walnuts

FROSTING:

3 oz. cream cheese, softened

1 Tbsp. fat-free milk

1 tsp. vanilla extract

2-1/2 cups confectioners' sugar

Dash salt

1. In a large bowl, beat sugars, eggs, oil, applesauce and vanilla until well blended. Combine the flours, baking powder, salt, cinnamon, allspice and baking soda; gradually beat into sugar mixture until blended. Stir in carrots and walnuts.

2. Pour into a 13-in. x 9-in. baking pan coated with cooking spray. Bake at 350° for 40-45 minutes or until a toothpick inserted near the center comes out clean. Cool completely on a wire rack.

3. For frosting, in a small bowl, beat the cream cheese, milk and vanilla until fluffy. Add confectioners' sugar and salt; beat until smooth. Spread over top of cake. Store in the refrigerator.

Nutrition Facts: 1 piece equals 223 calories, 8 g fat (1 g saturated fat), 30 mg cholesterol, 183 mg sodium, 36 g carbohydrate, 1 g fiber, 3 g protein.

Makeover Pecan Upside-Down Cake

PREP: 20 min. **BAKE:** 30 min. + cooling
YIELD: 20 servings

MAE JOHNSON • DE RIDDER, LOUISIANA

This moist and tender cake is packed with pecans and sweetness. Although still not a "light" dessert, it has nearly a third fewer calories and 43 percent less fat than the original! Try it in the morning with a cup of coffee or serve it with milk as an afternoon snack.

1/2 cup reduced-fat butter, melted

1/2 cup packed brown sugar

1/4 cup dark corn syrup

1-1/2 cups pecan halves

1 pkg. (18-1/4 oz.) butter pecan cake mix

1 cup reduced-fat sour cream

1/3 cup unsweetened applesauce

2 eggs

2 egg whites

1 tsp. vanilla extract

1. In a small bowl, combine the butter, brown sugar, corn syrup and pecans. Spread evenly into a 13-in. x 9-in. baking pan coated with cooking spray. Set aside.

2. In a large bowl, combine remaining ingredients; beat with a mixer on low speed for 30 seconds. Beat on medium for 2 minutes. Transfer to prepared pan.

3. Bake at 350° for 30-35 minutes or until a toothpick inserted near the center comes out clean. Cool for 5 minutes before inverting onto a serving platter. Serve warm or at room temperature.

Editor's Note: This recipe was tested with Land O'Lakes light stick butter.

Nutrition Facts: 1 piece equals 238 calories, 12 g fat (4 g saturated fat), 31 mg cholesterol, 236 mg sodium, 32 g carbohydrate, 1 g fiber, 3 g protein.

Pecans are packed with vitamins and minerals, including vitamins A and E, thiamin, zinc and magnesium. They're also **rich in protein** and fiber and have no cholesterol or sodium, making them a heart-smart snack!

MAKEOVER PECAN UPSIDE-DOWN CAKE

Makeover Mint Layer Brownies ⑤

PREP: 25 min. **BAKE:** 25 min. + chilling **YIELD:** 2 dozen

MARINDA SMITH • QUEEN CREEK, ARIZONA

This slimmed-down recipe, with just half the fat and cholesterol of the original treat, is still divinely decadent and makes a great meal finale!

1/2	cup reduced-fat butter
1-1/2	cups sugar
2	eggs
2	egg whites
1/2	cup unsweetened applesauce
2	squares (1 oz. *each*) unsweetened chocolate, melted
1	tsp. vanilla extract
1	cup all-purpose flour
1/3	cup baking cocoa
1/2	tsp. salt

MINT LAYER:

1/3	cup reduced-fat butter, softened
2	cups confectioners' sugar
1/4 to 1/2	tsp. peppermint extract
2	drops green food coloring, optional

ICING:

1	cup (6 oz.) semisweet chocolate chips
6	Tbsp. butter

1. In a large bowl, cream butter and sugar until light and fluffy. Add eggs, then egg whites, beating well after each addition. Beat in the applesauce, chocolate and vanilla (mixture will appear curdled).

2. Combine the flour, cocoa and salt; stir into butter mixture just until blended. Pour into a 13-in. x 9-in. baking dish coated with cooking spray. Bake at 350° for 22-28 minutes or until a toothpick inserted near the center comes out clean. Cool completely on a wire rack.

3. For mint layer, in a small bowl, beat butter until fluffy. Add the confectioners' sugar, extract and food coloring if desired; beat until smooth. Spread over cooled brownies. Refrigerate until firm.

4. For icing, in a microwave, melt chocolate chips and butter; stir until smooth. Gently pour over the top. Refrigerate until set. Cut into bars.

Editor's Note: This recipe was tested with Land O'Lakes light stick butter.

Nutrition Facts: 1 brownie equals 218 calories, 10 g fat (6 g saturated fat), 33 mg cholesterol, 134 mg sodium, 33 g carbohydrate, 1 g fiber, 2 g protein.

Chocolate Angel Food Cake Ⓕ ⑤

PREP: 35 min. **BAKE:** 30 min. + cooling
YIELD: 16 servings

REBECCA BAIRD • SALT LAKE CITY, UTAH

This eye-appealing cake brings mild chocolate flavor and a touch of elegance to any meal. And there's only 1 g of fat per serving!

12	egg whites
1	cup cake flour
1/3	cup baking cocoa
3/4	tsp. cream of tartar
1-1/2	tsp. vanilla extract
1/4	tsp. almond extract
1/8	tsp. salt
1-2/3	cups sugar

ICING:

1-3/4	cups confectioners' sugar
1/3	cup baking cocoa
1/3	cup reduced-fat sour cream
1	Tbsp. fat-free milk
3/4	tsp. vanilla extract

1. Place egg whites in a large bowl; let stand at room temperature for 30 minutes. Sift flour and cocoa together twice; set aside.

2. Add the cream of tartar, extracts and salt to egg whites; beat on medium speed until soft peaks form. Gradually add sugar, about 2 Tbsp. at a time, beating on high until stiff glossy peaks form and sugar is dissolved. Gradually fold in flour mixture, about 1/2 cup at a time.

3. Gently spoon into an ungreased 10-in. tube pan. Cut through batter with a knife to remove air pockets. Bake on the lowest oven rack at 350° for 30-40 minutes or until lightly browned and entire top appears dry. Immediately invert pan; cool completely, about 1 hour.

4. Run a knife around side and center tube of pan. Remove cake to a serving plate.

5. For icing, in a small bowl, beat the confectioners' sugar, cocoa, sour cream, milk and vanilla until smooth. Drizzle over cake. Refrigerate leftovers.

Nutrition Facts: 1 slice equals 195 calories, 1 g fat (trace saturated fat), 2 mg cholesterol, 64 mg sodium, 43 g carbohydrate, 1 g fiber, 4 g protein.

MAKEOVER MINT LAYER BROWNIES

Chocolate Orange Cake

PREP: 25 min. **BAKE:** 20 min. + cooling
YIELD: 12 servings

LINDA DALTON • STOUGHTON, MASSACHUSETTS

I love the combination of chocolate and orange and this recipe complements both. Since I process oats to add to the flour, they're undetectable, so it's our healthy little secret. It's a wonderful snack any time of year.

2	tsp. plus 1/3 cup baking cocoa, *divided*
1/3	cup quick-cooking oats
2/3	cup reduced-fat sour cream
1/3	cup sugar blend
2	eggs
3	Tbsp. Triple Sec or orange juice
2	Tbsp. butter, melted
5	tsp. canola oil
1	tsp. vanilla extract
2/3	cup all-purpose flour
1	tsp. baking powder
1/2	tsp. baking soda
1/4	tsp. salt
1/4	cup miniature semisweet chocolate chips
2	tsp. grated orange peel

FROSTING:

4	oz. reduced-fat cream cheese
1/4	cup confectioners' sugar
2	tsp. grated orange peel
2	tsp. orange juice

1. Coat an 8-in. square baking dish with cooking spray and sprinkle with 2 tsp. cocoa; set aside. Place oats in a small food processor; cover and process until ground. Set aside.

2. In a large bowl, beat the sour cream, sugar blend, eggs, Triple Sec, butter, oil and vanilla until well blended. Combine the flour, oats, baking powder, baking soda, salt and remaining cocoa; gradually beat into sour cream mixture until blended. Stir in chocolate chips and orange peel.

3. Transfer to reserved dish. Bake at 350° for 20-25 minutes or until a toothpick inserted near the center comes out clean. Cool completely on a wire rack.

4. For frosting, in a small bowl, beat cream cheese until fluffy. Add the confectioners' sugar, orange peel and juice; beat until smooth. Frost top of cake. Refrigerate leftovers.

Editor's Note: This recipe was tested with Splenda sugar blend.

Nutrition Facts: 1 piece equals 192 calories, 9 g fat (4 g saturated fat), 51 mg cholesterol, 210 mg sodium, 22 g carbohydrate, 1 g fiber, 5 g protein. **Diabetic Exchanges:** 2 fat, 1-1/2 starch.

> The sugar blend in Chocolate Orange Cake shaves 5 g carbohydrates and **21 calories** from the recipe. Prefer granulated sugar? Use 2/3 cup instead of the blend.

Gluten-Free Toffee Bars S

PREP: 25 min. **BAKE:** 15 min. + standing
YIELD: 2-1/2 dozen

PAM GIANETTI • GIRARD, OHIO

These nutty, crunchy bars are perfect for those with gluten intolerance.

2/3	cup butter, softened
1	cup packed brown sugar
1	egg yolk
1/3	cup unsweetened applesauce
1	tsp. vanilla extract
1	cup white rice flour
1/3	cup potato starch
1/3	cup tapioca flour
4-1/2	tsp. cornstarch
4-1/2	tsp. gluten-free garbanzo and fava flour
2-1/2	tsp. xanthan gum
3/4	tsp. salt
1	cup (6 oz.) semisweet chocolate chips
1/2	cup finely chopped pecans

1. In a small bowl, cream butter and brown sugar until light and fluffy. Add egg yolk; mix well. Beat in applesauce and vanilla. In a small bowl, combine the rice flour, potato starch, tapioca flour, cornstarch, garbanzo and fava flour, xanthan gum and salt; gradually add to creamed mixture and mix well.

2. Spread into a 15-in. x 10-in. x 1-in. baking pan coated with cooking spray. Bake at 350° for 15-20 minutes or until lightly browned. Sprinkle with chocolate chips; let stand for 5 minutes. Spread chocolate chips over crust. Sprinkle with pecans. Let stand until chocolate is set. Cut into bars.

Editor's Note: This recipe was tested with Bob's Red Mill garbanzo and fava flour.

Nutrition Facts: 1 bar equals 136 calories, 7 g fat (4 g saturated fat), 18 mg cholesterol, 94 mg sodium, 18 g carbohydrate, 1 g fiber, 1 g protein. **Diabetic Exchanges:** 1 starch, 1 fat.

Gluten-Free Pecan Pumpkin Cake

PREP: 30 min. **BAKE:** 40 min + cooling
YIELD: 12 servings

KATHY RAIRIGH • MILFORD, INDIANA

Here's a delicious pumpkin cake for the holidays. But don't just bake it then—it's wonderful all year long!

- 1 cup sugar
- 1 cup canned pumpkin
- 3 Tbsp. canola oil
- 2 egg whites
- 1 egg
- 1 tsp. vanilla extract
- 1-1/2 cups brown rice flour
- 1/2 cup potato starch
- 1/4 cup tapioca flour
- 1-1/2 tsp. baking powder
- 1 tsp. baking soda
- 3/4 tsp. xanthan gum
- 1/2 tsp. salt
- 1/2 tsp. pumpkin pie spice
- 1/4 cup chopped pecans
- 1/3 cup packed dark brown sugar
- 1/2 tsp. ground cinnamon
- 3 Tbsp. cold butter

Confectioners' sugar, optional

1. In a bowl, beat first six ingredients until blended. In a separate bowl, combine the next eight ingredients; reserve 1/4 cup for topping. Gradually beat remaining mixture into pumpkin mixture until blended. Spread batter into a 9-in. springform pan coated with cooking spray.

2. In a bowl, combine pecans, brown sugar, cinnamon and reserved flour mixture. Cut in butter until mixture resembles coarse crumbs; sprinkle over batter.

3. Bake at 350° for 40-45 minutes or until a toothpick inserted near the center comes out clean. Cool on a wire rack for 20 minutes. Remove sides of pan. Cool completely. Sprinkle with confectioners' sugar if desired.

Nutrition Facts: 1 slice equals 264 calories, 9 g fat (2 g saturated fat), 25 mg cholesterol, 294 mg sodium, 45 g carbohydrate, 2 g fiber, 3 g protein.

Makeover Cake with Coconut-Pecan Icing

PREP: 20 min. **BAKE:** 25 min. + cooling
YIELD: 20 servings

RIVKA KAHAN • BROOKLYN, NEW YORK

My family is absolutely crazy about this soft, moist cake with its rich-tasting, super chocolaty icing. My dad would finish half the pan if he could!

- 1/3 cup shortening
- 3/4 cup sugar
- 1/3 cup sugar blend
- 2 eggs
- 1/2 cup unsweetened applesauce
- 1 tsp. vanilla extract
- 1 cup cake flour
- 1 cup all-purpose flour
- 1/4 cup baking cocoa
- 1 tsp. baking soda
- 3/4 tsp. salt
- 1-1/2 cups buttermilk

ICING & GARNISH:
- 1/3 cup reduced-fat butter, cubed
- 3 Tbsp. baking cocoa
- 2 Tbsp. fat-free milk
- 2 cups confectioners' sugar
- 1-1/4 cups chopped pecans, toasted, *divided*
- 3/4 cup flaked coconut, toasted, *divided*
- 3/4 tsp. vanilla extract

1. In a large bowl, beat the shortening, sugar and sugar blend until crumbly, about 2 minutes. Add eggs, one at a time, beating well after each addition. Beat in applesauce and vanilla (batter will appear curdled). Combine the flours, cocoa, baking soda and salt; add to shortening mixture alternately with buttermilk, beating well after each addition.

2. Pour into a 13-in. x 9-in. baking pan coated with cooking spray. Bake at 350° for 25-30 minutes or until a toothpick inserted near the center comes out clean. Place on a wire rack.

3. For icing, in a small saucepan, melt butter. Stir in cocoa until smooth. Add milk and bring to a boil. Remove from the heat. Stir in the confectioners' sugar, 3/4 cup pecans, 1/2 cup coconut and vanilla until smooth. Spread over warm cake. Sprinkle with remaining pecans and coconut. Cool completely. Refrigerate leftovers.

Editor's Note: This recipe was tested with Splenda Sugar Blend and Land O'Lakes light stick butter.

Nutrition Facts: 1 piece equals 271 calories, 12 g fat (4 g saturated fat), 26 mg cholesterol, 213 mg sodium, 39 g carbohydrate, 2 g fiber, 4 g protein.

MAKEOVER CAKE WITH COCONUT-PECAN ICING

Makeover Strawberry Cake

PREP: 10 min. **BAKE:** 20 min. + cooling
YIELD: 16 servings

GAIL LONG • PELHAM, ALABAMA

My family just loves this wonderful and easy cake that's as pretty as it is tasty!

1	pkg. (18-1/4 oz.) white cake mix
1	pkg. (.3 oz.) sugar-free strawberry gelatin
4	egg whites
1/3	cup canola oil
1	cup frozen unsweetened strawberries, thawed
1/2	cup water

ICING:
1/3	cup butter, softened
2-1/3	cups confectioners' sugar

1. Line two 9-in. round baking pans with waxed paper. Coat pans with cooking spray and sprinkle with flour; set aside. In a large bowl, combine cake mix and gelatin. Add egg whites and oil; beat until well blended.

2. In a small bowl or food processor, mash the strawberries in their juice. Set aside 3 Tbsp. for icing. Add water and remaining berries to the batter; mix well. Pour into prepared pans. Bake at 350° for 20-25 minutes or until a toothpick inserted near the center comes out clean. Cool for 10 minutes before removing from pans to wire racks to cool completely.

3. For icing, in a small bowl, combine butter and reserved strawberries. Gradually beat in confectioners' sugar until light and fluffy.

4. Place one cake layer on a serving platter; top with half of the icing. Repeat layers.

Nutrition Facts: 1 slice equals 287 calories, 11 g fat (4 g saturated fat), 10 mg cholesterol, 264 mg sodium, 44 g carbohydrate, trace fiber, 3 g protein.

MAKEOVER STRAWBERRY CAKE

Quick Chocolate Snack Cake ⑤

PREP: 25 min. **BAKE:** 20 min. + cooling
YIELD: 18 servings

ANGELA OELSCHLAEGER • TONGANOXIE, KANSAS

I recently learned I'm diabetic. I never thought I'd be able to curb my sweet tooth—until I made this!

1/3	cup prune baby food *or* unsweetened applesauce
1	cup sugar
1/2	cup sugar blend
1/2	cup egg substitute
1/2	cup water
1/3	cup canola oil
1	tsp. vanilla extract
3/4	cup baking cocoa
2/3	cup all-purpose flour
2/3	cup whole wheat pastry flour
1/2	tsp. baking soda
1/4	tsp. salt
1/2	cup semisweet chocolate chips

1. In a large bowl, beat the baby food, sugar, sugar blend, egg substitute, water, oil and vanilla until well blended. Combine the cocoa, flours, baking soda and salt; gradually beat into prune mixture until blended. Transfer to a 13-in. x 9-in. baking dish coated with cooking spray.

2. Bake at 350° for 20-25 minutes or until a toothpick inserted near the center comes out clean. Sprinkle with chips. Cool on a wire rack.

Editor's Note: This recipe was tested with Splenda sugar blend.

Nutrition Facts: 1 piece equals 170 calories, 6 g fat (1 g saturated fat), 0 cholesterol, 82 mg sodium, 29 g carbohydrate, 1 g fiber, 2 g protein. **Diabetic Exchanges:** 2 starch, 1 fat.

Berry Patch Pie ⑤

PREP: 30 min. + cooling **YIELD:** 8 servings

HEALTHY COOKING TEST KITCHEN

Enjoy a gorgeous, made-for-summer pie with this mouth-watering recipe. Each bite bursts with sweet, juicy berries.

Pastry for single-crust pie (9 in.)
3/4	cup sugar
1/4	cup cornstarch
2	cups halved fresh strawberries
1-1/2	cups fresh raspberries
1	cup fresh blackberries
1	cup fresh blueberries
1	Tbsp. lemon juice

1. On a lightly floured surface, unroll pastry. Transfer to a 9-in. pie plate. Trim pastry to 1/2 in. beyond edge of plate; flute edges. Line unpricked pastry with a double thickness of heavy-duty foil. Bake at 450° for 8 minutes. Remove foil; bake 5-7 minutes longer or until golden brown. Cool on a wire rack.

2. Meanwhile, in a large saucepan, combine sugar and cornstarch. Stir in berries and lemon juice. Cook, stirring occasionally, over medium heat until mixture

just comes to a boil; pour into prepared crust. Cool completely on a wire rack.

Nutrition Facts: 1 piece equals 250 calories, 7 g fat (3 g saturated fat), 5 mg cholesterol, 101 mg sodium, 46 g carbohydrate, 4 g fiber, 2 g protein.

Lactose-Free Chocolate Chip Cookies S

PREP: 15 min. + chilling **BAKE:** 15 min./batch
YIELD: 3 dozen

SARAH ANN MANTHE • BROOKFIELD, WISCONSIN

Though vegan-friendly and dairy-free, these pack all that classic cookie flavor into each and every bite!

1	cup maple syrup
3/4	cup sugar
1/2	cup canola oil
1/2	cup unsweetened applesauce
3-1/2	tsp. vanilla extract
3/4	tsp. molasses
3	cups all-purpose flour
3	tsp. baking powder
1-1/2	tsp. baking soda
3/4	tsp. salt
1	pkg. (10 oz.) dairy-free semisweet chocolate chips

1. In a large bowl, beat the syrup, sugar, oil, applesauce, vanilla and molasses until well blended. Combine the flour, baking powder, baking soda and salt; gradually add to syrup mixture and mix well. Stir in chocolate chips. Cover and refrigerate for 1 hour.

2. Drop by heaping tablespoonfuls 2 in. apart onto baking sheets lightly coated with cooking spray. Bake at 350° for 11-13 minutes or until edges are lightly browned. Remove to wire racks.

Editor's Note: This recipe was tested with Enjoy Life semisweet chocolate chips.

Nutrition Facts: 1 cookie equals 147 calories, 6 g fat (2 g saturated fat), 0 cholesterol, 136 mg sodium, 23 g carbohydrate, 1 g fiber, 2 g protein. **Diabetic Exchanges:** 1-1/2 starch, 1 fat.

Can't find the dairy-free chocolate chips that this recipe calls for? Check the baking aisle and the health or natural-food aisle of your grocery store. You can also substitute them with **carob chips**. Carob chips are similar in shape and size to regular chocolate chips, but they contain no chocolate whatsoever.

MAKEOVER MARBLED ORANGE FUDGE

MAKEOVER PEACH BOWL PIZZA

CRANBERRY APPLE CRISP

Treat Yourself

Moist cupcakes, bubbling fruit crisps, chocolate tortes and frosty ice cream delights–you can enjoy all of these favorites and more! Stop here when you need a decadent delight, and dig in without an ounce of guilt.

Cranberry Apple Crisp S

PREP: 15 min. **BAKE:** 40 min. **YIELD:** 8 servings

CAROLYN DIPASQUALE • MIDDLETOWN, RHODE ISLAND

I left the fibrous, vitamin-rich apple peels on and replaced most of the butter with canola oil. I'm so pleased with the results.

    5   medium tart apples, sliced
    1   Tbsp. all-purpose flour
    1   can (16 oz.) whole-berry cranberry sauce
TOPPING:
    3/4 cup quick-cooking oats
    1/3 cup packed brown sugar
    1/4 cup all-purpose flour
    2   Tbsp. plus 2 tsp. wheat bran
    2   Tbsp. canola oil
    2   Tbsp. butter, melted
    3/4 tsp. ground cinnamon
    Fat-free vanilla frozen yogurt, optional

1. In a large bowl, combine apples and flour; toss to coat. Stir in cranberry sauce. Transfer to a 13-in. x 9-in. baking dish coated with cooking spray.

2. In a small bowl, combine topping ingredients; sprinkle over apple mixture. Bake, uncovered, at 350° for 40-45 minutes or until topping is golden brown and fruit is tender. Serve with frozen yogurt if desired.

Nutrition Facts: 1 serving (calculated without frozen yogurt) equals 259 calories, 7 g fat (2 g saturated fat), 8 mg cholesterol, 36 mg sodium, 50 g carbohydrate, 4 g fiber, 2 g protein.

Frozen Hot Chocolate S

PREP/TOTAL TIME: 15 min. + freezing
YIELD: 4 servings

LILLIAN JULOW • GAINESVILLE, FLORIDA

Make it an occasion for chocolate lovers with this yummy, icy treat. For a stiffer consistency, freeze the mixture for 8 hours.

    3/4 cup sugar
    1/2 cup baking cocoa
    2-3/4 cups 2% milk, *divided*
    1/4 cup reduced-fat whipped topping
    4   tsp. chocolate syrup

1. In a large saucepan, combine sugar and cocoa. Gradually add milk, reserving 2 Tbsp. for blending; cook and stir until heated through and sugar is dissolved. Remove from the heat and let cool.

2. Transfer to an 8-in. square dish. Freeze for 2 hours or until edges begin to firm. Stir and return to freezer. Freeze 4 hours longer or until firm.

3. Just before serving, transfer to a food processor; cover and process with remaining milk until smooth. Garnish with whipped topping and chocolate syrup.

Nutrition Facts: 1 cup equals 285 calories, 5 g fat (3 g saturated fat), 13 mg cholesterol, 88 mg sodium, 57 g carbohydrate, 2 g fiber, 8 g protein.

Makeover Peach Bowl Pizza

PREP: 30 min. + cooling **YIELD:** 16 slices

SARAH FILSON • GALVA, ILLINOIS

Imagine a crispy, crumbly, shortbread crust covered in a layer of fluffy, sugary cream cheese and topped with juicy fresh peaches—that's exactly what you're getting in this fantastic pizza dessert!

    1-1/4 cups all-purpose flour
       6 Tbsp. sugar
    1/4   tsp. salt
       9 Tbsp. cold butter
       1 pkg. (8 oz.) reduced-fat cream cheese
    1/2   cup confectioners' sugar
    1/4   tsp. almond extract
       1 cup reduced-fat whipped topping
       4 medium peaches, peeled and diced

1. In a large bowl, combine the flour, sugar and salt. Cut in butter until crumbly. Press onto an ungreased 12-in. pizza pan. Bake at 350° for 15-18 minutes or until lightly browned. Cool on a wire rack.

2. In a small bowl, beat the cream cheese, confectioners' sugar and extract until smooth; fold in whipped topping. Spread over crust. Arrange the peaches on top. Refrigerate leftovers.

Nutrition Facts: 1 slice equals 180 calories, 10 g fat (7 g saturated fat), 27 mg cholesterol, 142 mg sodium, 20 g carbohydrate, 1 g fiber, 3 g protein.

Frozen Peach Yogurt F S

PREP: 20 min. Process: 20 min. + freezing
YIELD: 6 cups

With its fresh and sweet flavor, you'll be glad that each bite of this cool and creamy treat delivers bone-strengthening benefits!

- 4   medium peaches, peeled and sliced
- 1   envelope unflavored gelatin
- 1   cup fat-free milk
- 1/2   cup sugar
- Dash salt
- 2-1/2   cups reduced-fat vanilla yogurt
- 2   tsp. vanilla extract

1. Place peaches in a blender. Cover and process until blended; set aside. In a small saucepan, sprinkle gelatin over milk; let stand for 1 minute. Heat over low heat, stirring until gelatin is completely dissolved. Remove from the heat; stir in sugar and salt until sugar dissolves. Add the yogurt, vanilla and reserved peaches.

2. Fill cylinder of ice cream freezer two-thirds full; freeze according to the manufacturer's directions. When ice cream is frozen, transfer to a freezer container; freeze for 2-4 hours before serving.

Nutrition Facts: 3/4 cup equals 149 calories, 1 g fat (1 g saturated fat), 4 mg cholesterol, 83 mg sodium, 29 g carbohydrate, 1 g fiber, 6 g protein. **Diabetic Exchanges:** 1 starch, 1/2 fruit, 1/2 reduced-fat milk.

> The hype is true! If you don't get enough **calcium**, your body robs it from your bones. Eating reduced-fat dairy items is a great way to get more calcium into your diet.

FROZEN PEACH YOGURT

Candy Bar Cupcakes

PREP: 30 min. **BAKE:** 20 min. + cooling
YIELD: 1-1/2 dozen

Everyone in my family loves cupcakes, so I experimented to create these treats that fit everyone's tastes. I also tried to make them healthier. Guests at your next gathering are sure to enjoy them as much as we do.

- 1   cup sugar
- 1   cup buttermilk
- 1/4   cup canola oil
- 1   tsp. vanilla extract
- 1-1/2   cups all-purpose flour
- 1/3   cup baking cocoa
- 1   tsp. baking soda
- 1/2   tsp. salt

FILLING:
- 6   oz. fat-free cream cheese
- 2   Tbsp. confectioners' sugar
- 1   egg
- 2   Snickers candy bars (2.07 oz. *each*), finely chopped

FROSTING:
- 1/3   cup butter, cubed
- 1/3   cup packed brown sugar
- 3   Tbsp. fat-free milk
- 1-1/2   cups confectioners' sugar

1. In a large bowl, beat the sugar, buttermilk, oil and vanilla until well blended. Combine the flour, cocoa, baking soda and salt; gradually beat into sugar mixture until blended.

2. For filling, in a small bowl, beat cream cheese and confectioners' sugar until light and fluffy. Add egg; mix well. Stir in candy bars.

3. Fill 18 paper-lined muffin cups one-third full with batter. Drop filling by tablespoonfuls into the center of each (cups will be about half full). Bake at 350° for 20-25 minutes or until a toothpick inserted in the filling comes out clean. Cool for 10 minutes before removing from pans to wire racks to cool completely.

4. For frosting, in a small saucepan, melt butter. Stir in brown sugar. Bring to a boil; cook for two minutes, stirring occasionally. Remove from the heat; stir in the milk, then confectioners' sugar. Cool until the frosting reaches spreading consistency. Frost the cupcakes.

Nutrition Facts: 1 cupcake equals 250 calories, 9 g fat (3 g saturated fat), 23 mg cholesterol, 248 mg sodium, 40 g carbohydrate, 1 g fiber, 4 g protein.

GRILLED PEACH CRISPS

Grilled Peach Crisps S

PREP/TOTAL TIME: 25 min. **YIELD:** 8 servings

MICHELLE SANDOVAL • ESCALON, CALIFORNIA

Most of the fat and sugar is eliminated from this grilled version of peach cobbler. A perfect finish to a summer barbecue, this dessert always impresses our guests.

   2 Tbsp. sugar
   1 tsp. ground cinnamon
   4 medium peaches, halved and pitted
   4 cups reduced-fat vanilla ice cream
   1 cup reduced-fat granola

1. In a small bowl, combine sugar and cinnamon; sprinkle over cut sides of peaches. Let stand for 5 minutes.

2. Coat grill rack with cooking spray before starting the grill. Place peaches cut side down on grill rack. Grill, covered, over medium heat for 8-10 minutes or until peaches are tender and begin to caramelize.

3. Place peaches in dessert bowls. Serve with ice cream and granola.

Nutrition Facts: 1 serving equals 193 calories, 4 g fat (2 g saturated fat), 18 mg cholesterol, 83 mg sodium, 36 g carbohydrate, 2 g fiber, 5 g protein.

Lemon-Apricot Fruit Pops
F S C

PREP: 15 min. + freezing **YIELD:** 6 servings

AYSHA SCHURMAN • AMMON, IDAHO

With just 31 calories, 4 tsp. sugar and lots of vitamin C, this is one, refreshing summer dessert everyone will find room for no matter how full they are!

   1 cup sliced fresh apricots
  1/2 cup ice cubes
  1/4 cup lemon juice
  1/4 cup orange juice
   4 tsp. sugar
   1 tsp. grated lemon peel
   1 tsp. minced fresh mint, optional
   6 Popsicle molds *or* paper cups (3 oz. *each*) and Popsicle sticks

1. In a blender, combine the first six ingredients; stir in mint if desired. Fill each mold or cup with 1/4 cup apricot mixture; top with holders or insert sticks into cups. Freeze.

Nutrition Facts: 1 fruit pop equals 31 calories, trace fat (trace saturated fat), 0 cholesterol, trace sodium, 8 g carbohydrate, 1 g fiber, trace protein. **Diabetic Exchange:** 1/2 fruit.

Makeover Marbled Orange Fudge F S C

PREP: 30 min. + chilling   **YIELD:** 2-1/2 lbs

JANA MOSES • WEST LINN, OREGON

Packed with orange flavor, marshmallow creme and white chocolate chips, this makeover is like eating an orange Creamsicle ice cream bar...in amazing fudge form.

2-1/2	cups sugar
2/3	cup evaporated milk
1/2	cup butter, cubed
1	pkg. (10 to 12 oz.) white baking chips
1	jar (7 oz.) marshmallow creme
3	tsp. orange extract
12	drops yellow food coloring
9	drops red food coloring

1. Line a 13-in. x 9-in. pan with foil and coat with cooking spray; set aside. In a small heavy saucepan, combine the sugar, evaporated milk and butter. Cook and stir over low heat until sugar is dissolved. Bring to a boil; cook and stir for 4 minutes. Remove from the heat; stir in chips and marshmallow creme until smooth.

2. Remove 1 cup and set aside. Add extract and food coloring to the remaining mixture; stir until blended. Pour into prepared pan. Pour reserved marshmallow mixture over the top; cut through mixture with a knife to swirl. Cover and refrigerate until set.

3. Using foil, lift fudge out of pan. Discard foil; cut fudge into 1-in. squares. Store in an airtight container in the refrigerator.

Nutrition Facts: 1 piece equals 45 calories, 2 g fat (1 g saturated fat), 3 mg cholesterol, 10 mg sodium, 7 g carbohydrate, 0 fiber, trace protein. **Diabetic Exchange:** 1/2 starch.

Makeover Crunchy Pumpkin Dessert Squares

PREP: 15 min. **BAKE:** 1 hour + cooling
YIELD: 20 servings

CINDY STYLES • GOLDSBORO, NORTH CAROLINA

The Healthy Cooing Test Kitchen home economists lightened my original recipe to feature 100 fewer calories per serving! Even with reduced-fat ingredients, you'll agree it's a decadent dessert worthy of praise. It's a wonderful alternative to traditional pumpkin pie.

1 can (30 oz.) pumpkin pie filling
1 can (12 oz.) fat-free evaporated milk
3 eggs
1 pkg. (18-1/4 oz.) yellow cake mix
2/3 cup chopped pecans
1 cup reduced-fat butter, melted
1-1/4 cups fat-free whipped topping

1. In a large bowl, combine the pie filling, milk and eggs; beat on medium speed until smooth. Pour into an ungreased 13-in. x 9-in. baking pan. Sprinkle with cake mix and pecans; drizzle with butter.

2. Bake at 350° for 60-65 minutes or until a toothpick inserted near the center comes out clean. Cool completely on a wire rack. Garnish with whipped topping. Refrigerate leftovers.

Editor's Note: This recipe was tested with Land O'Lakes light stick butter.

Nutrition Facts: 1 piece equals 246 calories, 10 g fat (4 g saturated fat), 44 mg cholesterol, 335 mg sodium, 36 g carbohydrate, 1 g fiber, 4 g protein.

Makeover Frosted Banana Bars S

PREP: 15 min. **BAKE:** 20 min. + cooling
YIELD: 3 dozen

SUSAN STUFF • MERCERSBURG, PENNSYLVANIA

I've made these banana bars many times, always with favorable comments and requests for the recipe. With this makeover, you don't have to be shy about grabbing seconds of this treat!

3 Tbsp. butter, softened
1-1/2 cups sugar
2 eggs
1-1/2 cups mashed ripe bananas (about 3 medium)
1/4 cup unsweetened applesauce
1 tsp. vanilla extract
2 cups all-purpose flour
1 tsp. baking soda
Dash salt
FROSTING:
1 pkg. (8 oz.) reduced-fat cream cheese
1/3 cup butter, softened
3 cups confectioners' sugar
2 tsp. vanilla extract

1. In a large bowl, beat butter and sugar until crumbly, about 2 minutes. Add eggs, one at a time, beating well after each addition. Beat in the bananas, applesauce and vanilla. Combine the flour, baking soda and salt; stir into butter mixture just until blended.

2. Transfer to a 15-in. x 10-in. x 1-in. baking pan coated with cooking spray. Bake at 350° for 20-25 minutes or until a toothpick inserted near the center comes out clean. Cool in pan on a wire rack.

3. For frosting, in a small bowl, beat cream cheese and butter until fluffy. Add confectioners' sugar and vanilla; beat until smooth. Frost bars. Refrigerate leftovers.

Nutrition Facts: 1 bar equals 149 calories, 4 g fat (3 g saturated fat), 23 mg cholesterol, 89 mg sodium, 26 g carbohydrate, trace fiber, 2 g protein. **Diabetic Exchanges:** 2 starch, 1 fat.

Creamy Butterscotch Pudding

PREP: 10 min. **COOK:** 15 min. + chilling
YIELD: 4 servings

EMR •TASTE OF HOME ON-LINE COMMUNITY

Deciding to make a real homemade dessert one night, I mixed up this pudding. It's from my favorite cookbook with a few added tweaks—and much better than any store-bought version!

1/2 cup packed dark brown sugar
2 Tbsp. plus 2 tsp. cornstarch
1/8 tsp. salt
2 cups fat-free milk
2 egg yolks, lightly beaten
1 Tbsp. butter
1-1/2 tsp. vanilla extract

1. In a small saucepan, combine the brown sugar, cornstarch and salt. Add milk and egg yolks; stir until smooth. Cook and stir over medium heat until mixture comes to a boil. Cook and stir 1-2 minutes longer or until thickened.

2. Remove from the heat; stir in butter and vanilla. Cool to room temperature, stirring several times. Pour into four individual dessert dishes. Cover and refrigerate for 1-2 hours or until chilled.

Nutrition Facts: 1/2 cup equals 221 calories, 5 g fat (3 g saturated fat), 112 mg cholesterol, 161 mg sodium, 38 g carbohydrate, trace fiber, 5 g protein.

CREAMY BUTTERSCOTCH PUDDING

Chocolate Raspberry Torte

PREP: 30 min. **BAKE:** 25 min. + cooling
YIELD: 16 servings

SHARON KURTZ • EMMAUS, PENNSYLVANIA

For an elegant ending to any meal, impress guests with this gorgeous guilt-free torte. The chocolate cake by itself is truly wonderful, but the light, creamy raspberry filling really makes it special.

2	cups sugar
1	cup water
1	cup buttermilk
2	eggs
1/2	cup unsweetened applesauce
1/4	cup canola oil
2	tsp. vanilla extract
2	cups all-purpose flour
1	cup baking cocoa
1	tsp. baking powder
1/2	tsp. salt
1/2	tsp. baking soda
1	pkg. (8 oz.) reduced-fat cream cheese
1/2	cup confectioners' sugar
1/4	cup seedless raspberry jam

Fresh raspberries, mint sprigs and additional confectioners' sugar, optional

1. In a large bowl, beat the sugar, water, buttermilk, eggs, applesauce, oil and vanilla until well blended. Combine the flour, cocoa, baking powder, salt and baking soda; gradually beat into the sugar mixture until blended.

2. Transfer to two 9-in. round baking pans coated with cooking spray. Bake at 350° for 25-30 minutes or until a toothpick inserted near the center comes out clean. Cool for 10 minutes before removing from pans to wire racks to cool completely.

3. In a small bowl, beat the cream cheese, confectioners' sugar and jam until blended. Split each cake into two horizontal layers. Place a bottom layer on a serving plate; spread with a third of the filling. Repeat layers twice. Top with remaining cake layer. Garnish with raspberries, mint and additional confectioners' sugar if desired.

Nutrition Facts: 1 slice (calculated without optional garnish) equals 281 calories, 8 g fat (3 g saturated fat), 37 mg cholesterol, 223 mg sodium, 49 g carbohydrate, 2 g fiber, 5 g protein.

Gingered Cranberry Granita

F **S**

PREP: 20 min. + freezing **YIELD:** 4 servings

LISA KEYS • MIDDLEBURY, CONNECTICUT

This is elegant, easy and refreshing and requires no special equipment to prepare it.

2	cups cranberry juice
1/4	cup plus 3 Tbsp. sugar, *divided*
4	orange peel strips (1 to 3 in.)
1	Tbsp. minced candied or crystallized ginger
4	fresh mint leaves

1. In a small saucepan, bring the cranberry juice, 1/4 cup sugar and orange peel to a boil. Cook and stir until sugar is dissolved. Remove from heat; stir in the ginger.

2. Place remaining sugar in a small bowl. Remove orange peel from syrup; add to sugar, one piece at a time, and shake to coat. Place in a single layer on a foil-lined plate. Let stand overnight. Cover remaining sugar; set aside.

3. Transfer cranberry mixture to an 8-in. square dish; cool to room temperature. Cover and freeze overnight.

CHOCOLATE RASPBERRY TORTE

GINGERED CRANBERRY GRANITA

BLUEBERRY WALNUT BARS

4. Just before serving, lightly moisten mint with cold water; dip in remaining sugar to coat. Using a fork, scrape granita into dessert dishes. Garnish with mint and candied orange peel.

Nutrition Facts: 1 serving equals 156 calories, trace fat (trace saturated fat), 0 cholesterol, 5 mg sodium, 40 g carbohydrate, trace fiber, 1 g protein.

Blueberry Walnut Bars ⑤

PREP: 20 min. **BAKE:** 10 min. + cooling
YIELD: 12 servings

DAWN ONUFFER • CRESTVIEW, FLORIDA

With power-packing oats, walnuts and blueberries, kids aren't the only ones that are going to love this sweet treat. Health-minded parents can feel good about these bars, too.

2/3	cup ground walnuts
1/2	cup graham cracker crumbs
2	Tbsp. plus 1/3 cup sugar, *divided*
1/3	cup old-fashioned oats
3	Tbsp. reduced-fat butter, melted
1	pkg. (8 oz.) reduced-fat cream cheese
1	Tbsp. orange juice
1/2	tsp. vanilla extract
1/2	cup reduced-fat whipped topping
2	Tbsp. blueberry preserves
1-1/2	cups fresh blueberries

1. Combine the walnuts, cracker crumbs, 2 Tbsp. sugar, oats and butter. Press onto the bottom of an 8-in. square baking dish coated with cooking spray. Bake at 350° for 9-11 minutes or until set and edges are lightly browned. Cool on a wire rack.

2. In a large bowl, beat cream cheese and remaining sugar until smooth. Beat in orange juice and vanilla. Fold in whipped topping. Spread over crust.

3. In a microwave-safe bowl, heat the preserves on high for 15-20 seconds or until warmed; gently stir in the blueberries. Spoon over filling. Refrigerate until serving.

Editor's Note: This recipe was tested with Land O'Lakes light stick butter.

Nutrition Facts: 1 bar equals 167 calories, 9 g fat (4 g saturated fat), 17 mg cholesterol, 125 mg sodium, 19 g carbohydrate, 1 g fiber, 3 g protein. **Diabetic Exchanges:** 2 fat, 1 starch.

Being blue may not be so bad after all! Foods that are blue and purple **pack a bounty** of nutrition. Vibrant violets such as berries and eggplant offer vitamins and fiber as well as antioxidants that can help keep cancer at bay.

Butterscotch Bliss Layered Dessert c

PREP: 20 min. + chilling **YIELD:** 24 servings

JANICE VERNON • LAS CRUCES, NEW MEXICO

Four easy layers come together for a fantastic treat that's perfect for cooling down hot summer nights. Take this to a party, and we guarantee you'll bring home an empty dish every time!

1-1/2 cups graham cracker crumbs
Sugar substitute equivalent to 1/2 cup sugar, *divided*
   6 Tbsp. butter, melted
   2 pkg. (8 oz. *each*) reduced-fat cream cheese
   3 cups cold fat-free milk, *divided*
   2 pkg. (1 oz. *each*) sugar-free instant butterscotch pudding mix
   1 carton (8 oz.) frozen reduced-fat whipped topping, thawed
 1/2 tsp. rum extract

1. In a small bowl, combine the cracker crumbs, 1/4 cup sugar substitute and butter. Press into a 13-in. x 9-in. dish coated with cooking spray.

2. In a small bowl, beat the cream cheese, 1/4 cup milk and remaining sugar substitute until smooth. Spread over crust.

3. In another bowl, whisk remaining milk with the pudding mix for 2 minutes. Let stand for 2 minutes or until soft-set. Gently spread over cream cheese layer. Combine whipped topping and extract; spread over the top. Refrigerate for at least 4 hours.

Editor's Note: This recipe was tested with Splenda no-calorie sweetener.

Nutrition Facts: 1 piece equals 136 calories, 8 g fat (6 g saturated fat), 21 mg cholesterol, 245 mg sodium, 12 g carbohydrate, trace fiber, 3 g protein. **Diabetic Exchanges:** 1 starch, 1 fat.

Ginger Mango Grunt s

PREP: 25 min. **COOK:** 25 min. **YIELD:** 8 servings

ROXANNE CHAN • ALBANY, CALIFORNIA

These tender dumplings in a fruit sauce are loaded with vitamins C and A to ward off illness and nourish skin.

 1/2 cup all-purpose flour
   3 Tbsp. yellow cornmeal
4-1/2 tsp. sugar
   1 tsp. baking powder
 1/4 tsp. ground ginger
 1/8 tsp. salt
   2 Tbsp. cold butter
   3 Tbsp. egg substitute

3/4 cup mango nectar, *divided*
  1 jar (24 oz.) refrigerated mango slices, drained
1/2 cup reduced-sugar orange marmalade
  1 Tbsp. lemon juice
1/2 cup golden raisins
1/4 cup chopped candied *or* crystallized ginger
1/4 cup sliced almonds

1. In a small bowl, combine the first six ingredients. Cut in butter until mixture resembles coarse crumbs. Combine egg substitute and 1/4 cup nectar; stir into the flour mixture just until moistened.

2. Place the mango slices, marmalade, lemon juice and remaining nectar in a blender. Cover and process until chunky.

3. Transfer to a large skillet; stir in raisins. Bring to a boil. Drop batter in eight mounds onto the simmering mango mixture. Reduce heat; cover and simmer for 20 minutes or until a toothpick inserted in a dumpling comes out clean (do not lift the cover while simmering). Sprinkle with ginger and almonds.

Nutrition Facts: 1 serving equals 232 calories, 5 g fat (2 g saturated fat), 8 mg cholesterol, 136 mg sodium, 47 g carbohydrate, 2 g fiber, 3 g protein.

Streusel Apples

PREP: 30 min. **BAKE:** 30 min. **YIELD:** 9 servings

MARIE HATTRUP • THE DALLES, OREGON

With its custard-like filling and sweet crumb layer, this old-fashioned treat is irresistible!

  1 egg, lightly beaten
4-1/2 tsp. lemon juice
  5 cups sliced peeled tart apples
1/2 cup golden raisins
1/2 cup chopped walnuts
1/3 cup sugar
1/3 cup all-purpose flour
  1 tsp. baking powder
  1 tsp. ground cinnamon
1/4 tsp. salt
TOPPING:
1/3 cup all-purpose flour
1/3 cup packed brown sugar
  1 tsp. ground cinnamon
  1 tsp. grated lemon peel
1/4 tsp. salt
  3 Tbsp. cold butter

1. In a large bowl, combine egg and lemon juice. Add the apples, raisins and walnuts; toss to coat. Combine the sugar, flour, baking powder, cinnamon and salt; sprinkle over apple mixture and toss to coat. Spoon into an 8-in. square baking dish coated with cooking spray.

2. For topping, combine the flour, brown sugar, cinnamon, lemon peel and salt. Cut in butter until mixture resembles coarse crumbs. Sprinkle over apple mixture. Bake at 375° for 30-35 minutes or until filling is bubbly and top is golden brown. Serve warm.

Nutrition Facts: 1 piece equals 241 calories, 9 g fat (3 g saturated fat), 34 mg cholesterol, 207 mg sodium, 40 g carbohydrate, 3 g fiber, 3 g protein.

Soft Orange Custard

PREP: 15 min. **BAKE:** 35 min. **YIELD:** 5 servings

SUE FRIEND • LYNDEN, WASHINGTON

This creamy custard with a splash of sunshiny citrus flavor will brighten any gray day. It's a light, lovely dessert!

  2 Tbsp. butter, softened
2/3 cup sugar
  2 eggs, lightly beaten
  2 Tbsp. all-purpose flour
1/4 tsp. salt
1/4 cup orange juice
1-1/2 tsp. grated orange peel
  1 tsp. lemon juice
  1 cup fat-free milk

1. In a small bowl, beat butter and sugar on medium speed for 1 minute. Add the eggs, flour and salt. Beat for about 2 minutes or until thickened. Add the orange juice, orange peel and lemon juice. Stir in milk.

2. Pour into five 6-oz. ramekins or custard cups. Place ramekins in a 13-in. x 9-in. baking pan. Add 1 in. of boiling water to pan. Bake, uncovered, at 325° for 35-40 minutes or until a knife inserted near the center comes out clean. Remove ramekins from water bath. Serve warm or chilled. Refrigerate leftovers.

Nutrition Facts: 1/2 cup equals 208 calories, 7 g fat (4 g saturated fat), 98 mg cholesterol, 215 mg sodium, 33 g carbohydrate, trace fiber, 5 g protein. **Diabetic Exchanges:** 2 starch, 1 fat.

SOFT ORANGE CUSTARD

Makeover Cranberry Trifle

PREP: 10 min. + chilling **COOK:** 15 min.
YIELD: 15 servings

SONYA LABBE • SANTA MONICA, CALIFORNIA

You'd never guess that this showstopper fruit trifle has been lightened up because it boasts all of the original's festive flavor, but only half the fat and way fewer calories!

- 1 pkg. (16 oz.) frozen unsweetened strawberries, thawed
- 1 pkg. (12 oz.) fresh or frozen cranberries
- 1 cup sugar
- 1/2 cup water
- 4 tsp. grated orange peel
- 1 pkg. (8 oz.) reduced-fat cream cheese
- 1/4 cup packed light brown sugar
- 1/2 tsp. vanilla extract
- 1 carton (8 oz.) frozen whipped topping, thawed
- 2 loaves (10-3/4 oz. *each*) frozen reduced-fat pound cake, thawed and cubed

1. In a large saucepan, combine the first five ingredients. Cook over medium heat until the berries pop, about 15 minutes. Cool completely.

2. Meanwhile, in a large bowl, beat the cream cheese, brown sugar and vanilla until smooth. Fold in whipped topping.

3. Place a third of the cake cubes in a 3-qt. trifle bowl; top with a third of the cranberry mixture and a third of the cream cheese mixture. Repeat layers twice. Cover and refrigerate for at least 2 hours before serving.

Nutrition Facts: 1 cup equals 316 calories, 12 g fat (6 g saturated fat), 33 mg cholesterol, 254 mg sodium, 49 g carbohydrate, 2 g fiber, 4 g protein.

Cinnamon-Raisin Bites F S C

PREP/TOTAL TIME: 25 min. **YIELD:** 2 dozen

HANNAH BARRINGER • LOUDON, TENNESSEE

These scone-like snacks are equally good straight out of the oven or at room temperature!

- 2 cups all-purpose flour
- 3 tsp. baking powder
- 1/2 tsp. salt
- 1/2 tsp. ground cinnamon
- 1/4 tsp. ground nutmeg
- 1 cup fat-free milk
- 1/4 cup canola oil
- 1/4 cup honey
- 1/2 cup raisins

1. In a large bowl, combine the flour, baking powder, salt, cinnamon and nutmeg. In a small bowl, combine the milk, oil and honey; add to the dry ingredients and stir just until moistened. Stir in raisins.

2. Drop by tablespoonfuls onto baking sheets coated with cooking spray. Bake at 425° for 8-10 minutes or until lightly browned. Remove to wire racks.

Nutrition Facts: 1 piece equals 82 calories, 2 g fat (trace saturated fat), trace cholesterol, 104 mg sodium, 14 g carbohydrate, trace fiber, 2 g protein. **Diabetic Exchanges:** 1 starch, 1/2 fat.

MAKEOVER CRANBERRY TRIFLE

CINNAMON-RAISIN BITES

Makeover Strawberry Rhubarb Crunch S

PREP: 15 min. **BAKE:** 25 min. **YIELD:** 8 servings

HEALTHY COOKING TEST KITCHEN

Now all you rhubarb fans out there can maximize that mouth-watering flavor without having to ladle on the sugar. This light recipe lets you enjoy one of springtime's quintessential treats and feel good about each bite you take.

1/2	cup sugar
2	Tbsp. cornstarch
2-1/2	cups sliced fresh strawberries
2	cups diced fresh or frozen rhubarb
1	tsp. vanilla extract
2/3	cup all-purpose flour
1/2	cup quick-cooking oats
1/4	cup brown sugar blend
1/2	tsp. ground cinnamon
1/4	cup cold butter

Reduced-fat whipped topping or reduced-fat strawberry ice cream, optional

1. In a large saucepan, combine sugar and cornstarch. Stir in strawberries and rhubarb until blended. Bring to a boil; cook and stir for 1-2 minutes or until thickened. Remove from the heat; stir in vanilla. Pour into an 8-in. square baking dish coated with cooking spray.

2. In a small bowl, combine the flour, oats, brown sugar blend and cinnamon; cut in butter until crumbly. Sprinkle over fruit mixture. Bake at 350° for 25-30 minutes or until filling is bubbly and topping is golden brown. Serve with whipped topping or ice cream if desired.

Editor's Note: This recipe was tested with Splenda brown sugar blend.

Nutrition Facts: 1 serving (calculated without whipped topping or ice cream) equals 210 calories, 6 g fat (4 g saturated fat), 15 mg cholesterol, 45 mg sodium, 37 g carbohydrate, 2 g fiber, 2 g protein.

> **To splurge or conserve?** When serving **rhubarb crunch**, note that 2 tablespoons of whipped cream equal 52 calories and 6 g fat. An equal amount of reduced-fat whipped topping, offers just 20 calories and 1 g fat.

BANANAS FOSTER SUNDAES

Bananas Foster Sundaes S

PREP/TOTAL TIME: 15 min. **YIELD:** 6 servings

LISA VARNER • GREENVILLE, SOUTH CAROLINA

I have wonderful memories of eating Bananas Foster in New Orleans and, as a dietitian, wanted to find a healthier version. I combined the best of two recipes and added my own tweaks to create this Southern treat.

1	Tbsp. butter
3	Tbsp. brown sugar
1	Tbsp. orange juice
1/4	tsp. ground cinnamon
1/4	tsp. ground nutmeg
3	large firm bananas, sliced
2	Tbsp. chopped pecans, toasted
1/2	tsp. rum extract
3	cups reduced-fat vanilla ice cream

1. In a large nonstick skillet, melt butter over medium-low heat. Stir in the brown sugar, orange juice, cinnamon and nutmeg until blended. Add bananas and pecans; cook, stirring gently, for 2-3 minutes or until bananas are glazed and slightly softened. Remove from the heat; stir in extract. Serve with ice cream.

Nutrition Facts: 1/3 cup banana mixture with 1/2 cup ice cream equals 233 calories, 7 g fat (3 g saturated fat), 23 mg cholesterol, 66 mg sodium, 40 g carbohydrate, 2 g fiber, 4 g protein.

Strawberry-Raspberry Ice F S

PREP: 10 min. + freezing **YIELD:** 3-1/2 cups

SANDRA SAKAITIS • ST. LOUIS, MISSOURI

This is so refreshing on a hot, sunny day. The bright color and flavor of this icy dish will lure everyone right to it! It's also packed with tons of vitamin C from the fruits and juices, making it ideal to enjoy in cold-weather months when sickness abounds.

1	pkg. (16 oz.) frozen sweetened sliced strawberries, partially thawed
2	cups frozen unsweetened raspberries, partially thawed
1/3	cup sugar
3	Tbsp. lime juice
2	Tbsp. orange juice

Fresh raspberries and lime wedges, optional

1. Place the strawberries, raspberries, sugar and juices in a blender. Cover and process for 2-3 minutes or until smooth.

2. Transfer mixture to a 13-in. x 9-in. dish. Freeze for 1 hour or until edges begin to firm.

3. Stir and return to freezer. Freeze 2 hours longer or until firm.

4. Just before serving, transfer to a food processor; cover and process for 2-3 minutes or until smooth.

5. Scoop into individual dishes; garnish with raspberries and lime wedges if desired.

Nutrition Facts: 1/2 cup equals 118 calories, trace fat (trace saturated fat), 0 cholesterol, 3 mg sodium, 31 g carbohydrate, 2 g fiber, 1 g protein. **Diabetic Exchanges:** 1 starch, 1/2 fruit.

Coconut Rice Pudding S

PREP: 5 min. **COOK:** 1 hour **YIELD:** 4 servings

SARAH HOWARD • FONTANA, CALIFORNIA

Serve this cozy dessert warm or cold to suit your taste. The best part is it takes just 5 minutes of prep time.

1	can (14 oz.) light coconut milk
1-1/3	cups fat-free milk
1/2	cup uncooked long grain rice
1/4	cup packed light brown sugar
1	tsp. vanilla extract
1/2	tsp. ground cinnamon

1. In a large saucepan, bring the coconut milk, milk, rice and brown sugar to a boil over medium heat. Reduce heat; cover and simmer for 50-55 minutes or until thick and creamy, stirring occasionally. Remove from the heat; stir in vanilla.

2. Spoon into dessert dishes. Sprinkle with cinnamon. Serve warm or cold.

Nutrition Facts: 3/4 cup equals 243 calories, 7 g fat (5 g saturated fat), 2 mg cholesterol, 61 mg sodium, 38 g carbohydrate, trace fiber, 4 g protein.

STRAWBERRY-RASPBERRY ICE

Makeover Peanut Ice Cream Delight

PREP: 20 min. + freezing **YIELD:** 24 servings

ASHLEY NEUMANN • METAMORA, MICHIGAN

The economists in the Healthy Cooking Test Kitchen kept the full-fat ice cream in this dessert, while trimming it down at the same time. Cool vanilla ice cream is the perfect match for the chocolate wafer crust and chocolate-caramel topping. You won't believe this is light!

1	pkg. (9 oz.) chocolate wafers, crushed
1/3	cup reduced-fat butter, melted
1/2	gallon vanilla ice cream, softened
1	cup salted peanuts

CHOCOLATE SAUCE:

1	can (14 oz.) fat-free sweetened condensed milk
4	squares (1 oz. *each*) semisweet chocolate, chopped
2	Tbsp. butter
1	tsp. vanilla extract
1	jar (12-1/4 oz.) caramel ice cream topping

If you'd like to make Makeover Peanut Ice Cream Delight but want to save **even more calories** and fat, consider using fat-free ice cream instead of the traditional variety. You'll slash another 29 calories per serving from the dessert as well as 5 g fat.

MAKEOVER PEANUT ICE CREAM DELIGHT

1. In a small bowl, combine wafer crumbs and butter; press onto the bottom of a 13-in. x 9-in. dish. Spread ice cream over crust; sprinkle with peanuts. Cover and freeze for at least 1 hour.

2. For chocolate sauce, in a small heavy saucepan, combine the milk, chocolate and butter. Cook and stir over medium-low heat until chocolate is melted. Remove from the heat; stir in vanilla. Cool.

3. Drizzle chocolate sauce over peanuts. Cover and freeze for 2 hours or until firm. Drizzle each serving with 2 tsp. caramel topping.

Editor's Note: This recipe was tested with Land O'Lakes light stick butter.

Nutrition Facts: 1 piece equals 296 calories, 13 g fat (6 g saturated fat), 28 mg cholesterol, 218 mg sodium, 42 g carbohydrate, 1 g fiber, 6 g protein.

"S'more, Please" Trifle

PREP/TOTAL TIME: 55 min + chilling **YIELD:** 16 servings

LORI ANN PANCHISIN • HOLLY HILL, FLORIDA

Don't worry about having more than 1 day's worth, there won't be leftovers of this! If your clan loves the classic combination of graham crackers, chocolate and marshmallow, they'll dig right into this trifle version. The recipe calls for reduced-fat ingredients, but the results are delicious.

1	pkg. (18-1/4 oz.) chocolate cake mix
1	can (12 oz.) diet lemon-lime soda
2-1/2	cups plus 2 Tbsp. fat-free milk, *divided*
2	pkg. (1.4 oz. *each*) sugar-free instant chocolate pudding mix
1	carton (8 oz.) frozen fat-free whipped topping, thawed
1/2	cup dark chocolate chips
10	whole reduced-fat graham crackers, *divided*
1	jar (7 oz.) marshmallow creme

Grated chocolate, optional

1. In a large bowl, combine cake mix and soda; beat on low speed for 30 seconds. Beat on medium for 2 minutes. Pour into a 13-in. x 9-in. baking pan coated with cooking spray. Bake at 350° for 30-35 minutes or until a toothpick inserted near the center comes out clean. Cool completely on a wire rack.

2. Meanwhile, in a large bowl, whisk 2-1/2 cups milk and the pudding mix for 2 minutes. Let stand for 2 minutes or until soft-set. Fold in whipped topping; set aside.

3. In a microwave, melt the chocolate chips and the remaining milk; stir until smooth. Coarsely crush five crackers; set aside. Cut the cake into 1-in. cubes.

4. In a 3-qt. trifle bowl or glass bowl, layer half of the cake cubes, pudding, crushed crackers, chocolate mixture and marshmallow creme. Repeat layers. Refrigerate for at least 1 hour before serving.

5. Just before serving, coarsely crush the remaining crackers; sprinkle over the top. Garnish with grated chocolate if desired.

Nutrition Facts: 3/4 cup (calculated without grated chocolate) equals 300 calories, 6 g fat (3 g saturated fat), 1 mg cholesterol, 463 mg sodium, 59 g carbohydrate, 2 g fiber, 4 g protein.

Gingerbread Cupcakes

PREP: 25 min. **BAKE:** 20 min. + cooling
YIELD: 21 cupcakes

BUGZBUNNY • TASTE OF HOME ON-LINE COMMUNITY

With heartwarming molasses, allspice and cinnamon, these cupcakes taste like the holidays!

2/3 cup sugar
1/2 cup canola oil
2 egg whites
1 egg
1 cup unsweetened applesauce
1 cup molasses
1-1/2 cups all-purpose flour
1 cup whole wheat flour
2-1/2 tsp. baking soda
1 tsp. ground ginger
1 tsp. ground cinnamon
1 tsp. ground allspice
1/2 tsp. salt
1-1/3 cups reduced-fat whipped topping

1. In a large bowl, beat the sugar, oil, egg whites and egg until well blended. Add applesauce and molasses; mix well. In a small bowl, combine the flours, baking soda, ginger, cinnamon, allspice and salt; gradually beat into applesauce mixture until blended.

2. Fill paper-lined muffin cups two-thirds full. Bake at 350° for 18-22 minutes or until a toothpick inserted near the center comes out clean. Cool for 10 minutes before removing from pans to wire racks to cool completely.

3. Just before serving, top each cupcake with 1 Tbsp. whipped topping.

Nutrition Facts: 1 cupcake equals 189 calories, 6 g fat (1 g saturated fat), 10 mg cholesterol, 221 mg sodium, 32 g carbohydrate, 1 g fiber, 2 g protein. **Diabetic Exchanges:** 2 starch, 1 fat.

This handy index lists every recipe by food category, major ingredient and/or cooking method, so you can easily locate recipes to suit your needs.
•*Table-ready in 30 minutes or less.*

This handy index lists every recipe alphabetically, so you
can easily find the dishes you enjoy most.
•*Table-ready in 30 minutes or less.*

Reference Index

Use this index to find the many recipe hints located throughout this cookbook.